Computer Architecture

Computer Architecture
Design and performance

Second edition

Barry Wilkinson

Department of Computer Science
University of North Carolina, Charlotte

Prentice Hall

London   New York   Toronto   Sydney   Tokyo   Singapore
Madrid   Mexico City   Munich

First published 1991
This edition published 1996 by
Prentice Hall Europe
Campus 400, Maylands Avenue
Hemel Hempstead
Hertfordshire, HP2 7EZ
A division of
Simon & Schuster International Group

Printed and bound in Great Britain by
Hartnolls Limited, Bodmin, Cornwall

Library of Congress Cataloging-in-Publication Data

Wilkinson, Barry
    Computer architecture: design and performance / Barry Wilkinson.
    – 2nd ed.
      p. cm
    Includes bibliographical references and index.
    ISBN 0-13-518200-X
    1. Computer architecture. I. Title
QA76.9.A73W54   1996   95-46401
004.2'2–dc20   CIP

British Library Cataloguing in Publication Data

A catalogue record for this book is available
from the British Library

ISBN 0-13-518200-X

---

1 2 3 4 5   00 99 98 97 96

*To my wife, Wendy
and my daughter, Johanna*

Contents

Preface   xiii
About the Author   xv

Part I Computer design techniques   1

1   Computer systems   3

   1.1   The stored program computer   3
       1.1.1 Concept   3
       1.1.2 Improvements in performance   12
   1.2   Microprocessor systems   14
       1.2.1 Development of microprocessor families   14
       1.2.2 Microprocessor architecture   17
   1.3   Architectural developments   20
       1.3.1 Pipelined processor design   20
       1.3.2 Processor-memory interface   22
       1.3.3 External memory and memory hierarchy   26
       1.3.4 Multiple processor systems   28
       1.3.5 Performance and cost   29
   1.4   Reduced instruction set computer   30
       1.4.1 Motives   30
       1.4.2 RISC examples   36
   Discussion questions   39

2   Instruction set design   41

   2.1   Processor characteristics   41
   2.2   Instruction formats   44
       2.2.1 Register-register instructions   44
       2.2.2 Register-register-constant (immediate) format   46
       2.2.3 Register-memory format   47

2.2.4 Branch format   49
2.2.5 Jump instructions   55
2.2.6 Procedure calls   56
2.3 Internal operation   62
2.4 Centralized control unit design   70
2.4.1 Hardwired logic design   70
2.4.2 Microprogrammed approach   72
2.5 Concluding comments   77
Problems   77

3 Cache memory systems   **80**

3.1 Cache memory   80
3.1.1 Operation   80
3.1.2 Hit ratio   84
3.2 Cache memory organizations   86
3.2.1 Fully associative mapping   86
3.2.2 Direct mapping   89
3.2.3 Set-associative mapping   91
3.2.4 Sector mapping   93
3.3 Fetch and write mechanisms   94
3.3.1 Fetch policy   94
3.3.2 Instruction and data caches   94
3.3.3 Write operations   96
3.3.4 Write-through mechanism   96
3.3.5 Write-back mechanism   98
3.4 Replacement policy   99
3.4.1 Objectives and constraints   99
3.4.2 Random replacement algorithm   100
3.4.3 First-in first-out replacement algorithm   100
3.4.4 Least recently used algorithm for a cache   101
3.5 Cache performance   105
3.6 Second-level caches   109
3.7 Disk caches   110
Problems   112

4 Memory management   **115**

4.1 Memory hierarchy   115
4.2 Paging   117
4.2.1 General   117
4.2.2 Translation look-aside buffers   121
4.2.3 Address translation   122
4.2.4 Page size   127

	4.2.5	Multilevel page mapping	129
4.3		Replacement algorithms	130
	4.3.1	General	130
	4.3.2	Random replacement algorithm	132
	4.3.3	First-in first-out replacement algorithm	133
	4.3.4	Clock replacement algorithm	134
	4.3.5	Least recently used replacement algorithm	134
	4.3.6	Working set replacement algorithm	135
	4.3.7	Performance and cost	137
4.4		Virtual memory systems with cache memory	141
	4.4.1	Addressing cache with real addresses	141
	4.4.2	Addressing cache with virtual addresses	143
	4.4.3	Access time	145
4.5		Segmentation	147
	4.5.1	General	147
	4.5.2	Paged segmentation	150
	4.5.3	8086 family segmentation	151
		Problems	153

5 Pipelined processor design 157

5.1		Overlap and pipelining	157
	5.1.1	Technique	157
	5.1.2	Pipeline data transfer	159
	5.1.3	Performance and cost	160
5.2		Instruction overlap and pipelines	163
	5.2.1	Instruction fetch/execute overlap	163
	5.2.2	Further overlap	165
	5.2.3	Pipeline for our RISC processor	168
5.3		Instruction pipeline hazards	171
	5.3.1	Resource conflicts	171
	5.3.2	Procedural dependencies and branch instructions	173
	5.3.3	Data dependencies	182
	5.3.4	Forwarding	188
	5.3.5	Multithreaded processor	192
5.4		Superscalar processors	192
	5.4.1	Implementing out-of-order instruction issue	196
	5.4.2	Centralized instruction window	197
	5.4.3	Distributed instruction window	199
	5.4.4	Register renaming	200
	5.4.5	Reorder buffer	201
5.5		Interrupt handling	203
5.6		Arithmetic pipelines	204
	5.6.1	General	204

5.6.2 Floating point pipelines   205
5.6.3 Fixed point arithmetic pipelines   208
5.6.4 Reservation tables and feedback pipelines   210
5.6.5 Pipeline scheduling and control   212
5.7 Pipelining in vector computers   217
Problems   219

Part II Shared memory multiprocessor systems   225

6   Multiprocessor systems and programming   227

6.1 General   227
6.2 Multiprocessor classification   229
     6.2.1 Flynn's classification   229
     6.2.2 Other classifications   231
6.3 Array computers   231
     6.3.1 General architecture   231
     6.3.2 Features of some array computers   233
     6.3.3 Bit-organized array computers   236
6.4 General purpose (MIMD) multiprocessor systems   238
     6.4.1 Architectures   238
     6.4.2 Shared memory multiprocessor systems   240
6.5 Potential for increased speed   245
6.6 Programming multiprocessor systems   252
     6.6.1 Concurrent processes   252
     6.6.2 Constructs for specifying parallelism   253
     6.6.3 Dependency analysis   258
     6.6.4 Critical sections   263
     6.6.5 Semaphores   267
Problems   271

7   Bus-based multiprocessor systems   274

7.1 Sharing a bus   274
     7.1.1 General   274
     7.1.2 Bus request and grant signals   276
     7.1.3 Multiple bus requests   277
7.2 Priority mechanisms   279
     7.2.1 Parallel priority   279
     7.2.2 Serial priority   285
     7.2.3 Polling   291
7.3 Performance of single bus network   293
     7.3.1 Methods and assumptions   293

		7.3.2 Bandwidth and execution time	295
		7.3.3 Access time	297
	7.4	System and local buses	299
	7.5	Crossbar switch multiprocessor systems	300
		7.5.1 Architecture	300
		7.5.2 Modes of operation and examples	301
		7.5.3 Bandwidth of crossbar switch	303
	7.6	Multiple bus multiprocessor systems	306
		7.6.1 Multiple bus networks	306
		7.6.2 Bandwidth of multiple bus systems	308
	7.7	Overlapping connectivity networks	309
		7.7.1 Overlapping crossbar switch networks	310
		7.7.2 Overlapping multiple bus networks	314
		7.7.3 Generalized arrays	315
	7.8	Caches in multiprocessor systems	316
		7.8.1 Cache coherence	318
		7.8.2 Write policy	319
		7.8.3 Methods of achieving cache coherence	322
		Problems	331

8 Interconnection networks   **335**

	8.1	Dynamic interconnection networks	335
		8.1.1 General	335
		8.1.2 Single stage networks	337
		8.1.3 Multistage networks	337
		8.1.4 Bandwidth of multistage networks	346
		8.1.5 Hot spots	347
		8.1.6 Overlapping connectivity multistage interconnection networks	351
	8.2	Static interconnection networks	356
		8.2.1 General	356
		8.2.2 Exhaustive static interconnections	357
		8.2.3 Limited static interconnections	357
		8.2.4 Altering the number of links between nodes	363
		8.2.5 Evaluation of static networks	367
		Problems	370

Part III Multiprocessor systems without shared memory   **373**

9 Message-passing multiprocessor systems   **375**

	9.1	General	375
		9.1.1 Architecture	375

     9.1.2 Communication paths   378

  9.2 Programming   387

     9.2.1 Message-passing routines   388

     9.2.2 Process structure   389

  9.3 Message-passing system examples   392

     9.3.1 Cosmic cube and derivatives   392

     9.3.2 Workstation clusters   394

  9.4 Transputer   397

     9.4.1 Philosophy   397

     9.4.2 Processor architecture   398

  9.5 Occam   400

     9.5.1 Structure   400

     9.5.2 Data types   401

     9.5.3 Data transfer statements   402

     9.5.4 Sequential, parallel and alternative processes   402

     9.5.5 Repetitive processes   406

     9.5.6 Conditional processes   407

     9.5.7 Replicators   408

     9.5.8 Other features   409

  Problems   410

10 Multiprocessor systems using the dataflow mechanism   414

  10.1 General   414

  10.2 Dataflow computational model   415

  10.3 Dataflow systems   420

     10.3.1 Static dataflow   420

     10.3.2 Dynamic dataflow   422

     10.3.3 VLSI dataflow structures   427

     10.3.4 Dataflow languages   429

  10.4 Macrodataflow   434

     10.4.1 General   434

     10.4.2 Macrodataflow architectures   435

  10.5 Summary and other directions   438

  Problems   438

References and further reading   **441**

Index   **453**

Preface

Intense effort continues to be made to improve the performance of present computer systems as the demands placed upon them increases dramatically. This book is concerned with the essential design techniques to improve the performance of computer systems. Many design techniques to improve performance involve the use of *parallelism* in which more than one operation is performed simultaneously. Parallelism can be achieved by using multiple functional units at various levels within the computer system and much of this book is concerned with such techniques involving the use of parallelism.

The first edition of the book was divided into three parts, Part I describing the fundamental methods to improve the performance of computer systems, Part II describing multiprocessor systems using shared memory, and Part III describing computer systems not using shared memory. The second edition retains the basic format of the first edition but opportunity has been taken to expand the treatment of most parts and to introduce recent advances and examples. In Part I, opportunity has also been taken to develop the intermediate subject area between basic processor operation and advanced processor design by having a new chapter on processor design, concentrating upon the design of the instruction set and implementation. This enables more advanced processor design to be developed better and a later chapter in Part I now covers pipelined and superscalar processors in detail.

Chapter 1 begins with an introduction to computer systems, microprocessor systems and the scope for improved performance. This chapter introduces the topics dealt with in detail in the subsequent chapters. The concept of the reduced instruction set computer (RISC) is introduced. The RISC processor is chosen for discussion of processor designs in subsequent chapters. Chapter 2 develops alternatives for the instructions of a RISC processor and discusses the trade-offs. How the processor can be designed using a centralized unit control is described. Chapters 3 and 4 concentrate upon memory – Chapter 3 on cache memory and Chapter 4 on main memory/secondary memory management. The importance of cache memory has resulted in a full chapter on the subject, rather than a small section combined with main memory/secondary memory as often found elsewhere. Chapter 5 continues the design of a processor started in Chapter 2 and deals with pipelining as applied within a processor, this being the basic technique for parallelism within a processor. Substantial additional material is provided on superscalar designs.

Chapter 6, the first chapter in Part II, introduces the design of shared memory multi-processor systems, including a new section on caches protocols in shared memory systems. Chapter 7 concentrates upon using buses to interconnect processors and memories, buses being common for smaller multiprocessor systems. Chapter 8 considers alternative interconnection networks suitable for larger multiprocessor systems, notable dynamic multistage interconnection networks and static link networks.

Chapter 9, the first chapter in Part III, presents multiprocessor systems having local memory only. Message-passing concepts and architectures are described, including networks of workstations. The transputer is outlined, together with its language, Occam. Virtually all computers use the stored program concept in which the actions to be performed are described in a program held within the memory of the system. Chapter 10 explores an alternative called the dataflow technique.

The text is intended to serve as a course text for senior level/graduate computer science, computer engineering, and electrical engineering courses in computer architecture and multiprocessor system design. The text should also appeal to design engineers working on single processor and multiprocessor applications. The material presented is a natural extension to material in introductory computer organization/computer architecture courses. The book can be used in a variety of ways. Material from Chapters 1 to 6 could be used for a senior computer architecture course, whereas for a course on multiprocessor systems, Chapters 6 to 10 could be studied in detail. Alternatively, for a computer architecture course with greater scope, material could be selected from all or most chapters, though generally from the first parts of sections. It is assumed that the reader has a basic knowledge of logic design, computer organization, and computer architecture. Exposure to computer programming languages, both high level programming languages and low level microprocessor assembly languages, is also assumed.

I would like to record my appreciation to Christopher Glennie of Prentice Hall for his guidance throughout the preparation of this book. His work developing a questionnaire and summarizing the very significant responses from many adopters of the first edition was very helpful in the development of the second edition. I wish to record my deep thanks to the anonymous reviewers for taking the time to provide helpful comments. Special thanks are extended to my students in the graduate courses CPGR 6182, CPGR 5141, and CPGR 5145 at the University of North Carolina, Charlotte, who have continued to help me refine the material.

Barry Wilkinson
University of North Carolina
Charlotte

About the Author

Barry Wilkinson is an Associate Professor in the Department of Computer Science at the University of North Carolina at Charlotte. He has previously held faculty positions at Brighton Polytechnic (now the University of Brighton), England (1984–1987), State University of New York, College at New Paltz (1983–1984), University College, Cardiff, Wales (1976–1983), and the University of Aston, England (1973–1976). From 1969 to 1970, he worked on process control computer systems at Ferranti Ltd. He is the author of *Computer Peripherals* (with D. Horrocks, Hodder and Stoughton, 1980, 2nd edn, 1987) and *Digital System Design* (Prentice Hall, 1987, 2nd edn, 1992). In addition to these books, he has published many articles and papers in major journals. He received the BSc degree in Electrical Engineering (with 1st class hons) from the University of Salford in 1969, and MSc and PhD degrees from the University of Manchester (Department of Computer Science), England, in 1971 and 1974 respectively.

PART I

Computer design techniques

CHAPTER
1 | *Computer systems*

In this chapter, the basic operation of the traditional stored program digital computer and the microprocessor implementation are reviewed, assuming the reader is already familiar with basic computer organization. The limitations of the single processor computer system are outlined and methods to improve the performance are suggested. One of the fundamental techniques of increasing performance – the introduction of separate functional units operating concurrently within the system – is also given.

1.1 The stored program computer

1.1.1 Concept

The computer system in which operations are encoded in binary, stored in a memory and performed in a defined sequence is known as a *stored program computer*. Most computer systems presently available are stored program computers. The concept of a computer which executes a sequence of steps to perform a particular computation can be traced back over 100 years to the mechanical decimal computing machines proposed and partially constructed by Charles Babbage. Babbage's Analytical Engine of 1834 contained program and data input (punched cards), memory (mechanical), a central processing unit (mechanical with decimal arithmetic) and output devices (printed output or punched cards) – all the key features of a modern computer system. However, a complete, large scale working machine could not be finished with the available mechanical technology and Babbage's work seems to have been largely ignored for 100 years, until electronic circuits, which were developed in the mid-1940s, made the concept viable.

It was soon recognized that the binary number representation would be the most suitable for electronic computers, because only two voltages or states are needed to represent each digit (0 or 1).[1] Binary representation is used throughout a computer system for the number representation and arithmetic and corresponding Boolean values

---

[1] Multiple valued representation and logic have been, and are still being, investigated.

are used for logical operations and devices. The true binary programmable electronic computers began to be developed by several groups in the mid-1940s, notably von Neumann and his colleagues in the United States. Stored program computers are often called *von Neumann computers*, after his work. (Some pioneering work was done by Zuse in Germany during the 1930s and 1940s, but this work was not widely known at the time.) During the 1940s, immense development of the stored program computer took place and the basis of complex modern computing systems was created. There are alternative computing structures with stored instructions which are not executed in a sequence related to the stored sequence (e.g., dataflow computers, which are described in Chapter 10) or which may not even have instructions stored in memory at all (e.g., neural computers).

The basic von Neumann stored program computer has:

1. A memory used for holding both instructions and the data required by those instructions.
2. A control unit for fetching the instructions from memory.
3. An arithmetic processor for performing the specified operations.
4. Input/output mechanisms and peripheral devices for transferring data to and from the system.

The control unit and the arithmetic processor of a stored program computer are normally combined into a *central processing unit* (CPU), or simply a *processor*, which results in the general arrangement shown in Figure 1.1.

The binary encoded instructions are known as *machine instructions*. The operations specified in the machine instructions are normally reduced to simple operations, such as arithmetic operations, to provide the greatest flexibility. Arithmetic and other simple

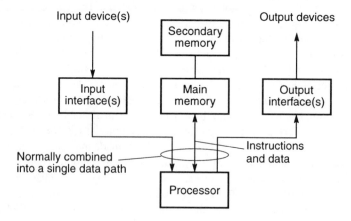

Figure 1.1 Stored program computer

operations operate on one or two operands and produce a numeric result. More complex operations are created from a sequence of simple instructions by the user. From a fixed set of machine instructions available in the computer (the *instruction set*) instructions are selected to perform a particular computation. The list of instructions selected is called a *computer program*. Normally a *programmer* writes the program in a high level language such as C. The program is then translated into machine instructions by a *compiler*, though it may be necessary very occasionally for the programmer to write programs in *assembly language* (which corresponds closely to machine language). The machine instruction program is stored in the memory and, when the system is ready, each machine instruction is read from (main) memory and executed.

The instructions being executed (or about to be executed) and their associated data are held in the *main memory*. This is organized such that each binary word is stored in a location identified by a number called an *address*. Memory addresses are allocated in strict sequence, with consecutive memory locations given consecutive addresses. Individual storage locations in the main memory may be accessed in any order and at very high speed. Memory supporting this form of access is known as *random access memory* (RAM) and is essential for the main memory of the system. Main memory usually consists of semiconductor memory and mostly of read-write semiconductor memory which is volatile (memory whose information is lost when the power is removed). In *read-write memory*, a location can be read or altered by the processor. It is usually necessary to have some main memory which is non-volatile (memory whose information is not lost when the power is removed) to hold instructions to execute when the computer is first turned on. One form of semiconductor memory, *read-only* semiconductor memory, though still random access, can only be read by the processor but is non-volatile. The information is written into the read-only memory, either during manufacture of the memory, or subsequently by a special electrical process. (More information on the different forms of memory can be found in books on logic design or introductory computer organization.)

The size of each main memory location having a unique address is usually 8 bits because then each memory location can hold the binary pattern for one alphanumeric character (as would be found on a keyboard). Eight bits is called a *byte*. The specific pattern for each character is defined in a code. The code widely used is the ASCII code (American Standard Code for Information Interchange). Clearly 8 bits are insufficient for holding very large numbers. Eight bits would only provide for integer numbers ranging from −128 to +127 using 2's complement binary numbers. Multiple consecutive bytes are used to store larger numbers, for example 2 bytes (16 bits), 4 bytes (32 bits), or 8 bytes (64 bits). The address of the resultant word is given by the lowest address of the bytes. For example, if locations 100, 101, 102 and 103 are used to store a 32-bit number, the address of the number is 100. Location 100 might store the least significant byte of the number, 101 the next significant byte and so on. This is known as *little endian* addressing. Alternatively location 100 could store the most significant byte of the number, 101 the next most significant byte and so on. This is known as *big endian* addressing. Some processors use little endian addressing (for example the Intel 8086 family, including the Intel 486). Some processors use big endian addressing (for example the Motorola MC68000 family). The choice of addressing is usually insignificant except when transferring data from one system to another system, or when individual bytes of a number must be manipulated separately. The Intel 486 does have specific instructions for converting between big endian and little endian.

There is usually additional memory, known as *secondary memory* or *backing store*, provided to extend the capacity of the memory system more economically than when main memory alone is used. Secondary memory can also provide the necessary large amounts of non-volatile memory. Secondary memory usually consists of non-volatile magnetic disk memory which is much less expensive per bit than semiconductor memory. However, this magnetic secondary memory is not capable of providing the required high speed of data transfer, nor can it locate individual storage locations in a random order at high speed (i.e., it is not truly random access memory).

Using the same memory for data and instructions is a key feature of the von Neumann stored program computer. Having data memory and program memory separated, with separate data transfer paths between the memory and the processor, is possible. This arrangement is occasionally called the *Harvard architecture*. The Harvard architecture may simplify and improve memory read/write mechanisms, particularly as programs are normally only read and not altered during execution while data might be read or altered. Also, data and instructions can be brought into the processor simultaneously with separate memories. However, using one memory to hold both the program and the associated data gives more efficient use of memory and it is usual for the bulk of the main memory in a computer system to hold both. The early idea that stored instructions could be altered during execution was quickly abandoned with the introduction of other methods of modifying instruction execution.

Each machine instruction needs to specify the operation to be performed, e.g., addition, subtraction, etc. This is specified in the operation or *opcode* part of the instruction, usually the first part of all instructions. The opcode is usually between 6 and 8 bits. Six bits would provide for 2^6 (64) different operations. A specific binary pattern will be used for each operation, for example 000000 for addition, 000001 for subtraction, etc. (It may not be that simple as different forms of operands even with the same basic operation may be given different opcodes and sometimes other parts of the instruction modify the operation being specified.)

The operands also need to be specified, either explicitly in the instruction or implicitly by the operation. Often, each operand is specified in the instruction by giving the address of the location holding it. This results in a general instruction format having three addresses:

1. Address of the first operand.
2. Address of the second operand.
3. Address of the location for holding the result of the operation.

A further address could be included, that of the next instruction to be executed. This is the *four-address instruction format*. The EDVAC computer, which was developed in the 1940s, used a four-address instruction format (Hayes, 1988) and this format has been retained in some microprogrammed control units (see later), but the fourth address is always eliminated for machine instructions by arranging that the next instruction to be executed is immediately following the current instruction in memory. This results in a *three-address instruction format*. To obtain a decision-making power, it is then necessary to provide a method of specifying a change of execution order often dependent upon a calculated result. This is normally achieved by including instructions in the instruction set which alter the subsequent execution sequence if specific conditions exist at that time.

If each of the three addresses in the three-address format are memory locations, then the length of the instruction could be significant. For example, suppose each memory address has 32 bits, a common size, and the opcode has 8 bits, the whole instruction would be 104 bits (13 bytes). We really want to keep the instruction length as short as possible, much shorter than this, to keep the machine program short and its execution fast. This can be achieved by eliminating addresses in the instruction or by shortening the address.

The third address can be eliminated to obtain the *two-address instruction format* by always placing the result of arithmetic or logic operations in the location where the first operand was held; this overwrites the first operand. The second address can be eliminated to obtain the *one-address instruction format* by having only one place for the first operand and result. This location, which would be within the processor itself rather than in the memory, is known as an *accumulator*, because it accumulates results. However, having only one location for one of the operands and for the subsequent result is too limiting. Instead, a small group of storage locations within the processor is usually provided called (data) *registers*. The registers to be used are selected by a small field in the instruction. The corresponding instruction format is the *one-and-a-half-address instruction format* or register type. All the addresses can be eliminated to obtain the *zero-address instruction format*, by using two known locations for the operands. These locations are specified as the first and second locations of a group of locations organized as a last-in-first-out queue called a stack. The zero-address instruction format can be useful for evaluating arithmetic expressions, but is rarely used today as the basis of a processor design. The various memory addressing formats are shown in Figure 1.2.[2]

Once data registers are introduced into a processor for holding operands, it is best to use the registers totally for holding all the operands of the computations and the results, rather than memory locations. Such operations could be called register-register operations. Registers can be accessed more quickly than memory locations and hence can achieve a higher computational speed. A set of data registers is commonly provided inside the processor and arithmetic operations can be performed upon the contents of these registers, producing a result which is loaded into a register. Compilers will allocate registers to variables declared in the program when possible. The number of registers provided in a processor is a compromise between providing sufficient to reduce having to use memory locations and not requiring too many bits in the instruction to specify the

---

[2] The order of 1st operand, 2nd operand and result fields in the instruction can vary between processor designs. We will use the order: result, 1st operand, 2nd operand in Chapter 2 and subsequently.

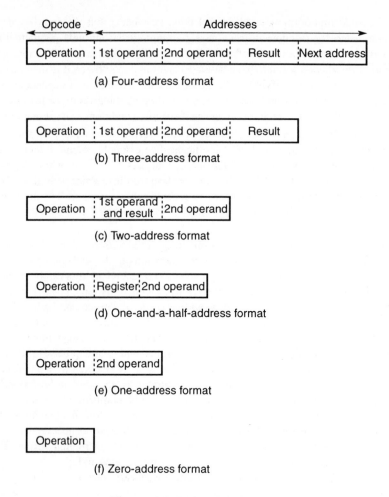

Figure 1.2 Instruction formats

registers. Also a larger number of registers requires more to save on a context switch and consumes more space in the processor. Finally, it may not be that easy for a compiler to use a large number of registers effectively. There may be say up to thirty-two such registers. Thirty-two registers would require 5 bits for each register specified.

There are two possible instruction formats for register-register instructions:

1. Two-register format
2. Three-register format.

In the two-register format, the result is stored in the same location as one of the operands, overwriting and destroying one operand. The format requires two registers to be specified in the instruction. In the three-register format, the result can be stored in a different register, which provides for greater flexibility. (It is allowable, of course, to specify the same register for one operand and the result.) Three registers have to be specified in the instruction, consuming 15 bits with 32 registers. This format is usually used in Reduced Instruction Set Computers (RISCs), whereas Complex Instruction Set Computers (CISCs) often use the two-register format, see later. Apart from data registers, the processor has a number of other registers for holding memory addresses (*address registers*) and for holding control information. The exact allocation of registers is dependent upon the design of the processor.

Various methods (*addressing modes*) can be used to identify the location of an operand. The actual address of the operand after all address computations have been performed is called the *effective address*. Five different common methods are:

1. *Immediate addressing* – when the operand is part of the instruction.
2. *Absolute addressing* – when the address of an operand is held in the instruction.
3. *Register direct addressing* – when the operand is held in a register specified in the instruction.
4. *Register indirect addressing* – when the address of the operand location is held in a register which is specified in the instruction.
5. Various forms of *relative addressing* – when the address of the operand is computed by adding an offset held in the instruction to the contents of specific register(s).

Immediate addressing enables a constant to be specified in the instruction and is useful for loading registers with initial values. Absolute addressing enables a memory location to be accessed by its address. However, this addressing mode does not allow the address to be changed during the computation. Register indirect addressing provides this facility by using a register to hold the address. Then by altering the contents of this register, different memory locations can be accessed. Relative addressing provides a memory address which is some distance from a base address and is essential for programs which are to be placed in different places in memory for execution. A common form of relative addressing is used with branch instructions, instructions which change the flow of execution. These instructions will specify the location of the next instruction to be executed if not the next sequential instruction, by providing the location address as a number of locations from the branch instruction (when using relative addressing). Wherever the branch instruction is loaded into memory for execution, the instruction address will always be the same number of locations away. Register indirect addressing often also incorporates a displacement or offset (*register indirect addressing with offset*). The offset is held in the instruction and is added to the contents of the address register to form the effective address. This is in fact a form of relative addressing as the location address is relative to a point of reference, in this case the contents of a general-purpose register.

Some processors, notably the Motorola MC68000 family, differentiate between registers which can only hold data operands and registers which can only hold addresses (data registers and address registers respectively). This means less bits are needed to specify the register because whether a data register or address register is to be used is selected by context. It also provides a structure to machine instruction programs and all programmers/compilers must use certain registers for data and others for addresses. Other processors, such as the Intel 8086 family, do provide some registers which are intended mainly for addresses, but these registers can also be used for data if required.

There are several variations and extensions of the addressing modes described. For example, register indirect addressing can incorporate automatic increment or decrement of the contents of the address register before or after the memory location is accessed. This might be useful for accessing consecutive items in a list. A processor could be provided with very many addressing modes but this adds to the complexity of the processor. As a completely opposite approach, a minimum subset could be provided; just sufficient to perform all normal memory accesses. For example, immediate addressing and register indirect addressing together can be used to create absolute addressing (by simply loading a register with the address first) and most other addressing modes.

The length of a machine instruction might be the same for every type of instruction or there might be several different instruction lengths, depending upon the design of the processor. Providing many different types of addressing modes tends to lead to instructions of different lengths. The minimal approach of having a few addressing modes will lead to all instructions having the same size, say 32 bits. If every instruction has 32 bits, for example, the program counter will increment by four after every instruction has been fetched. If instructions are of different lengths, multiple byte or word accesses are needed from memory to fetch the complete instruction.

The internal design of a simple processor is shown in Figure 1.3. An internal bus, or more usually three internal buses, connect the major parts, which consist of an ALU (Arithmetic and Logic Unit), a registers file, a control unit and a number of specialized registers. One such register is the *Instruction Register* (IR) which holds the instruction being executed. The ALU performs basic arithmetic and logical operations such as addition and subtraction as would be specified in machine instructions. The control unit orchestrates the actions within the processor by sending signals to the various components. The *program counter* (PC), also called the *instruction pointer* (IP), is a register inside the processor holding the address of the next instruction to be executed. The contents of the PC are usually incremented each time an instruction word has been read from memory in preparation for the next instruction word, which is often in the next location. (The name program counter is unfortunate since it does not count programs; it identifies the next instruction in the program.) The contents of the program counter can be purposely altered by the execution of "jump" instructions, used to change the execution sequence. This facility is essential to create significant computations and different computations which depend upon previous computations.

The operation of the processor can be divided into two distinct steps, a *fetch cycle* and an *execute cycle*. In the fetch cycle, as illustrated in Figure 1.3(a), an instruction is obtained from the memory and loaded into the instruction register. The program counter is incremented to point to the next instruction. In the execute cycle, as illustrated in Figure 1.3(b), the operation is performed which includes fetching any operands and storing the result. In this design, there is a centralized control unit which generates the

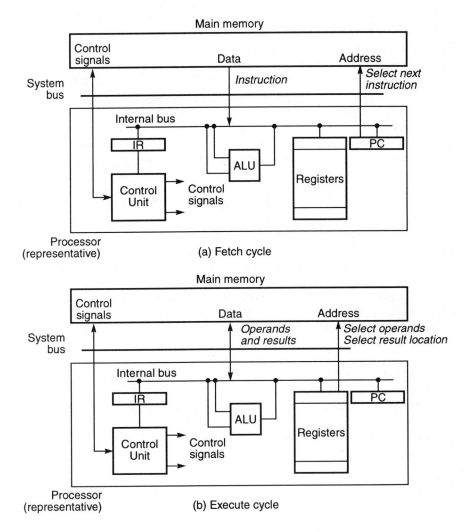

Figure 1.3 CPU mode of operation
(PC, program counter; IR, instruction register; ALU, arithmetic and logic unit)

required signals to cause information to transfer from one place to another within the processor and to cause internal components to take actions.

The operations required to fetch and to execute an instruction can be divided into a number of sequential steps. The signals for each step are generated by the control unit of the processor. The control unit can be designed using interconnected logic gates and counters to generate the required signals (a *random logic* approach). Alternatively, each step could be binary-encoded into a *microinstruction*. A sequence of these microinstructions is formed for each machine instruction and the sequence is then stored in a high speed memory within the internal control unit of the processor. This memory is called a *control memory*. The sequence of microinstructions is known as a *microprogram* (or *microcode*) and one sequence must be executed for each machine instruction read from the main memory. This technique was first suggested by Wilkes in the early 1950s (Wilkes, 1951) but was not put into practice in the design of computers until the 1960s, mainly because the performance was limited by the control memory, which needs to operate much faster than the main memory. Normally the control memory would be non-volatile read-only memory. If the control memory were made so that its contents could be alterable (read/write memory), it would be possible to alter the machine instruction set of the computer by rewriting the microprograms. This leads to the concept of *emulation*, in which a computer behaves at the machine instruction level like a different computer. This can be achieved by rewriting the microprograms of the computer to create exactly the same instruction set as another computer so that machine instruction programs written for the emulated computer will run on the microprogrammed computer.

The microprogrammed approach is particularly convenient for implementing complex instructions and was popular in the 1970s but lost favor since the early 1980s as a way of designing a processor with the advent of processors having simpler instruction sets. We will demonstrate the microprogrammed technique in Chapter 2.

To summarize, we can identify the main operating characteristics of the stored program computer as follows:

1. Only elementary operations are performed (e.g., arithmetic addition, logical operations).
2. The user (programmer) or compiler selects operations to perform the required computation.
3. Encoded operations are stored in a memory.
4. Strict sequential execution of stored instructions occurs (unless otherwise directed).
5. Data may also be stored in the same memory.

The reader will find a full treatment of basic computer architecture and organization in Stallings (1987) and Mano (1982).

1.1.2 Improvements in performance

Since the 1940s the development of stored program computer systems has concentrated upon three general areas:

1. Improvements in technology.
2. Software development.
3. Architectural enhancements.

Improvements in technology, i.e., in the type of components used and in fabrication techniques, have led to dramatic increases in speed. Component speeds have typically doubled every few years during the period. Such improvements are unlikely to continue for electronic components because switching times now approach the limit set by the velocity of electrical signals (about 2/3 speed of light, 0.2 m ns^{-1}) and the delay through interconnecting paths will begin to dominate. In fact, this limit has been recognized for some time and has led some researchers to look at alternative technologies, such as optical technology (optical computers).

After the overall design specification has been laid down and cost constraints are made, one of the first decisions made at the design stage of a computer is the choice of technology. In the 1970s, this was normally between TTL/CMOS (transistor-transistor logic/complementary metal oxide semiconductor) and ECL (emitter-coupled logic) for high performance systems. Factors to be taken into account include the availability of very large scale integration (VLSI) components and the consequences of the much higher power consumption of ECL. ECL has a very low level of integration compared to CMOS but has still been chosen for the highest performance systems because, historically, it is much faster than MOS (metal oxide semiconductor). However, MOS technology continues to improve and most systems today use this technology. Predictions need to be made as to the expected developments in technology, especially those developments that can be incorporated during the design phase of the system. For example, it might be possible to manufacture a chip with improved performance, if certain design tolerances are met (see Maytal *et al.*, 1989).

A computer system can be characterized by its instruction execution speed, the internal processor cycle time or clock period, the capacity and cycle time of its memory, the number of bits in each stored word (*word length*) and by features provided within its instruction set among other characteristics. The performance of a high performance computer system is often characterized by the basic speed of machine operations, e.g., millions of operations per second, MOPS (or sometimes millions of instructions per second, MIPS). These operations are further specified as millions of floating point operations per second, MFLOPS, or even thousands of MFLOPS, called gigaflops, GFLOPS, especially for large, high performance computer systems. A computer is considered to be a *supercomputer* if it can perform hundreds of millions of floating point operations per second ($\times 100$ MFLOPS) with a word length of approximately 64 bits and a main memory capacity of millions of words (Hwang, 1985). However, as technology improves, these figures may need to be revised upwards. A Cray X-MP computer system, one of the fastest computer systems developed in the early 1980s, has a peak speed of about 2 GFLOPS. This great speed has only been achieved through the use of the fastest electronic components available, the most careful physical design (with the smallest possible distances between components), very high speed pipelined units with vector processing capability, a very high speed memory system and, finally, multiple processors, which were introduced in the Cray X-MP and the Cray 2 after the single processor Cray 1.

The internal *cycle time* (*clock period*) specifies the period allotted to each basic internal operation of the processor. In some systems, notably microprocessor systems (see Section 1.2), the clock frequency is a fundamental figure of merit, especially for otherwise similar processors. A clock frequency of 100 MHz would correspond to a clock period of 10 ns.

If *every* instruction is completed after every 10 ns clock period, the instruction rate would be 100 MIPS. However, some instructions may take longer than others and we would have to take the average. The actual rate will depend upon the mix of instructions. The value for MIPS would be given by the number of instructions executed in program/execution time $\times 10^{-6}$. For floating point instructions, the value for MFLOPS would be given by the number of floating point instructions in program/execution time $\times 10^{-6}$. Various benchmark programs exist with representative mixes of instructions. For example, the SPECint92 and SPECfp92 UNIX benchmarks are sometimes quoted by manufacturers, especially when comparing their processors to those of their competitors.

One or more periods may be necessary to fetch an instruction and execute it, but very high speed systems can generate results at the end of each period by using pipelining and multiple unit techniques. The Cray X-MP computer had a 9.5 ns clock period in 1980 and finally achieved its original design objective of an 8.5 ns clock period in 1986, by using faster components (August *et al.*, 1989). Each subsequent design has called for a shorter clock period, e.g., 4 ns and 1 ns for the Cray 2 and Cray 3, respectively. Other large "mainframe" computer systems have had cycle times/clock periods in the range 10–30 ns. For example, the IBM 308X, first delivered in 1981, had a cycle time of 26 ns (later reduced to 24 ns) using TTL circuits mounted on ceramic thermal conduction modules. The IBM 3090, a development of the 3080 with faster components, first introduced in 1985, had a cycle time of 18.5 ns (Tucker, 1986).

Software development, i.e., the development of programming techniques and the support environment, have included various high level languages such as PASCAL, FORTRAN and C and more recently C++. Also complex multitasking operating systems have been developed for controlling more than one user on the system. Some developments in software have led to variations in the internal design of the computer. For example, computers have been designed for the efficient handling of common features of high level languages by providing special registers or operating system operations in hardware. Most computer systems now have some hardware support for system software.

In this text, we are concerned with architectural developments, i.e., developments in the internal structure of the computer system to achieve improved performance. Such developments will be considered further in the next section. First though, let us examine the most striking technological development in recent years – the development of the microprocessor – as this device is central to the future development of multiprocessor systems, particularly those systems with large numbers of processors.

1.2 Microprocessor systems

1.2.1 Development of microprocessor families

Since the late 1960s, logic components in computer systems have been fabricated on integrated circuits (chips) to achieve high component densities. Technological developments in integrated circuits have produced more logic components in a given area, allowing more complex systems to be fabricated on the integrated circuit, first in small scale integration (SSI, 1 to 12 gates) then medium scale integration (MSI, 12 to 100 gates), large scale integration (LSI, 100 to 1000 gates), through to very large scale integration (VLSI, usually much greater than 1000 gates). This process led directly to the microprocessor, a complete processor on an integrated circuit. The early microprocessors required the equivalent of large scale integration.

Later integration methods are often characterized by the applied integrated circuit design rules specifying the minimum features, e.g., 1.25 µm and then 0.8 µm, 0.6 µm, 0.5 µm line widths. Smaller line widths increase the maximum number of transistors fabricated on one integrated circuit and reduce the gate propagation delay time. The number of transistors that can be reasonably fabricated on one chip with acceptable yield even at 1.25 µm design rules is in excess of one million, but this number is dependent upon the circuit complexity. Repetitive cells, as in memory devices, can be fabricated at higher density than irregular designs.

Microprocessors are often manufactured with different guaranteed clock frequencies, e.g., 60 MHz, 75 MHz, 90 MHz, or 100 MHz. There is a continual improvement in the clock frequencies due to an improved level of component density and the attendant reduced gate propagation delay times. By increasing the clock frequency the processor immediately operates more quickly and in direct proportion to the increase in clock frequency, assuming that the main memory can also operate at the higher speed.

Microprocessors are designated 4-bit, 8-bit, 16-bit, 32-bit, or 64-bit depending upon the basic unit of data processed internally. For example, a 32-bit microprocessor will usually be able to add, subtract, multiply or divide two 32-bit integer numbers directly. A processor can usually operate upon smaller integer sizes in addition to their basic integer size. A 32-bit microprocessor can perform arithmetic operations upon 8-bit and 16-bit integers directly. Specific machine instructions operate upon specific word sizes. An interesting computer architecture not taken up in microprocessors (or in most other computer systems), called a *tagged architecture*, uses the same instruction to specify an operation upon all allowable sizes of integers. The size is specified by bits (a tag) attached to each stored number.

The first microprocessor, the Intel 4004, introduced in 1971, was extremely primitive by present standards, operating upon 4-bit numbers and with limited external memory, but it was a milestone in integrated circuits. Four-bit microprocessors are now limited to small system applications involving decimal arithmetic, such as pocket calculators, where 4 bits (a nibble) can conveniently represent one decimal digit. The 4004 was designed for such applications and, in the ensuing period, more complex 8-bit, 16-bit and 32-bit microprocessors have been developed, in that order, mostly using MOS integrated circuit technology. Binary-coded decimal (BCD) arithmetic is incorporated into these more advanced processors as it is not subject to fractional number rounding errors which is convenient for financial applications.

Eight-bit microprocessors became the standard type of microprocessor in the mid-1970s, typified by the Intel 8080, Motorola MC6800 and Zilog Z-80. At about this time, the microprocessor operating system CP/M, used in the 8080 and the Z-80, became widely accepted and marked the beginning of the modern microprocessor system as a computer system capable of being used in complex applications. Eight-bit processors are now generally limited to embedded controller applications, for example, domestic appliances and electronics and automobile applications, where great precision may not be needed. Some 8-bit microprocessors are particularly designed for embedded control applications, such as the Intel 8051 processor.

Sixteen-bit microprocessors started to emerge as a natural development of the increasing capabilities of integrated circuit fabrication techniques towards the end of the 1970s, e.g., the Intel 8086 and Motorola MC68000, both introduced in 1978. Subsequent versions of these processors were enhanced to include further instructions, circuits and, in particular, memory management capabilities and on-chip cache memory. In the Intel 8086 family, the 80186 included additional on-chip circuits and instructions and the 286 included memory management. In the Motorola family, the MC68010 included memory management. Thirty-two bit versions also appeared in the 1980s (e.g., the Intel 386 with paged memory management, the Motorola MC68020 with cache memory and the MC68030 with instruction/data cache memories and paged memory management). The Intel 486 and Motorola MC68040 continued the trend of adding facilities within the chip.

Floating point numbers were originally processed by additional special processors intricately attached to the basic microprocessor. With increased integrated circuit densities, floating point facilities are often integrated into the processor chip. Floating point numbers correspond to real numbers in high level languages and are numbers represented by two parts, a mantissa and an exponent, such that the number $= $ mantissa $\times$ base^{exponent}, where the base is normally 2 for binary representation. For further details see Mano (1982). Both the Motorola MC68040 and Intel 486 incorporate floating point units. (There is a version of the MC68040 without an internal floating point unit.)

A characteristic in the development of microprocessors has been the increase on clock speeds, from around 1 MHz on early microprocessors in the 1970s, around 8–20 MHz in the 1980s, to 50–100 MHz range in the mid 1990s. Usually the processor can be designed to operate internally much faster than the external memory. The technique of *clock doubling* (and *clock tripling*) appeared in the early 1990s in which the internal components of the processor operate at twice (or quadruple) the speed of the external interface. An example of a processor using this technique is the Intel 486 DX2 (and DX4). It is particularly convenient for upgrading a processor with a faster clock doubling which can be done simply by inserting the new processor into the socket of the old processor. We will discuss an alternative to this approach, namely by increasing the number of data lines, later.

Microprocessors so far mentioned generally achieve an average execution of no more than one instruction in each clock cycle. They also operate on single numbers intrinsically. Such processors are called *scalar processors*. In the drive to obtain higher performance and greater execution speed, processor designs emerged in the early 1990s in which more than one instruction can be executed in each cycle. Such processors are called *superscalar processors*. An example of a superscalar processor is the Intel Pentium processor which is a superscalar version of their 486 processor and the replacement for the 486, achieving significantly greater computational speed.

Superscalar operation is usually achieved by duplicating components in the processor, notably the functional units (ALUs and the like), such that each unit can operate separately on different instructions. Superscalar designs are considered in Chapter 5. We can note here that designing a superscalar processor which can execute two instructions simultaneously is attractive if two instructions exist which are independent and hence could be executed simultaneously. In many applications there will be some instructions that could be executed simultaneously but it will be limited to perhaps groups of 2–3 instructions at any instant and certainly not greater than groups of 6–7 instructions will be found that are independent. Hence the superscalar approach can only be applied effectively for a small groups of instructions.

Processors are usually developed in "families" such that processors would be able to execute programs of earlier processors. This is a very important commercial consideration and maintains the software base of the processors. Applications do not necessarily have to be rewritten for the newer processors (though they probably would be in due course to utilize the features of the new processor).

Perhaps the most important development to occur in processor design emerged in the late 1970s and early 1980s, called the *Reduced Instruction Set Computer* (RISC) which we will describe later, as it is a significant departure for the increasing complexity of processors. We will discuss the RISC later, but first let us describe the basic architecture of a microprocessor system.

1.2.2 Microprocessor architecture

The basic architecture of a microprocessor system is shown in Figure 1.4 and consists of a microprocessor, a semiconductor memory and input/output interface components all connected through a common set of lines called the *bus*. The memory holds the program currently being executed, those to be executed and the associated data. There would normally be additional secondary memory, usually disk memory and input/output interfaces are provided for external communication. The bus-based architecture is employed in all microprocessor systems, but microprocessor systems were not the first or only

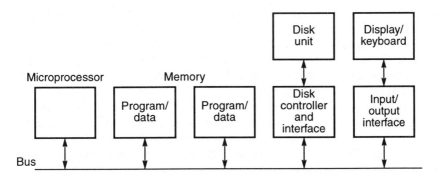

Figure 1.4 Fundamental parts of a microprocessor system

computer systems to use buses; the PDP 8E minicomputer, introduced in 1971, used a bus called Omnibus and the PDP 11, first introduced in 1970, used a bus called Unibus. The expansibility of a bus structure has kept the technique common to most small and medium size computer systems.

The bus is the communication channel between the various parts of the system and can be divided into three parts:

1. Data lines.
2. Address lines.
3. Control lines.

The data lines carry the instructions from the memory to the processor during each instruction fetch cycle and data between the processor and memory or input/output interfaces during instruction execute cycles, dependent upon the instruction being executed. Eight-bit microprocessors have eight data lines, 16-bit microprocessors have sixteen data lines (unless eight lines are used twice for each 16-bit data transfer, as in some low cost 16-bit microprocessors). Similarly, 32-bit microprocessors can have thirty-two data lines. Some 32-bit processors have 64 data lines in which two 32-bit words can be transferred simultaneously. For example the Intel Pentium is a 32-bit processor but has 64 data lines. Notice that the microprocessor bit size – 8-bit, 16-bit, 32-bit, 64-bit, or whatever – does not specify the number of data lines. It specifies the basic size of the data being processed internally and the size of the internal arithmetic and logic unit (ALU).

If the instructions are of variable length, the instructions fetched from memory to the processor comprise one or more 8-bit words (bytes), or one or more 16-bit words, depending upon the design of the microprocessor. The instructions of all 8-bit microprocessors have one or more bytes, typically up to 5 bytes. One byte is provided for the operation including information on the number of subsequent bytes and two bytes each for each operand address when required. Sixteen/32-bit microprocessors can have their instructions in multiples of bytes or in multiples of 16-bit words, generally up to 6 bytes or three words (excluding RISCs, see later).

When the data bus cannot carry the whole instruction in one bus cycle, additional cycles are performed to fetch the remaining parts of the instruction. Hence, the basic instruction fetch cycle can consist of several data bus transfers and the timing of microprocessors is usually given in terms of bus cycles. Similarly the operands (if any) transferred during the basic execute cycle may require several bus cycles. In all, the operation of the microprocessor is given in read and write bus transfer cycles, whether these fetch instructions or transfer operands/results.

During a bus cycle, the bus transfer might be to the processor, when an instruction or data operand is fetched from memory or a data operand is read from an input/output interface, or from the processor, to a location in the memory or an output interface to transfer a result. Hence, the data lines are bidirectional, though simultaneous transfers in both directions are impossible and the direction of transfer must be controlled by signals within the control section of the bus.

The address lines carry addresses of memory locations and input/output locations to be accessed. A sufficient number of lines must be available to address a large number of memory locations. Typically, 8-bit microprocessors in the 1970s provided for sixteen address lines, enabling 2^{16} (65 536) locations to be specified uniquely. More recent microprocessors have more address lines, e.g., the 16-bit 8086 has twenty address lines (capable of addressing 1 048 576 bytes, i.e., 1 megabyte), the 16-bit 286 and MC68000 have twenty-four (capable of addressing 16 megabytes) and the 32-bit MC68020/30/40 and Intel 386/486/Pentium have thirty-two (capable of addressing 4096 megabytes, i.e., 4 gigabytes). Thirty-two address lines became a standard for the early 1990s. Sixty-four address lines would provide an enormous main memory addressing capability (2^{64} bytes).

Processors usually have the capability of selecting either an 8-bit word, a 16-bit word (consisting of two consecutive byte locations), a 32-bit word (consisting of four consecutive byte locations) and a 64-bit word (consisting of eight consecutive byte locations) if the data path has 64 bits. To make this selection (with either read or write operation), separate signals are provided. For example the Intel 486 has address lines A_2 to A_{31} to select the 32-bit word and four separate signals BE0, BE1, BE2 and BE3 to select the bytes within the word (BE0 for D_0 to D_7, BE1 for D_8 to D_{15}, BE2 for D_{16} to D_{23}, BE3 for D_{24} to D_{31}). To select a 16-bit word two of these signals would be activated. The Pentium is similar but with a 64-bit data path, uses address lines A_3 to A_{31} and byte enable signals BE0, BE1, BE2, BE3, BE4, BE5, BE6 and BE7 to select the byte(s), as shown in Figure 1.5. Other processors may achieve the same result with different signals. For example BE0 to BE3 in the 486 are essentially encoded into two size signals, SIZ1 and SIZ0, on the MC68040. The full 32-bit address is provided by A_{31} to A_0 to give the address of the first byte of the transfer. SIZ1 = 0, SIZ0 = 0 indicates a 32-bit (4 byte)

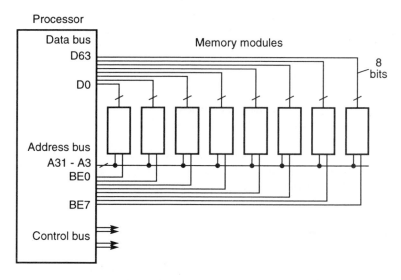

Figure 1.5 Processor signals with 64-bit data bus

transfer, SIZ1 = 0, SIZ0 = 1 indicates a byte transfer, SIZ1 = 1, SIZ0 = 0 indicates a 16-bit (2 byte) transfer and SIZ1 = 1, SIZ0 = 1 indicates a 16-byte (line) transfer. In any event, we refer to the processors as having 32 address lines.

The control lines carry signals to activate the data/instruction transfers and other events within the system; there are usually many control lines on recent processors. The control signals, as a group, indicate the time and type of a transfer. The types of transfer include transfers to or from the processor (i.e., read or write) and involve memory and input/output interfaces which may be differentiated.

A trend with the continual development of microprocessors is the increase in the number of data, address and control lines, as evidenced by the increasing numbers of pins on the packages. Early microprocessors could be packaged in small 40–48-pin dual-in-line packages (with pins along two opposite edges). Processors now have packages with an enormous number of pins. The Intel Pentium processor for example has 273 pins arranged in a two-dimensional matrix on a 2.16" square package (though 99 pins are used for the supply voltage, V_{cc} and V_{ss}, and 6 pins are not used.)

1.3 Architectural developments

There have been many developments in the basic architecture of the stored program computer to increase its speed of operation. Most of these developments can be reduced to applying parallelism, i.e., causing more than one operation to be performed simultaneously, but significant architectural developments have also come about to satisfy requirements of the software or to assist the application areas. A range of architectural developments has been incorporated into the basic stored program computer without altering the overall stored program concept. In general, important architectural developments can be identified in the following areas:

1. Those concerned with the internal design of the processor.
2. Those around the processor-memory interface.
3. Those concerned with the memory system hierarchy.
4. Those involving use of multiple processor systems.

Let us briefly review some of these developments, which will be presented in detail in the subsequent chapters. Perhaps the single most important development in processor design to have occurred is the Reduced Instruction Set Computer (RISC), which we consider at the end of this chapter.

1.3.1 Pipelined processor design

One of the basic techniques which can improve the performance of a processor is the pipeline technique, a technique known for many years and always applied in high performance systems. As we have noted, the operation of the processor is centered on two composite operations:

1. Fetching an instruction.
2. Executing the fetched instruction.

First, an instruction is read from memory using the program counter as a pointer to the memory location. Next, the instruction is decoded, that is, the specified operations are recognized. In the fetch/execute partition, the instruction decode occurs during the latter part of the fetch cycle and once the operation has been recognized, the instruction can be executed. The operands need to be obtained from registers or memory at the beginning of the execute cycle and the specified operation is then performed on the operands. The results are usually placed in a register or memory location at the end of the execute cycle.

The execution of an instruction and the fetching of the next instruction can be performed simultaneously in certain circumstances; this is known as *instruction fetch/ execute overlap*. The principal condition for success of the instruction fetch/execute overlap is that the particular instruction fetched can be identified before the previous instruction has been executed. (This is the case in sequentially executed instructions. However, some instructions will not be executed sequentially, or may only be executed sequentially after certain results have been obtained.)

The two basic cycles, fetch and execute, can be broken down further into the following three steps which, in some cases, can be overlapped.

1. Fetch instruction.
2. Decode instruction and fetch operands.
3. Execute operation.

The execute operation can be broken into individual steps dependent upon the instruction being executed. Simple arithmetic operations operating upon integers may only need one step while more complex operations, such as floating point multiplication or division, may require several steps.

In high speed processors, the sequence of operations to fetch, decode and execute an instruction are performed in a pipeline. In general, a pipeline consists of a number of stages, as shown in Figure 1.6, with each stage performing one sequential step of the overall task. Where necessary, the output of one stage is passed to the input of the next stage. Information required to start the sequence enters the first stage and results are

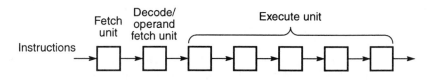

Figure 1.6 Processor pipeline

produced by the final (and sometimes intermediate) stage.

The time taken to process one complete task in the pipeline will be at least as long as the time taken when one complex homogeneous functional unit, designed to achieve the same result as the multistage pipeline, is used. However, if a sequence of identical operations is required, the pipeline approach will generate results at the rate at which the inputs enter the pipeline, though each result is delayed by the processing time within the pipeline. For sequential identical operations, the pipeline could be substantially faster than one homogeneous unit.

Clearly, instruction operations are not necessarily identical, nor always sequential and predictable and pipelines need to be designed to cope with non-sequential, dissimilar operations. Also, it is not always possible to divide a complex operation into a series of sequential steps, especially into steps which all take the same length of time. Each stage need not take the same time, but if the times are different, the pipeline must wait for the slowest stage to complete before processing the next set of inputs. However, substantial speed-up can be achieved using the pipeline technique and virtually all computer systems, even modern microprocessors, have a pipeline structure.

Chapter 5 will study the pipeline technique in detail. There are many complexities in the operation of a pipeline, notably that instructions cannot be processed independently.

1.3.2 Processor-memory interface

The processor-memory interface is concerned with:

1. Carrying instructions from the memory to the processor during instruction fetch.
2. Carrying data between the processor and the memory during instruction execution.

Naturally, it is important that the transfer of instructions/data takes place at least as fast as the information can be digested by the destination (processor or memory). It is not necessary to exceed this requirement and, when systems are being designed, attempts are made to match the processor and memory data rates. If the maximum processor and memory information transfer rates are different, the system speed may be constrained by the slower device. Normally the processor can operate at a higher speed than the main memory.

Increasing the communication bandwidth

The *bandwidth* is the amount of information that can be transferred across a communication link, given as bits/sec. The bandwidth can be increased by simply increasing the number of wires in the link. Increasing the number of data lines from 32 data lines to 64 data lines would double the bandwidth. Reducing the *latency* (the time to transfer one bit) is much more difficult. The speed of light (and hence electricity) is not easy to change!

A general technique for increasing the effective rate of a slow unit is to duplicate the unit and make more than one transfer simultaneously. For example, if there is a factor of 8 between the access times of the source and the destination, such that the destination can accept information at eight times the rate at which the source can generate information, then the source could be replicated eight times. Then eight transfers could be made to the destination simultaneously.

The technique can be used to match the speed of memory to the speed of the processor, by duplicating the memory modules. For example, suppose instructions are fetched from memory one at a time. If two memory modules are provided, with separate data paths to the processor, two instructions could be fetched from the memory simultaneously, increasing the transfer rate by a factor of 2. The same double word address is sent to both memory modules. If a factor of n increase in transfer rate is required, then n memory modules could be provided. There can be any number of memory modules, each with a separate data path, though in most applications a number which is a power of 2 would be used. To obtain blocks of sequentially addressed locations, the most significant part of the full address would specify the address of the n-word block and the least significant part of the address would specify the word within the n-word block. Using multiple memory modules in this way constrains transfers to be blocks of sequential locations and only works effectively if all (or most) items transferred are actually required; in essence, we are increasing the memory word length.

It is possible to send different addresses to each memory module so that n unrelated locations in different memory modules can be accessed simultaneously. This scheme is known as *memory interleaving*. It is important to differentiate between wide word length memory transfers and true memory interleaving. In the former, a block of consecutive locations can be accessed simultaneously and, in the latter, locations not in order can be accessed simultaneously, if these locations are in different memory modules.

In memory interleaving, we divide the memory address field into two parts, one to select the memory module and the other to select the location within the memory module. The memory module can be selected by either the least or the most significant bits; the latter is known as *low order interleaving* and the former as *high order interleaving*. These two alternative address formats are shown in Figure 1.7. Low order interleaving is suitable for single processor interleaved memory, so that consecutive memory locations

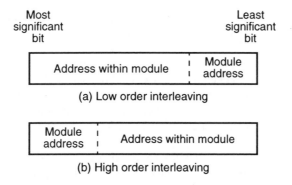

Figure 1.7 Address formats for interleaving

Microprocessor   Memory modules

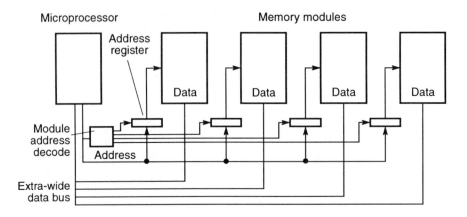

Figure 1.8 Memory interleaving with wide data bus

are in different memory modules and can be accessed simultaneously. With, for instance, four modules and low order interleaving, the first module addresses would be 0, 4, 8, 12, 16, ..., the addresses in the second module would be 1, 5, 9, 13, 17, ..., those in the third module, 2, 6, 10, 14, 18, ..., and in the fourth module, 3, 7, 11, 15, 19, ... In general, with n-way low order interleaving, the first module addresses would be 0, n, $2n$, $3n$, ... and the same stride in the other modules. (Normal memory systems divided into memory modules use the high order format, but only one module is addressed at a time and there is no overlap between memory operations.)

Figure 1.8 shows an interleaved memory organization for a single processor system using a separate data bus for each memory module to the processor. The memory module addresses select the modules and the module word addresses generated are loaded into address buffers in succession. As each address is loaded, the module can proceed to identify the location and provide read or write access. For read, data appear on each of the data buses in succession after the memory access time has elapsed. For write, the data is produced by the processor on the data bus and taken in succession by the memory modules. This organization might be suitable for a cache system which is also divided into modules.

A single data bus can be used, as shown in Figure 1.9. It is necessary to provide each memory module with a data buffer register to hold the data to be written into the module or read out. The timing of this system is shown in Figure 1.10(a). It is possible to supply the same address to all modules simultaneously so that consecutive words can be accessed (for the low order interleaved address format). The timing of this is shown in Figure 1.10(b).

Memory interleaving can be used in a pipelined system, as described in Chapter 5, to fetch more than one instruction simultaneously. After these instructions are fetched, each one is executed in sequence. The interleaving releases the processor-memory interface for subsequent operand accesses.

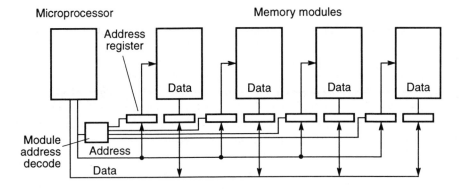

Figure 1.9 Memory interleaving with single bus

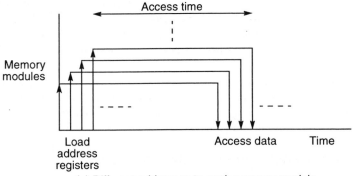

(a) Different addresses to each memory module

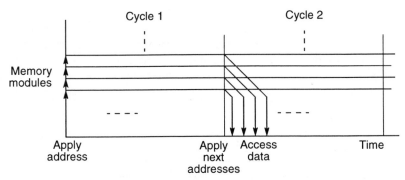

(b) Same address to each memory module

Figure 1.10 Interleaved memory timing

Prefetch buffers

If we increase the communication bandwidth sufficiently, it may be that the processor cannot always keep up with the instructions/data that could be fetched. Instructions and data can be prefetched before needed and held in a first-in first-out *prefetch buffer*. Normally the prefetched instructions are sequential instructions in the program. The prefetch buffer will help counter the effects of varying completion times of instructions and perhaps the effects of the memory bus being used by other devices. Microprocessors often have such "prefetch buffers" to hold instructions prior to execution. For example the Intel 486 has a 32-byte prefetch buffer. In this case, the prefetch buffer also enables instructions of varying lengths to be formed before execution.

Cache

A very significant improvement in performance can be made if high speed memory called a *cache* is introduced between the processor and the main memory, as shown in Figure 1.11. Program instructions and data are first loaded into the cache and then accessed by the processor. Assuming that the information is required more than once, which is usually true of program instructions, substantial improvements in overall speed can be achieved Most microprocessor systems now have cache memory inside their chip or externally. Separate caches can be provided for instructions (code) and for data, or a *unified* cache can be provided holding both. At first, these caches were quite small. Motorola MC68040 has a 4 Kbyte instruction cache and a 4 Kbyte data cache. The Intel 486 has an 8 Kbyte unified cache, though the Pentium has separate instruction and data caches (both 8 Kbytes). The trend is to provide larger and larger separate caches, and even two levels of cache memory. However the cache must operate faster than the main memory for the idea to make sense. Chapter 3 considers the design of cache memory systems.

1.3.3 External memory and memory hierarchy

The external memory system so far described consists of the main, random access memory supported by non-random access secondary memory, the latter usually being based upon magnetic technology. The most common is magnetic disk memory in which information is recorded in concentric tracks in a magnetic surface of a disk as it rotates. Magnetic disk memory operates several orders of magnitude slower than the main memory. Whereas main memory *access time* (the time to retrieve or alter the stored information) is in the order of 20–100 ns, access time on a disk is in the range 5–20 ms and it

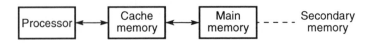

Figure 1.11 Cache memory

is difficult to improve substantially on this because of the mechanical nature of the disks. There has been gradual improvement over the years. We can use the same technique of duplicating modules to increase the communication bandwidth with disks. A file to be stored is divided into blocks and consecutive blocks are stored and accessed in an inter-leaved fashion from different disk units as shown in Figure 1.12. This is known as *file striping*. The size of the block could be one byte or multiple bytes. Using a single byte from each disk is likely to require that the disks be synchronized. With n disks, the data transfer bandwidth will increase by a factor of n. File striping does not help with the time to find the first location on the disks.

Inexpensive disks can be used to replace one larger disk and provide fault tolerance. If one disk becomes faulty and the data has been recorded on more than one disk or, more likely, error checking/correcting codes are in place, the system can reconfigure to use the remaining disks. The term *RAID* (redundant array of inexpensive disks) has been invented to describe using multiple disks in this fashion. Organization of magnetic disks is outside the scope of this book. Flynn (1995) has an excellent advanced treatment of disk organi-zations.

What is within the scope of this book is the way the different types of memory are managed. Various types of magnetic memory may be present, including exchangeable magnetic floppy disk memory, Winchester magnetic disk memory and magnetic tape memory. Optical disk technology, such as CD-ROMs, offers vast capacity for large amounts of data in one unit and becomes another level in the memory hierarchy. A sub-stantial part of architectural enhancements is concerned with making this memory hierarchy easy and efficient to use and assisting multiprogramming.

Multiprogramming is the term used to describe system programming when more than one user program is executed, in effect concurrently, by executing parts of each program in sequence. In the presence of a memory hierarchy it is necessary to transfer programs

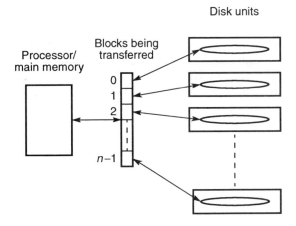

Figure 1.12 Multiple disks with file striping

from the secondary memory into the main memory before the program code can be executed. Similarly, data must be transferred into the main memory before being read or altered. Since only a limited amount of space is available in the main memory, programs or data not immediately required may need to be transferred out of the main memory and stored in the secondary memory until required. Moving programs or data into and out of the main memory requires a memory management scheme, preferably one which is hidden from the user and activated automatically.

The principal memory management method is known as *virtual memory*. This creates an automatic mechanism for arranging that data or program code is in the main memory, ready for execution, without the programmer having to program the main memory/ secondary memory transfers. The stored information is divided into fixed sized blocks which are moved between the main and secondary memories. The operand addresses used within the programs are not altered, but a hardware translation mechanism is in place to translate the addresses as they are generated by the processor so that they refer to the actual memory locations. The scheme is a significant and widely used architectural development. (Chapter 4 deals with memory management in detail.)

1.3.4 Multiple processor systems

The application of more than one processor working in a coherent manner on a single task within a single computer system has been studied since at least 1960 (Conway, 1963) and is an obvious method of increasing the speed of the system. One would expect that if n processors worked continuously and simultaneously on a single problem (a *multiprocessor*), the results would be obtained n times faster than if one processor were applied to the problem. However, it is not always easy to partition a problem so that n processors can operate simultaneously and, even if this were possible, an interprocessor communication overhead generally exists in the multiprocessor version. But multiprocessor solutions are necessary to achieve substantial increases in speed over existing high speed single processor systems and a large part of this text is devoted to the design of multiprocessor systems, particularly the possible architectural arrangements that could be employed for coupling the processors.

Multiprocessor systems can be developed from a single processor system by simply adding one or more processors, all of which share the same memory, resulting in the so-called shared memory multiprocessor system. Each processor might have local memory, but would use the shared memory to pass information between processors and to obtain shared programs/information – Part II of this text is largely devoted to such multiprocessor systems. In a bus-based system, additional processors can be added to the bus, as shown in Figure 1.13 – this approach has been taken by microprocessor system designers and will be discussed in Chapter 7. Generally, the approach is only suitable for small numbers of processors because of bus and memory contention, though multiple buses and a hierarchy of buses can be used to extend the system.

Alternatively, multiprocessor systems can use direct connections between processing elements. This approach leads to multiple processors which operate independently, passing information to other processing elements perhaps through a message-passing

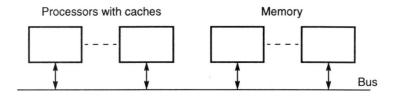

Figure 1.13 Single bus multiple microprocessor system

protocol, rather than through a shared memory system. Message-passing multiprocessor systems are easier to expand to large numbers of processors and are more suitable for VLSI fabrication with large numbers of processors. They do not suffer from the problems of maintaining consistency between the shared and local memories or from the problems of controlling access to shared information. Such multiprocessor systems are considered in Part III, together with dataflow computer systems.

1.3.5 Performance and cost

Cost is a major factor in design decisions and there are trade-offs between increased architectural (and technological) complexities and increased cost. There are often diminishing returns for added complexity and a point is reached when the added costs cannot be justified. For example, a cache memory inserted between the processor and main memory can substantially improve the performance and the larger the cache, the greater the improvement. However, a point is reached when the increased cost of further cache memory does not materially improve the performance, or if there is a significant improvement, the cost is not justified. There are various ways of organizing a cache (see Chapter 3) and each has different cost and performance implications. Unfortunately, it may not be immediately clear which organization should be chosen, as performance is highly dependent upon the programs being executed and the choice has to be made after considering likely applications of the system and general program characteristics. In a multiprocessor design (Part II and Part III), the use of more than one processor has to be justified in terms of performance and cost (hardware cost and programming cost) when compared to high speed single processor systems. In a multiprocessor system, a significant hardware factor is the method of interconnecting the processors. It is theoretically possible to connect all the processors together and allow them to communicate simultaneously, but such exhaustive interconnections incur heavy cost penalties and limited interconnection networks (see Chapter 8) need to be evaluated in terms of effect on performance and the cost. Multiprocessors also have to be evaluated in terms of programming costs.

1.4 Reduced instruction set computer

While the processors such as the Intel 8086 family and Motorola MC68000 family continued to be enhanced and developed, the early 1980s saw the development of a completely new direction for processor design, that of reducing the complexity of instructions leading to the *reduced instruction set computer* (RISC). This is a major change which has had a profound influence on the design of all processors, including the continuing development of existing processor families.

1.4.1 Motives

The general argument for providing additional operations and addressing modes was that they can be performed at greater speed in hardware than as a sequence of primitive machine instructions. We now call processors with instructions that can perform "complex" operations *complex instruction set computers* (CISCs). Complex instructions can be identified in the following areas:

1. To replace sequences of primitive arithmetic operations.
2. For alternative indirect methods of accessing memory locations.
3. For repetitive arithmetic operations.
4. In support of procedure calls and parameter passing.
5. In support of the operation system.
6. In support of multiprocessor systems.

Support for common repetitive operations is appealing because one instruction could initiate a long sequence of similar operations without further instruction fetches. Examples include instructions to access strings and queues and many CISCs have support for strings and queues. The Intel 8086 family has several instructions which access a consecutive sequence of memory locations. The Motorola MC68000 family has postincrement and predecrement addressing modes, in which the memory address is automatically incremented after a memory access and decremented prior to a memory access respectively. (Similar addressing can also be found in the VAX family.) Multiple operations are needed during procedure calls and returns. In addition to saving and restoring the return address, more complex call and return instructions can save all the main processor registers (or a subset) automatically. Mechanisms for passing procedure parameters are helpful, as procedure calls and returns occur frequently and can represent a significant overhead. Other composite operations also include checking for error conditions. For example, the MC68000 has a "check register against bounds" (CHK) instruction to compare the value held in a register with an upper bound. If the upper bound is exceeded, or the register value is below zero, an exception (internal interrupt) occurs. The upper bound is held in another register or in memory. More than one arithmetic/logic operation could be specified in one instruction, for example, to add two operands and shift the result one or more places left or right, as in the Nova minicomputer of the early 1970s. Clearly the number of instances in a program that such operations are required in sequence is limited.

Apart from adding more complex operations, complex addressing modes have also been introduced into systems. Addressing modes can be combined, for example index register addressing and base register addressing (i.e., base plus index register addressing). Indirect addressing could be multilevel. In multilevel indirect memory addressing, the address specifies a memory location which holds either the address of the operand location or, if the most significant bit is set to 1, the remaining bits are interpreted as an address of another memory location. The contents of this location are examined in the same manner. The indirection mechanism will continue until the most significant bit is 0 and the required operand address is obtained. Such multilevel indirection was provided in the NOV computer of the 1970s. Multilevel indirection is an example of a mechanism which is relatively simple to implement but which is of limited application and is now rarely found.

CISCs often have between 100 and 300 instructions and 8–20 addressing modes. An often quoted extreme example of a CISC is the VAX-11/780, introduced in 1978, having 303 instructions and 16 addressing modes with complex instruction encoding. Microprocessor examples include the Intel 386, with 111 instructions and 8 addressing modes, and the Motorola MC68020, with 109 instructions and 18 addressing modes. The Intel 486 increased the number of address modes of the 386 further to 11 and added instructions mostly for the now integrated floating point unit. (There were six other completely new instructions.) Almost always, the development came about by extending previous system designs and because of the view that the greatest speed can be achieved by providing operations in hardware rather than using software routines.

One of the effects of complex instructions is the need to specify different parameters in different instructions which has led to variable length instructions, usually in units of bytes or 16-bit words. Totally variable length instructions, using Huffman coding, can be used and, in one study, led to a 43 per cent saving in code size (Katevenis, 1985). The Intel 432 microprocessor uses bit-encoded instructions, having from 6 to 321 bits. Instructions can be limited to be multiples of bytes or words, which leads to 35 and 30 per cent savings, respectively. Limiting instructions in this way is often done because it matches the memory byte/word fetch mechanism. For example, an MC68000 instruction can be between one and five 16-bit words. An 8086 instruction can be between 1 and 6 bytes. The VAX-11/780 takes this technique to the extreme with between 2 and 57 bytes in an instruction.

All this complexity was questioned in the late 1970s. The basic questions asked were *"What effect on the design of the processor does all these extra instruction have on the operation of the processor?"* and *"Do the extra instructions indeed increase the speed of the system?"*

To discover which instructions are more likely to be used, extensive analyses for application programs are needed. It has been found that though high level languages allow very complex constructs, many programs use simple constructs. Tanenbaum (1990) identifies, on average, 47 per cent of program statements to be assignment statements in various languages and programs, and of these assignment statements, 80 per cent are simply assigning a value to a constant. Other studies have shown that the complex addressing modes are rarely used. For example, DEC found during the development of the VAX architecture that 20 per cent of the instructions required 60 per cent of the microcode but were only used 0.2 per cent of the time (Patterson and Hennessy, 1985). This observation led to the micro VAX-32 having a slightly reduced set of the full VAX instruction set (96 per cent) but a very significant reduction in complexity.

Hennessy and Patterson (1990) presented instruction frequency results for the VAX, IBM 360, Intel 8086 and their paper design, DLX processor. Table 1.1 is based upon the

Table 1.1 8086 Instruction usage

	MASM Assembler (%)	Turbo C compiler (%)	Lotus 1-2-3 (%)	Average (%)
Operand access				
Memory	37	43	43	41
Immediate	7	11	5	8
Register	55	46	52	51
Memory addressing				
Indirect	12	9	15	12
Absolute	36	18	34	30
Displacement	52	73	51	59
Instruction type				
Data transfer				
MOV	30	30	21	29
PUSH/POP	12	18	8	12
LEA	3	6	0	3
Arithmetic/logical				
CMP	9	3	3	7
SAL/SHR/RCR	0	3	12	5
INC/DEC	3	3	3	5
ADD	3	3	3	3
OR/XOR	1.5	4.5	3	3
Other each				3
Control/call				
JMP	3	1.5	1.5	2
LOOP	0	0	12	4
CALL/RET	3	6	3	4
Conditional branch	12	12	6	10

8086 results. Three programs are listed, all running under MS-DOS 3.3 on an 8086 processor IBM PC. The first is the Microsoft assembler, MASM, assembling a 500-line assembly language program. The second is the Turbo C compiler compiling the Dhrystone benchmark and the third is a Lotus 1-2-3 program calculating a 128 cell worksheet four times. The Dhrystone benchmark was developed as a benchmark program embodying operations of a "typical" program. This benchmark, and the other widely quoted benchmark program – the Whetstone benchmark – have been criticized as not being able to predict performance (see, for example, Hennessy and Patterson (1990), pp. 73 and 183). The test done here refers to the compiler, not to the execution of the Dhrystone benchmark. (More favored benchmarks are the SPECint92 and SPECfp92.)

Of course, each instruction frequency study will give different results depending upon benchmark programs, the processor and other conditions. However, register accesses generally account for a large percentage of accesses, and a significant percentage are move operations (for example 51 per cent register addressing, 29 per cent MOV and 12 per cent PUSH/POP in Table 1.1). Conditional branch instructions also account for a significant percentage of instructions (10 per cent in Table 1.1) and, though not shown in Table 1.1, instructions using small literals are very commonly used for counters and indexing lists.

CISC processors take account of differing instruction usage by using compact instruction encoding for frequently used instructions. The following frequently used operations are candidates for compact encoding:

1. Loading a constant to a register.
2. Loading a small constant (say 0 to 15) to a register.
3. Loading a register or memory with 0.
4. Arithmetic operations with small literals.

The MC68000 has "quick" instructions (move/add/subtract quick) in compact encoding with small constants. Similarly, the 8086 family has compact encoding for some register operations. In fact, using compact encodings makes the processor design even more complex.

A significant consequence of complex instructions with irregular encoding is the need for complex decode logic and complex logic to implement the operations specified. Most CISCs use microcode to sequence through the execution steps, an ideal method of implementing complex instructions. This can lead to a very large control store holding the microcode. Again, an extreme example is the 456 Kbyte microcode control store of the VAX-11/780. A consequence of bit-, byte- and word-encoded instructions is that the decoding becomes a sequential operation. Decoding continues as further parts of the instruction are received.

The general philosophy of the reduced instruction set computer design is to transfer the complexity into software when this results in improved overall performance. The most frequent primitive operations are provided in hardware. Less frequent operations are provided only if their inclusion does not adversely affect the speed of operation of the existing operations. The prime objective is to obtain the greatest speed of operation through the use of relatively simple hardware.

The following issues lead to the RISC concept:

1. The effect of the inclusion of complex instructions.
2. The best use of transistors in VLSI implementation.
3. The overhead of microcode.
4. The use of compilers.

Inclusion of complex instructions

The inclusion of complex instructions is a key issue. As we have mentioned, it was already recognized prior to the introduction of RISCs that some instructions are more frequently used than others. The CISC solution was to have shorter instruction lengths for commonly used instructions; the RISC solution is not to have the infrequently used instructions at all. To paraphrase Radin (1983), even if adding complex instructions only added one extra level of gates to a ten-level basic machine cycle, the whole CPU has been slowed down by 10 per cent. The frequency and performance improvement of the complex functions must first overcome this 10 per cent degradation and then justify the additional cost.

Use of transistors

One of the arguments put forward for the RISC concept concerns VLSI implementation. In the opening paragraph of his award-winning thesis, Katevenis (1985) makes the point that "it was found that hardware support for complex instructions is not the most effective way of utilizing the transistors in a VLSI processor". There is a trade-off between size/complexity and speed. Greater VLSI complexity leads directly to decreased component speeds due to circuit capacitances and signal delays. With increasing circuit densities, a decision has to be made on the best way to utilize the circuit area. Is it to add complex instructions at the risk of decreasing the speed of other operations, or should the extra space on the chip be used for other purposes, such as a larger number of processor registers, caches or additional execution units, which can be performed simultaneously with the main processor functions? The RISC proponents argue for the latter. Many RISCs employ silicon MOS technology; however, the RISC concept is also applicable to the emerging, lower density gallium arsenide (GaAs) technology and several examples of GaAs RISC processors have been constructed.

Microcode

A factor leading to the original RISC concept was changing memory technology. CISCs often rely heavily on microprogramming (microcode) in which a fast control memory inside the processor holds microinstructions specifying the steps to perform for each machine instruction. Microprogramming was first used at a time when the main memory was based upon magnetic core stores and faster read-only control memory could be provided inside the control unit. With the move to semiconductor memory, the gap between the achievable speed of operation of main memory and control memory narrows. Now, a considerable overhead can appear in a microprogrammed control unit, especially for simple machine instructions.

Compilers

There is an increased prospect for designing optimizing compilers with fewer instructions. Some of the more exotic instructions are rarely used, particularly in compilers which have to select an appropriate instruction automatically, as it is difficult for the compiler to identify the situations where the instructions can be used effectively. A key part of the RISC development is the provision for an optimizing compiler which can take over some of the complexities from the hardware and make best use of the registers. Many of the techniques that can be used in an optimizing RISC compiler are known and can be used in CISC compilers.

Further advantages of the RISC concept include simplified interrupt service logic. In a RISC, the processor can easily be interrupted at the end of simple instructions. Long, complex instructions would cause a delay in interrupt servicing or necessitate complex logic to enable an interrupt to be serviced before the instructions had completed. A classic example of a complex instruction which could delay an interrupt service is a string instruction.

There are claims against the RISC concept. Disadvantages include the fact that if the machine instructions are simple, it is reasonable to expect the programs to be longer. There is some dispute over this point, as it is argued that compilers can produce better optimized code from RISC instruction sets, and in any event, more complex instructions are longer than RISC instructions. Certain features identified with a RISC might also improve a CISC. For example, RISCs usually call for a large number of general purpose registers. A large register file could improve the performance of a CISC. Similarly, optimizing compilers using information on the internal structure of the processor can improve the performance of a CISC.

Though the RISC philosophy can be achieved after various architectural choices, there are common characteristics. The number of different instructions is limited to about 128, or fewer, carefully selected instructions which are likely to be most used. These instructions are preferably encoded in one fixed-size word and execute in one cycle without microcoding. Perhaps only four addressing modes are provided. Indexed and PC-relative addressing modes are probably a minimum requirement; others can be obtained from using these two addressing modes. All instructions conform to one of a few instruction formats. Memory operations are limited to load and store and all arithmetic/logical operations operate upon operands in processor registers. Hence it is necessary to have a fairly large number of general purpose processor registers, perhaps thirty-two integer registers. A three-register address instruction format is commonly chosen for arithmetic instructions, i.e., the operation takes operands from two registers and places the result in a third register. This reduces the number of instructions in many applications and differs from many CISC microprocessors, which often have two-register, or one-register/one-memory, address instructions. In keeping all instructions to a fixed size, some do not use all the bits in the instruction for their specification, and unused bits would normally be set to zero.

Such wastage is accepted for simplicity of decoding. Chapter 2 will begin assuming that we will use the RISC approach in the design of processors.

1.4.2 RISC examples

IBM 801

The first computer system designed on RISC principles was the IBM 801 machine, designed over the period 1975–79 and publicly reported in 1982 (see Radin, 1983). The work marks the time when increasing computer instruction set complexity was first questioned. The 801 establishes many of the features for subsequent RISC designs. It has a three-register instruction format, with register-to-register arithmetic/logical operations. The only memory operations are to load a register from memory and to store the contents of a register in memory. All instructions have 32 bits with regular instruction formats. Immediate operands can appear as 16-bit arithmetic/logical immediate operands, 11-bit mask constants, 16-bit constant displacement for PC-relative branch instructions and 26-bit offset for PC-relative addressing or absolute addressing. The system was constructed using SSI/MSI ECL components with a cycle time of 66 ns.

Programming features include:

- 32 general purpose registers.
- 120 32-bit instructions.
- Two addressing modes: base plus index; base plus immediate.
- Optimizing compiler.

A four-stage pipeline is employed having the stages: instruction fetch; register read or address calculation; ALU operation; register write.

A key aspect of the 801 project was the design of an optimizing compiler. The project depended upon being able to transfer complexity from the architecture into an optimizing compiler. From a source code program, intermediate language code is first produced and then optimized by the compiler. Conventional optimizing techniques applicable to any system are used. For example, constants are evaluated at compile time, loops are shortened by moving constant expressions to outside the loop, intermediate values are reused when possible and some procedures are expanded in-line.

The location of registers to variables in the program is a critical part of the optimization. In a register assignment procedure, the variables are mapped onto the available set of registers in such a manner as to minimize memory accesses. The algorithm used in the IBM project is based upon the notion that the register allocation problem can be seen as a graph coloring problem. In this approach, each node of a graph represents a variable to be held in a register. A variable is *live* if it has been assigned a value which will be used again before being recomputed. If two variables are simultaneously live, an arc connects the nodes. Each node is assigned a color. The problem then reduces to finding colors for the nodes such that each connected node has a different color, the so-called graph coloring problem. If this requires n colors, to fully assign all the variables to registers

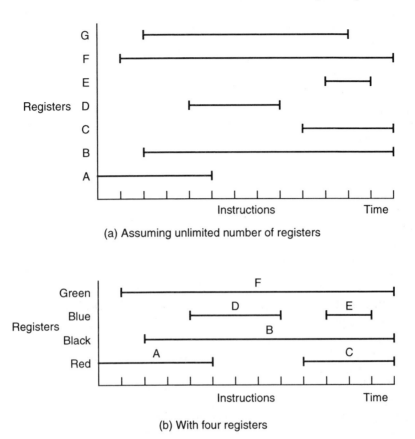

(a) Assuming unlimited number of registers

(b) With four registers

Figure 1.14 Register allocation with limited number of registers

would require *n* colors. Allocation of variables to registers is illustrated in Figure 1.14. The *lifetime* of each variable is identified, the time between the first and last use of the variable. In Figure 1.14(a) one register is assigned to each variable, A, B, C, D, E, F and G. In Figure 1.14(b), we assume four registers are available, corresponding to the colors, red, black, blue and green, and a possible assignment is shown. Those variables which cannot be allocated registers are held in memory, for example G in Figure 1.14. In the 801, 17 registers were made available, so a 17-color solution was sought. The graph coloring algorithm is fully described by Chaitin *et al.* (1981).

Notice that the lifetime of a variable may not always represent its usage. A variable with a short lifetime might be referenced many times, and hence should be held in register, while another variable might have long lifetime but is not referenced very often and would have a lower overhead if held in memory. Figure 1.14 does not show this aspect. It may be, for example, that G is used more frequently than F, and it might be

Table 1.2 Features of early VLSI RISCs

Features	RISC I	RISC II	MIPS
Registers	78	138	16
Instructions	31	39	55
Addressing modes	2	2	2
Instruction formats	2	2	4
Pipeline stages	2	3	5

better to allocate G to Green and use Green at other times for F. At the times that Green is assigned to G, F must be return to memory.

Early university research prototypes – RISC I/II and MIPS

The first university-based RISC project was probably at the University of California at Berkeley (Patterson, 1985; Katevenis, 1985), very closely followed by the MIPS (Microprocessor without Interlocked Pipeline Stages) project at Stanford University. Both projects resulted in the first VLSI implementations of RISCs, the Berkeley RISC I in 1982, and the Stanford MIPS and the Berkeley RISC II, both in 1983. These early VLSI RISCs did not have floating point arithmetic, though it was anticipated that floating point units could be added to operate independently of other units in the processor. Floating point operations are regarded as candidates for inclusion in the instruction set, especially for numeric applications. Features of these early VLSI RISCs are shown in Table 1.2. All processors are 32-bit, register-to-register processors and do not use microcode. Regular instruction formats are used. The large number of registers in the RISC I/II processors were used in a register window construction described in Chapter 5. Only 32 registers were accessible in a program at any instant in time. Thirty-two registers have become a standard for RISCs.

Commercial RISCs

Both the RISC I/II and MIPS led to commercial RISC processors. The SUN Sparc processor is derived from the Berkeley RISC II processor but with sixty-nine instructions (Hwang, 1993). The MIPS Computer System Corporation was established purposely to develop the Stanford MIPS processor, and a series of processors have appeared, including the R2000, R3000, R4000, R5000, etc. At about the same time as these processors were being developed, other manufactures started to become interested in the idea.

The Motorola MC88100 RISC 32-bit microprocessor, introduced in 1988 (Motorola, 1988a), is one of the first RISCs to be produced by a major CISC microprocessor manufacturer. The main characteristics of the MC88100 are:

- Register-to-register (three-address) instructions, except load/store.
- Thirty-two general purpose registers.
- Fifty-one instructions.
- All instructions fixed 32-bit length.
- No microcode.
- Four pipelined execution units that can operate simultaneously.
- Separate data and address paths (Harvard architecture).

Later RISCs also incorporated superscalar operation (executing more than one instruction in one clock cycle). Examples of RISCs with superscalar operation include the IBM RS 6000, DEC 21064 (Alpha) and the PowerPC family. The *scalarity* (the number of instructions that can be executed simultaneously) in these processors is between 2 and 4, and the number of function units available for the instructions is usually between 2 and 6 (at least the same as the scalarity as defined here). During this continual development, the trend has been to increase the scalarity and to move from 32 bits to 64 bits, and to increase the addressing to 40+ bits. Examples of 64-bit superscalar processors include the Alpha 21164, MIPS 10 000, PowerPC 620 and the UltraSparc (all having a scalarity of 4, and 40-bit or 41-bit addressing).

Discussion questions

1.1 Why are memory locations organized as locations each holding one byte even in a 32-bit processor? What would be the effects of only having 32-bit locations on the design of the system (i.e. not having byte locations)? What are the advantages and disadvantages?

1.2 The trend is to move to higher precision integer capability within a processor. Where would 64-bit integers be useful in computing? Are there areas where even higher precision is warranted? Do you expect the length of instructions to also be increased from 32 bits to 64 bits (or another size)?

1.3 Suppose technology has advanced to enable 64 RISC processors to be fabricated on one chip or a single superscalar RISC processor with a scalarity of 64 (capable of executing 64 instructions simultaneously) to be fabricated on one chip. Discuss the two options and write a report recommending one option.

1.4 Why was microprogramming invented? Why is it not currently used?

1.5 Were the first processors developed in the 1940s and 1950s RISC processors? Discuss.

1.6 Suggest one reason why the RISC concept was not used widely in the 1970s (apart from the term not conceived!).

1.7 Name one memory addressing mode usually not found in RISC processors. Name two other characteristics common to (most) RISCs.

1.8 Discuss whether you expect the number of address bits to increase over the next ten years and why?

2 | *Instruction set design*

In this chapter, we focus on the design of a reduced instruction set processor. We will explore the alternatives for instructions and establish an instruction set. This instruction set is representative of many reduced instruction computers. Next we describe actions necessary to implement the instructions within the processor, concentrating upon designs using a centralized control unit. This chapter establishes the instruction formats and mnemonics which will be used in subsequent chapters. Chapter 5 continues the detailed design of the processor, by exploring the complexities of pipeline processors, and advanced techniques for increasing the performance of the processor. Chapter 5 could be studied immediately after Chapter 2, or after the intermediate Chapters 3 (on cache memory), and 4 (on memory management).

2.1 Processor characteristics

The processor is of course the central part of any computer system, and hence we begin with the design of the processor. In Chapter 1, we reviewed the general mode of operation of computers and the processor. Irrespective of the processor, all processors operate by fetching instructions from memory, and executing the fetched instructions. The first design characteristic is to establish the instructions and formats that the processor will recognize. We have two approaches here; first we could take the instructions and formats of an existing processor. Alternately we could invent a hypothetical processor. The disadvantage of choosing an existing processor is that certain decisions may have been made to make the processor compatible with other processors or because of particular technological constraints. Of course one may be familiar with a particular processor as a user, and the instructions would also be familiar. The advantage of using a hypothetical processor is that various design decisions can be investigated. We will use the hypothetical approach. This means that an instruction set and formats needs to be invented. However, we will design our processor instruction set to be very close to processors of real reduced instruction set computers (RISCs). In Chapter 1, we established the reduced instruction set computer as an attractive design approach. Apart from this type of processor being very popular for new processor designs, it also has a simple type of instruction set and instruction formats, making the design "cleaner". It is an attractive design choice for studying processor design. Fortunately most real RISC processors have adopted very similar instructions and instruction formats, and we can extract the common traits of RISC processors. (Conversely, complex instruction set computers, CISCs, of different families have widely different instructions and formats.)

There is no precise definition of a RISC processor, and what constitutes a reduced instruction or a complex instruction. Generally a complex instruction is one which can involve many internal steps to complete execution of the instruction, whereas a reduced instruction could be completed in a few major steps. RISCs do have a number of important common traits due to the underlying belief of their designers that *simpler is faster.*

Use of memory and registers

A major common trait of an RISC processor in terms of its instruction set is the decision to use memory only to store data, and to use registers for all arithmetic operations. It is not possible, as it is in some CISCs, to perform arithmetic on operands stored in memory directly. The theme in RISCs is to design for maximum speed avoiding the use of memory whenever possible because memory is slower to access than registers. For greater flexibility, a three-register instruction format is used for arithmetic operations such as addition. Thirty-two registers are commonly chosen for the register file within the processor for storing integers. This is a compromise between providing compilers with enough registers, and having too many registers to save before a context switch. Also as we increase the number of registers (in powers of 2), the access time of the register file usually increases, so we do not want to create a slow register file by increasing its size. Memory must of course be accessed, to bring in data to load into registers and to store operands from registers to memory. Such instructions are called *load* and *store* respectively, and will be the major instructions for accessing memory. The use of load and store instructions lead to processors of this type as having a *Load/Store instruction format.*

The thirty-two registers will be called R0–R31. Some of the registers will be given certain uses in additional to their general purpose nature. One register, R0, will permanently store the number zero, and cannot be used for any other purpose. This is a common design approach, and done because it is very convenient to have a register holding zero for clearing locations, and for comparison operations. R0 will be used in ADD instructions when all we actually wish to do is move the contents of one register to another register. A "move" instruction will not be provided explicitly. The lack of a move instruction is not an overhead because, as we shall see, operands pass through an arithmetic and logic unit (ALU) for all instructions. The uses of other registers will be developed as we go.

Operand and instruction size

In VLSI (very large scale integration), the number of bits processed simultaneously by the processor is closely linked to the allowable complexity of the fabrication technology.

A 16-bit processor (a processor being able to process 16-bit numbers intrinsically) is obviously less complex than a 32-bit processor (a processor being able to process 32 bits intrinsically). Fabrication technology had advanced so that by, 1990, 32-bit processors, or even 64-bit processors, could reasonably be designed on one VLSI chip. (Of course with the RISC philosophy of "simpler is faster" we must decide whether we should use the available chip area for a 64-bit processor, or design a 32-bit processor and use the remaining "real estate" on the chip for other things.) Thirty-two bits provide a reasonable precision for integers, though 64 bits may be more attractive for floating point numbers. Some processors even support 128 bits. For example, the Intel i860 RISC processor (Intel, 1992b) has 128-bit load and store operations.

We shall choose to consider a 32-bit integer processor as this has become very common. There are very few significant architectural differences between processors with different operand sizes in terms of control techniques – the main differences are in the number of gates to make up the registers and ALUs and other functional components and the number of internal data lines to connect the functional units. The one factor in the instruction set design which may appear with increasing integer size is the need to specify the size of the number being processed, 8 bits, 16 bits, 32 bits, 64 bits (or greater). The size of 8 bits is provided principally to handle ASCII characters. The other sizes are provided for increasing precision at the expense of increasing memory requirements. A typical way to handle the different sizes in the instruction specification is to have a size field in the instruction, say two bits with 00 = 8 bits, 01 = 16 bits, 10 = 32 bits and 11 = 64 bits. Once such a decision is made, we may have compatibility issues if subsequently a compatible processor is needed with larger word lengths. We do not show a size field in subsequent instructions, assuming all transfers are 32 bits. It is left as an exercise to incorporate a size field (Problem 2.1).

Whether the number of bits in the operands and the number of bits in the instruction are the same is a design decision. Clearly both need to be related to the smallest address-able unit in memory which has been established universally as the byte (8 bits). Therefore instructions need to be multiples of bytes rather some arbitrary length, for efficiency. Complex instruction set processors usually have instructions of different lengths (variable length instructions). We shall have all instructions the same length for ease of decoding (fixed length instructions), and will choose 32 bits for the instructions. This length is commonly chosen for RISCs, but it does cause problems, notably that it is not possible to specify a 32-bit constant in a 32-bit instruction, since we need at least an opcode, and a register specified. Similarly we cannot specify a 32-bit address in the instruction. Such problems could be alleviated by using a longer instruction, such as 48 bits or 64 bits. Then there would be many instructions which do not need all these bits in their instruc-tion. Choosing 32-bit instructions will make it necessary to have a sequence of two instructions to form a 32-bit constant. This will be accomplished by loading the upper 16 bits of the register with a 16-bit constant, and then loading the lower 16 bits with a 16-bit constant. We have avoided this complexity for loading zero, by using R0 to hold a (32-bit) zero, so loading zero can be done in one instruction.

Size of the memory address

The number of bits provided to address the main memory must be chosen. It may be related to the size of the registers within the processor if these are to hold addresses. Having n bits in the address allows 2^n locations to be addressed (without any other addressing mechanisms in place, see Chapter 4 on memory management). As the allowable complexity of chips increases, so more bits are provided to address memory. Early microprocessors (and minicomputers) of the 1970s used 16-bit addresses, providing for 64 Kbytes, but this was soon recognized as insufficient, and increased to 20 bits (in the Intel 8086), 24 bits (in the Motorola MC68020) and finally to 32 bits for many processors in the time period 1985–1995. Choosing 32 bits is convenient if the registers in the processor also have 32 bits. Sixty-four bits is also a possibility to ensure longevity of the design, especially if the registers are increased to 64 bits. We shall assume 32-bit addresses providing for main memory up to 2^{32} bytes (4 gigabytes).

2.2 Instruction formats

The purpose of this section is to design the instruction formats and main instructions for our processor. Not every possible instruction will be enumerated. However, all instructions must conform to one of the basic instruction formats. In subsequent sections and chapters we will develop designs for the processor.

We shall number the bits in the instruction 0 to 31, with bit 31 being on the left side. (Some manufacturers/designers number the bits in the opposite direction; there is no particular consensus.) To specify one of the thirty-two registers requires 5 bits in the instruction for each register specified. Most instructions require two or three registers specified, each requiring 5 bits in the instruction. Six bits are allocated for the primary opcode (operation), bits 26 to 31, allowing up to sixty-four different operations. Sometimes a secondary field (*sub-opcode*) is used for some instructions which do not use all the other bits, to expand the number of operations. For example, the main opcode could specify a class of arithmetic operations, and a sub-opcode in the rest of the instruction specify the actual arithmetic operation. We shall explore alternative instruction formats in this section.

There are five classes of instructions:

2.2.1 Register-register instructions

Our design calls for operands to be held in registers for speed and efficiency. The central operations are concerned with performing an arithmetic/logic operation on two operands, each held in a register, and placing the result in a register. We classify these operations as *register-register*. We need 15 bits in the instruction format to specify the three registers. Figure 2.1 shows the instruction format chosen for the register-register instructions. Eleven bits, bits 0 to 10, are unused. The reason for this arrangement is partly because a

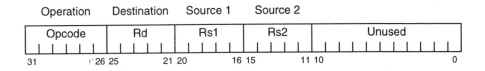

Figure 2.1 Register-register instruction format (R-R-R format)

6-bit opcode and two register fields occupies 16 bits, leaving 16 bits for the upper and lower 16-bit constants for loading a 32-bit constant in register-constant operation (see next class of operations). We want to keep the fields in the same place in all instruction formats that use the field, i.e., all instructions which have a destination register (Rd) will use bits 21 to 25, all instructions which use source registers use bits 16 to 20 for one source (Rs1) and bits 11 to 15 for the other source register (Rs2). If the instruction only uses one source register, as in adding a constant to a register, then the source register will be specified in the first source field, Rs1, bits 16 to 20. Having unused bits in the instruction might seem wasteful and inefficient in storage. However code efficiency is not a primary factor to consider – what is much more important is how fast the instruction can be decoded and executed.

An example of a register-register instruction would be:

```
ADD R2,R3,R4    ;R2 = R3 + R4
```

As above, we will illustrate machine instructions in an *assembly language*, consisting of the opcode as a mnemonic, the operands with the destination first, and finally a comment written in a C-like notation separated from the instruction by a semicolon. Though we chose to use the destination first in the assembly language as in the machine instruction, this is by no means standard; some use the destination last, and not necessarily in the same position as in the machine instruction.

Using one register, R0, to hold zero, we can create a register move operation with addition, i.e., to copy the contents of R4 into R5 we use:

```
ADD R5,R4,R0    ;R5 = R4 (+0)
```

so that a specific register move instruction is unnecessary. The addition operation does not normally cause the processor to operate slower because operands of all instructions are arranged to pass through an adder.

The arithmetic operations which we would expect to be provided include addition, subtraction, multiplication and division, operating upon integers, shift/rotate left or right one or more bits, and bit-wise logical operations such as AND, OR, NOT, and exclusive-OR. AND and OR are especially useful for setting, resetting and testing the value of specific bits in a number. They are regarded as essential in the instruction set. They are also very simple to implement. Floating point numbers normally have their own arithmetic operations of addition, subtraction, multiplication and division, and it may be that integer multiplication/division are not provided, only floating point multiplication and division.

Shift/rotate instructions only require one operand; the other operand could specify the number of shifts, i.e., Rs1 hold the number to be shifted and Rs2 holds the number of places to be shifted. Even though it is questionable whether these instructions are widely used, and also their implementation may be complex for high speed, shift and rotate instructions are usually incorporated into processors.

We could use the remaining currently unused bits in the instruction to specify a sub-operation, perhaps an operation associated with a functional unit, such as an arithmetic/logic unit, and then the primary opcode specifies a class of operations processed by the functional unit. This would provide for more operations than could be specified in the primary opcode, and is done in some RISCs. Unfortunately bits 0 to 10 will be used in other instructions with arithmetic operations, so that consistency could not be guaranteed across instruction classes. Problem 2.2 explores the use of a sub-opcode.

2.2.2 Register-register-constant (immediate) format

It is a very common requirement to be able to add a constant to a register, or do another arithmetic operation using one operand as a constant. This is generally referred to as the immediate addressing mode, because the constant is part of the instruction and immediately follows the rest of the instruction. We have already established that we will not be able to specify a 32-bit constant in the instruction, but often the constant required is a small constant. A convenient and reasonable small constant size has 16 bits because then two instructions can hold two 16-bit constants forming a 32-bit constant. Figure 2.2 shows our format for the register-register-constant instructions. Again the opcode has 6 bits and the register fields remain in the same place as the register-register instructions. One source register is simply replaced by the 16-bit constant. Now we do not have any unused bits in the instruction, though as we have indicated, this is not particularly important. An example is:

```
ADD R2,R3,16              ;R2 = R3 + 16
```

The constant is held in the instruction. In such cases, the term *literal* is sometimes used to convey the idea of the value being literally available. In our assembly language, a constant is written simply as the number without any additional notation; the 16 means

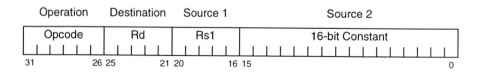

Figure 2.2 Register-constant instruction format (R-R-I format)

the constant 16. Sometimes an additional symbol is used to indicate a constant, for example the # symbol, i.e. #16 means the constant 16. This is only necessary if 16 on its own could mean something else, notably the address 16. We shall use the notation [16] to mean the memory address 16.[1]

The register-register-constant format could be used with all the arithmetic/logical operations provided in the register-register format, including shift/rotate operations in which the number of shift positions is given by the constant.

2.2.3 Register-memory format

Although all operands are processed in registers, they must first be loaded into registers from memory (unless entered as program input, or declared as immediate constants). Register-memory (load and store) instructions need to specify the address of a memory location, and many addressing mechanisms have been devised for computing the (effective) address over the years. However, one addressing mode, register indirect addressing with offset, provides an addressing mode from which most other addressing can be created, and register indirect addressing with offset will be chosen as the principal memory addressing mode. In register indirect addressing, a register holds the address of the memory location. Optionally an offset given as a constant in the instruction can be added to the address to create the final address used to access memory. The load instruction loads a destination register with the contents of the memory, and the store instruction stores the contents of a source register in the addressed memory location. Hence two registers need to be specified in these instructions, one source or destination register, and one register holding the memory address. Additionally an offset constant needs to be given in the instruction. Typical instructions would be:

```
LD R1,100[R2]        ;Contents of memory location
                     ;whose address is given by contents
                     ;of R2 + 100 is copied in R1
ST 200[R8],R6        ;R6 is copied into memory location
                     ;whose address is given by R8 + 200
```

Hence a format similar to the register-constant instruction format could be used as shown in Figure 2.3. For a load, Rd specifies the register to be loaded, and for a store, Rd specifies the register to be copied to memory. In both cases Rs1 specifies the register holding the address. It is rather unfortunate that in a load, Rd is the destination, and in a store, Rd is the source. We shall see that this causes a minor complexity to the processor design – the only way around this is to use the three-register format and use the previously unused bits as the offset as shown in Figure 2.4. Then the offset could only be 11

---

[1] To add to the confusion of notations that exist, some RISC designers use ( ) rather than [ ] to show a memory address; [ ] has been common with CISCs. In RISCs, even when a notation is used for memory address, sometimes the # is still used for constants. The # does tend to make it absolutely clear that a constant is specified.

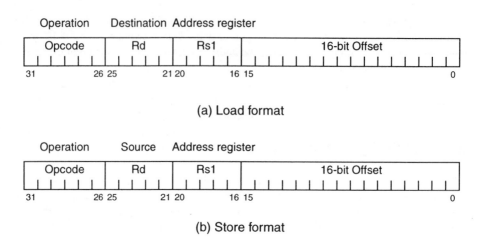

(a) Load format

(b) Store format

Figure 2.3 Load/store instruction formats (using R-R-I format) - version 1

bits, i.e., an offset of $+2^{10} - 1$ through to -2^{10} using a 2's complement for the number representation of the offset. Actually the unused bits in the instruction could be used for some purpose, for example additional offset bits (probably rather complex to implement for the store instruction).

Though in our notation we place the destination first and the source second in the assembly language, and this is also done in the machine instruction, some RISC designs

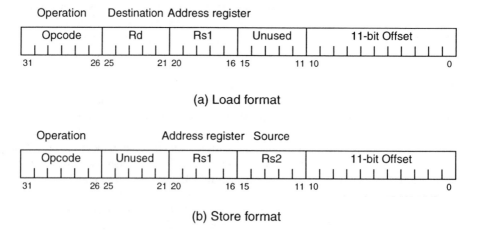

(a) Load format

(b) Store format

Figure 2.4 Load/store instruction formats (using R-R-I format) - version 2

do not maintain this for the ST, i.e. the instruction might be written as ST R6,200[R8]. (Even the mnemonics vary. LW and SW is sometimes used to indicate a 32-bit word load and store.)

2.2.4 Branch format

All instructions sets must provide for changing the program sequence dependent upon some computed values, otherwise we lose the decision-making power of the computer. In high level languages such as C and PASCAL, we have IF statements, e.g.:

```
if (x != y) && (z < 0) {
    a = b + 5;
    b = b + 1;
}
```

(in C). Compilers must translate such statements into machine instructions. At the machine instruction level, we will need more than one instruction to implement this high level language sequence. It would be unreasonable to try to provide a unique machine instruction for this IF statement because of the vast number of possible IF statements that could be written. We could not provide an instruction for each one. (Actually many programmers do not write very complex constructs, even though it may be possible in the language.) It is also not a good idea to try to match the machine instruction set with a particular high level language. Instead, we wish to extract the essential primitive operations for machine instructions. Clearly we need some form of "conditional jump" instruction at the machine instruction level in which the sequence of execution can be changed dependent upon a specified condition.

We could decompose the above IF statement, and any other complex IF construct into simple IF statements of the form:

```
if (x relation y) goto L1;
```

where relation would be any of the usual relations allowed in high level languages, e.g. <, >, >=, <=, ==, !=. This simple IF statement can be implemented with machine instructions. Then more complex constructs can be implemented from simpler IF constructs. For example, depending upon the compiler, the previous C statement could be compiled into the equivalent machine instructions of the statements:

```
    if (x == y) goto L1;
    if (z => 0) goto L1;
    a = b + 5;
    b = b + 1;
L1:
```

There is more than one way of creating the basic IF statement, if (x relation

y) `goto L1`, with machine instructions. Each way has a particular impact upon the internal design of the processor and in coding.

In general the `goto L1` part requires the target instruction address L1 to be specified. Normally the "target" address is given as a number of locations from the address of the present (or next) instruction as an offset, and this offset is added to the program counter to obtain the absolute address (i.e., *PC-relative addressing* is used). This is because mostly the instructions are used to implement small changes in sequences or program loops of relatively short length. Also it is good programming practice to limit sequence changes to a short distance from the current location to avoid difficult to read code. It also helps make the code *relocatable*. (This means that the code can be loaded anywhere in memory without having to change the branch and other addresses.) PC-relative addressing requires an *effective memory address* to be computed in much the same way as register-indirect addressing, except the register is the program counter and need not be specified. (Recall the effective address is the address obtained after all fetches and calculations have occurred to obtain the memory address.)

In addition to a conditional branch instruction, we also need an unconditional change of sequence. Instructions to implement this are called here *jump instructions*. Jump instructions will be discussed in the next section. We will also use jump instructions to make a change to a distant location, by providing jump instructions with register-indirect addressing. When register-indirect addressing is applied to jump instructions (and to branch instructions), the contents of a register specified in the instruction holds the target address.

Conditional branch instructions can be visualized as providing the two directions in a branch of a road, or branches of a tree. Perhaps the most commonly known method of implementing conditional branch machine instructions is by using the condition code register.

Condition code register approach

The *condition code register* (or Flag register) is a special-purpose register within the processor, normally closely linked to the ALU. Individual bits in the condition code register indicate a particular aspect of the result of the last arithmetic instruction, such as whether the result is zero or not zero (Z flag in the condition code register = 1 or 0), whether a final carry was generated or not generated (C flag in the condition code register = 1 or 0), whether an overflow occurred or did not occur (O flag in the condition code register = 1 or 0), whether the result is negative or positive (S flag in the condition code register = 1 or 0). In relation to a processor model given in Chapter 1 (Figure 1.3), the condition code register becomes a register accessible by (certain) instructions and becomes part of the state of the processor, as shown in Figure 2.5. The position of each flag in the condition code register is an arbitrary design decision.

To implement the basic IF statement, first an arithmetic instruction is executed which sets the flags in the condition code register according to the result of the arithmetic instruction. The most common arithmetic instruction performed to set the flags is the *compare instruction* which is similar to a subtract instruction except the result is not stored anywhere, only the flags are set according to the result. If the result is zero, the

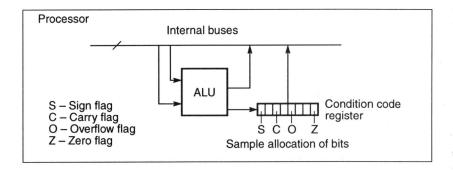

Figure 2.5 Condition code register

zero flag is set to 1. If the result is negative the sign flag is set to 1, etc. It is possible to have more than one flag set (but not of course the zero flag and sign flag, as zero is regarded as a positive number). Then, a conditional branch instruction examines the values stored in the condition code register to compute whether the specific condition exists. It may be that more than one flag needs to be examined for the condition. For example whether one number is equal to or greater than another may require the zero flag and the negative flag (and perhaps others) to be examined.

The instruction set must be provided with all expected conditions that may be wanted. A typical list of conditions includes:

Mnemonic	Condition	High level language notation
BL	Branch if less than	<
BG	Branch if greater than	>
BGE	Branch if greater or equal to	>=
BLE	Branch if less or equal to	<=
BE	Branch if equal	==
BNE	Branch if not equal	!=

The comparison could be between 2's complement numbers or between pure positive numbers (bit patterns that represent only positive numbers). Normally the two types of numbers must be differentiated in the system when it comes to comparing their values. For example the number 1111101 is less than 00000101 using 2's complement representation (−3 is less than +5). However, 1111101 is greater than 00000101 using pure positive representation (125 is greater than 5). This means that the number of arithmetic conditions provided effectively doubles. Checking relationships between signed numbers and between unsigned numbers requires different combinations of flags. (Problem 2.5 involves determining the combinations of flags.) In addition checking individual flags such as the carry flag and overflow flag must be provided.

In effect we have decomposed the IF statement such as:

```
        if (x == y) goto L1
```

into two parts:

```
        (x - y); Set condition codes S, O, C, Z, etc.
        if (certain condition codes set) goto L1
```

The condition code register approach has been extremely common and can be found in complex instruction set processors such as the Intel 8086 family and Motorola MC68000 family, and earlier microprocessors. For example to implement:

```
        if (x == y) goto L1;
```

in an 8086 with X in the AX register and Y in the BX register, a typical sequence would be:

```
    CMP AX,BX       ;Perform the operation AX - BX and
                    ;store conditions in condition code
                    ;register (F register)
    JZ L1           ;jump to instruction labelled L1 if
                    ;zero result (AX = BX)
```

(The 8086 uses the term jump even for conditional branch instructions.)

Having a sequence of two instructions is rather unfortunate when designing high performance processors because the two instructions must be performed in sequence without any other instruction in between which can affect the condition code register.[2] Also the first instruction must be executed to completion before the second can start. As we shall see, high performance processors usually start subsequent instructions before previous ones have completed if they can, and may on occasion execute instructions not in program order. Such strategies could not be employed with the above condition code sequence. Finally the condition code register is part of the processor state and must be saved on a "context switch" (when a program sequence is interrupted temporarily), though this in itself is not a major factor.

Having said all the disadvantages, the condition code register approach is still very popular. One way to mitigate the problems of having two closely linked and dependent instructions in a pipelined processor (see Chapter 5) is to place unrelated instructions which do not affect the conditional code register between the compare instruction and the conditional branch instruction, separating the two instructions in the pipeline. A compiler could rearrange existing instructions in the program in this way, though not many

---

[2] Only arithmetic and logical instructions are designed to affect the condition code register in this approach. Instructions such as register move and load/store do not affect the condition codes, and could be inserted in between, though this could make the code harder to understand.

unrelated instructions can usually be found. (This is similar in concept to the delayed branch instruction described in Chapter 5.)

Avoiding the use of a condition code register

An alternative which both avoids the use of a condition code register and eliminates the necessity of a sequence of two sequential instructions is to combine the two instructions into one conditional branch instruction. This instruction compares the contents of two registers, and branches upon a specified condition, e.g. for "equals":

```
BEQ R1,R2,L1    ;Branch to L1 if R1 = R2
```

A separate instruction is needed for each condition. (Of course, a separate branch instruction is also needed in the condition code approach for each condition.) Generally an instruction which tests for greater than (or less than) is, together with the branch on equals, sufficient for any of the tests given. Suppose we had the instruction:

```
BL R1,R2,L1    ;Branch to L1 if R1 < R2
```

This could be used to create all tests, though some tests would require a two-instruction sequence. These are the instructions for each test:

Condition	Code sequence
R1 < R2	BL R1,R2,L1
R1 > R2	BL R2,R1,L1
R1 >= R2	BL R2,R1,L1 BEQ R1,R2,L1
R1 <= R2	BL R1,R2,L1 BEQ R1,R2,L1
R1 == R2	BEQ R1,R2,L1
R1 != R2	BL R1,R2,L1 BL R2,R1,L1

To eliminate the two-instruction sequences, two more instructions are needed, BGE (branch if greater than or equal) and BNE (branch if not equal).

Testing for zero is a very common operation in programs and we could provide a "branch if zero", BEQZ, and "branch if not zero", BEQNZ, instructions specifically, i.e.:

```
BEQZ   R3,L1    ;Branch to L1 if R3 == 0
BEQNZ R3,L1     ;Branch to L1 if R3 != 0
```

though in our case it is easy to accomplish with R0, i.e.:

```
BEQ R3,R0,L1    ;Branch to L1 if R3 == 0
BNE R3,R0,L1    ;Branch to L1 if R3 != 0
```

One advantage of having special instructions for testing for zero is there would be more space in the instruction to specify L1 as a bigger offset. Also it may be that a very fast circuit could be provided to test for zero, rather than using an ALU. (A very fast circuit could also be provided for BEQ to test for two numbers being equal.)

Yet another design alternative is to have an instruction which performs a compare operation, creating condition code values which are loaded into a general-purpose register specified in the instruction rather than loading a special condition code register. Then the subsequent branch instruction would inspect the register loaded with the condition codes. This approach also allows us to separate the two instructions in the program more easily. An example of this type of approach would be the "set on less" instruction found on the MIPS RISC processor. The "set on less" instruction sets the destination register to 1 if one source register is less than the other source register. Then a "branch on not equal or not zero" can be used for the relationship "less than", i.e.:

```
STL R3,R2,R1    ;R3 = 1 if R2 < R1
BNE R3,R0,L1    ;Branch to L1 if R3 ≠ 0, if R2 < R1
```

In all cases, the choice of instructions in RISCs is very closely dependent upon implementation details, and the effect on the overall throughput of the processor with the introduction of certain instructions in the instruction set. The condition "equals" requires a comparator, which would operate quite fast. Other conditions such as "equal or greater" would require a full subtracter, which is slower to operate.

Selected branch format

We shall choose the single instruction approach with the complete set of four instructions:

```
BEQ R2,R1,L1
BNE R2,R1,L1
BL  R2,R1,L1
BGE R2,R1,L1
```

A suitable instruction format is shown in Figure 2.6, where R2 is Rd, R1 is Rs and L1 = PC + 16-bit offset. Again we are using the destination register field for a source register. The distance possible with a 16-bit 2's complement number is -2^{15} through to $2^{15} - 1$ locations. Since all instructions are 32 bits, instructions could be aligned on word boundaries, and the locations could be considered as 32-bit words.

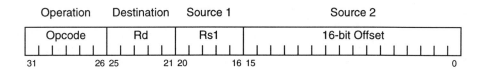

Figure 2.6 Branch instruction format (using R-R-I format)

2.2.5 Jump instructions

The jump instruction causes an unconditional change of execution sequence to a new location. Such instructions are necessary to implement more complicated IF constructs or IF–THEN–ELSE constructs. They are also often useful in implementing FOR and WHILE loops in which the condition for exiting is performed at the beginning of the loop. Then the unconditional jump instruction can be used at the end of the loop to return to the beginning. Using J as the opcode mnemonic, we have the instruction:

```
J L1              ;jump to L1
```

As with branch instructions, PC-relative addressing is used. No registers need be specified, so a format such as in Figure 2.7 is suitable where the offset to L1 is stored in the instruction. Here only the opcode and offset need be specified. The branch instructions described previously could also be made unconditional, e.g.:

```
BEQ R1,R1,L1     ;branch if R1 = R1
```

but the jump format provides for a greater offset in the instruction, a 26-bit offset instead of a 16-bit offset, using PC-relative addressing. The distance possible with a 26-bit 2's complement number is -2^{25} through to $2^{25} - 1$ locations. Again the locations could be assumed to be 32-bit locations.

In addition to PC-relative addressing, normal register-indirect addressing could be provided with both branch and jump instruction but more particularly with jump instructions. An "address register" would be specified in the instruction holding the address of

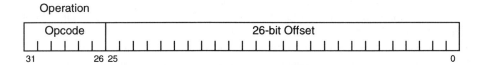

Figure 2.7 Jump instruction format (I format)

Operation   Address register

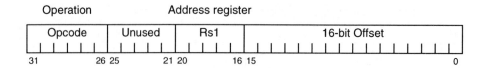

Figure 2.8 Jump instruction format with register indirect addressing

the location holding the next instruction to be executed. Such an instruction could be used, for example, to implement the SWITCH/CASE statements in a high level language. It may also be necessary for procedure return operations (see next section).

For jump, we might have:

```
J [R1]              ;jump to location whose address is in
                    ;R1
```

or even:

```
J 100[R1]           ;jump to location whose address is in
                    ;R1 plus 100.
```

Now the target address is specified as an absolute address, rather than as a relative address. (Problem 2.5 explores using relative addressing in which the contents of R1 plus the offset is interpreted as the offset.) So far, we do not have an instruction format with a single register field. A suitable format is shown in Figure 2.8. This provides for a 16-bit offset. We have avoided using the destination register field as a source register field at the expense of a reduced offset size. It might be possible to use the unused field for a new purpose, for example, to specify a destination register which will be loaded with the effective address computed. Now we are moving into the CISC realm again. (How often would such an operation be useful, and what would be the impact on the speed of the processor? Problem 2.6 explores this aspect.) Notice the notation [ ] here does not mean "contents of memory whose address is …" as in load/store instructions.

2.2.6 Procedure calls

An essential ingredient of high level language programs is the facility to execute procedures, code sequences to perform computations that are needed repeatedly through a main program. Rather than duplicate the code, one copy of the code is provided, and the code is "called" from the main program at the various places it is needed. After each execution of the code, control is returned to the main program to the location immediately after the procedural call. It is usually expected during the execution of a program, that a procedure might call another procedure, and that procedure could call yet another procedure, and so on. It is also usually allowable for a procedure to call itself (a *recursive* procedure). Procedures also make the overall program better structured. When a procedural call is made, often parameters are transferred to the procedure, to be used in the procedural computation at that point. Procedures may or may not return a value at the end of the computation. (Sometimes a procedure that returns a value is called a *function*.)

There are two issues to resolve in implementing procedures. First, a mechanism must be in place to be able to jump to the procedure from various locations in the *calling* program (or procedure), and to be able to return from the *called* procedure to the right place in the calling program (or procedure). Second, a mechanism must be in place to handle passing parameters to the procedure, and to return results (if a function). Also usually when a procedure is called, registers being used by the calling procedure must be saved, so that they can be reused by the called procedure. On return to the calling procedure, the registers have to be restored.

CALL/RET instructions

Special machine instructions can be provided for both the procedural call and the procedural return in the complex instruction set tradition. These instructions are often called CALL and RET respectively. A procedural CALL is simply an unconditional jump to the start of the procedure, with the added feature that the *return address* (the address of the next instruction after the call) is retained somewhere. A procedural RET, returning to the main program after execution of the procedure, is simply an unconditional jump to the location having the address given by the return address. The mechanism is shown in Figure 2.9, with two calls to the same procedure.

In both cases, it is necessary to store the return addresses of each procedural call in the order that the procedures are called, and be able to extract these return addresses in reverse order to effect the correct returns. A suitable data structure for holding the return addresses is a last-in-first-out queue (LIFO), in which the last return address placed on the queue is the first return address to be extracted from the queue. Only one end of the queue need be accessed, the end that new items are placed or taken off. Such a queue is called a *stack*.

Stacks

Stacks can be implemented in main memory or using registers within the processor. Historically main memory stacks have been used for procedures because they allow almost limitless nesting and recursion of procedures. A register called a *stack pointer* is provided inside the processor to hold the address of the "top" of the stack (the end of the stack where items are loaded are retrieved). As items are placed on the stack, the stack grows, and as items are removed from the stack, the stack contracts. Normally memory stacks are made to grow downwards, i.e., items are added to locations with decreasing addresses. Suppose 32-bit addresses are stored on the stack. Then 4 bytes would be needed for each address, and the stack pointer would be decremented by four each time an address is added to the stack, and incremented by four as addresses are removed from the stack. Part of the operation of the CALL instruction is to decrement the stack pointer, and part of the RET instruction would be to increment the stack pointer. Depending upon

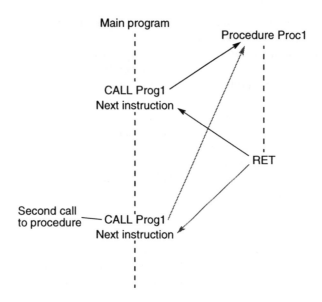

Figure 2.9 Procedure calls using CALL and RET instruction

the conventions chosen by the designer, after the CALL or RET the stack pointer would point to the top location of the stack or the next free location for the stack.

A stack could be created inside the processor using a set of dedicated registers. The first microprocessor (the Intel 4004) did have an internal stack, and internal stacks have appeared subsequently for applications when a small number of procedures are expected. The particular advantage of an internal stack is the speed of operation, which would be much greater than using external memory – and we would rather avoid the use of external memory in a RISC if possible. However, such an arrangement can only provide a finite number of locations.

Passing parameters using a stack

Procedures usually require parameters to be passed to them, and sometimes return values. The stack can also be used to hold parameters which are passed to a called procedure and passed back from the called procedure. Processors which use CALL and RET instructions also usually provide instructions for passing items on the stack, and for taking items off the stack, called PUSH and POP instructions. The PUSH instruction will decrement the stack pointer before (or after) an item is copied onto the stack, and the POP increments the stack pointer after (or before) an item is copied from the stack. Before the call and return address is pushed onto the stack, parameters are pushed onto the stack. Then within the procedure, the parameters are "popped" off the stack.

The stack can also be used to save the contents of registers prior to the call (or immediately after the call inside the procedure). Upon return (or immediately before) the registers can be restored from the contents of the stack. Saving/restoring registers is probably best done inside the called procedure.

Passing parameters and providing registers for local variables using the register window approach

Since procedures are heavily used in most applications, saving and restoring registers represents a significant overhead. The Berkeley RISC project (Patterson, 1985; Katevenis, 1985) introduced concept of providing internal registers called the *register window* to simplify and increase the speed of passing parameters between nested procedures and to provide local registers for each procedure. The idea has been adopted in some subsequent processors which have followed the Berkeley design such as the SUN Sparc processor.

In the register window approach, an internal register file is created inside the processor to hold return addresses and parameters passed between procedures, as shown in Figure 2.10. Each procedure can access a set of registers in this file allocated for its use, a register window. The central registers are used only within the procedure. The upper

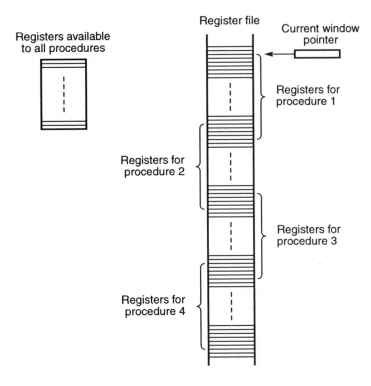

Figure 2.10 RISC register window

portion can be accessed by the procedure and by the procedure that called it. The lower portion can be accessed by the procedure and the procedure it calls, i.e., both the upper and lower portions of the registers allocated to one procedure overlap with the allocation of registers of other procedures. When a procedure is called (from another procedure, the main program initially), the register window moves to the next one, and after a return from a procedure it moves back. In this way, it is not necessary to save parameters in memory during procedure calls, assuming a sufficient number of registers is provided for the nesting of procedures. A set of registers is also provided that is accessible by all procedures, for global variables. To identify the current register window, a current window pointer is provided.

It has been found that procedures are not usually nested to a depth of greater than eight and very rarely greater than ten or eleven, and calls and returns may oscillate over this depth, especially over any reasonably short period of the computation. However it may be that the nesting could go deeper over the life of the program. To handle these characteristics efficiently, the register file is accessed in circular fashion. To take a specific example, consider, the Berkeley RISC II, which has 138 registers configured as eight windows, each of twenty-two registers and ten global registers.[3] The register windows can be viewed arranged in a circular fashion, as shown in Figure 2.11. The current window pointer, CWP, points to the window that can be accessed. The specific register being accessed is specified by the register number in the instruction (0–31). Register numbers between 0 and 9 always refer to the global registers irrespective of the current window. Register numbers between 10 and 31 refer to registers in the current register window. The register address is made up of a 3-bit window address concatenated to the 5-bit register number. Note how a register in an overlapping group has two addresses. For example, register 1:26 in window 1 is also register 2:10 in window 2.

We would expect that during a period in the computation, the procedures would nest to a limited extent, and the circular nature of the windows accommodates this characteristic well. However should the nesting go deeper, main memory must be used to store some of the register contents. Another potential disadvantage occurs when multiple tasks are performed which would necessitate allocating some of the registers for particular tasks or saving registers when tasks are swapped.

Selected procedural call mechanism

There are two issues here. First we would like to avoid complex instructions such as CALL/RET instructions which perform multiple operations (CISC-type instructions). Second, we would like to avoid using memory at all for storing return addresses, parameters and saving registers, as procedure calls could be very frequent. If operations are frequent, it should be provided according to the RISC philosophy (assuming it does not impact too adversely upon the rest of the operations). The register window approach seems attractive for register usage and passing parameters. It can be used to store return

---

[3] The Berkeley RISC I, which introduced the register window concept, had six windows, each of fourteen registers with four overlapping registers to each adjacent windows, and eighteen global registers.

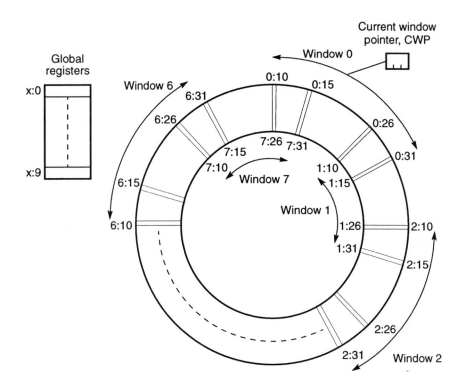

Figure 2.11 RISC II register window

addresses, but still we need memory to store an overflowing register file.

A final possibility is to reduce the CALL/RET instructions into sequences of simpler instructions. We will choose this approach. A single internal register is used for holding the return address, register R31. A call instruction "jump and link", JAL, will jump to the location whose address is specified in the instruction and store the return address in R31. A return is simply an unconditional jump to the location whose address is given in R31 – for this, a register indirect jump can be used, without having to provide a special return instruction. The JAL instruction can use the format shown in Figure 2.7. The mechanism will of course only work for one level of procedure call. For nesting, R31 will be stored in a memory stack, using another register as a stack pointer, R29. This in essence creates a stack in which the top location is a register (R31) and the remaining locations are in memory. The code required would look like:

```
SUB R29,R29,4   ;Decrement stack pointer (4 bytes)
ST  [R29],R31   ;Store last return address on stack
```

```
JAL Proc_label  ;jump to proc_label, and store
                ;return address in R31
LD R31,0[R29]   ;After return from call, restore
                ;previous return address in R31
ADD R29,R29,4   ;Increment stack pointer
```

assuming the stack grows towards lower addresses. To return at the end of the procedure we simply have:

```
J [R31]             ;jump to location whose address is in
                    ;R31
```

We have two alternatives for saving registers, either before the call (*caller save*) as above or after the call (*callee save*). To store parameters as well on the stack before the call, we would have:

```
SUB  R29,R29,4
ST   [R29],R31
SUB  R29,R29,4
ST   [R29],parameter1
SUB  R29,R29,4
ST   [R29],parameter2
JAL Proc_label
```

Now we have defined the main instruction formats, we are in a position to design our processor. Of course additional instructions will be needed in the instruction set. However, we will assume that any new instruction will use one of the formats described.

2.3 Internal operation

Model

We illustrated the internal structure of a simple processor in Figure 1.3. This structure contains an operand register file, a number of dedicated registers notably the instruction register, and the program counter, an arithmetic and logic unit (ALU), and a control unit. The first approach to designing this processor will use a centralized control unit which generates the signals in one place to cause information to pass from one site inside the processor to another. In our first design, we shall use three internal buses interconnecting the registers and ALU. Two of these buses carry the values from two sources (when both used), and the third bus carries the result to the destination. This is appropriate for our three-register instruction format. The overall layout is shown in Figure 2.12.

A number of common registers and other components are identified in this figure, which we will refer to throughout:

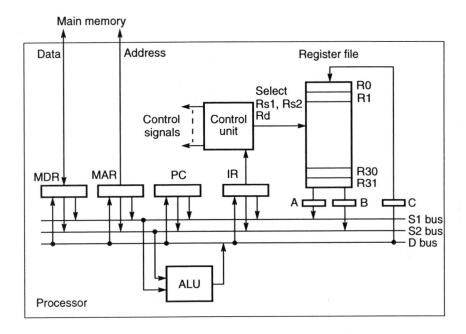

Figure 2.12 Processor with centralized control

Registers:

PC	Program counter – holding the address of the next instruction.
IR	Instruction register – holding the current instruction being executed.
MDR	Memory data register – holding data to be sent to the memory or received from memory.
MAR	Memory address register – holding the address of the memory location being accessed during a memory read or memory write operation.
A	Holds contents of first selected source register, Rs1, from register file.
B	Holds contents of second selected source register, Rs2, from register file.
C	Holds value to be stored in selected destination register, Rd, in register file.

Other components:

Register file	A set of general-purpose registers, R0 to R31, specified by the instructions.
ALU	Arithmetic and logic unit – component for performing the basic arith-

metic such as addition and subtraction and logic operations such as logic AND and OR.

S1, S2, D — Internal buses for transferring information between the registers and other components.

Control unit — The unit which generates the signals required to perform the data transfers and other actions within the processor. The control unit will use the contents of the IR register to determine which signals it must generate and in what sequence. Different types of instruction will have different sequences.

We have added several registers to the model in Figure 1.3. Two registers are provided in the interface to the main memory, MDR and MAR, which are not "visible" to the programmer (i.e., cannot be specified in any machine instruction). We assume that when MAR is loaded with a memory address, this address will be sent to the memory, which would be done for memory access instructions. For memory read instructions (LD instructions), MDR will be loaded by the memory. For memory write instructions (ST instructions), MDR will be loaded by the processor. When loaded by the processor, it is assumed that the contents will be sent to the addressed memory location. Also not visible are registers A, B, and C. These registers are provided to interface to the general-purpose register file. Registers A and B hold data read from the source registers specified in the instruction (Rs1 and Rs2) and register C holds the data to be loaded into the destination register specified in the instruction (Rd).

In the first instance we have provided connection for all registers to both source buses, to the destination bus, enabling a full range of paths to be established. It may be that some of these paths would not be useful. For example, the MDR may never be loaded from the program counter. We leave it as an exercise to identify those connections not needed.

In our design, information passes internally from one register to another. We can indicate this action in a *register transfer notation*. For example:

$$R_A \leftarrow R_B$$

means transfer the contents of R_B to R_A, where R_A and R_B are registers inside the processor. Of course, there must be a path between R_B and R_A, otherwise some intermediate transfers would be necessary. The only way from a source to a destination in our design is through the ALU, so we will have:

$$ALU_{o/p} \leftarrow R_B$$
$$R_A \leftarrow ALU_{o/p}$$

One source bus, say, S1 bus, will be used to transfer R_B to the ALU. The result from the ALU needs to be transferred to R_A in this example. The output of the ALU is in effect a source of information and will be named $ALU_{o/p}$. The D bus will be used to transfer the output of the ALU to R_A. We will omit this intermediate step in the following sequences because some implementations may not use the ALU to make the connection between registers. Problem 2.12 explores how to eliminate the intermediate steps. Of course sometimes the data must pass through the ALU, to perform an arithmetic or logic operation.

As we mentioned in Chapter 1, the basic operation of a processor can be divided into two phases, a fetch cycle and an execute cycle, which is present in all processors in some form. Now let us specify the information transfers that are necessary in each of these cycles. Later we will examine how the transfers can be implemented.

Fetch cycle

In the fetch cycle, the contents of the program counter provides the address of the instruction in memory. This address must be placed on the address lines of the memory. This occurs by loading the memory address register, MAR. After a delay dependent upon the access time of the memory, the memory data bus will carry the instruction, assumed to be a single 32-bit word. This will be loaded into the memory data register, MDR, and then the contents of this register must be passed to the instruction register. Normally at the end of the fetch cycle, the program counter is incremented by 4 to point to the next instruction.[4] Describing these actions in our notation, the fetch cycle becomes:

```
MAR ← PC
IR ← MDR
PC ← PC + 4
```

The first step must be performed before the second, though the second and third steps could be performed together if suitable data paths and components are available in the processor. Ignoring implementation details that might prevent simultaneous operations, we have:

```
MAR ← PC
IR ← MDR; PC ← PC + 4
```

where the ; shows simultaneous actions. Processors are designed to operate synchronously (for the most part) in that each action or group of simultaneous actions start at the beginning of a clock period. The clock period is related to the processor's clocking frequency. For example, a 100 MHz processor has a 10 ns clock period.

Since the fetch cycle of an instruction is independent of the type of instruction and the steps are always the same, they can be generated by hardwired logic (if the instructions are of fixed length). Such logic is not shown specifically in Figure 2.12 but is assumed to be part of the control unit.

---

[4] If all instructions are 32-bit words (4 bytes), the least significant two bits of the program counter will always be zero.

Execute cycle

The steps in the second phase, executing an instruction, will depend upon the actual instruction that must be executed. In most cases, operands have to be fetched from registers in the register file, i.e., Rs1 and Rs2. Rs1 and Rs2 are selected using the register addresses provided in the machine instruction. The contents of these two source registers are loaded into registers A and B, i.e., we perform the steps:

```
A ← Rs1
B ← Rs2
```

Since generally the register fields remain in the same place in the instruction irrespective of the instruction type, it is possible to extract the register identifiers from the instruction without having to recognize (*decode*) the specific operation (opcode), i.e., bits 16 to 20 specify one source register, bits 11 to 15 specify the other source register. (Problem 2.4 explores alternative positions in the instruction for the register fields while still allowing these registers to be selected before decoding the instruction.) We could arrange for the two steps to be performed automatically for all instructions even if two source registers are not used, such as in an unconditional jump instruction which may not have any source registers specified (see Figure 2.7). For those instructions that do not have source registers, the contents of A and B are not used subsequently. This does not cause a performance degradation because we have dedicated paths between the register file and the A and B registers. We also have a dedicated path from the C register to the register file.

The subsequent steps depend upon the particular instruction class (as given by the opcode). The opcode can be decoded by hardware within the control unit. Now let us look at the major classes of instruction:

Arithmetic/logic instructions – register-register

For arithmetic and logic instructions using three registers such as ADD R1,R2,R3, we need to transfer the contents of the A register and the contents of the B register to the ALU to perform the arithmetic/logic operation. The result from the ALU needs to be transferred to the C register. The S1 bus will be used to transfer A to the ALU, the S2 bus will be used to transfer B to the ALU and the D bus will be used to transfer the output of the ALU to the C register. Once the C register is loaded, the C register is copied into the destination register in the register file. Thus we have the steps:

```
C ← A <operation> B
Rd ← C
```

The destination address is found in a fixed place in the instruction and hence the final step is almost automatic, and could be assumed.

We could have decomposed the steps further, specifying the buses, i.e.:

```
S1bus ← A; S2 bus ← B
```

```
Dbus ← S1 bus <operation> S2 bus
C ← Dbus
```

The operation is found from the opcode, or sub-opcode if used. We see now that sub-opcode might be a convenient way of specifying operations within a class of instructions. However, arithmetic/logic instructions with a constant (literal) specification cannot use a sub-opcode, and the same basic operation would have to be specified in the main opcode for operations with literals.

Arithmetic/logic instructions – register-constant

Arithmetic and logic instructions using two registers and a constant such as ADD R1,R2,44 is similar to the arithmetic/logic instruction using three registers except that one source is a constant which is held in the least significant (rightmost) 16 bits of the instruction. Hence we need to extract the constant from these 16 bits of the IR register. Using the notation IR_{15-0} for the least significant 16 bits of the IR register, we have:

```
C ← A <operation> IR₁₅₋₀
```

This implies that we must have a mechanism of extracting bits 0 to 15 from the IR register. A suitable path is provided from IR to the internal S1 and S2 buses in Figure 2.12, from which the constant can be sent to the ALU.

Remember that we do not provide an explicit move instruction to transfer the contents of one register to another; rather we rely upon ADD with R0. We have not provided a direct path from sources to destinations. All sources can reach all destinations, if necessary through the ALU.

Memory reference (load/store) instructions

In both load and store instructions, the address of the memory location is specified by the contents of a source register, Rs1 using version 1 load/store formats (Figure 2.3), plus an offset in the least significant 16 bits of the instruction. The computed address must be loaded into the memory address register, MAR, i.e.:

```
MAR ← A + IR₁₅₋₀
```

The ALU can be used for this operation. Subsequent steps depend upon whether the memory reference is a load or a store.

For load instruction, the contents of the addressed memory location will pass through the memory data register to the destination register, C, i.e., the complete sequence is:

```
MAR ← A + IR₁₅₋₀
C ← MDR
Rd ← C
```

Sufficient time must elapse between issuing the memory address and reading MDR to allow the memory to provide the data.

For a store instruction we have the problem of dealing with the source register being specified in the destination field of the instruction. One solution is to arrange so that the C register is automatically loaded with the current contents of Rd, in addition to A and B being loaded, i.e., the instruction decode/operand fetch sequence would be:

```
A ← Rs1
B ← Rs2
C ← Rd
```

We then redirect C to the memory destination. The contents of the source register will pass through the memory data register to the addressed memory location, i.e., the complete sequence is:

```
MAR ← A + IR₁₅₋₀
MDR ← C
```

However this approach would require a register file with three read ports. An alternative solution, keeping the source register in the destination field, would be to have some form of hardware redirection when the ST instruction is decoded, so that the B register is used, i.e.:

```
MAR ← A + IR₁₅₋₀
MDR ← B
```

For example, in the instruction ST R4, [R2], A is loaded from R2 and B is loaded from R4. The path from B to MDR is not provided directly in our model of Figure 2.12. The ALU would need to be used to establish a path, after it has been used for MAR. If a path were available, MAR and MDR could be loaded simultaneously.

Branch instructions

In branch instructions, the condition specified in the instruction has to be checked. If the condition is true, the target address is computed and loaded into the program counter. Branch conditions between Rs1 and Rs2 could be checked by examining the result of subtracting Rs1 from Rs2:

```
condition ← A <operation> B
```

The target address is computed by adding the offset in the instruction to the program counter:

```
ALUₒ/ₚ ← PC + IR₁₅₋₀
```

The target address could be computed at the same time as evaluating the condition if sufficient resources are available. Unfortunately, computing the target address also requires an ALU, and the internal data paths. This is one reason why some RISCs limit the condition to A = 0, which can be checked by providing fast zero detecting hardware.

The final step is to load the program counter if the condition exists:

$$\text{IF condition} = \text{TRUE PC} \leftarrow \text{ALU}_{o/p}$$

otherwise the program counter points to the next instruction, as in non-control instructions.

Jump instructions

The basic PC-relative addressed jump instruction simply adds the offset in the instruction to the program counter. Whereas the offsets previously are 16 bits, there are 26 bits in the offset in jump instructions, so there has to be a mechanism of extracting the lower 26 bits from the instruction register. Given suitable data paths, the steps are:

$$\text{PC} \leftarrow \text{PC} + \text{IR}_{25-0}$$

For register indirect addressed jump instructions such as J 100 [R2], the sequence is:

$$\text{PC} \leftarrow \text{A} + \text{IR}_{15-0}$$

where R2 is selected by A. For a procedural call, the jump and link instruction, JAL, is provided here, which is similar to the jump instruction with the added feature that the return address is loaded into R31, i.e.:

$$\text{R31} \leftarrow \text{PC}$$
$$\text{PC} \leftarrow \text{PC} + \text{IR}_{25-0}$$

given that the PC will be pointing to the next instruction after the fetch cycle.

Control instructions

Apart from computational instructions, other instructions are needed. Often these instructions do not have any operands specified, only an operation. An instruction which does nothing except consume a processor cycle, called a No-op instruction (NOP), is always present in the instruction set. This instruction is used to separate dependencies between instructions (see Chapter 5), and to pad out programs after instructions have been removed during debugging. The most convenient encoding for a NOP is an instruction format with all 0's (32 zeros) as then memory initialized to zero would behave as NOP instructions. Other control instructions include an HALT instruction which stops execution completely. To continue after a HALT instruction normally requires some form of interrupt mechanism. We refer the reader to computer organization books for further details (for example Tanenbaum, 1990).

2.4 Centralized control unit design

Now we have the basic instructions for our processor and the steps that must be performed for each instruction, let us look at the various possible design approaches, using a centralized control unit. The more powerful decentralized approaches will be considered in Chapter 5.

2.4.1 Hardwired logic design

Let us start by using arithmetic instructions as our example. The complete list of steps for fetching and executing the arithmetic instructions (register-register instructions) is:

```
MAR ← PC
IR ← MDR
PC ← PC + 4
A ← Rs1; B ← Rs2
C ← A <operation> B
```

Each step or group of steps that can be performed simultaneously is a state of the machine. We can describe the sequence of states in a *state diagram* (sometimes called a *finite state diagram* as there will be a finite number of states to reach a conclusion). A state diagram for the fetch cycle for our processor is shown in Figure 2.13. (The full state diagram including all instruction sequences would of course be very large, and we will show it in parts.) After the fetch cycle, the instruction must be decoded, and the required sequence selected for the decoded instruction. The method of decoding an instruction is unspecified here; simply a state marked for it. Normally the opcode (the first six bits of the instruction in our case) uniquely identifies the instruction, and an "n to 2^n decoder" where $n = 6$ in our case is sufficient for decoding.

Let us assume that a register-register instruction such as addition has been decoded. The state diagram for this class of instruction is shown in Figure 2.14. First, operands must be fetched from the register file. Next the arithmetic operation must be performed and finally the result has to be stored in the register file. Almost all instructions require operands to be fetched. Figure 2.14(a) shows the steps without the intermediate ALU path, while Figure 2.14(b) shows the intermediate ALU step which occurs in our implementation, but not necessarily in all implementations.

Each state requires specific signals to be generated. For example to transfer the contents of one register to another we require a signal to cause the contents of the source register to be loaded onto a bus, and a signal to cause the contents of the bus to be loaded into the destination registers shown in Figure 2.15. Therefore one hardware implementation is to have one signal for each source, and one signal for each destination. Once the

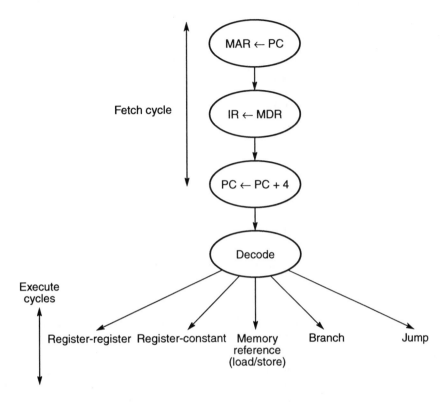

Figure 2.13 State diagram for fetch cycle

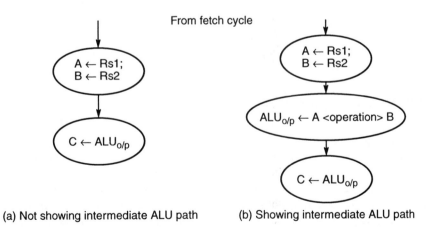

Figure 2.14 State diagram for execute cycle of register-register instructions

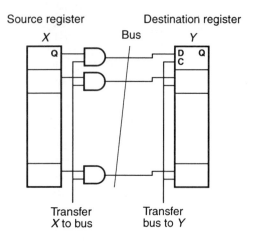

Source register · Destination register

X · Bus · Y

Q · D C · Q

Transfer
X to bus

Transfer
bus to Y

Figure 2.15 Logic signals for register transfer

signals have been generated, the logic moves onto the next state, and so on. There are several logic design approaches for implementing state diagrams. We could use a binary counter, where each output number is decoded into specific signals. The binary counter generates numbers corresponding to state numbers, state, 0, state 1, ... Each number is decoded into a set of signals, for example MAR ← PC requires one signal to load PC onto a bus, one signal to transfer the contents of the bus to MAR, leading to the circuit in Figure 2.16.

Clearly more than this is necessary for dealing with each instruction, as each instruction may have a different number of states (not necessarily a power of 2). One approach is to use some of the outputs to select the next state, thus replacing the counter. The initial state is selected by the opcode of the instruction, so that the appropriate sequence is followed. The idea of having each state specify the next state is embodied in the microprogrammed approach.

2.4.2 Microprogrammed approach

The microprogrammed approach was introduced in Chapter 1 as a structured way of generating the control signals. In the microprogrammed approach the operations for each state are encoded in binary in an instruction known as *microinstruction* (a small instruction). Each microinstruction will cause the signals necessary to transfer data from one place to another in the processor, and activates the ALU (and any other functional units) if it is necessary for the operations. A list of microinstructions is necessary for each machine instruction, and the whole list for the instruction set of the processor is called a *microprogram*. The microprogram is held in a very high speed memory within the control

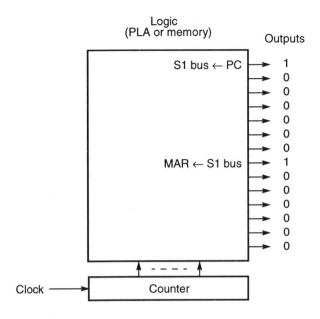

Figure 2.16 Using a counter and decoder to generate control signals

unit of the processor.

The general arrangement of a microprogrammed control unit is shown in Figure 2.17. An instruction is fetched into the instruction register by a standard instruction fetch microprogram. The machine instruction "points" to the first microinstruction of the microprogram sequence for that machine instruction. The microinstruction is executed, and then the next and so on just as a machine instruction program. Microprograms are very much like machine instruction programs in execution, and some of the same techniques can be applied to both. A *microinstruction program counter* can be present to hold the address of the next microinstruction to be executed, just as a machine instruction program counter holds the address of the next instruction to be executed. The execution sequence can be altered by conditions occurring within or outside the processor. In particular, microinstruction sequences of conditional branch instructions may be altered by conditions indicated in the processor condition code register. The address of the next microinstruction, should the conditions be met, is provided in the microinstruction. (It is possible to provide the next addresses in all microinstructions, and potentially eliminate the microinstruction program counter.) Just as in machine instruction level procedures are present, microinstruction procedures (subroutines) can be created to reduce the size of the microprogram. A stack is used to hold the return address of machine instruction procedures, and a control memory stack can be provided to hold the return address for a microinstruction subroutine.

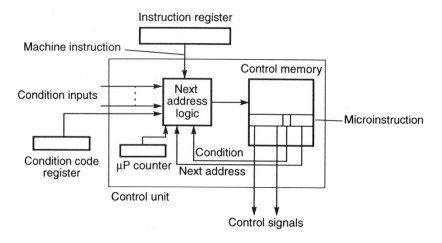

Figure 2.17 Microprogrammed control unit

In general, the microinstruction is divided into two fields, one known as a *micro-order* giving the signals and actions to be generated for the step, and one, the *next address field*, giving the address of the next microinstruction to be executed if some condition exists. The condition is specified in another field of the microinstruction. Conditions will relate to those conditions which alter machine instructions, such as arithmetic/logic result conditions (the conditions in the condition code register), interrupts being present, and error conditions being present. The micro-order field can have one bit for each signal to be generated, binary encoded fields, or a combination. A two-level approach is also possible, in which a short microinstruction points to a set of much longer nanoinstructions held in another control memory.

There are two types of micro-order format:

1. Horizontal micro-order format.
2. Vertical micro-order format.

In the horizontal micro-order format (the original Wilkes method) one bit is provided for each logic signal that can be generated by the microinstruction, as shown in Figure 2.18(a). For example, if there were 100 possible signals, there would be 100 bits in the micro-order. To generate a particular signal, the corresponding bit in the micro-order would be set to a 1. More than one signal could be generated simultaneously if required by setting more bits to a 1.

In the vertical micro-order format, the bits are encoded into fields to reduce the number of bits in the micro-order, as shown in Figure 2.18(b). Bits are formed into groups specifying signals that cannot be activated together. For example, for a basic register transfer operation, only one destination register can be selected at a time. If there were 15

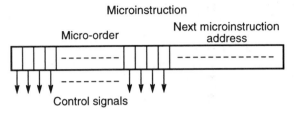

(a) Horizontal micro-order format

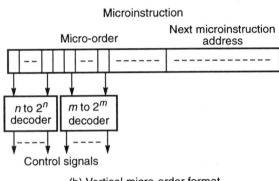

(b) Vertical micro-order format

Figure 2.18 Micro-order formats

possible destination registers, 4 bits could be used (one pattern, say 0000, might be reserved for no destination). As another example, external signals might be generated from the microinstruction. Suppose the external data transfer request signals were memory read, memory write, input read, and output write. These signals would be all mutually exclusive and could not occur together. Hence they could be encoded into three binary digits (with up to three other signals). Again one encoded pattern, say 000, must be reserved to no signal at all.

The horizontal method is the most flexible but results in a long microinstruction whereas the vertical method is more efficient but requires logic to decode the patterns and hence the speed of operation is reduced. Also it is less flexible in that mutually exclusive signals must be identified and new signal combinations cannot be introduced later in the system after the design is implemented.

Usually a combination of both methods are used in microinstruction encoding; groups of actions that cannot be performed together are usually encoded, rather than one bit for each action, to reduce the number of bits needed. Single bits are used for actions that can be performed together or there are small groups of independent actions. Some encoded fields must use one pattern, say all zeros, to indicate no operation. A common application of encoding is selecting one of several registers as a source of data or as the destination of data. Encodings are also used to select one function from many in an ALU, e.g., add, subtract, shift, multiply, divide, etc. This encoded pattern would then be sent to the ALU. Similarly selecting conditions, say zero, not zero, carry, no carry, etc., could be encoded vertically. Single bits might be used for specifying the direction of memory accesses. The operation could be memory read or memory write. One bit could specify read and another write. Suppose the bits are called RD (for read) and WR (for write). For read, RD = 1, and for write, WR = 1, with RD = WR = 0 for no memory access operation. Encoding memory read or write would require the same number of bits.

In our example, all the data transfers that pass through the three internal buses, S1, S2 and D, and all source/destination registers connect to all buses. We could have three fields in the microinstruction, one for one source, one for the second source, and one for the destination. The data transfers along these buses could be specified in microinstruction fields as shown in Figure 2.19. A binary pattern is allocated for each possibility in each field. For example if there are between four and seven possible sources and possible destinations, three bits would be needed in each of these fields. For simplicity, we have reserved zero in each field for no selection. The pattern 001 could specify the A register in the source fields, and pattern 010 the B register. In the destination field, the pattern 001 could specify the C register. Hence the microinstruction to perform

$$C \leftarrow A$$

has the pattern:

```
... 001 001 001 000 ...
    Dest ALU  Sources
```

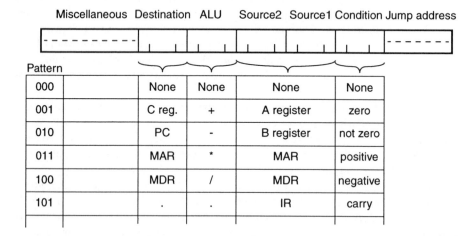

Figure 2.19 Microinstruction format

In a microprogrammed control unit, since a complete microprogram must be executed for each machine instruction, it follows that the speed of operation of executing each microinstruction must be much faster than that of the corresponding machine instruction. Therefore the control memory must operate much faster than that of the main memory holding the machine instruction (or cache memory if present). In a processor with a fixed set of machine instructions, the control memory can be read-only memory. More details of the design of a microprogrammed system can be found in (Tanenbaum, 1990, or Wilkinson, 1992c).

2.5 Concluding comments

In this chapter, we have developed the instruction formats for a RISC processor. We outlined the microprogrammed approach to the design of the control unit. Notable advantages of the microprogrammed method over a hardwired approach are:

Organized way to design the processor.
Easily develop and insert new instructions.
Can emulate other machines by having microcode for instructions native to other computers.
Good for complex instructions.

However there have been two developments which have made the microprogrammed technique less attractive. First, semiconductor memory is used throughout the processor and it is difficult to provide semiconductor control memory which is significantly faster than the main/cache memory. Second, the microprogrammed technique can incur a significant overhead in RISC processors with their simplified instructions sets. Often a RISC instruction might only require one or two microinstructions. We note that the microprogrammed approach is not amenable to a distributed control unit design. The pipeline technique has the potential of much higher speed than a centralized design and is particularly convenient for RISC processor instruction sets. We shall look at pipelining in Chapter 5.

PROBLEMS

2.1 Modify the instructions presented in this chapter to allow for an operand size of 8 bits, 16 bits or 32 bits where appropriate.

2.2 We chose not to use a sub-opcode in the register-register instructions. Explore the possibility of a sub-opcode, and identify the advantages and disadvantages of using a sub-opcode, as opposed to increasing the size of the primary opcode, or having different lengths for the opcode (most undesirable for a RISC).

2.3 There are several possible alternative positions for the register fields in the instruction. We chose in the text to place the destination register field first, then the two source registers. Assuming that the same instructions are to be implemented, identify all the possible ways to place the fields while still allowing preemptive selection of registers before decoding the instruction.

2.4 Obtain the combinations of flags in the condition code register that need to be set to recognize the relationships:

Branch if less than
Branch if greater than
Branch if greater or equal to
Branch if less or equal to
Branch if equal
Branch if not equal

for both signed and unsigned numbers, given that the flags are S (sign), Z (zero), O (overflow), and C (carry). *Prove your results.*

2.5 Suppose the register indirect jump instruction is designed such that the computed value is a relative displacement from the next address, e.g.:

```
J 100[R1]    ;jump to location distance away is
             ;given by the contents of R1 plus 100
```

Determine the execution steps required. Do you think this instruction would be useful and should be incorporated? Are there any disadvantages, for example with certain implementations? (See Chapter 5 on pipeline implementations.)

2.6 Investigate using the unused bits in instruction formats.

2.7 Name one situation in which part of the IR register might be transferred to the MAR register. Describe the buses and paths used to achieve this transfer using a register transfer notation.

2.8 Write the steps for classical (CISC) procedural call and return instructions (CALL and RET), for our processor model.

2.9 Work through all instructions presented in this chapter to establish which, if any, connections to the three internal buses, S1, S2 and D, in the processor of Figure 2.12, are not currently necessary.

2.10 Design the paths in the processor of Figure 2.12 to eliminate needing to pass information always through the ALU.

2.11 Design a processor along the lines of Figure 2.12 but using only one internal bus. Show how all register transfer steps to be accomplished, and develop the register transfer steps necessary to implement four selected instructions in this chapter. Use additional temporary registers as needed.

2.12 Repeat Problem 2.11, but with two buses.

3 Cache memory systems

This chapter studies the use of a relatively small capacity but high speed memory called a *cache*, which is inserted between the processor and main memory. The cache is introduced into the system to decrease the effective memory access time and hence increase the operational speed of the system. Virtually all computer systems use a cache.

3.1 Cache memory

3.1.1 Operation

The speed at which locations can be accessed in a memory is a critical factor in the system design. Semiconductor memory speeds are characterized by the memory access time and memory cycle time. The *memory access time* is the time between the submission of a memory request and the completion of transfer of information into or from the addressed location. Normally, the access time for a read and for a write operation is the same, and we will assume read and write access times to be the same in one memory. The *memory cycle time* is the minimum time that must elapse between two successive operations to access locations in the memory (read or write). Sometimes the access time and cycle time are almost the same, i.e. immediately a location has been accessed, another memory operation can be initiated, but often a short period must elapse after the access for the internal circuits to settle and be ready for the next read/write operation (i.e. a precharge period in some semiconductor designs). In high speed memory systems the cycle time is almost double the access time.

Processors (except early microprocessors) are generally able to perform operations on operands faster (perhaps one order of magnitude faster) than the access time of large capacity main memory. Though semiconductor memory which can operate at speeds comparable with the operation of the processor exists, it is not economical to provide all the main memory with very high speed semiconductor memory. The problem can be alleviated by introducing a small block of high speed memory called a *cache* between the main memory and the processor as shown in Figure 3.1. A cache consists of very high

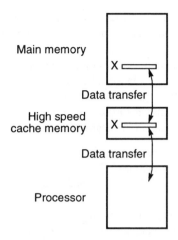

Figure 3.1 Cache memory

speed random access memory operating at the speed required by the processor. Program instructions and data are transferred to the cache, which are then accessed by the processor. Normally the original programs and data are kept in the main memory so that the contents of the cache are copies of main memory locations, such as location X in Figure 3.1. It is necessary that the original main memory address of any cached location is stored in some manner in the cache, as the processor will access the cache with the same main memory address as it would if it were accessing the main memory. Any data items to be changed by the processor are first written to the cache and either written to the main memory at the same time, or subsequently when the cache location is to be used by other main memory item, the cache being of finite size and can only hold copies of so many main memory locations.

A cache was first used in a commercial computer system by IBM in the IBM System/360 Model 85. The IBM 360 Model 85 cache was described and the term cache memory used by Conti in 1968 (Conti *et al.*, 1968). However, the concept of a cache can be found earlier. Wilkes describes the idea of slave memories in 1965 (Wilkes, 1965). Though most computers use cache memory, there is a notable exception; the Cray vector computers use files of register buffer storage instead of cache memory.

Instrumental to the success of a cache are certain characteristics of programs. If programs were executed purely in sequence, from one memory address onwards, and the same instructions were never re-executed, caches would cause an additional overhead as information would first have to be transferred from the main memory to the cache and then to the processor and vice versa. The access time would then be:

$$t_a = t_m + t_c$$

where t_c = cache access time and t_m = main memory access time. Fortunately though code is generally executed sequentially, virtually all programs repeat sections of code and repeatedly access the same or nearby data. This characteristic is embodied in the *Principle of Locality*, which has been found empirically to be obeyed by most programs. It applies to both instruction references and data references, though it is more likely in instruction references. It has two main aspects:

1. *Temporal locality* (locality in time) – individual locations, once referenced, are likely to be referenced again in the near future.

2. *Spatial locality* (locality in space) – references, including the next location, are likely to be near the last reference. (References to the next location are sometimes separated into a third aspect, known as *sequential locality*.)

Temporal locality is found in instruction loops, data stacks and variable accesses. Spatial locality describes the characteristic that programs access a number of distinct regions. Sequential locality describes sequential locations being referenced and is a main attribute of program construction. It can also be seen in data accesses, as data items are often stored in sequential locations. Temporal locality is essential for an effective cache. Spatial locality is helpful when we design a cache as we shall see, but it is not essential.

Taking advantage of temporal locality

When instructions are formed into loops which are executed many times, the length of a loop is usually quite small. Therefore once a cache is loaded with loops of instructions from the main memory, the instructions are used more than once before new instructions are required from the main memory. The same situation applies to data; data is repeatedly accessed. Suppose the reference is repeated n times in all during a program loop and, after the first reference, the location is always found in the cache, then the average access time would be:

$$\text{Average access time} = \frac{(nt_c + t_m)}{n} = t_c + \frac{t_m}{n}$$

where n = number of references. If $t_c = 25$ ns, $t_m = 200$ ns and $n = 10$, the average access time would be 45 ns, as opposed to 200 ns without the cache. This is a substantial increase in speed using a cache operating at eight times the speed of the main memory. It is assumed that there are no additional timing factors with the introduction of the cache and the processor must be able to handle the increased speed (ten 25 ns accesses and one 200 ns access). We note that as n increases, the average time approaches the access time of the cache. The increase in speed will, of course, depend upon the program. Some programs might have a large amount of temporal locality, while others have less. Also, the average access time gives only an indication of the system improvement. The actual improvement will be different because instruction execution speeds have components other than instruction fetch and operand fetch times.

Taking advantage of spatial locality

To take advantage of spatial locality, we will transfer not just one byte or word from the main memory to the cache (and vice versa) but a series of sequential locations called a *line* or a *block*. (Both terms are used in the literature – we shall use the term line.) For best performance, the line should be transferred simultaneously across a wide data bus to the cache, with one byte or word being transferred from each memory module. This also enables the access time of the main memory to be matched to the cache. The general arrangement is shown in Figure 3.2 (see also Section 1.3.2). Here, eight memory modules together create an 8-byte line for the cache. The addresses are distributed across the memory modules so that successive bytes are in successive memory modules as shown. The most significant part of the memory address is sent to all memory modules to access one location from each memory module simultaneously. The three least significant bits of the memory address identify the byte. Hence eight consecutive locations can be read into the cache, or written from the cache back to the main memory simultaneously. Of course this technique assumes that eight consecutive locations are required.

The number of memory modules, m say, is chosen to produce a suitable match in the speed of operation of the main and cache memories. For a perfect match, m would be chosen such that $mt_c = t_m$. The cache words could subsequently be accessed by the processor in sequential order from the cache in another mt_c seconds. Hence the average

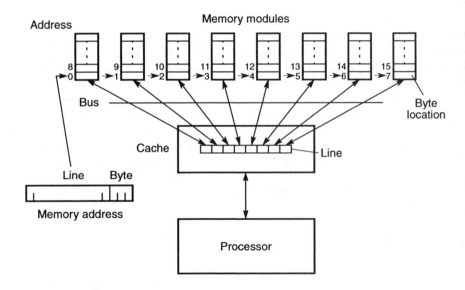

Figure 3.2 Cache memory with multiple memory modules (wide word length memory)

access time of these words when first referenced would be $2mt_c/m = 2t_c$. Should the words be referenced n times in all, the average access time would be:

$$\text{Average access time} = \frac{2t_c + (n-1)t_c}{n} = \frac{(n+1)t_c}{n}$$

For example, if a cache has an access time of 25 ns and the main memory has an access time of 200 ns, eight main memory modules would allow eight words to be transferred to the cache in 200 ns. With ten references in all, we have:

$$\text{Average access time} = \frac{(50 + 9 \times 25)}{10} = 27.5 \text{ ns}$$

The average access time is approximately t_c for large n, making the same rather broad assumptions as before. However, it does indicate that substantial speed improvements can be achieved by using the cache.

Notice that if the locality in programs was only instruction sequential locality, and if we could always rely on instructions being sequential, a cache would not be needed and wide word length memories would be sufficient to keep the processor content with instructions, with perhaps a single wide word length buffer. However, this is not the case and variations in sequential instruction fetches and data references need to be taken into account.

We have assumed that it is necessary to reference the cache before a reference is made to the main memory to fetch a word, and it is usual to look into the cache first to see if the information is held there. The advantage of the cache comes from information it holds and, although it may be necessary to make a second reference to the cache after the word has been fetched from the main memory to the cache, it is likely that the word can be sent to the cache and the processor simultaneously with suitable hardware and data paths. For write operations through the cache, the cache location will be altered. Write operations require an additional scheme to deal with the main memory; this is described in Section 3.3. Any word altered in the cache must be transferred back to the main memory eventually, and this transfer will reduce the average time. We will develop formulae to compute the average access time including the main memory write mechanism, but first let us assume read-only operations. In general, all formulae are applicable to both access time and cycle time.

3.1.2 Hit ratio

The probability that the required word is already in the cache depends upon the program and on the size and organization of the cache; typically 70–90 per cent of references will find their words in the cache. A *hit* occurs when a location in the cache is found immediately, otherwise a *miss* occurs and a reference to the main memory is necessary. The cache *hit ratio*, h, is defined as:

$$h = \frac{\text{Number of times required word found in cache}}{\text{Total number of references}}$$

The cache hit ratio (or *hit rate*) is also the probability that a word will be found in the cache. The *miss ratio* (or *miss rate*) is given by $1 - h$. In cache studies, the miss ratio is sometimes quoted rather than the hit ratio. The average access time, t_a is given by:

$$t_a = t_c + (1 - h)t_m$$

assuming again that the first access must be to the cache before an access is made to the main memory. Accesses made to the main memory add the time $(1 - h)t_m$ to the access time. For example, if the hit ratio is 0.85 (a typical value), the main memory access time is 100 ns and the cache access time is 25 ns, then the average access time is $25 + 0.15 \times 100 = 35$ ns.

Rearranging the equation we get:

$$\frac{t_a}{t_c} = 1 + (1 - h)\frac{t_m}{t_c}$$

The objective is to get the memory access time ratio, t_a/t_c, as close to 1 as possible which occurs when h is close to 1 and when t_m/t_c is close to 1. For a cache system, the ratio t_m/t_c is quite low, perhaps between 2 and 10. In that case, h in the range 70–90% will yield t_a/t_c quite close to 1.[1]

In all derivations in this chapter and generally, we assume that when the data is fetched from the main memory to the cache it is immediately available to the processor at that time without needing to read the cache again, i.e., there is a direct path between the main memory and the processor. We will use the above formula as the basis of our derivations.

There are alternative ways of describing the access time. For example, the cache access time, t_c, is the time taken to interrogate the cache and discover whether the data is present, and to produce it if it is. If the data item is not present, then it takes t_m seconds to fetch the data item to the processor, including any additional time to load the cache. We can separate the cache access time into a cache interrogate time, t_{ci}, and a subsequent cache read time, t_{cr}. Then the average access time is given by:

$$t_a = t_{ci} + ht_{cr} + (1 - h)t_m$$

or:

$$t_a = h(t_{ci} + t_{cr}) + (1 - h)(t_{ci} + t_m)$$

---

[1] The same formula applies to a paging system, and then the ratio t_m/t_c is much larger and the hit ratio is very high, see Chapter 3.

i.e., the access time if the data is in the cache (the hit time) is $t_{ci} + t_{cr}$, and the access time if the data is not in the cache (the miss time) is $t_{ci} + t_m$.

We can rearrange the above equation as:

$$t_a = t_{ci} + t_{cr} + (1 - h)(t_m - t_{cr})$$

or:

$$t_a = t_{hit} + (1 - h)t_{miss\_pen}$$

where t_{hit} = the time to access the data should be it in the cache (the hit time) and t_{miss_pen} is the extra time require if the data is not in the cache (the *miss penalty*).

Measuring access time in machine cycles

In a practical system, each access time will be given as an integer number of machine cycles (which is related to the clock frequency of the system). Also individual instructions take a specific number of machine cycles. Hence it can be convenient to calculate the access time in machine cycles. This can be applied to all our equations. For example in the previous equation, typically the hit time will be 1–2 cycles. The cache miss penalty is often in the order of 5–20 cycles.

3.2 Cache memory organizations

There are various ways that a cache can be arranged internally to store the cached data. In all cases, the processor references the cache with the main memory address of the data it wants. Hence each cache organization must use this address to find the data in the cache if it is stored there, or to indicate to the processor when a miss has occurred. The problem of mapping the information held in the main memory into the cache must be totally implemented in hardware to achieve improvements in the system operation. Various strategies are possible.

3.2.1 Fully associative mapping

Perhaps the most obvious way of relating cached data to the main memory address is to store both the memory address and data together in the cache. This is the *fully associative mapping* approach. A fully associative cache requires the cache to be composed of associative memory (content addressable memory, CAM) holding both the memory address and the data for each cached line. The incoming memory address is simultaneously compared with all stored addresses using the internal logic of the associative memory, as shown in Figure 3.3. If a match is found, the corresponding data is read out. Single words from anywhere within the main memory could be held in the cache, if the associative part of the cache is capable of holding a full address.

In all organizations, the data can be more than one word, i.e., a block of consecutive locations, or line, to take advantage of spatial locality. In Figure 3.4, a line constitutes four words, each word being 4 bytes. The least significant part of the address selects the particular byte, the next part selects the word, and the remaining bits form the address compared to the address in the cache. The whole line can be transferred to and from the cache in one transaction if there are sufficient data paths between the main memory and the cache. With only one data word path, the words of the line have to be transferred in separate transactions, and then an additional bit must be stored with each word in each line to indicate whether valid data is present in the cache (see later).

Usually main memory of the system is organized with each addressable memory location holding an 8-bit byte. Four consecutive bytes in memory constitutes a 32-bit word. The processor may require a byte, a 16-bit word or a 32-bit word (or greater size). There are different ways that the processor could specify the location (such as described in Chapter 1). When considering the address generated by the processor, we will assume throughout that the processor generates byte addresses, and some additional signals are generated to say whether a byte, two bytes, four bytes, or more bytes are required. A line of 4 bytes is a convenient minimum size for the line, as this will correspond to one 32-bit instruction. A line of 8 bytes would hold two 32-bit instructions. Though the minimum line size might be four bytes, it is necessary to be able to access individual bytes of the

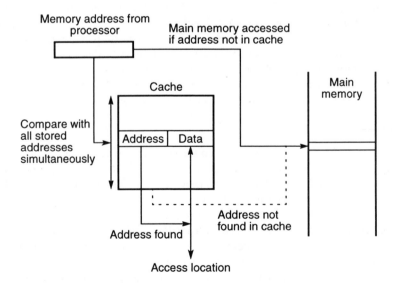

Figure 3.3 Cache with fully associative mapping

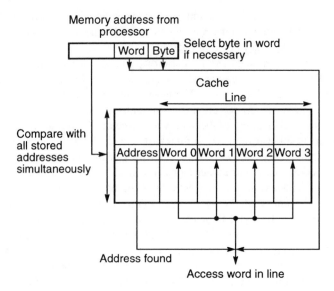

Figure 3.4 Fully associative mapped cache with multi-word lines

word; this is done after the word has been accessed by using the least significant bits of the address to identify the byte.

The fully associative mapping cache gives the greatest flexibility of holding combinations of lines in the cache and minimum conflict for a given sized cache, but is also the most expensive, due to the cost of the associative memory. It requires a replacement algorithm to select a line to remove upon a miss and the algorithm must be implemented in hardware to maintain a high speed of operation. The fully associative cache can only be formed economically with a moderate size capacity. Microprocessors with small internal caches often employ the fully associative mechanism.

Valid bits

In all caches, if the line size is greater than the size of the external data path to the main memory, multiple transfers will be necessary to fill the line from the main memory and to transfer altered lines back to the main memory. It is possible for the line not to hold all the words associated with the line at the time that words are being transferred into the cache one after the other; some words might be from a previous line. To handle this situation, each word in the cache is provided with a valid bit which is set when the word forms part of a line having the same address as the stored address. When a word is loaded, the corresponding valid bit is set. Each address tag in the cache identifies a line, though not all the words within the line may be part of the current line; they may be parts of previous lines. When the processor accesses the cache, the address tag from the processor is compared with all the address tags stored in the cache. If a match is found, the valid bit associated with the required word is checked to see whether the stored word is a valid part of the line. If it is valid, the word is accessed, otherwise the main memory is accessed and the cache loaded with the word. A suitable location is found in the cache, using, say, the least recently used algorithm implemented in hardware. The address tag is updated and the valid bit is set. All valid bits in the line, except that associated with the newly loaded word, are reset. Subsequent words of the line are loaded when they are requested and associated valid bits set then. The term *sub-block* is used to describe the unit requiring a valid bit. For a 32-bit data bus, the sub-block would be 32 bits; for a 64-bit data bus it would be 64 bits.

Even if a complete line can be transferred in one bus transaction, valid bits are usually required in all cache organizations to handle the start-up situation when a cache will hold random patterns of bits.

3.2.2 Direct mapping

The fully associative cache is expensive to implement because of requiring a comparator with each cache location, effectively a special type of memory. In *direct mapping*, the cache consists of normal high speed random access memory, and each location in the cache holds the data, at an address in the cache given by the lower significant bits of the main memory address. This enable the line to be selected directly from the lower significant bits of the memory address. The remaining higher significant bits of the address are stored in the cache with the data to complete the identification of the cached data.

First, consider the example shown in Figure 3.5. The address from the processor is

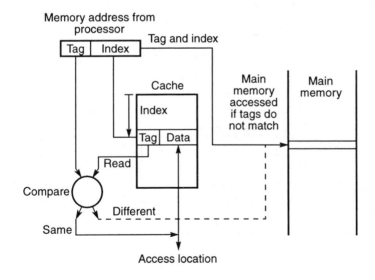

Figure 3.5 Cache with direct mapping

divided into two fields, a *tag* and an *index*. The tag consists of the higher significant bits of the address, which are stored with the data. The index is the lower significant bits of the address used to address the cache.

When the memory is referenced, the index is first used to access a word in the cache. Then the tag stored in the accessed word is read and compared with the tag in the address. If the two tags are the same, indicating that the word is the one required, access is made to the addressed cache word. However, if the tags are not the same, indicating that the required word is not in the cache, reference is made to the main memory to find it. For a memory read operation, the word is then transferred into the cache where it is accessed. It is possible to pass the information to the cache and the processor simultaneously, i.e., to *read-through* the cache, on a miss. The cache location is altered for a write operation. The main memory may be altered at the same time (*write-through*) or later. Write operations will be discussed in Section 3.3.2.

Figure 3.6 shows the direct mapped cache with a line consisting of more than one word. The main memory address is composed of a tag, a line, and a word within a line. All the words within a line in the cache have the same stored tag. The line part of the address is used to access the cache and the stored tag is compared with the required tag address. For a read operation, if the tags are the same, the word within the line is selected for transfer to the processor. If the tags are not the same, the line containing the required word is first transferred to the cache.

In direct mapping, the corresponding lines with the same index in the main memory will map into the same line in the cache, and hence only lines with different indices can be in the cache at the same time. A replacement algorithm is unnecessary, since there is

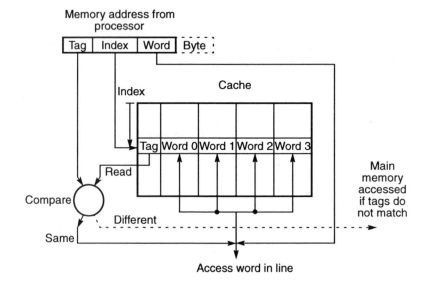

Figure 3.6 Direct mapped cache with a multi-word line

only one allowable location for each incoming line. Efficient replacement relies on the low probability of lines with the same index being required. However, there are such occurrences, for example, when two data vectors are stored starting at the same index and pairs of elements need to be processed together. To gain the greatest performance, data arrays and vectors need to be stored in a manner which minimizes the conflicts in processing pairs of elements. Figure 3.6 shows the lower bits of the processor address used to address the cache location directly. It is possible to introduce a mapping function between the address index and the cache index so that they are not the same. We will see this used in TLBs described in Chapter 4.

The following advantages can be identified for the direct mapped cache:

1. No replacement algorithm necessary.
2. Simple hardware and low cost.
3. High speed of operation.

Disadvantages include:

1. Performance drops significantly if accesses are made to locations with the same index.
2. Hit ratio lower than associative mapping methods (Sections 3.2.1 and 3.2.3).

However, as the size of cache increases, the difference in the hit ratios of the direct and associative caches reduces and becomes insignificant. The trend is for larger direct caches, which suit direct mapped caches. Hill (1988) presents a detailed case for the direct mapped cache.

3.2.3 Set-associative mapping

In the direct scheme described, all words stored in the cache must have different indices. The tags may be the same or different. In the fully associative scheme, lines can displace any other line and can be placed anywhere, but the cost of the fully associative scheme becomes prohibitive for large caches and large associative memories operate relatively slowly.

Set-associative mapping allows a limited number of lines, with the same index and different tags, in the cache and can therefore be considered as a compromise between a fully associative cache and a direct mapped cache. The organization is shown in Figure 3.7. The cache is divided into "sets" of lines. A four-way set associative cache would have four lines in each set. The number of lines in a set is known as the *associativity* or set size. Each line in each set has a stored tag which, together with the index (set number), completes the identification of the line. First, the index of the address from the processor is used to access the set. Then, comparators are used to compare all tags of the selected set with the incoming tag. If a match is found, the corresponding location is accessed, otherwise, as before, an access to the main memory is made.

The tag address bits are always chosen to be the most significant bits of the full

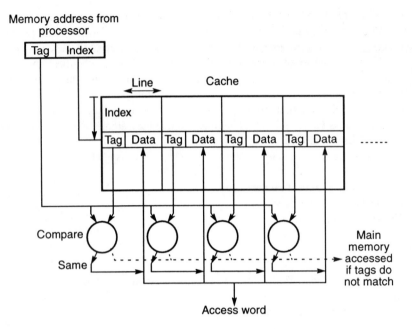

Figure 3.7 Cache with set-associative mapping

address, the line address bits are the next significant bits and the word/byte address bits form the least significant bits as this spreads out consecutive main memory lines throughout consecutive sets in the cache. This addressing format is known as *bit selection* and is used by all known systems. In a set-associative cache it would be possible to have the set address bits as the most significant bits of the address and the line address bits as the next significant, with the word within the line as the least significant bits, or with the line address bits as the least significant bits and the word within the line as the middle bits.

Notice that the association between the stored tags and the incoming tag is done using comparators and can be shared for each associative search, and all the information, tags and data, can be stored in ordinary random access memory. The number of comparators required in the set-associative cache is given by the number of lines in a set, not the number of lines in all, as in a fully associative memory. In a fully associative cache, each tag requires its own comparator within the content addressable memory element. In the set-associative cache, the set can be selected quickly and all the lines of the set can be read out simultaneously with the tags before waiting for the tag comparisons to be made. After a tag has been identified (assuming that a hit has occurred), the corresponding line can be selected.

The replacement algorithm for set-associative mapping need only consider the lines in one set, as the choice of set is predetermined by the index (set number) in the address. Hence, with two lines in each set, for example, only one additional bit is necessary in each set to identify the line to replace. Typically, the set size is 2, 4, 8, or 16. A set size of one line reduces the organization to that of direct mapping and an organization with one set becomes fully associative mapping. For a given number of lines, there is a design choice between increasing the number of sets or increasing the number of lines in each set, as the cache size = (number of sets) × (number of lines in each set).

The set-associative cache has been popular for the internal caches of microprocessors, and can be found in, for example, the Motorola MC68040 (4-way set associative), the Intel 486 (4-way set associative), Intel i860 (4-way set associative), and the Intel Pentium (two-way set associative).

3.2.4 Sector mapping

In sector mapping, the main memory and the cache are both divided into *sectors*, each sector composed of a number of lines. Any sector in the main memory can map into any sector in the cache and a tag is stored with each sector in the cache to identify the main memory sector address. However, a complete sector is not transferred to the cache or back to the main memory as one unit. Instead, individual lines are transferred as required. On cache sector miss, the required line of the sector is transferred into a specific location within one sector. The sector location in the cache is selected (by the replacement algorithm) and all the other existing lines in the sector in the cache are from a previous sector. To differentiate between lines of the sector given by the stored tag and old lines, a valid bit is associated with each line in each sector. When a new line of a new sector is read into the cache, the valid bit of the line is set, and all the other lines are marked as invalid. Subsequent accesses to the same sector but to invalid lines cause the required lines to be read in and the corresponding valid bits set.

We notice that though sectors can be placed anywhere, once the position of the sector is selected the line must be placed at the appropriate location within the sector, i.e. line i is placed in the ith location from the beginning of the sector, and the line bits act as an index. Hence the replacement algorithm need only consider sector addresses in its replacement algorithm.

Sector mapping was used on the first commercial cache system, IBM System/360 Model 85. In this computer system, there were sixteen sectors, each sector with sixteen lines. Each line consisted of 64 bytes, giving a total of 1024 bytes in each sector and 16 Kbytes in all. On a miss, 4 bytes were sent to the cache and also to the processor, using four-way interleaved memory; the remaining 60 bytes of the line being transferred subsequently. A true least recently used replacement algorithm was implemented in hardware (see Section 3.4).

Sector mapping might be regarded as a fully associative mapping scheme with valid bits, as in some microprocessor caches. Each line in the fully associative mapped cache corresponds to a sector, and each byte corresponds to a "sector line". Hence, though the sector mapping generally lost favor after the System/360 Model 85 (around 1968), perhaps because the hit ratio of the sector mapping was said to have been less than comparable to set-associative mapping, a form of it has reappeared in microprocessor systems. We note that the limited bus width of microprocessor systems prevents large numbers of words being transferred simultaneously.

3.3 Fetch and write mechanisms

3.3.1 Fetch policy

We can identify three strategies for fetching bytes or lines from the main memory to the cache, namely:

1. Demand fetch.
2. Prefetch.
3. Selective fetch.

Demand fetch is the name given to fetching a line when it is needed and is not already in the cache, i.e. to fetch the required line on a miss. This strategy is the simplest and requires no additional hardware or tags in the cache recording the references, except to identify the line in the cache to be replaced.

Prefetch is the name given to the strategy of fetching lines before they are requested. A simple prefetch strategy is to prefetch the $(i + 1)$th line when the ith line is initially referenced (assuming that the $(i + 1)$th line is not already in the cache) on the expectation that it is likely to be needed if the ith line is needed. Sequential prefetch can reduce the miss ratio by 50 per cent if the cache is large. Unfortunately, fetching the $(i + 1)$th line means that some other line must be displaced, and this line might be more likely to be referenced than the $(i + 1)$th line. On the simple prefetch strategy, not all first references will induce a miss, as some will be to prefetched lines. Prefetching could be limited to when there has been a miss to the ith line (*prefetching on a miss*).

Selective fetch describes the policy of not always fetching lines, dependent upon some defined criterion, and in these cases using the main memory rather than the cache to hold the information. For example, shared writable data might be easier to maintain if it is always kept in the main memory and not passed to a cache for access, especially in multiprocessor systems. Cache systems need to be designed so that the processor can access the main memory directly and bypass the cache. Individual locations could be tagged as non-cacheable.

3.3.2 Instruction and data caches

The basic stored program computer provides for one main memory for holding both program instructions and program data. The cache can be organized in the same fashion, with the cache holding both program instructions and data. This is called a *unified cache*. There are several advantages, though, if we separate the cache into two parts, one holding the data (a *data cache*) and one holding the program instructions (an *instruction* or *code cache*). First, the write policy would only have to be applied to the data cache (assuming instructions are not modified. Second, separate paths could be provided from the processor to each cache, allowing simultaneous transfers to both the instruction cache and the data cache. This is particularly convenient in a pipeline processor,[2] as different stages

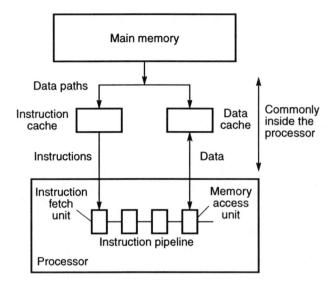

Figure 3.8 Separate instruction and data caches

of the pipeline access each cache (the instruction fetch unit accesses the instruction cache and the memory access unit accesses the data cache). Another advantage is that a designer may choose to have different sizes for the instruction cache and data cache, and have different internal organizations and line sizes for each cache. The general arrangement of separate caches is shown in Figure 3.8. Often the cache will be integrated inside the processor chip (whether a unified cache of separate instruction and data caches). Many microprocessors have separate caches, for example the Pentium (but not the Intel 486), and the Motorola MC68040.

Separate caches do have some complexities and constraints especially if introduced into an existing processor family. Most existing processors still allow a programmer to write self-modifying code (or a compiler to create such code), even though such actions would be *very strongly* discouraged. If allowed, a situation would occur with an instruction in both the instruction cache and the data cache. If modified in the data cache, the copy in the instruction cache would be different. Also the time that such modification occurred would depend upon the pipeline design, and might not occur before the instruction is fetched. Most existing processors also allow instructions and data to be loaded into consecutive or nearby locations in memory, so that it might be possible for a line to hold both data and instructions (if the line is sufficiently large). Again we would have two copies of cached lines, and a problem with consistency. Of course all these problems can be eliminated simply by insisting that instructions and data are separated in memory (as

---

² See Chapter 1 for the basic ideas of pipeline processors, and Chapter 5 more details.

they would normally be) and that self-modifying code is not written. Otherwise one mechanism is to invalidate the line in the instruction cache if the same line is written to in the data cache. This allows duplicated lines, but only when not altered.

3.3.3 Write operations

As reading the required word in the cache does not affect the cache contents, there can be no discrepancy between the cache word and the copy held in the main memory after a memory read instruction. However, in general, writing can occur to cache words and it is possible that the cache word and copy held in the main memory may be different. It is necessary to keep the cache and the main memory copy identical if input/output transfers operate on the main memory contents, or if multiple processors operate on the main memory, as in a shared memory multiple processor system.

If we ignore the overhead of maintaining consistency and the time for writing data back to the main memory, then the average access time is given by the previous equation, i.e. $t_a = t_c + (1 - h)t_m$, assuming that all accesses are first made to the cache. The average access time including write operations will add additional time to this equation which will depend upon the mechanism used to maintain data consistency. If it is not necessary to keep both main memory and cache memory contents consistent, for example in a system in which all processors and input/output devices access data through the one cache, then the average access time is given as before.

Though the average access time of the cache is a major factor in the performance of the system and will be computed for various read/write strategies in the next sections, the overall speed of computation is influenced by various factors. In particular, the instruction execution speed is determined by various internal operations in addition to instruction fetches and operand accesses. Also, differences in machine architecture can have a profound influence on the overall performance. An increase in the line size without any increase in the cache memory/main memory data paths might even result in a decrease in the overall performance as multiple transfers appear on the data path.

There are two principal alternative mechanisms to update the main memory, namely the *write-through* mechanism and the *write-back* mechanism (also called *copyback*).

3.3.4 Write-through mechanism

In the *write-through* mechanism, every write operation to the cache is repeated to the main memory, normally at the same time. The additional write operation to the main memory will, of course, take much longer than to the cache and will dominate the access time for write operations. Fortunately, there are usually several read operations between write operations (typically between three and ten). Smith (1982), for example, reports that in one of his studies, 16 per cent of references were write references, though for different programs the percentage varied from 5 per cent to 34 per cent. The average access time of write-through with transfers from main memory to the cache on all misses (read and write) is given by:

$$t_a = t_c + (1 - h)t_b + w(t_m - t_c)$$
$$= (1 - w)t_c + (1 - h)t_b + wt_m$$
$$= (1 - w)t_c + (1 - h + w)t_m \quad \text{if } t_b = t_m$$

where t_b = time to transfer line (block) to cache, assuming the whole line must be transferred together, and w = fraction of write references.

The term $(t_m - t_c)$ is the additional time to write the word to main memory whether a hit or a miss has occurred, given that both cache and main memory write operations occur simultaneously but the main memory write operation must complete before any subsequent cache read/write operations can proceed. If the size of the line matches the external data path size, a whole line can be transferred in one transaction and $t_b = t_m$. If the line is longer than the external data path, separate data transfers are needed for each word of a line. Then $t_b = bt_m$ when there are b transfers to transfer the complete line.

Suppose $t_c = 25$ ns, $t_m = 200$ ns, h = 99 per cent, $w = 20$ per cent, and the memory data path fully matches the cache line size. The average access time would be 62 ns, with misses accounting for 2 ns and write policy accounting for 35 ns. When the data path does not match the line size and more than one transfer is required, the misses become more significant. For example, if the line size is sixteen times larger than the external data path ($b = 16$), the average access time is 92 ns, with misses accounting for 32 ns and the write policy accounting for 35 ns.

On a cache miss, a line could be transferred from the main memory to the cache whether the miss was caused by a write or by a read operation. The term *fetch on write* is used to describe a policy of bringing a word/line from the main memory into the cache for a write operation. In write-through, fetch on write transfers are often not done on a miss, i.e., a *no fetch on write* policy. The information will be written back to the main memory but not kept in the cache. The term *allocate on write* is sometimes used for fetch on write because a line is allocated for an incoming line on cache miss. *Non-allocate on write* corresponds to no fetch on write.

The average access time with a no fetch on write policy is given by:[3]

$$t_a = t_c + (1 - w)(1 - h)t_b + w(t_m - t_c)$$
$$= (1 - w)(t_c + (1 - h)t_b) + wt_m$$

The hit ratio will generally be slightly lower than for the fetch on write policy because altered lines will not be brought into the cache and might be required during some read operations, depending upon the program. Suppose the hit ratio and other parameters were the same as before, then the average access time is 61.6 ns or, with $b = 16$, 85.6 ns.

The write-through scheme can be enhanced by incorporating buffers, as shown in

---

[3] When using probability theory, one needs to be careful to account for all combinations. The above result can also be obtained by considering each combination of read/write with hit/miss:

$$t_a = \underbrace{(1 - w)ht_c}_{\text{Read-hit}} + \underbrace{(1 - w)(1 - h)(t_c + t_b)}_{\text{Read-miss}} + \underbrace{wht_m}_{\text{Write-hit}} + \underbrace{w(1 - h)t_m}_{\text{Write-miss}}$$

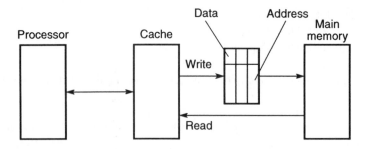

Figure 3.9 Cache with write buffer

Figure 3.9, to hold information to be written back to the main memory, freeing the cache for subsequent accesses. (Buffers are also found in write-back schemes, see Section 3.3.5). For write-through, each item to be written back to the main memory is held in a buffer together with the corresponding main memory address if the transfer cannot be made immediately. The capacity to store more than one data/address pair is preferable. A capacity of four data/address items is typically sufficient, as used on the Intel 486 with write-through cache. If the write-through is totally transparent to the cache operation, the average cycle time reduces to that given in Section 3.1.2. Buffers require considerable additional logic to ensure that any request to main memory (by the processor/cache mechanism or another device) checks the buffers. All memory reference addresses have to be compared to the addresses stored in the buffers.

Immediate writing to main memory when new values are generated ensures that the most recent values are held in the main memory and hence that any device or processor accessing the main memory should obtain the most recent values immediately, thus avoiding the need for complicated consistency mechanisms. There will be a latency before the main memory has been updated, and the cache and main memory values are not consistent during this period. If the processor fails, the system can be restored relatively easily. The main memory often has error detection/ correction circuitry based upon parity and Hamming codes, but the cache memory may not have this circuitry.

Write-through caches can be found in many systems, large and small, over the years. They can be found in many microprocessor cache systems, being easy to implement and to maintain on a single bus system. However, every write will generate main memory transfer, and bus traffic. This will be significant particularly if the bus is being used by other devices, such as other processors in a multiprocessor system (see Chapter 6 onwards).

3.3.5 Write-back mechanism

In the *write-back* mechanism, the write operation to the main memory is only done at line replacement time. At this time, the line displaced by the incoming line might be written back to the main memory irrespective of whether the line has been altered. The policy is known as simple write-back, and leads to an average access time of:

$$t_a = t_c + (1 - h)t_b + (1 - h)t_b = t_c + 2(1 - h)t_b$$

where one $(1 - h)t_b$ term is due to fetching a line from memory and the other $(1 - h)t_b$ term is due to writing back a line. Write-back normally handles write misses as fetch on write, as opposed to write-through, which often handles write misses as no fetch on write.

The write-back mechanism usually only writes back lines that have been altered. To implement this policy, a 1-bit tag is associated with each cache line and is set whenever the line is altered. At replacement time, the tags are examined to determine whether it is necessary to write the line back to the main memory. The average access time now becomes:

$$t_a = t_c + (1 - h)t_b + w_b(1 - h)t_b = t_c + (1 - h)(1 + w_b)t_b$$

where w_b is the probability that a line has been altered (fraction of lines altered). The probability that a line has been altered could be as high as the probability of write references, w, but is likely to be much less, as more than one write reference to the same line is likely and some references to the same byte/word within the line are likely. The hit ratio will be the same as the simple write-back and the same as the write-through with fetch on write. For relatively little extra hardware, the average access time has been reduced by $(1 - h + w_b)t_b$, which is quite significant. However, under this policy the complete line is written back, even if only one word in the line has been altered, and thus the policy results in more traffic than is necessary, especially for memory data paths narrower than a line, but still there is usually less memory traffic than write-through, which causes every alteration to be recorded in the main memory. The write-back scheme can also be enhanced by incorporating buffers to hold information to be written back to the main memory, just as is possible and normally done with write-through.

Apart from the two main types of write policies, write-back and write-through, additional mechanisms are necessary to cope with multiple caches in a multiple processor system. Most microprocessors are designed to be used in small-scale multiprocessor system where each processor will have its own cache and shares the same bus to the main memory. Additional mechanisms for multiprocessor operation are described in Chapter 6, Section 6.5.

3.4 Replacement policy

3.4.1 Objectives and constraints

When the required word of a line is not held in the cache, we have seen that it is necessary to transfer the line from the main memory into the cache, displacing an existing line if the cache is full. Except for direct mapping, which does not allow a replacement algorithm, the existing line in the cache is chosen by a *replacement algorithm*. For cache systems, the least recently used algorithm is most commonly used. We shall discuss these algorithms in the context of cache memory systems in the following sections.[4] The replacement mechanism must be implemented totally in hardware, preferably such that the selection can be made completely during the main memory cycle for fetching the new line. Ideally, the line replaced will not be needed again in the future. However, such future events cannot be known and a decision has to made based upon facts that are known at the time.

Replacement algorithms are classified as *usage-based* or *non-usage-based*. For a cache, usage and non-usage algorithms are both candidates for the replacement algorithm; a critical factor is often the amount of hardware necessary to implement the algorithm, as the differences in performance might be less important than the differences in cost.

A usage-based replacement algorithm for the fully associative cache needs to take the usage (references) to all stored lines into account. A usage-based replacement algorithm for a set-associative cache needs to take only the lines in one set into account at replacement time, though a record needs to be kept of relative usage of the lines in each set.

Whatever type of algorithm (usage-based or non-usage-based), there are generally fewer lines to consider in a set-associative cache than in a similar sized fully associative cache, and the logic is simpler. For a two-way set-associative cache, only one bit per set is needed to indicate which item should be replaced. The associativity of caches is often small (two or four) but some large systems have set sizes up to sixteen (e.g. IBM 3033) and then the required logic and its speed to implement the replacement algorithm must be carefully considered.

3.4.2 Random replacement algorithm

Perhaps the easiest replacement algorithm to implement is a pseudo-random replacement algorithm. A true random replacement algorithm would select a line to replace in a totally random order, with no regard to memory references or previous selections; practical random replacement algorithms can approximate this algorithm in one of several ways. For example, one counter for the whole cache could be incremented at intervals (for example after each clock cycle, or after each reference, irrespective of whether it is a hit or a miss). The value held in the counter identifies the line in the cache (if fully associative) or the line in the set if it is a set-associative cache. The counter should have sufficient bits to identify any line. For a fully associative cache, an n-bit counter is necessary if there are 2^n words in the cache. For a four-way set-associative cache, one 2-bit counter would be sufficient, together with logic to increment the counter.

3.4.3 First-in first-out replacement algorithm

The first-in first-out replacement algorithm removes the line which has been in the cache

---

[4] Replacement algorithms are also used in paging system described in Chapter 4. In that case, the algorithm can be implemented partially in software.

for the longest time. The first-in first-out algorithm would naturally be implemented with a first-in first-out queue of line addresses, but can be more easily implemented with counters, only one counter for a fully associative cache or one counter for each set in a set-associative cache, each with a sufficient number of bits to identify the line.

3.4.4 Least recently used algorithm for a cache

In the *least recently used* (LRU) algorithm, the line which has not been referenced for the longest time is removed from the cache. Only those lines in the cache are considered. The word "recently" comes about because the line is not the least used, as this is likely to be back in memory. It is the least used of those lines in the cache, and all of these are likely to have been recently used otherwise they would not be in the cache. The least recently used (LRU) algorithm is popular for cache systems and can be implemented fully when the number of lines involved is small. There are several ways the algorithm can be implemented in hardware for a cache, these include:

1. Counters.
2. Register stack.
3. Reference matrix.
4. Approximate methods.

In the counter implementation, a counter is associated with each line. A simple implementation would be to increment each counter at regular intervals and to reset a counter when the associated line had been referenced. Hence the value in each counter would indicate the age of a line since last referenced. The line with the largest age would be replaced at replacement time.

The algorithm for these *ageing registers* can be modified to take into account the fact that the counters have a fixed number of bits and that only a relative age is required as follows. When a hit occurs, the counter associated with the hit line is reset to 0, indicating that it is the most recently used, and all counters having a smaller value than the "hit line" counter originally are incremented by 1. All counters having a larger value are unaffected. On a miss when the cache is not full, the counter associated with the incoming line is reset to 0 and all other counters are incremented by 1. On a miss when the cache is full, the line with a counter set at the maximum value (three for a 2-bit counter and four sets) is chosen for replacement and then the counter is reset to 0, and all other counters incremented by 1. The counter with the largest value identifies the least recently used line. For example, suppose there are four lines in the set of a set-associative cache. A 2-bit counter is sufficient for each line. Let the counters in one set be C_0, C_1, C_2, and C_3. Initially, all the counters are set to 0. As an example, we obtain the sequence in Table 3.1 for the conditions specified.

In the register stack implementation, a set of n-bit registers is formed, one for each line in the set to be considered. The most recently used line is recorded at the "top" of the stack and the least recently used line at the bottom. Actually, the set of registers does not form a conventional stack, as both ends and internal values are accessible. The value held in one register is passed to the next register under certain conditions. When a line is refer-

Table 3.1 Least recently used algorithm using counters – set size of four lines

Location referenced (when tag changes)		C_0	C_1	C_2	C_3	Subsequent actions
Address tag	Hit/Miss					
	Initialization	0	0	0	0	
5	Miss	0	1	1	1	Line 0 filled
6	Miss	1	0	2	2	Line 1 filled
5	Hit	0	1	2	2	Line 0 accessed
7	Miss	1	2	0	3	Line 2 filled
8	Miss	2	3	1	0	Line 3 filled
6	Hit	3	0	2	1	Line 1 accessed
9	Miss	0	1	3	2	Line 0 replaced
10	Miss	1	2	0	3	Line 2 replaced

enced, starting at the top of the stack, the values held in the registers are shifted one place towards the bottom of the stack until a register is found to hold the same value as the incoming line identification. Subsequent registers are not shifted. The top register is loaded with the incoming line identification. This has the effect of moving the contents of the register holding the incoming line number to the top of the stack. It is left as a logic design exercise to devise the required logic. It will be found that the logic is fairly substantial and slow, and not really a practical solution, given the alternative reference matrix method.

The reference matrix method centers around a matrix of status bits. There is more than one version of the method. In one version (Smith, 1982), the upper triangular matrix of a $B \times B$ matrix is formed without the diagonal, if there are B lines to consider. The triangular matrix has $(B \times (B - 1))/2$ bits. When the ith line is referenced, all the bits in the ith row of the matrix are set to 1 and then all the bits in the ith column are set to 0. The least recently used line is one which has all 0's in its row and all 1's in its column, which can be detected easily by logic. The method is demonstrated in Figure 3.10 for $B = 4$ and the reference sequence 2, 1, 3, 0, 3, 2, 1, ..., together with the values that would be obtained using a register stack. Maruyama (1975) extends the reference matrix method to select m least recently used lines where m can be greater than 1.

The reference matrix method can be derived from the following definition (for 4 lines):

$B_5 = 1$ when line 3 is more recently used than line 2.
$B_4 = 1$ when line 3 is more recently used than line 1.
$B_3 = 1$ when line 3 is more recently used than line 0.

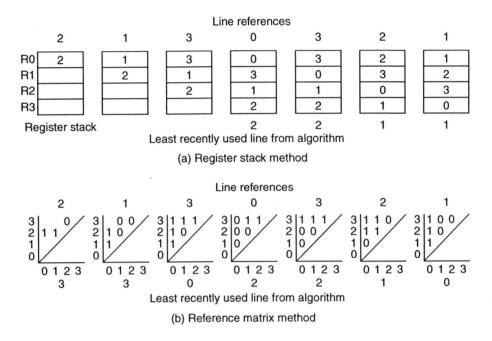

Figure 3.10 Least recently used replacement algorithm implementation

$B_2 = 1$ when line 2 is more recently used than line 1.
$B_1 = 1$ when line 2 is more recently used than line 0.
$B_0 = 1$ when line 1 is more recently used than line 0.

where B_5, B_4, B_3, B_2, B_1 and B_0 are the bits of the matrix (B_0 the first row, B_1 and B_2 the second row, and B_3, B_4, B_5 the third row). The Motorola MC88200 uses this method.

When the number of lines to consider increases above about four to eight, approximate methods are necessary for the LRU algorithm. Figure 3.11 shows a two-stage approximation method with eight lines, which is applicable to any replacement algorithm and has been used with the least recently used algorithm (IBM 370/168-3). The eight lines in Figure 3.11 are divided into four pairs, and each pair has one status bit to indicate the most/least recently used line in the pair (simply set or reset by reference to each line). The least recently used replacement algorithm now only considers the four pairs. Six status bits are necessary (using the reference matrix) to identify the least recently used pair which, together with the status bit of the pair, identifies the least recently used line of a pair.

The method can be extended to further levels. For example, sixteen lines can be divided into four groups, each group having two pairs. One status bit can be associated with each pair, identifying the line in the pair, and another with each group, identifying the group in a pair of groups. A true least recently used algorithm is applied to the groups. In fact, the

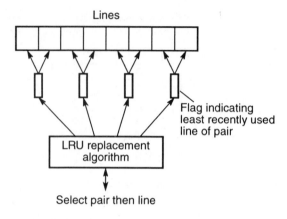

Figure 3.11 Two-stage replacement algorithm

scheme could be taken to its logical conclusion of extending to a full binary tree, and this has been done in the Intel 486 processor. Here there are four lines in a set. One status bit, B_0, specifies which half of the lines are most/least recently used. Two more bits, B_1 and B_2, specify which line of pairs are most recently/least recently used, as shown in Figure 3.12. Every time a cache line is referenced (or loaded on a miss), the status bits are updated. For example, if line L_2 is referenced, B_2 is set to a 0 to indicate that L_2 is the most recently used of the pair L_2 and L_3, B_0 is set to a 1 to indicate that L_2/L_3 is the most recently used of the four lines, L_0, L_1, L_2 and L_3. To identify the line to replace on a miss, the status bits are examined. If $B_0 = 0$, then the line is either L_0 or L_1. If then $B_1 = 0$, it is L_0. If $B_1 = 1$ it is L_1. If $B_0 = 1$, then the line is either L_2 or L_3. If then $B_2 = 0$, it is L_2. If $B_2 = 1$ it is L_3. For n lines $\log_2 n$ status bits will be needed, which is the least of all the implementations described. It is left as an exercise (Problem 3.16) to determine how well this algorithm approximates to the true least recently used algorithm.

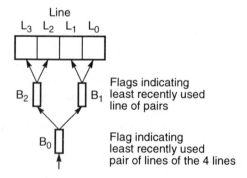

Figure 3.12 Replacement algorithm using a tree selection

3.5 Cache performance

For any given cache, if the size of the cache is increased, the miss ratio decreases and generally the performance of the system increases. The actual miss ratio depends very heavily on the programs being executed and the overall workload such that an exact fixed value of miss ratio cannot be found for any particular computer system. The miss ratio also depends upon the cache organization chosen, the size of the internal divisions of the cache, the write policy and the replacement algorithm.

In the design phase of a computer system incorporating a cache, there are three basic methods of obtaining an estimate of the miss ratio:

1. Trace-driven simulation.
2. Direct measurement.
3. Mathematical modelling.

The trace-driven method is perhaps the most popular, giving miss ratios in actual situations which can be varied. In this method, programs are selected for execution on a computer system not necessarily having a cache. (It does not matter whether the system has a cache of any kind but the system should have a processor of the type in the system under investigation.) A record of the instruction and data references is kept. The processor trace facility (assuming there is one) is generally used. After each test program instruction has been executed, a trace interrupt causes a special routine to be executed; this records the instruction and data references. The routine usually has to recognize the effective addresses of the test program instructions, but this is relatively straightforward to accomplish. For example, the Intel 8086 family (and many other processors) has an instruction which returns the effective address rather than the addressed operand (LEA instruction - load effective address) which can be used in many cases. There are also operating system utilities that will trace programs as they are being executed, and record memory references (and other information).

Specific cache organizations are then simulated, using the instruction/data references that have been gathered, to determine the miss ratio. Generally, a very large number of references needs to be gathered to obtain accurate figures, usually at least several hundred thousand references. When the cache simulation is begun, a relatively large number of initial misses will be due to the cache containing no information. This of course occurs in practice; such *cold starts* produce a disproportionate number of misses. Also occurring in practice are *context switch misses*, which occur frequently in a multiprogramming environment. In such an environment, the computer system will execute part of one program and will then return to the operating system to select another program. It will then execute part of this program and the procedure will be repeated with all user programs. Even in a single-user system, there will be operating system calls causing a change in context. However, many trace/simulation experiments will assume that warm start results are required. For warm start results (when the effects of the start-up and context changes are not considered) traces of perhaps 300 000–1 000 000 references, or thereabouts, are required. Since trace programs will operate substantially more slowly than the test program alone, experiments need to be performed for many hours. There are techniques for substantially reducing the number of references but still obtaining accurate values and the reader is directed to Stone (1987) for further details. Other trace experiments have been directed towards transient behavior of cold start and context switch environments (Strecker, 1983).

Figure 3.13 shows representative warm start results obtained by the trace method for three programs, A, B and C, and is based on the results of Smith (1987a). There can be significant differences between individual programs; in fact there can be enormous differences. As expected, as the overall size of the cache is increased, the hit ratio initially decreases significantly but this change reduces as the cache size is increased further and after a certain cache size, the change in miss ratio becomes unnoticeable.

When computed as a function of line size, as shown in Figure 3.14, for a given cache size, the miss ratio decreases with increasing cache size but often a minimum is reached and then the miss ratio increases. Hence there is an optimum value for the line size for a particular cache size. For example, a good line size for a 256-byte cache, according to Figure 3.13, would be perhaps 64 bytes. As the cache size is increased, the optimum line size increases. The overall effect is caused partly by program locality, when programs reference more than one contiguous area and fewer of these areas can reside in the cache simultaneously as the line size increases. For example, when the number of lines is half the cache size, only two different contiguous areas could be stored in the cache simultaneously. More significantly, as the line size increases, there is more contiguous information in the cache and more likelihood that some of this information will not be wanted. This unwanted information displaces information that might be wanted in the future (an effect called *memory pollution*). We note also that as the line size increases, more infor-

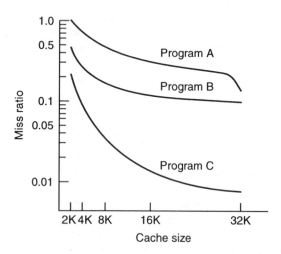

Figure 3.13 Miss ratio against cache size

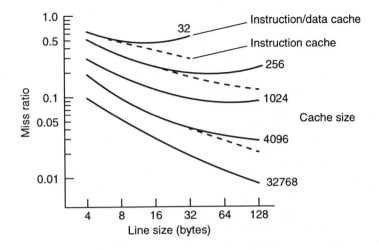

Figure 3.14 Miss ratio against block size

mation must be transferred into the cache on a miss which decreases the operational speed if more than one bus transfer is necessary.

The miss ratio for a particular cache organization differs for instruction references and data references. For data references, we might get a more pronounced "knee" in the miss ratio curve as plotted against line size, particularly for small cache sizes, whereas for instruction fetches (shown by the dashed lines in Figure 3.14) there is a general decrease in miss ratio for increasing line size. This effect is because instructions are more likely to be referenced sequentially and more of the information in larger lines is likely to be needed. (However, data items are also often stored in contiguous locations.)

The memory reference sequence could be obtained by direct measurement by attaching special monitoring hardware to the computer system to record the memory references. (In fact, for the study reported by Smith (1987a) simulation trace references and hardware monitored references were both used.) Monitoring hardware is feasible for relatively slow and medium speed systems, including microprocessor systems, but might be difficult, if not impossible, to implement for the fastest computer system operating at full speed. It might be possible to decrease the speed of operation of these fast computer systems by decreasing the clock rate so that the memory references could be captured. Once the sequence has been obtained, it can be processed by a cache simulation program, as before.

One advantage of direct measurement is that all memory references can be obtained. Some instructions might not be easily traced in software, notably operating system reserved instructions. Also, hardware monitors operate at a much greater speed than software monitors and may be left on a system during a normal operation without appreciably affecting the operation. In contrast, software trace monitors slow the system down drastically. To simulate context switches, several programs can be traced and each program executed during the cache simulation for, say, 20 000 references in sequence. For example, in the study by Smith (1987a), twenty-seven program traces were selected from five different types of computer system as a representative sample.

An alternative method of gathering cache results is to construct the cache physically in a system and make direct measurements. As a design tool before finally deciding on the cache size and organization, the method has the disadvantage that cache parameters cannot be easily altered. However, it can be performed after a cache design has been selected to confirm that the choice was appropriate.

Mathematical models of caches can be developed based upon differential equations, statistical and probabilistic techniques. After a mathematical model has been obtained, it is generally compared to experimental simulation results. Mathematical curve fitting expressions can also be derived based upon trace-driven results, and extrapolated for designs not covered in the trace-driven simulation.

The contents of a cache in a multiprogrammed system will exhibit constant changes from one program to another. During the transition between programs, a much higher miss ratio will occur as the new program displaces the old program in the cache. The miss ratio will reduce until a steady state is reached with the cache holding the new program. This important aspect is called the *transient behavior* of caches and has been studied mathematically by Strecker (1983), and by Thiebaut and Stone (1987). Strecker has developed a formula for the rate of change of the number of locations filled in the cache as:

$$\frac{dn}{dt} = m(n)p(n)$$

where $m(n)$ is the miss ratio with n locations filled in the cache and $p(n)$ is the probability that a miss results in a new location being filled. ($p(n)$ is 0 if the cache is filled, 1 if the cache is not filled and any free location can be used, i.e., in a fully associative cache, and less than 1 with direct and set-associative caches, which place restraints upon the availability of locations for incoming lines.) Strecker assumes that the probability is numerically equal to the fraction of free cache locations, i.e.:

$$p(n) = \frac{s - n}{s}$$

where s is the size of the cache. The reasonably good approximation to the miss ratio is given as:

$$m(n) = \frac{a + bn}{a + n}$$

where a and b are constants to be found from trace results. Hence we obtain:

$$\frac{dn}{dt} = \frac{(a+bn)(s-n)}{(a+n)s}$$

It is left as an exercise to solve this equation (see Strecker, 1983).

Thiebaut and Stone (1987) introduced the term *footprint* to describe the active portion of a process that is present in the cache. Footprints of two processes reside in the cache during a transition from one program to another. Probabilistic equations are derived (see Stone, 1987). Mathematical modeling is useful in helping to see the effect of changing parameters, but mathematical models cannot capture the vast differences in programs.

3.6 Second-level caches

When the cache is integrated into the processor, it will be impossible to increase its size should the performance not be sufficient. In any case, increasing the size of the cache may create a slower cache. As an alternative, which has become very popular, a second larger cache can be introduced between the first cache and the main memory as shown in Figure 3.15. This *"second-level"* cache is sometimes called a *secondary cache*. The second-level cache is usually at least an order of magnitude larger than the first-level cache, for example 256 Kbytes for the second-level cache and 8 Kbytes for the first-level cache.

On a memory reference, the processor will access the first-level cache. If the information is not found there (a first-level cache miss occurs), the second-level cache will be accessed. If it is not in the second cache (a second-level cache miss occurs), then the main memory must be accessed. Memory locations will be transferred to the second-level cache and then to the first-level cache, so that two copies of a memory locations will exist

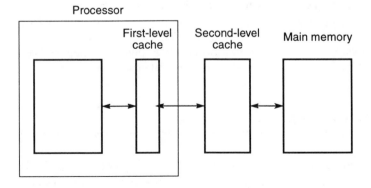

Figure 3.15 Two-level caches

in the cache system at least initially, i.e., locations cached in the second-level cache also exist in the first-level cache. This is known as the *Principle of Inclusion.* (Of course the copies of locations in the second-level cache will never be needed as they will be found in the first-level cache.) Whether this continues will depend upon the replacement and write policies, but it is usually assumed to continue for analytical purposes (Flynn, 1995). The replacement policy practiced in both caches would normally be the least recently used algorithm. Normally write-through will be practiced between the caches, which will maintain duplicate copies. The line size of the second-level cache will be at least the same if not larger than the line size of the first-level cache, because otherwise on a first-level cache miss, more than one second-level cache line would need to be transferred into the first-level cache line.

We can use extend our previous equations to cover a second-level cache. Expanding t_c in:

$$t_a = t_c + (1 - h)t_m$$

we get:

$$t_a = [t_{c1} + (1 - h_1)t_{c2}] + (1 - h_2)t_m$$

where t_{c1} is the first-level cache access time, t_{c2} the second-level cache access time, t_m the main memory access time, h_1 is the first-level cache hit ratio, and h_2 is the combined first/second-level cache hit ratio, considering the two caches are one homogeneous cache system. The hit ratio h_1 will be greater than the hit ratio h_2. Clearly we could extend the cache system and the analysis to cover a greater memory hierarchy, and one way is to introduce a disk cache.

Most microprocessor families provide for second-level caches, using separate cache controllers for such external caches. The Intel 486 has the 8291 cache controller chip, the Pentium has the 82491 cache controller, and Motorola has similar cache controller chips. The interface between the processor and the second-level cache must operate very fast, and a separate second-level cache bus can be provided. This bus has been called a *backside* bus (as opposed to a *frontside* bus connecting to the main memory). The Intel P6, the replacement for the Pentium (Halfhill, 1995), has such buses, and also packages both the processor and the second-level cache onto a single multichip module to achieve the high speed of operation, and provide a conveniently packaged product.

3.7 Disk caches

The concept of a cache can be applied to the main memory/disk interface. A disk cache is a random access memory introduced between the disk and the normal main memory of the system. It can be placed within the disk unit as shown in Figure 3.16, or within the computer system proper. The disk cache has considerable capacity, perhaps greater than 8

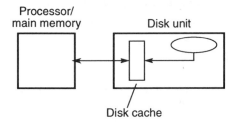

Figure 3.16 Disk cache in disk unit

Mbytes, and holds blocks of information from the disk which are likely to be used in the near future. The blocks are selected from previous accesses in much the same way as lines are placed in a main memory cache. A disk cache controller activates the disk transfers. The principle of locality, which makes main memory caches effective, also makes disk caches effective and reduces the effective input/output data transfer time, perhaps from 20–30 ms to 2–5 ms, depending upon the size of the transfer to the main memory. The disk cache is implemented using semiconductor memory of the same type as normal main memory, and clearly such memory could have been added to the main memory as a design alternative. It is interesting to note that some operating systems, such as UNIX, employ a software cache technique of maintaining an input/output buffer in the main memory.

The unit of transfer between the disk and the disk cache could be a sector, multiple sectors or one or more tracks. A minimum unit of one track is one candidate (Grossman, 1985), as is transferring the information from the selected sector to the end of the track. A write-through policy has the advantage of simplifying error recovery. Not all the information from/to the disk needs to pass through the disk cache and some data/code might be better not using the cache. One possibility is to have a dynamic cache on/off mechanism which causes the cache to be bypassed in selected circumstances.

Perhaps one of the main attractions of placing the additional cache memory in the disk unit is that existing software and hardware may not need to be changed and substantial improvements in speed can be obtained in an existing system. Most commercial disk caches are integrated into the disk units. Examples include the IBM 3880 Model 23 Cache Storage Controls with an 8–64 Mbyte cache. Disk caches have also been introduced into personal computer systems. It is preferable to be able to access the disk cache from the processor and to allow disk cache transfers between the disk cache and disk simultaneously, as disk transfers might be one or more tracks and such transfers can take a considerable time. Some early commercial disk caches did not have this feature (for example the IBM 3880 Model 13).

Disk caches normally incorporate error detection and correction. For example, the disk cache incorporated into the IBM 3880 Model 23 has error detection/correction to detect all triple-bit errors, and correct all double-bit errors and most triple-bit errors. The earlier IBM 3880 Model 13, having a 4–8 Mbyte cache, could detect double errors and correct single-bit errors (Smith, 1985). Both these disk drives maintain copies of data in the cache using a least recently used replacement algorithm.

PROBLEMS

3.1 Choose suitable memory interleaving to obtain an average access time of less than 50 ns given that the main memory has an access time of 150 ns and a cache has an access time of 35 ns. If ten locations hold a loop of instructions and the loop is repeated sixty times, what is the average access time?

3.2 What is the average access time of a system having three levels of memory, a cache memory, a semiconductor main memory and magnetic disk secondary memory, if the access times of the memories are 20 ns, 200 ns and 2 ms, respectively? The cache hit ratio is 80 per cent and the main memory hit ratio is 99 per cent.

3.3 A computer employs a 16 Mbyte 32-bit word main memory and a cache of 8 Kbytes. Determine the number of bits in each field of the address in the following organizations:

1. Direct mapping with a line size of one word.
2. Direct mapping with a line size of eight words.
3. Set-associative mapping with a set size of four and line size of one word.

3.4 Derive an expression for the hit ratio of a direct mapped cache assuming there is an equal likelihood of any location in the main memory being accessed (in practice this assumption is not true). Repeat for a two-way set-associative mapped cache. Determine the size of memory at which the direct mapped cache has a hit ratio within 10 per cent of the set-associative cache.

3.5 A cache memory has a total of 256 lines (blocks) of 16 bytes each. The processor generates 32-bit (byte) addresses. Draw the cache configuration giving the number of bits in each field of the addresses if the cache is direct mapped. Assume the cache is full when a new series of addresses are being accessed which are not currently in the cache. The following addresses (in hexadecimal) are produced by the processor, in sequence:

```
00053272105
00053502120
00053271130
00053272106
00053502124
00053261130
00053272104
```

Whenever a byte is requested from memory, the complete line is fetched. How many misses will be generated? (Note: one hexadecimal digit corresponds to four binary digits.)

3.6 Derive an expression for the average access time of a system with cache memory given the following:

Line size	$= b$ bytes
Time to interrogate cache to discover whether matching tag exists	$= t_i$
Time to read data from cache if matching tag exists	$= t_c$
Time to access 1, 2, or 4 consecutive bytes in main memory (read or write)	$= t_m$
Fraction of write references	$= \omega$

Write policy is write-through, with no fetch on write. Writing to main memory is overlapped with writing to the cache. A line must be completely loaded into the cache before the next cache access. Make (but state) any other reasonable necessary assumptions. Explain the purpose of each term in your equation.

3.7 Design the logic to implement the least recently used replacement algorithm for four lines using a register stack.

3.8 Design the logic to implement the least recently used replacement algorithm for four lines using the reference matrix method.

3.9 Determine the conditions in which a write-through policy creates more misses than a simple write-back policy, given that the hit ratio is the same in both cases.

3.10 Determine the conditions in which a write-through policy with no fetch on write creates more misses than a write-through policy with fetch on write, given that fetch on write creates a 10 per cent higher hit ratio.

3.11 Determine the average access time in a computer system employing a cache given that the main memory access time is 70 ns, the cache access time is 20 ns and the hit ratio is 85 per cent. The write-through policy is used and 20 per cent of memory requests are write requests.

3.12 Repeat Problem 3.10 assuming a write-back policy is used, and the block size is sixteen words fully interleaved.

3.13 Define the least recently used replacement algorithm, without using the words, "least", "recent", and "used".

3.14 Using ageing counters to implement the least recently used algorithm, as described in Section 3.4.4, derive the numbers held in the counters after each in the following sequence:

2, 6, 9, 7, 2, 3, 2, 9, 6, 2, 7, 4

given that the cache holds four lines.

3.15 Show how a reference matrix as described in Section 3.4.4 can be used to implement the least recently used algorithm with the sequence:

2, 6, 9, 7, 2, 3, 2, 9, 6, 2, 7, 4

given that the cache holds four lines.

3.16 Study how well the tree algorithm described in Section 3.4.4 approximates to the least recently used algorithm, with four lines, by working through the reference sequence in Problem 3.15.

3.17 Solve the equation given in Section 3.5:

$$\frac{dn}{dt} = \frac{(a + bn)(s - n)}{(a + n)s}$$

for n where n locations are filled in the cache, s is the size of the cache, and a and b are constants.

3.18 A disk cache is introduced into a system and the access time reduces from 20 ms to 6.3 ms. What is the access time of the disk cache, given that the hit ratio is 70 per cent?

CHAPTER

4 | *Memory management*

This chapter studies the methods of managing the memory hierarchy in a computer system, called memory management. Memory management relieves the programmer of the problems of ensuring that the required programs are in the main memory for execution. Memory management has been present in virtually all larger computers since the early 1970s. We will consider the two principal and complementary memory management methods, paging and segmentation (and their combination), together with their hardware requirements. Paging is principally concerned with the memory hierarchy, while segmentation is concerned with organizing programs in the memory.

4.1 Memory hierarchy

The total memory in a computer system is composed of various memory types, in particular a main random access memory and a secondary, usually non-random access memory (disk memory being called direct access memory). The main memory must have high speed, random access quality and programs and data must reside there for the processor to access the information (whether instructions or data). We have seen in Chapter 3 that another level of memory, cache memory, is usually inserted between the main memory and the processor. Two levels of cache memory may also be present. The secondary memory usually consists of magnetic disk memory, including exchangeable and non-exchangeable disk systems; other types of secondary memory include CD-ROM storage and magnetic tape systems (sometimes called mass memory). Large optical and magneto-optical disk systems might be present to hold vast amounts of information. With several types of memory present, information will reside in the slowest memory when it is not in use, and be brought to the faster secondary memories as its use becomes more imminent. Exchangeable media such as floppy disks would be used as appropriate, for example when programs must be moved from one computer system to another, unattached, computer system.

The memory hierarchy needs a method to arrange that the required information is in the main memory when it is to be read or altered by the processor; such methods are called

115

memory management. We will concentrate upon the main memory/secondary memory interface rather than any strategy for transferring information between different secondary/mass memory devices. When necessary, we will assume that the secondary memory is disk memory, and will refer to the secondary memory as disk memory unless the secondary memory is not disk memory.

The simplest memory management method is *overlaying* – when programs or sections of programs are transferred into the main memory, as required, under program control (by explicit program routines) and overwrite existing programs. This method places a heavy burden on the programmer but early computers in the 1950s and 1960s used it, as did early single-user microprocessor systems, including the MS-DOS operating system (see Duncan, 1986). Overlaying can be automated to some extent. The MS-DOS operating system program linker utility, LINK (Microsoft, 1987), provides for semiautomated overlays. LINK can create overlaid programs, specified by the user, in which parts of the program, which are specified as needed, will be loaded during run time and will occupy the same memory space as previously executed programs. Such techniques conserve memory space at the expense of much slower execution.

We note that the magnetic disk memory operates much more slowly than the semiconductor main memory – at least three orders of magnitude slower than main memory. Data can be accessed in a semiconductor main memory in the range 50–150 ns, while the latency before the required data is even reached on a disk might be in the range 10–30 ms. The gap widens as integrated circuit technology improves, given that disk memory latency time (time to locate one sector on the disk) and associated data rate are limited by mechanical factors.[1] The processor often cannot continue with the current program while transfers are in progress between the main memory and the disk memory. The processor in a single-user system will be idle and waiting for the transfer to be completed, even though this may be done by a separate direct memory access (DMA) device. Hence, reducing the number of transfers to a minimum is very important to achieve the highest performance.

One apparent solution recognized and suggested at a very early stage in the development of computers (for example by a group at MIT during the period 1957–61) was to provide a very large amount of main memory, sufficient to hold all the programs currently being executed or about to be executed. Though a brute force method, and not really a good technological solution at a time when main memory was a very expensive and valuable resource, the provision of a large amount of main memory has recently become routine and inexpensive and extremely large amounts of main memory may be common in the future. Certain applications, for example some graphics applications, find that a large amount of main memory is better than a smaller amount plus a memory management scheme to transfer information between the main and disk memories.

The trend is for larger and larger amounts of main memory, and larger and larger application programs. The memory management problem simply reappears on a larger scale,

---

[1] Though the access time of disks cannot be reduced by using arrays of disks, the data transfer rate after the locations on the disks have been found can be reduced by simultaneous access to individual disks.

though with larger main memory, it is more likely that complete application programs can be held in their entirety in the main memory. Then the memory management mechanism is active mainly during program load time, rather than throughout the execution of the program.

Given that we have main memory and disk memory for economic reasons (and also to give media exchangeability), a truly automatic method of transferring blocks of words into and out of the main memory is highly desirable to relieve the burden of programming transfers. The method should take into account the blocks likely to be required in the near future, to reduce disk transfers. Computer systems, particularly in a multiprogramming environment in which many programs, or parts of many programs, reside in the main memory, require an efficient mechanism for handling the storage of various information and also require memory protection mechanisms. These involve preventing specified memory operations on specified parts of the memory, notably the memory holding the operating system and other user programs.

The part of the system that implements memory management is called the *memory management unit* (MMU) which is normally within the processor, though early systems had separate MMUs attached to the processor. Memory management normally incorporate features for memory protection. Hence, we can identify two separate issues for memory management:

1. Handling the main and disk memory hierarchy.
2. Providing memory protection.

Memory protection will be considered later in the chapter. First, we will consider the original memory management method called *paging* which was introduced to handle the memory hierarchy.

4.2 Paging

4.2.1 General

At about the same time as the MIT group was proposing very large main memory, a group at Manchester University (Kilburn *et al.*, 1962) developed a method, originally called a *one-level store* and now called *paging*, which has become the standard method of managing the memory hierarchy. The objective of the original one-level store was to make the main core memory and secondary drum memories seem as though all the memory was main random access memory, hence the term one-level. The term *virtual memory* is now normally used, as the user is given the impression of a very large main memory space (a virtual memory space) which hides the actual memory space (the real memory space). Separate addresses are used for the virtual memory space and the real memory space. The actual memory addresses are called *real addresses* and the program generated addresses are called *virtual addresses*.

The real and virtual memory spaces are both divided into blocks of words called *pages*. All pages are the same size, which might be between 64 bytes and 4 Kbytes, depending upon the design. The virtual and real memory addresses are each divided into a *page field* and a word within the page field called a *line field*. The processor generates program dependent virtual addresses which assume that all the memory can be addressed directly. At any instant, each virtual address has a corresponding real address in the physical memory, either in the main memory or in the secondary memory, and *page tables* are maintained to record the correspondence between the virtual and real pages. Each virtual address generated by the processor is translated into the actual address in main memory by reference to the page tables. If the page is not currently in the main memory, a *page fault* occurs and a software routine is activated to bring it in automatically, updating the page tables accordingly.

Figure 4.1 shows an overall view of a virtual memory system. Notice that only the page field of the address need be translated since the line field is the same in both the virtual address and the real address. Figure 4.2 shows a snap-shot of a system with 32 pages in the main memory and 192 pages in secondary memory (as implemented in the original Atlas computer; nowadays there would be many more pages, but the concept is the same).

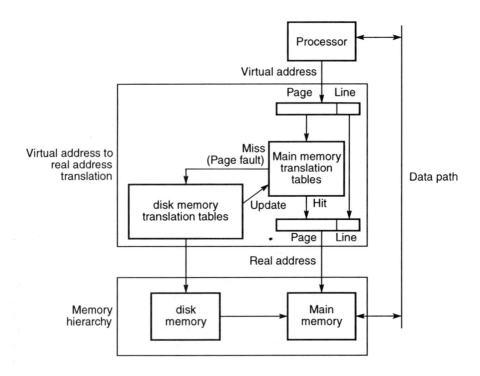

Figure 4.1 Virtual memory system

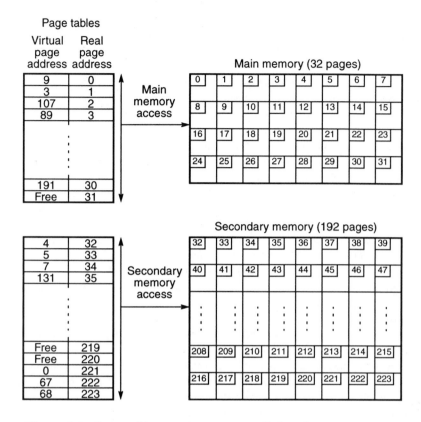

Figure 4.2 Page addresses in a very small virtual memory system

With only 32 pages, the complete main memory translation table can be implemented in a very fast specialized unit (i.e., completely in "hardware"). Nine bits are allocated to specify the line and 11 bits are used to specify the page in main memory or secondary memory. Secondary memory page addresses are shown starting at 32. The page tables are shown, with a possible distribution of pages in the system.

In the assignment of virtual pages to real pages shown in some virtual pages are unassigned (not used). Real page 31, the last page in the main memory, is currently free. Suppose virtual page 3 is requested by the processor. First, hardware is activated to check whether the page is in the main memory. The hardware finds that the page is currently residing in real page 1 and the page can be referenced. However, suppose virtual page 7 is now requested by the processor. The check shows that the page is not currently residing in the main memory and a software routine is activated to search for its location in the secondary memory. In this case, the page is found in real page 34 in the secondary memory. The page could be transferred into the free (real) page 31 in the main memory, and is subsequently referenced by the processor; now the main memory is full. If a reference is made to another page in the secondary memory, an existing page in the main memory must be returned to the secondary memory before the new page is transferred into the main memory, unless a valid copy is held in the secondary memory. Then the main memory copy can be simply overwritten. Kilburn *et al.* (1962) suggest keeping a vacant page in the main memory to allow the transfer to the main memory to take place first, and any writing back to the secondary memory can be done while the processor continues with normal processing.

There are various possible ways of translating the virtual page number into the corresponding real page number which we will discuss later, but they must operate on every memory reference. We hope that the page will usually be found in the main memory and that the high speed hardware translation can be used successfully on main memory pages. We will look at the situation when there are too many pages in the main memory for hardware translation to be used for all main memory pages. Software address translation is used for pages currently in the secondary memory. In addition, if necessary, a *page replacement algorithm* selects a page to be removed from the main memory to make room for the incoming page from secondary memory prior to use.

Though introduced simply to make all the memory look as one, it was also known at the time (Kilburn *et al.*, 1962) that paging allowed an operating system to relocate programs and parts of programs between the main and the secondary memories without altering any of the program addresses. Such relocation is essential and forms the basis of all operating system activities of moving user programs.

Main memory sizes have increased since 1962 and are now usually many megabytes. Even a main memory of 1 Megabyte (1 048 576 bytes), with a page size of 512 bytes, would give 2048 pages in the main memory. The secondary memory is normally several orders of magnitude greater than the main memory. Page addresses are numbered from zero onwards in the main memory and could continue through to the pages on the secondary memory as shown in Figure 4.2, which was done in the original one-level store. However, in practice, secondary memory normally has its own addressing scheme. For example, a disk memory stores its information arranged on concentric tracks; each track is divided into a number of sectors. One page might be stored on one sector, or on more than one sector, depending upon the size of the page and sector. The disk is usually organized so that one page can be located on the disk surface as one unit addressed in terms of track and sector.

The number of bits in the virtual address is normally specified by the addressing capability of the processor, i.e., by the number of address bits generated by the processor. The number of bits in the virtual and real addresses need not be related except that the number of bits provided to address the words within a page must be the same. The virtual address space is usually much larger than the real address space, in keeping with the original motive of giving the programmer the illusion of a very large main memory. However, it is possible for the two to be the same size, or to have a smaller virtual than real address space. This has been used to expand the addressing capability on computers with a limited addressing capability. For example, a processor with only 16-bit addressing (as was the case with early microprocessors) would be limited to using 64 Kbytes of main

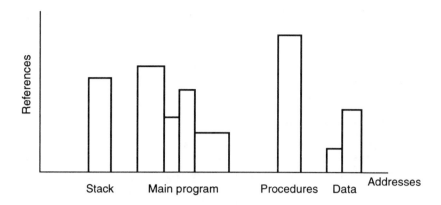

Figure 4.3 Program page references

memory without a virtual memory system or another address translation mechanism. With a virtual address translation with a larger real address, the addressing space could be expanded. The same virtual address might then translate to different real addresses, depending upon the context and program. Whether this mechanism could actually be called virtual memory is debatable. Having the same size for both the virtual and real main memory address spaces would be quite natural for processors which can generate large virtual addresses.

In Chapter 3, we identified a characteristic of computer programs called the Principle of Locality. Individual locations, once referenced, are likely to be referenced again in the near future (temporal locality) and references, including the next location, are likely to be near the last reference (spatial locality). Just as the Principle of Locality causes caches to be successful, the Principle of Locality makes paging successful. Figure 4.3 shows a histogram of typical page references. References are grouped into particular regions and many, if not all, locations are referenced several times. One region will commonly be for the stack holding procedure return addresses and procedure parameters. Another memory area will be for local variables, which are often stored together. A major area will be for the main program and called procedures might be in other, separate, areas, especially if shared with other programs.

Let us now consider methods of performing the virtual–real address translation. The chosen method must be implemented in hardware as a translation has to be performed on every memory reference, and the translation time directly adds to the overall instruction execution time.

4.2.2 Translation look-aside buffers

The number of pages in a modern computer system is too large to hold all the main memory page table in a very high speed look-up table. Given the program characteristics embodied in the Principle of Locality, we expect that one particular set of pages (the so-

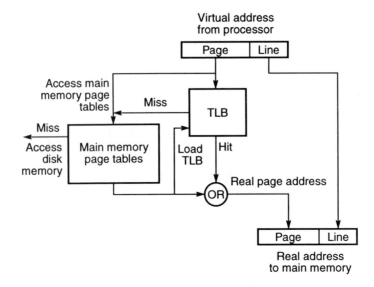

Figure 4.4 Translation look-aside buffer

called *working set*) will be referenced until a change of context occurs. Hence, only those page addresses predicted as most likely to be used need be translated in hardware. The rest of the page references are initially handled by reading a main memory page look-up table, and subsequently the high speed hardware page look-up table is updated. The high speed page address translation memory holding the most likely referenced page entries is known as a *translation look-aside buffer* (TLB) (also called a *translation buffer*, TB, a *directory look-aside table*, DLT, or an *address translation cache,* ATC). The TLB acts very much like a data cache by holding those items most likely to be referenced – hence the term address translation cache. Figure 4.4 shows a system with a TLB.

Because the TLBs do not translate all addresses into real addresses, even though the location may be in the main memory, a high speed translation and TLB entry replacement algorithms are necessary for those virtual addresses not translated immediately by the TLB.

4.2.3 Address translation

There are three basic hardware techniques to translate the virtual page address into a real page address:

1. (Pure) direct mapping.
2. Associative mapping.
3. Set-associative mapping.

In all cases, after translation the real page address is concatenated with the line number to form the complete virtual address.

Direct mapping

The (pure) *direct mapping* approach is shown in Figure 4.5.[2] All real page addresses are stored in a high speed random access memory page table, in locations whose addresses are the virtual page addresses of the stored real page addresses. Consequently, a real page address can be found directly from the memory by using the virtual page address to address the page table. For example, the virtual page address 34 selects location 34 in the page table, and location 34 holds the corresponding real page address for virtual page address 34.

The direct mapping technique as described is not suitable for a TLB. If fact, it translates all virtual addresses whether in main memory or disk memory, and would be a very

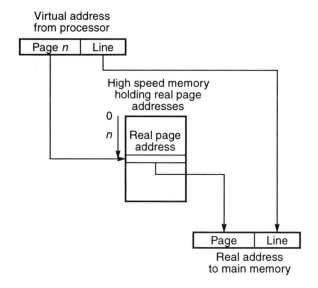

Figure 4.5 Direct mapping address translation

---

[2] We differentiate between the direct mapping used in caches and the direct mapping described here by calling the direct mapping here "pure" direct mapping because the location is directly found by the input virtual address. In caches called direct mapped caches, only part of the address (the index) is used to find the location. The remaining part of the address must match the stored tag part of the address in the location. This is applicable to TLBs but will be described as one-way set-associative mapping later.

large table, impractical for very high speed table. It would be very wasteful because most of the entries would refer to disk memory pages. Hence the direct method will be suitable as an approach for the main memory and second memory page tables, and will be the basis of these tables. A multilevel version of the direct mapping for such tables is described in Section 4.2.5.

Fully associative mapping

The (fully) *associative mapping* approach is shown in Figure 4.6. Here both the real page address and the corresponding virtual page address are stored together in a high speed memory. The incoming virtual page is compared with all the stored virtual pages simultaneously and, if a match is found, the real page is read out. Each virtual page entry requires a comparator. The original Kilburn one-level store employed associative mapping with 32 page registers and 32 comparators.

Associative mapped cache memory (Section 3.2.1) is similar in operation and as in associative mapped cache memory, a special type of memory, an *associative* (or *content addressable* (CAM) *memory*) which incorporates comparators, can be used to store the virtual page addresses. In such a memory a location is identified by its contents, rather than by an assigned address. CAMs are random access memories with a comparator associated with each stored location. They can be designed to operate at high speed approaching the speed of high speed random access memory, but they are relatively expensive. When used for associative mapping, the content addressable memory is coupled to normal random access memory, giving two parts to the memory. The CAM section holds

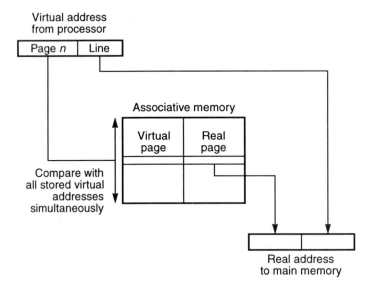

Figure 4.6 Fully associative mapping address translation

the virtual page addresses and the RAM section the real page addresses. When a virtual address is generated by the processor, the virtual page address is compared with all virtual page addresses stored in the CAM simultaneously, using comparison logic within the associative memory. If a match is found, the corresponding real page address held in the RAM part is read out.

In associative mapping, the page table look-up is a two-stage process. First, a comparison is done between the submitted page address and each of the stored page addresses. This process is indivisible; all the comparisons are performed simultaneously in hardware – sequential comparisons would be too slow. The next step depends upon whether a match is found. If a match was found, the real address is obtained and a main memory access occurs. If a match is not found, a page fault occurs and a page replacement routine is activated.

The fully associative method is used in some TLBs within microprocessor integrated circuits and specialized integrated circuit TLBs, an example being the Motorola MC88200 Cache/Memory Management Unit for the MC88100 reduced instruction set processor (Motorola, 1988b). The MC88200 has two fully associative TLBs. One, the *Block Address Translation Cache*, provides for translating addresses of ten 512-Kbyte blocks used principally for the operating system and other "high-use software". The other, the *Page Address Translation Cache*, provides for translating addresses of fifty-six 4-Kbyte pages used principally by the user. The virtual address space is divided into equal system and user spaces. However large fully associative TLBs may be expensive to create and will operate slower than set-associative TLBs. Most TLBs are now set-associative. This does not come without a performance consideration as we shall see.

Set-associative mapping

Set-associative mapping is a combination of direct and associative mapping. In the set-associative method, the virtual addresses and real addresses are divided into a most significant tag field, an index (row) field and a least significant word (offset) field. The corresponding page field often consists of the tag and index fields together. High speed random access memory is organized in blocks, each of which contains 2^i locations, where there are i index bits, as shown in Figure 4.7. Each location holds a virtual tag/real page address pair and the blocks are arranged such that one pair from each block is accessed via the index simultaneously. The virtual tags read are compared with the virtual tag presented by the processor and, if a match is found, the corresponding real page is taken and concatenated with the word (offset). The one-way set-associative mapping described here corresponds to the direct mapping in caches described in Chapter 3.

With only one tag/real address at each location, as shown in Figure 4.7, all the virtual page addresses to be translated must have different indices, but there is a fair probability that more than one virtual address will have the same index. A set-associative table can be designed so that there is more than one tag/real page entry at each index, and all the tags can be compared simultaneously. Figure 4.8 shows a set-associative table with two tag/real address entries for each index. The number of entries that can be compared simultaneously is called the *set size* or *associativity*. The associativity is normally given as *s*-way for a set size of *s*.

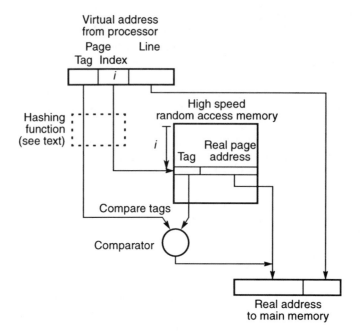

Figure 4.7 Set-associative mapping address translation (one-way)

Many systems use two- or four-way set-associative TLBs. For example the Intel 486 has a 32-entry four-way set-associative TLB. The Motorola 68040 has two 64-entry four-way set-associative TLBs (called *Address Translation Caches*, ATCs, by Motorola, and Intel sometimes), one for the data cache and one for the instruction cache (see later for use of TLBs with instruction and data caches). The Intel i860 uses a 64-entry four-way set-associative TLB. The VAX-8600 uses a one-way 512 word buffer.

The set-associative TLB with an index directly addressing the TLB has the major disadvantage that only n pages with virtual addresses having the same lower page bits (index bits) can be translated with a set size of n. The set size is often only one or two. The chance of virtual addresses having the same lower page bits is quite high, especially as virtual pages are likely to be assigned from zero onwards. To counteract this effect, higher page bits could be used instead of the lower page bits or, alternatively, a mixture of some lower and some higher bits could be used. In a system with user and supervisor address spaces separated by the most significant address bit, it may be advantageous to use the most significant bit in the index, so that the TLB is evenly divided between system and user addresses. This technique was used in the VAX-11/780 translation buffer. In this buffer, the system pages remain when user pages are purged on a task switch.

Another solution is to use a hardware hashing technique to "randomize" the virtual page address before accessing the TLB. Hashing is a general computer technique for converting one number into another (usually one with fewer bits) such that any expected

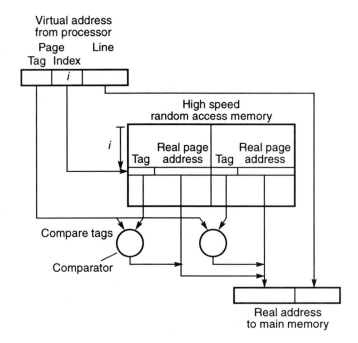

Figure 4.8 Set-associative mapping address translation (two-way)

sequence of input numbers will generate different and unique hashed numbers. As applied to TLBs, the hashing function would be applied to the page bits of the virtual address to create a new index to access the TLB, as shown in Figure 4.7. (It could also be applied to Figure 4.8 but is unnecessary for a fully associative TLB.) The hashing function has to be applied in hardware. Various hashing functions are known and some can reasonably be implemented in hardware. These hashing functions are mostly based upon logical exclusive-ORing bits in the input number. Figure 4.9 shows the simple hashing function used on the IBM 3033. In this hashing function, two pages with the same initial index only hash into pages with the same index when the upper five page bits used in the hashing are the same as the lower five index bits, and generally, in any page, sequential indices are made non-sequential. (It is left as an exercise to determine when the sequential nature continues through the hashing.)

4.2.4 Page size

The size of the page times the size of the TLB gives the amount of memory that will be directly handled by the TLB. For example if the page size were 4 Kbytes and there were 256 entries in the TLB, the memory coverage would be 1 Mbyte. Various page sizes are used in paging schemes, from small pages of 64 bytes through to very large pages of 512

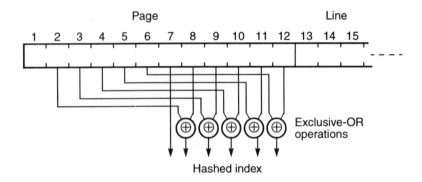

Figure 4.9 IBM 3033 page hashing function

Kbytes. A common page size has been 4 Kbytes. Some systems provide for different page sizes for flexibility, selected by context or by setting bits in registers, and separate page tables might be provided for each page size. For example, there could be different page sizes for data and for code. A small page of 64 bytes might be suitable for code while a larger page of 512 bytes might be suitable for data. A very large page size of say 4 Mbytes might suit graphics applications. Two page sizes can be selected in the Intel Pentium, either 4-Kbyte or 4-Mbyte pages. Different page sizes might also be appropriate for system and user pages. A larger page size might be better for system software, which resides in the main memory. For example, the Motorola MC88200 has 4-Kbyte pages for the users and 512-Kbyte pages for the system software.

If a small page size is chosen, the time taken in transferring a page between the main memory and the disk memory is short, and a large selection of pages from various programs can reside in the main memory. A small page also reduces the storing of superfluous code which is never referenced (e.g., an error routine which is never selected). However, a small page size necessitates a large page table, and *table fragmentation* increases. This is the term used to describe the effect of memory being occupied by mapping tables and hence being unavailable for code/data.

Conversely, a large page size requires a small page table but the transfer time is generally longer. Unused space at the end of each page is likely to increase – an effect known as *internal fragmentation*; on average, the last page of a program is likely to be 50 per cent full. The magnetic disk memory also constrains the page size to that of a disk sector, or to a multiple of a sector, unless additional sector buffer storage is provided to enable one page from several in a sector to be selected. Making the sector small increases the proportion of recorded information given over to sector identification on the disk. Overall, the number of words in each page has to be chosen as a compromise between the various factors.

4.2.5 Multilevel page mapping

The full page table giving all the virtual/real page associations for the main memory requires considerable memory when the main memory address has say 32 bits (a standard for 32-bit microprocessors). In two-level page mapping the virtual address is divided into three fields; a page directory field, a page within a page directory field and a line (or offset) within a page. The page directory field points to an entry in a directory table which gives the start address of the page table for that directory. The page field then selects the start address of the real page which, concatenated to the line, gives the complete real address. Two-level mapping requires more table entries in total than when the directory and page fields are combined into one page field and it has the disadvantage that two table references are required to extract the page address. However, it has the distinct advantages that the individual tables are much smaller and that only some of these tables need reside in the main translation memory simultaneously. It would be reasonable to place the most recently used tables in high speed translation look-aside buffers.

The system can be extended to more than two levels. A tree structure can be formed by a hierarchy of pointers, as shown in Figure 4.10, though two levels of tables are often sufficient. Such structures enable easy manipulation of the tables and reduction of the full table by eliminating the page tables of those pages which are not used. The first table in the memory is usually located by a dedicated register, sometimes called a *table descriptor register*. An example of multilevel page mapping is the MC68040 which provides for 3 levels of translation.

Paging, as described, does not allow pages to be shared between processes, and yet

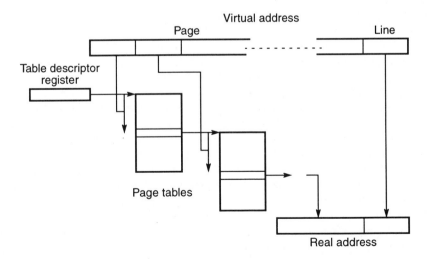

Figure 4.10 Page table organization

sharing system software between processes is a common requirement. A paging solution is to divide the virtual address space into two or more distinct spaces, one or more for user programs and one or more for the system software. The most significant bit(s) of the virtual address can be used to select the region, and the rest can be divided into a directory, page and line fields. The system space can use a one-level translation, using both the directory and page fields combined into a large page field, to select an entry in a single page table which holds the real page addresses and which is available to all users. The user space could use two-level translations using different page tables selected by different directory pointers and only available to the associated process. The VAX-11/780 computer system designers chose this solution partly because it represented an evolution of the earlier PDP-11/70 (the two alternatives considered were true segmentation and *capabilities* (see Strecker, 1978).

4.3 Replacement algorithms

4.3.1 General

A *page fault* occurs whenever the page referenced is not already in the main memory, i.e. when a valid page entry cannot be found in the address translator (both TLB and the main memory page tables). When this occurs the required page must be located in the disk memory using the disk memory page tables, and a page in the main memory must be identified for removal if there is no free space in the main memory. Disk memory/main memory transfers are relatively slow and are performed by a separate direct memory access (DMA) controller or input/output processor; thus the processor can select another process for execution while these transfers are being done.

There are various replacement algorithms that can be used to select the page to be removed from the main memory to make room for the incoming page. As we saw in Chapter 3, replacement algorithms are needed in cache memory. There is a significant difference in a paging system. We may have a very large number of pages to consider, not just the pages entries in the TLB but those in the whole main memory page table. In fact the page to remove from the main memory is very unlikely to have an entry in the TLB as these will have the most recently or most used pages. The algorithm to select the page from the main memory to replace will not be implemented totally in hardware; a combination of hardware and software is required. The algorithm itself is only executed when a page fault occurs and we can accept the overhead of a software algorithm. The algorithm to replace an entry in the TLB will be implemented totally in hardware, and can be based upon the same methods used in caches (see Chapter 3).

In some ways, the main memory page replacement algorithm is an operating system issue rather than an architectural issue. However we do need to know what hardware support will be required for common software replacement algorithms. There are three policies to consider when handling page faults in a virtual memory system:

1. Fetch policy – to determine when pages are loaded into the main memory.
2. Placement policy – to determine where the pages are to be placed in the main memory.
3. Replacement policy – to determine which page in the main memory to remove or overwrite.

The normal fetch policy is called *demand paging*, which is the term used to describe the fetch policy of waiting until a page fault occurs and then loading the required page from the disk memory. There has been a debate on the possibility of fetching pages before they are required in some prescribed prefetch policy. However, most paging systems employ demand paging. It appears that demand paging will result in the same or fewer page faults than are incurred by a prefetch paging policy (see Denning, 1970). A general metric for evaluating replacement algorithms is the number of page faults created.

With regard to the placement policy, we have assumed that when a page fault occurs, a page is removed from the main memory to make room for the incoming page and that the required page is brought into the same main memory location. Apart from using the same locations for the outgoing and incoming pages, alternative placement policies are possible if free space is maintained in the main memory. A placement policy might be created to maintain a certain amount of free main memory in the presence of variable memory usage.

As with cache memory replacement algorithms, page replacement algorithms can be classified as:

1. Usage-based algorithms.
2. Non-usage-based algorithms.

In a usage-based algorithm the choice of page to replace is dependent upon how many times each page in the main memory has been referenced. Non-usage-based algorithms use some other criteria for replacement. To implement usage-based algorithms, hardware is necessary to record when pages are referenced.

The simplest and most common hardware is to incorporate a *use* (or *accessed*) bit with each page entry in the page tables. The use bit of an entry is set if the corresponding page is referenced and is automatically reset when the bit is read. Use bits are read under program control to determine whether the pages have been used. To catch every increase in usage, use bits need to be scanned after each reference. Clearly this produces an unacceptable overhead, and the use bits are usually scanned at a much reduced rate to obtain an approximation of the usage, perhaps after 1 ms of process time. (Easton and Franaszek (1979) made a study of the use bit scanning technique in usage-based replacement algorithms.) To obtain a true value for usage, hardware counters could be introduced to record each reference, but this is not normally done.

Apart from a use bit, each entry in a page table has other bits to assist or improve the replacement algorithm, including a *modified* (or *written*, *changed* or *dirty*) bit. The modified bit is set if a write operation is performed on any location within the page. It is not necessary to write an unaltered page back to the disk memory if a copy has been maintained there, and this increases the speed of operation. Very occasionally, there is an unused bit associated with each page, which is set to 1 when the page is loaded into main memory and reset to 0 when subsequently referenced. This bit may be helpful to make sure that a page demanded is not removed before being used. Protection bits concerned with controlling access to pages are also present; these will be discussed later.

Paging replacement (usage-based or non-usage-based) algorithms can be classified as suitable as:

1. A global algorithm.
2. A local algorithm.

They may be classified as both. *Global replacement algorithms* make their selection of main memory page among all those existing in the main memory, irrespective of the programs associated with the pages. *Local replacement algorithms* make a selection only from those pages related to the "page-faulted" program, and do not consider those pages in the main memory associated with other programs. In general, local algorithms should be better than global algorithms in a multiprogramming environment because, for one reason, global policies do not take into account the fact that different programs may have different working set sizes and may take a page out of the working set of a program which is executed next, which would lead to *thrashing*. Denning (1970) used the term thrashing to describe the phenomenon of excessive page transfers that can occur in a multiprogramming environment when the memory is overcommitted; he attributed the term to Saltzer (Denning, 1980).

A process or program has a group of pages. In a multiprogramming environment all groups of pages might be the same size (known as a *fixed partition*) or different sizes (known as a *variable partition*). Cache memory always has a fixed partition. Early paging replacement algorithms naturally have a fixed partition but can be extended to variable partitions. Some later algorithms naturally have a variable partition. A fixed partition is easier to implement than a variable partition, but the latter is more flexible and reduces the memory requirements, typically by 30 per cent.

Let us now consider the main page replacement policies and their implementation.

4.3.2 Random replacement algorithm

In the *random replacement algorithm*, a page is chosen randomly at page fault time; there is no relationship between the pages or their use. This algorithm does not take the principle of locality of programs into account and hence would not be expected to work very well. (It is generally believed that replacement algorithms which take account of the characteristics of programs expounded in the principle of locality will work better.) The generation of page numbers for random replacement can be done using a numerical pseudorandom number generator, or by counting the occurrences of some event. The random replacement algorithm is simple to implement but is not widely used. It has been applied to TLBs. For example, the VAX 11/780 translation buffer (TLB), and more recently the TLB in the Intel i860 RISC processor (Intel, 1992b), use the random replacement policy.

4.3.3 First-in first-out replacement algorithm

In the *first-in first-out replacement algorithm*, the page existing in the main memory for the longest time is chosen at page fault time. This algorithm is naturally a fixed global policy but could be modified to operate locally. The algorithm can be described by a first-in first-out queue, which holds the list of all pages currently in the main memory. As a new entry is inserted, all the entries move down one place and the last entry is taken out and specifies the page to be removed. Each page in the queue may be referenced many times before the next page is referenced, and the number of references to one page between page changes does not affect the algorithm. Initially, when the main memory is empty, page faults occur when pages are first referenced. Each time a new page is referenced the page entries are moved one place to the right (conceptually, not the actual page entries). When the memory partition is full and a page fault occurs, the page deleted (and if necessary returned to the disk memory) is given by the entry at the rightmost end of the queue.

The algorithm requires no extra hardware to record memory references (as some other algorithms do) because the queue is maintained and updated only at page fault time with page fault information, and can be maintained in software. It does not matter how many times a page is referenced between page faults, though it is expected that it will be referenced many times (and of course at least once).

The algorithm can be implemented using a circular list holding the page entries, as shown in Figure 4.11. A pointer indicates the current rightmost end of the queue and the leftmost entry of the queue is immediately before the pointed entry. Upon a page fault, the page deleted and replaced is that indicated by the pointer. The pointer is then incremented to point to the next entry.

The first-in first-out algorithm anticipates that the program will move from one page to the next in a linear, sequential fashion, but it is not at all certain that such characteristics

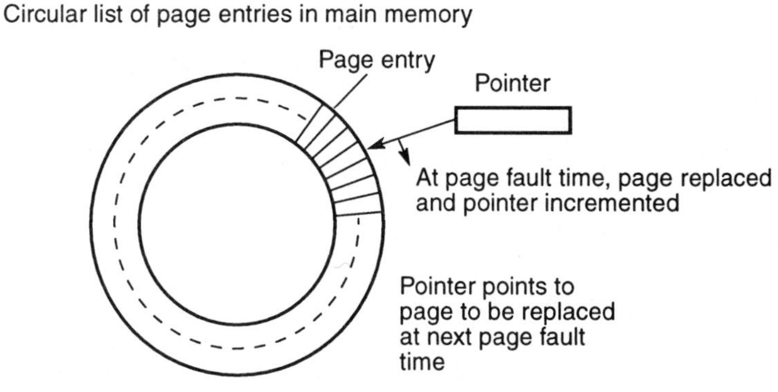

Figure 4.11 First-in first-out replacement algorithm using a circular list

are found in practice. More often, programs reference a group of pages repeatedly, but in various patterns, as different procedures are called. The first-in first-out algorithm performs particularly badly when the partition consists only of a loop of pages, sequentially and repeatedly executed, because every time execution moves from the last page back to the first page, a page fault will occur. For example, for the sequence of changes in page references:

1, 2, 3, 4, 5, 1, 2, 3, 4, 5, 1, 2, 3, 4, 5, …

and four pages in the main memory partition, the first-in first-out algorithm will generate a fault on every page change. In fact, virtually all fixed partition algorithms give bad results on this sequence and the best strategy here would be a *last-in first-out replacement algorithm* (a rarely used algorithm) which replaces the page just left, giving a page fault on every fourth page change on the above sequence.

Loop characteristics are, of course, a common characteristic of programs. However, large loops do not often occur; small loops with one or two pages are more likely, and all pages can be kept in memory simultaneously.

4.3.4 Clock replacement algorithm

The first-in first-out algorithm can be modified to avoid removing pages being referenced by moving over pages in the queue which have been referenced (and hence are likely to be accessed again). This algorithm is known as the *clock algorithm* because a pointing movement is used like that of the hand of a clock. The algorithm is also known as the *first-in-not-used-first-out algorithm*. It requires the addition of a use bit set by the hardware when the page is referenced. The algorithm can be described as a circular list of page entries, corresponding to the pages in main memory, and a pointer which identifies the next page to be replaced, as shown in Figure 4.12. When a page replacement is necessary, the use bit of the page entry identified by the pointer is examined. If the use bit is set to 1, the bit is reset to 0 and the pointer advanced to the next page entry. This process is repeated until a use bit is already reset to 0. Then, the corresponding page is replaced and the pointer advanced to the next page entry. Whenever a page is referenced subsequently, the associated use bit is set to 1. Various modifications can be made to the clock algorithm (see Easton and Franaszek (1979) for further details).

4.3.5 Least recently used replacement algorithm

In the *least recently used (LRU) replacement algorithm*, the page which has not been referenced for the longest time is transferred out at page fault time. The least recently used algorithm can be described as a "stack" holding the list of pages in the main memory in the order in which they have been referenced. Whenever a reference is made, the order of the list has to be updated. This means that the page entry is placed at the top of the list and all other page entries are moved down one place. As with the first-in first-out algorithm, the LRU algorithm fails badly on a single loop of pages. It produces identical

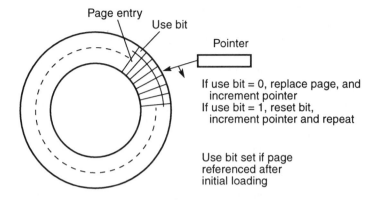

Figure 4.12 First-in-not-used first-out replacement algorithm

results to the first-in first-out algorithm on a sequence of pages in which pages in memory are not re-entered, because the page which has been longest in the memory is also the page referenced the longest time ago. However, the LRU algorithm would seem to match program characteristics.

The LRU algorithm poses some practical problems for a true implementation if there are many pages to consider because a record has to be made of references to each page (whether or not a page fault has occurred) during the execution of the programs. A common approximation to the LRU algorithm in a paging system is to employ the use bits. At intervals, say after every 1 ms as recorded by the system interrupt timer, all of the use bits are examined by the operating system and automatically reset when read. A record of the number of times the bits are found set to 1 would give an approximation of the usage in units of the interval selected. The approximation becomes closer to a true LRU algorithm as the interval is decreased. This method can also be implemented by having separate queues for different activity pages, a high activity queue, a medium activity queue and a low activity queue. Page entries are moved from one queue to the lower queue if the page was not referenced during the last time interval, and moved to the higher activity queue if it was referenced. Pages in the lowest activity queue move to a replacement queue for those pages which can be replaced.

4.3.6 Working set replacement algorithm

The *working set*, $w(t, T)$, at time t is defined as the collection of pages referenced by the process during the process time interval $(t - T, t)$. The working set function, $w(t, T)$, as a function of T and fixed t, increases monotonically, because the working set with an increased interval, $w(t, T + d)$, must include those pages of the original interval, $w(t, T)$, for a specified t. The working set must include sufficient pages for the program to run. The working set as a function of time, t, is not expected to change radically when only one process is being executed. Abrupt changes would occur when a new process is started, as in a multiprogramming environment.

The *working set algorithm*, which follows directly from the concept of programs having working sets (Denning, 1968), replaces the page which has not been referenced during the immediately preceding interval, T, given in terms of process time (or number of page references). The set of pages maintained are those which have been referenced during this interval. As time passes, a "window" moves along, capturing the working set of pages, as shown in Figure 4.13. It is possible for the memory allocation not to be full. For example, given a memory allocation of four pages, if the last five references were pages 5, 2, 6, 8 and 2, the pages in the set would be the three pages 2, 6 and 8.

Pages are added to the working set when a page fault occurs. Theoretically, pages are removed from the working set as soon as they have not been referenced during the preceding interval, though in practice such removal is only done at page fault time. The number of pages could grow very large, limited only by the number of references possible to different pages in the time interval, though the possibility of every single reference being to a different page is very remote. If the window is measured in terms of page references, then the maximum number of pages is given by the window size. In a pure working set policy, pages could be released at times other than at page fault time, though most implementations wait until a page fault. If pages are only taken from the working set at the time of a page fault, there may be more than one page which was not referenced during the preceding interval. The least recently used algorithm can be employed to choose and remove only one or two pages.

The partition for this algorithm is naturally variable and uses a local policy, whereas the previous algorithms are naturally fixed and global. (The previous algorithms can be modified to operate locally using process stacks/queues.) An interval needs to be chosen for the window; this interval is normally kept constant. The strength of the working set

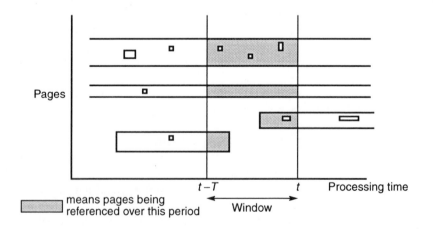

Figure 4.13 Working set reference patterns

algorithm is that it only keeps those pages likely to be required in memory, and does not use unnecessary memory.

A pure implementation would record the window interval in process time. The interval is never measured in actual seconds as there may be times when the process is suspended or delayed (such as during interrupt processing). One "counter" implementation would be to assign a hardware counter to each page, together with an identifier register, to indicate whether the page is part of the current window. When a page is referenced in the current window, the associated counter is reset to 0. All of the counters of the current window are incremented at regular intervals. If a counter overflows, the associated page is taken from the current window and is a candidate for removal at page fault time. If each counter has b bits and clock pulses are generated every p process seconds, then $T = p2^b$. The value of T is chosen by the system to give the best performance (i.e. the system is "tuned").

A major disadvantage of the working set algorithm is the necessity to record references between page faults and the need for hardware counters for a pure implementation. An approximate implementation could use the use bit scanning technique, as in approximate LRU algorithm implementations, by reading use bits in the page table at intervals using the system interrupt timer and record the pages referenced since the last scan. Baer (1980) describes a working set implementation using the scanning routine.

A replacement algorithm called the *page fault frequency algorithm* (Chu and Opder-beck, 1976) resembles the working set algorithm but has a dynamically variable window. This algorithm maintains a set of most recently used pages. The set varies in size, depending upon the frequency of page faults, given threshold values. With more page faults, the set grows to attempt to reduce the frequency of the page faults. However, it is known that the algorithm can exhibit erratic behavior.

4.3.7 Performance and cost

Replacement algorithm

The question of the selection of the replacement algorithm now arises – there are several possible algorithms to choose from and the choice rests upon performance and cost. The optimal replacement algorithm could be defined as one which creates the minimum number of page faults. We would expect that the minimum number of page faults is generated when the pages discarded from the memory are those which are not wanted again for the longest time in the future, which is known as the *principle of optimality*. This algorithm was described by Belady (1966) and is known as MIN (minimum page fault algorithm) or the optimal replacement policy (OPT). It operates like the least recently used algorithm, but on page references in the future. Stone presents an argument that MIN/OPT should be the optimum replacement algorithm (Stone, 1987) and some mathematical proofs exist for specific assumptions. However, the principle of optimality does not always hold (see Denning, 1970).

The MIN/OPT algorithm extended to variable partitioning is called the *variable space page replacement algorithm*, VMIN (Prieve and Fabry, 1976), or an optimal variable replacement algorithm, and it operates in a similar way to the working set algorithm on page references in the future. In VMIN, the window is an interval from the present to a point in the future, i.e., an interval $(t, t + \theta)$. At each page reference (time, t), the page is kept if the next reference to the page is in the interval $(t, t + \theta)$, otherwise the page is removed. VMIN generates the same sequence of page faults as the working set (Denning and Slutz, 1978) and has the interesting effect of anticipating transitions between disjointed working sets. Of course MIN and VMIN cannot be implemented in practice, but serve as benchmarks for comparison with practical algorithms.

In any selected replacement algorithm we would hope that, if the memory allocation is increased, the number of page faults decreases or at least stays the same. This would always be true if an allocation of m pages includes the pages in an allocation of $m - 1$ pages. Algorithms with this characteristic are known as *stack algorithms*. The stack characteristic is useful for studying different replacement algorithms using a known reference string and different memory partitions.

Particular practical algorithms will perform well under certain conditions. For example, the FIFO algorithm (not a stack algorithm) works well for programs in which pages are referenced in a long sequence, but otherwise can perform poorly. LRU works well for programs which repeatedly reference a set of pages. Global algorithms seem to perform worse than local algorithms in a multiprogramming environment and the working set algorithm appears to produce close to optimal results. Denning makes a strong case for his working set algorithm, arguing that the cost/complexity of implementation (its major disadvantage) should not be a deterrent.

Cost

The memory hierarchy in a system has mainly come about due to cost considerations. The cost of a memory system is normally characterized by the cost per bit of the memory. At each level of memory hierarchy, the cost per bit reduces, sometimes substantially, and the memory capacity (the number of locations in the memory system) increases. The access time also increases significantly, and there is a trade-off between cost and speed. The average cost of a memory system per bit having main and disk memories in the hierarchy is given by:

$$C_{av} = \frac{c_m m_m + c_s m_s}{m_m + m_s}$$

where c_m and c_s are the costs per bit of the main and disk memories and m_m and m_s are the capacities of the memories. The average access time will depend upon how often the required information is in the highest speed memory (connected to the processor).

In a virtual memory system, a criterion which embodies the memory allocation and overall speed of execution is the *space-time product* (ST). This is the product of the memory used by a program and the execution time of the program. Since these are directly related to cost, the space-time product is regarded as an indication of the cost of executing the program. As memory requirements change over time, the space-time product becomes the integral of the set of resident memory pages over time while the program is being executed, including times for waiting for a missing page, i.e.:

$$ST(t_1, t_2) = \int_{t_2}^{t_1} M(t)\, dt$$

over the time interval t_1, t_2 and $M(t)$ pages at time t. For a fixed memory allocation, M, the space-time product reduces to:

$$ST = M(n + D.f)$$

where n = number of references, D = average time to transfer page from disk memory to main memory and f = number of page faults.

For a variable memory allocation, we take into account that the memory allocation can be different with different memory references (in particular after a page fault) to obtain:

$$ST = \sum_{t=1}^{T} M(t) + D \sum_{i=1}^{f} M(t_i)$$

$$= M_{av}T + D \sum_{i=1}^{f} M(t_i)$$

where T = total program execution time; t_i = time of the ith page fault; M_{av} = the average memory allocation over the execution period. The space-time product should normally be minimized to reduce costs, although no optimal policy always does this.

Access time

The goal of any memory management scheme is to ensure that when it is required, information is in the highest level of memory as often as possible. The probability that an item is found immediately in the highest level of memory considered is known as the *hit ratio* (h) for this memory. The access time is the time required between a memory request being made and the location being read or written. Read and write access times often have the same value. The average access time is given by:

$$t_a = ht_m + (1 - h)t_s$$

or, if all requests must first be made to the main memory, then:

$$t_a = t_m + (1 - h)t_s$$

where t_m is the total access time of accessing the main memory, including the address translation, and t_s is the additional access time for accessing the disk memory.

We are using the same terminology and formulae as in a cache memory system – both have two memories, a slower memory and a higher speed memory, with the objective of hiding the effects of the slower memory. However in a virtual memory system, there is a much greater gap between the access time of the two memories and the miss ratio has a much greater effect on the overall access time. The average access time in either system, ignoring additional time involved in write operations, can be given as:

$$t_a = t_{m1} + (1 - h)t_{m2}$$

where t_{m1} is the access time of the higher speed memory (cache in a cache system, main memory in a virtual memory system); t_{m2} is the access time of the lower speed memory (main memory in a cache system, disk memory in a virtual memory system) and $(1 - h)$ is equal to the miss ratio. Therefore:

$$t_a = t_{m2}(1/k + (1 - h))$$

where $k = t_{m2}/t_{m1}$ (the ratio of lower speed memory access time to higher speed memory access time). We can see that the average access time will be dominated by the miss ratio if the ratio of the memory access times (k) is large, as in the case of a virtual memory system. For example, with a 20 ms access time disk and a 200 ns access time high capacity semiconductor random access memory, $k = 100\ 000$. A miss ratio of 1 per cent creates an average access time of 200.2 ns, which is much larger than the main memory access time. Clearly, for a virtual memory system the miss ratio ought to be very low indeed to approach the access time of the main memory.

Conversely, the average access time will be dominated by the ratio of the access times of the memories when this difference is small, rather than by the miss ratio. For a cache system, the ratio of main memory access time to cache access time (k) is in the region of 3–10. For example, with a 200 ns access time main memory and a 25 ns access time cache, $k = 8$. A miss ratio of 1 per cent creates an average access time of 27 ns, which is close to the cache access time. The miss ratio for a cache system need not be as low as for a virtual memory system for the average access time to approach the access time of the cache.

Though outside the scope of this book, just as with cache memory, theoretical studies have been performed using mathematical models for program behavior to predict memory references, but most models cannot easily incorporate the transitions that occur between processes in a multiprogramming environment.

TLB performance

Another key aspect is the performance of the TLB. If the page address is not found in the TLB, a TLB miss occurs, and a significant overhead occurs in searching the main memory page tables, even when the page is already in the main memory. The TLB is like a data cache (with the possible exception of using hashing, which appears not to be always done). Hence the basic cache equations also apply to the TLB, i.e. the address

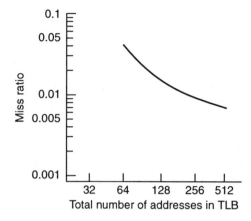

Figure 4.14 TLB miss ratio against size

translation time, t_t, is given by:

$$t_t = t_{tlb} + (1 - h_{tlb})t_{mt}$$

where t_{tlb} is the translation time of the TLB (hit or miss) and t_{mt} is the translation time looking in main memory tables on a TLB miss. The TLB miss ratio is given by $(1 - h_{tlb})$. Typically the TLB miss ratio (miss rate) is very low indeed, perhaps less than 0.05 per cent. Figure 4.14 shows a typical characteristic of a TLB for miss ratio against increasing TLB size (loosely based upon Flynn, 1995).

4.4 Virtual memory systems with cache memory

In a computer system with virtual memory and a cache, we can insert the cache after the TLB virtual/real address translation, so that the cache holds real address tags and the comparison of addresses is done with real addresses. Alternatively, we can insert the cache before the TLB virtual-real translation so that the cache holds virtual address tags and the comparison of addresses is done using virtual addresses. Let us first consider the former case, which is much less complicated and has fewer repercussions on the rest of the system design.

4.4.1 Addressing cache with real addresses

Though it is not necessary for correct operation, it is common to perform the TLB virtual-real translation at the same time as some independent part of the cache selection operation to gain an improvement in speed. The overlap is done in the following way. The address from the processor in a paged virtual memory system is divided into two fields, the most significant field identifying the page and the least significant field identifying the word (line) within the page. The division of page and line is fixed for a particular system and made so that a suitable sized line of information is transferred between the main and the disk memories. In a set-associative or direct mapped cache system, the address is also divided into fields – a most significant tag field and a less index significant field (to select the set or line). If the cache index field corresponds directly to the page address line field, then the set/line selection in the cache can be done while the virtual address translation is being done. This is because the page address line field is the same in both the virtual address and the real address. When the address translation has been done, and a real page address produced, this address can be compared with the tags selected from the cache, as shown in Figure 4.15 for a fully associative TLB and a direct mapped cache. A set-associative cache would be similar. On a cache miss, the real address is immediately available for selecting the line in main memory, assuming a page fault has not occurred and the line can be transferred into the cache directly. More likely a set-associative organization

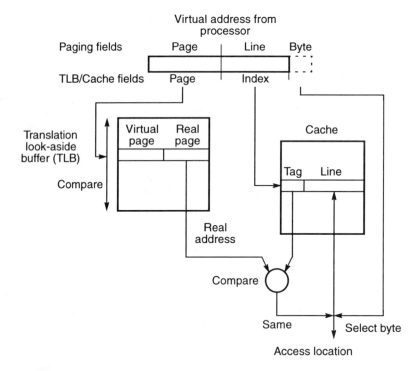

Figure 4.15 Fully associative translation look-aside buffer with a direct mapped cache

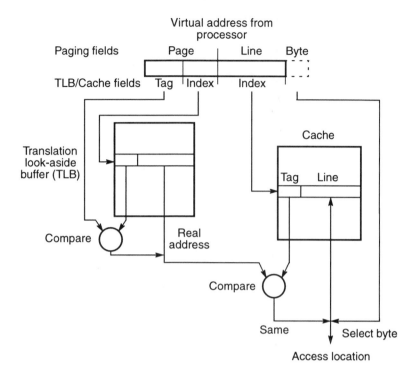

Figure 4.16 One-way set-associative translation look-aside buffer with a direct mapped cache

would be used for the TLB for economic reasons (and speed of operation). Then the page field must be divided to two subfields for the TLB as shown in Figure 4.16.

Clearly, as described, the overlap mechanism relies on the page size being the same as the cache size if the cache has a direct mapped organization. The overall size of a set-associative cache could be increased by increasing the set size. Some variations in the lengths of the fields are possible while still keeping some concurrent operations. In particular, the page size can be larger, so that there are more bits for the line than needed for the set/line selection in the cache. The extra bits are then concatenated with the real page address before being compared with the tags as shown in Figure 4.17.

4.4.2 Addressing cache with virtual addresses

If the cache is addressed with virtual addresses, these addresses are immediately available for selecting a word within the cache and there is a potential increase in speed over a real addressed cache. Only on a cache miss would it be necessary to translate a virtual address

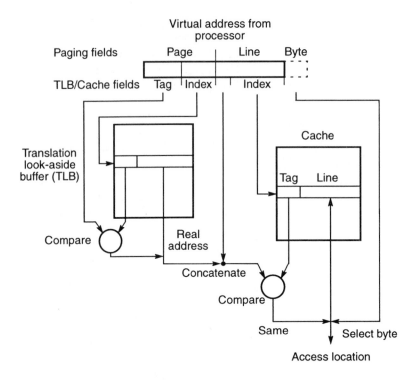

Figure 4.17 One-way set-associative translation look-aside buffer with a direct mapped cache and larger page size than cache size

into a real address, and there is more time then. Clearly, if the tag field of the virtual address is larger than the real address, the tag fields in the cache would be larger and there would be more associated comparators. Similarly, if the virtual address is smaller than the real address, the tag fields in the cache would be smaller and there would be fewer comparators. A particular advantage of a virtual addressed cache is that there is no need for overlap between the virtual/real address translation and the cache operation, as there is no translation mechanism for cache hits. So the division of addresses into fields in the virtual/real addresses and the division of fields in the cache selection mechanism can be designed separately and need not have any interrelationship.

Although the virtual addressed cache is an apparently attractive solution, it has a complication concerned with the relationship between virtual addresses in different processes which may be in the cache together. It is possible for different virtual addresses in different processes to map into the same real address. Such virtual addresses are known as *synonyms* – from the word denoting the same thing(s) as another but suitable for different contexts. Synonyms are especially likely if the addressed location is shared between processes, but can also occur if programs request the operating system to use different virtual addresses for the same real address. Synonyms can occur when an input/output device uses real addresses to access main memory accessible by the programs. They can also occur in multiprocessor systems when processors share memory using different virtual addresses. It is also possible for the same virtual address generated in different processes to map into different real addresses.

Process or other tags could be attached to the addresses to differentiate between virtual addresses of processes, but this adds a complication to the cache design, and would still allow multiple copies of the same real line in the cache simultaneously. Of course, synonyms could be disallowed by placing restrictions on virtual addresses. For example, each location in shared code could be forced to have only one virtual address. This approach is only acceptable for shared operating system code and is done in the IBM MVS operating system.

Otherwise, synonyms are handled in virtual addressed caches by the use of a *reverse translation buffer* (RTB), also called an *inverse translation buffer* (ITB). On a cache miss, the virtual address is translated into a real address using the virtual-real translation look-aside buffer (TLB) to access the main memory. When the real address has been formed, a reverse translation occurs to identify all virtual addresses given under the same real address. This reverse translation can be performed at the same time as the main memory cycle. If the real address is given by another virtual address already existing in the cache, the virtual address is renamed to eliminate multiple copies of the same line. The information from the main memory is not needed and is discarded. If a synonym does not exist, the main memory information is accepted and loaded into the cache.

When there are direct accesses to the main memory by devices such as a direct memory access (DMA) input/output device, the associated line in the cache, if present, must be recognized and invalidated. To identify the line, a real-virtual address translation also needs to be performed using a reverse translation buffer.

4.4.3 Access time

The average access time of a system with both a cache and a paged virtual memory has several components, depending on one of several situations arising - whether the real address (assuming a real addressed cache) is in the translation look-aside buffer, the cache or the main memory and whether the data is in the cache or the main memory. The translation look-aside buffer is used to perform the address translation when the virtual page is in the translation look-aside buffer. If there is a miss in the translation look-aside buffer, the translation is performed by accessing a page table which may be in the cache or in the main memory. There are six combinations of accesses, namely:

1. Address in the translation look-aside buffer, data in the cache.
2. Address in the translation look-aside buffer, data in the main memory.
3. Address in the cache, data in the cache.
4. Address in the cache, data in the main memory.
5. Address in the main memory, data in the cache.
6. Address in the main memory, data in the main memory.

Table 4.1 Access times and probabilities of the various access combinations

Access time		Probabilities	
25 + 25 + 25	= 75 ns	0.9 × 0.95	= 0.855
25 + 25 + 200	= 250 ns	0.9 × 0.05	= 0.045
25 + 25 + 25 + 25 + 25	= 125 ns	0.1 × 0.95 × 0.95	= 0.09025
25 + 25 + 25 + 25 + 200	= 300 ns	0.1 × 0.95 × 0.05	= 0.00475
25 + 25 + 200 + 25 + 25 + 25	= 325 ns	0.1 × 0.05 × 0.95	= 0.00475
25 + 25 + 200 + 25 + 25 + 200	= 500 ns	0.1 × 0.05 × 0.05	= 0.00025

(Part of the page table could be in the disk memory, but we will not consider this possibility.) Suppose there is no overlap between translation look-aside buffer translation and cache access (a rather unlikely situation) and the following times apply:

Translation look-aside buffer address translation time
(or to generate a TLB miss)   = 25 ns
Cache time to determine whether address in cache   = 25 ns
Cache data fetch if address in cache   = 25 ns
Main memory read access time   = 200 ns
Translation look-aside buffer hit ratio   = 0.9
Cache hit ratio   = 0.95

the access times and probabilities of the various access combinations are given in Table 4.1. The average access time is given by:

$$(75 \times 0.855) + (250 \times 0.045) + (125 \times 0.09025) + (300 \times 0.00475) + (325 \times 0.00475)$$
$$+ (500 \times 0.00025) = 89.75 \text{ ns } (64.125 \text{ ns on a cache hit})$$

If the virtual memory system also incorporates two-level paging or segments, further combinations exist. The calculation can easily be modified to take into account partial overlap between the TLB access and cache access.

4.5 Segmentation

4.5.1 General

The purpose of segmentation is to organize the programs in memory so that the operating system can relocate programs in the main and disk memory easily, and to provide protection from unauthorized access/execution. This is not the same purpose as paging which has a hardware motive, to manage the memory hierarchy in an automatic way. Segmentation, as a method of separating sections of program and data, dates from about the same time as the paging concept and was a main aspect of early Burroughs computers; it was first used in the B5000 and subsequently in other Burroughs systems. Since the early 1970s, segmentation has been combined with paging as a main memory management technique on most larger computer systems and more recently developed microprocessors. Let us first consider segmentation alone.

To be able to relocate complete programs, they are encapsulated into segments. A *segment* is a block of contiguous locations. Segments may be of different sizes since programs are of different sizes. Each address generated by the processor is composed of a *segment number* and a *displacement* within the segment. The displacement is also called an *offset* and the segment number is sometimes called the *base*. Rather than concatenate the segment and *offset* numbers, in a segmented system the segment number and the offset are added together to form the real address, because segments do not necessarily start at fixed boundaries. Segments are usually restricted to start at, say, 16 word boundaries so that the least significant bits of the segment address can be assumed to be 0. (Least significant 4 bits are 0 for 16 word boundaries.) The term *logical address* is used to describe the virtual address and *physical address* describes the real address. Segments can be shared between programs or may partially overlap if required.

An important aspect of the (symbolic) segmentation described here is that the segment number and offset are separate entities and any alteration to the offset by the program cannot affect the segment number. Once the maximum offset is reached (assuming that the segment grows with increasing addresses) adding one to the offset should create an error condition. A simple impure implementation of segmentation might cause the real address to wrap around to the beginning of the same segment. It would be unforgivable to implement a segmentation system that entered another segment when one was added to the maximum offset, though this effect is known in linear segmentation. It should not be possible to enter segments from other segments unless the access has been specifically allowed (as with shared system segments). In particular, data segments and code segments are separated, so that trying to execute data in data segments as code should generate an error condition. Similarly, trying to alter information in code segment should generate an error condition because code is normally assumed to be read-only and accessed only during a fetch cycle.

Figure 4.18 shows the usual method of translating logical addresses into physical addresses. The logical address has two parts, a segment number and an offset. The segment number specifies the logical segment and the offset specifies the number of

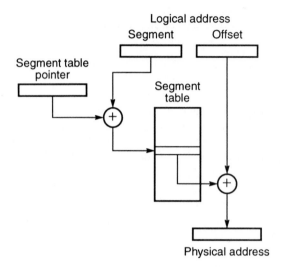

Figure 4.18 Segmentation address translation

locations from the beginning of the segment. The segment and offset fields are physically separate and are not obtained by simply dividing the address from the processor into two fields. The processor has to be designed to generate the segment and offset separately.

The translation mechanism usually employs direct mapping, as shown. The starting addresses of the physical segments are held in segment tables, and there is a different segment table for each active process. The starting address of the appropriate segment table is contained in a segment table pointer register and this is added to the segment number to locate the physical segment base address in the table. The base address read from the segment table is added to the offset to form the required physical address.

The segment table incorporates additional information, usually including:

1. Segment length.
2. Memory protection bits.
3. Bits for the replacement algorithm.

Segment length

Different segments can have different lengths. The length of each segment is stored in the length fields of the segment table entry to prevent programs referencing a location beyond the end of a particular segment. If the offset in the virtual address is greater than the stored length (limit) field, i.e. an attempt is being made to reference beyond the end of the segment, an error signal is generated, usually in the form of a system interrupt. A maximum segment length will be designed into a system, i.e. the length field will have a certain number of bits. Maximum segment lengths range from 64 Kbytes for early systems with small address spaces through to 4 gigabytes for 32-bit address spaces.

As an added facility for segments used to hold stacks that grow downwards (which is how most stacks grow), it is useful to know when one of the first 256 words (say) is being accessed, so that a warning that the end of the stack space is being reached can be given. A separate flag, which is set when such accesses are made, can be provided.

Memory protection

Memory protection involves preventing specified types of access to the addressed location and discarding or stopping the address translation occurring. The protection applies to all of the locations in the segment and not to particular locations. Note that segments should be produced for unified purposes, i.e. for data, for a procedure, etc. and the protection applied to the whole segment.

Typically, by setting bits in the segment tables, any segment can be assigned as:

1. Read-only.
2. Execute-only.
3. System-only.

Assigning a segment as read-only allows data to be protected from alteration. Assigning a segment as execute-only means that the segment can only be referenced during a fetch cycle, which prevents unauthorized copying of programs since execute-only code cannot be read as data. Segments that are shared by different processes could have different access rights for each process.

For the system-only assignment, it is necessary for the processor to have two operating modes, a normal mode which is for ordinary users, and a system mode dedicated to the operating system. Generally, when in the normal mode, there will be certain instructions (including input/output instructions) which cannot be executed. The only way to enter the system mode is through a system call to the operating system, either intentionally or due to an error condition. Hence, functions such as input/output can be totally controlled by the operating system without interference from the user programs. Though some memory management schemes do not have the full selection of protection bits, a system-only bit is regarded as the minimum protection that must be present.

Rather than having an "only" assignment, it is possible to have an "excluded" assignment, for example:

1. CPU excluded.
2. DMA excluded.

In CPU excluded, the segment cannot be accessed by the central processor, however, this leaves all other possible "bus masters", such as DMA input/output controllers. In DMA excluded, the DMA controllers are excluded, leaving the central processor and other bus masters, i.e. the other processors in a multiprocessor system. Multiple violations must be handled.

Replacement algorithm

The replacement algorithm in a segmented system can be similar to the replacement algorithm in a paged system except that it needs to take the varying size of the segments into account when allocating space for new segments. Typically, as in a paged system, replacement algorithm flags are associated with each logical/physical address entry in the segment table, in particular with the use (accessed) and modified (written) flags. As we have seen, the use flag is usually sufficient to implement a replacement algorithm or approximations to a replacement algorithm.

Placement algorithm

The variable size of segments causes some additional problems in main memory allocation. During operation, with segments returned to the disk memory, the main memory will become a "checkerboard", as shown in Figure 4.19, with holes between segments. Clearly, an incoming segment must be smaller than the main memory space available (hole) for the segment to be overwritten. However, leaving small spaces which cannot be used subsequently should be avoided, and is known as *external fragmentation*. Several placement algorithms for finding a suitable place in the main memory to hold an incoming segment have been proposed, including *first fit*, *best fit* and *worst fit*. In first fit, a table of memory allocation, in particular the available holes, is scanned from the beginning until a space which is big enough is found, and the segment is entered there. This algorithm can be modified to skip over spaces which would leave a very small, unusable space had the segment been placed there. The best fit scans the complete list of hole sizes to select the memory space which would leave the smallest hole and the worst fit selects the space which would leave the biggest hole, in the hope that this hole will be big enough for another segment.

To help fitting in segments, it is usually necessary to compact the memory by moving segments together and eliminating the holes between them, which is a very time consuming process. These problems have led to the incorporation of paging in most large systems that use segmentation.

4.5.2 Paged segmentation

Segmentation and paging can be combined, and usually are combined, to gain the advantages of both systems, i.e. the logical structure of segmentation and the hardware mapping between main and disk memory of paging. The paging aspect simplifies the memory allocation problem of a pure segmented system. When segmentation and paging

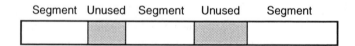

Figure 4.19 Checkerboard effect

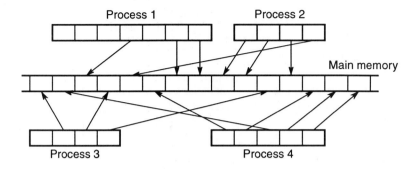

Figure 4.20 Paged segments in memory

are combined, but the concept of segments as logical units is kept, the segmentation is regarded as *symbolic segmentation* or *segmented name space*. Each segment is divided into a number of equal sized pages and the basic unit of transfer between main and disk memory is the page. It is not necessary to transfer the complete segment into the main memory as in the pure segmentation method; only those pages required need be transferred. Hence, the main memory might consist of pages from various segments, as shown in Figure 4.20, and pages of a new segment can be easily fitted into the memory.

The virtual address is divided into a segment number, a page number and displacement identifying the word within a page. The translation mechanism is shown in Figure 4.21. A segment table pointer selects a set of segment tables and the segment number selects a page table entry to select a page table. The page selects a real address which is concatenated with the displacement to obtain the full real address. In symbolic segmentation, length limit and other protection is naturally applied at the segment table level and replacement bits applied at the page table level. In a system with very large segments, segments can be paged using a two-level translation to reduce the number of page tables necessary for one task. There are potentially three levels of translation, one for the segment and two for the page as shown in Figure 4.22.

4.5.3 8086 family segmentation

The 16-bit 8086 microprocessor, introduced in 1978, is perhaps the first example of a microprocessor to incorporate a very restricted form of segmentation within the device (Intel, 1985a), though this nevertheless enables code and three forms of data to be separated in one program. However, it does not allow the facilities of true segmentation such as sharing and complete protection. The microprocessor contains four segment registers called the *code segment register* (CS), the *data segment register* (DS), the *stack segment register* (SS) and the *extra segment register* (ES) respectively. The address generated by the program is a 16-bit offset, without a segment number. A 16-bit offset allows segments up to 64 Kbytes. The particular segment is selected by context. Instruc-

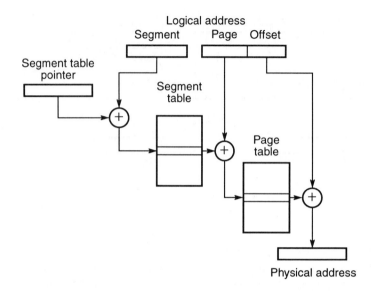

Figure 4.21 Paged segmentation address translation

tion fetch cycles always use the code segment with the offset provided by the program counter (called the instruction pointer, IP, in the 8086). Most data operations normally assume the use of the data segment register, though any segment register can be selected using an additional prefix instruction. Stack instructions always use the stack segment register. The extra segment is used for results of string operations. The segment registers have 16-bits. Four least significant 0s are added, giving a 20-bit base address and a 20-bit physical address.

Subsequent members of the 8086 family starting extended the memory management scheme of the 8086, though each extension had to be designed within the framework of the 8086 segment registers, leading to some very constrained and complicated designs. The 16-bit Intel 286 provided up to 2^{13} (8192) separately addressed segments, though only four, designated as CS, DS, SS and ES, can be used at a time and these are then used as in the 8086. Physical memory addressing was extended to 24 bits (16 Mbytes). The original segment registers within the device are now called *segment selectors* by Intel and are used as pointers to within main memory segment (descriptor) tables holding the segment information, in the form of a descriptor. A descriptor consists of a 24-bit segment base address, protection bits (access rights) and a length field. A multilevel translation in the manner of Figure 4.22 was used on the Intel 386 microprocessor (Intel, 1985b) and 486 microprocessor (Intel, 1994a), 32-bit developments of the 286, to include demand paging. Further information on the protection mechanisms provided can be found in the Intel literature (see, for example, Intel, 1987a, 1994a).

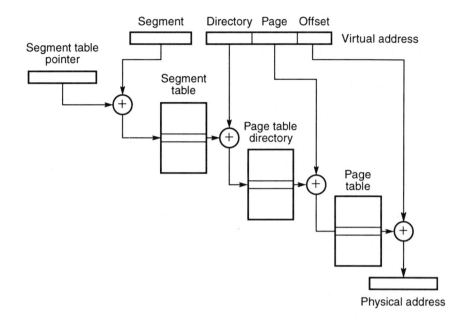

Figure 4.22 Two-level paging with segmentation

PROBLEMS

4.1 In a paged system, suppose the following pages are requested in the order shown:

12, 14, 2, 34, 56, 23, 14, 56, 34, 12

and the main memory partition can only hold four pages at any instant (in practice usually many more pages can be held). List the pages in the main memory after each page is transferred using each of the following replacement algorithms:

1. First-in first-out replacement algorithm.
2. Least recently used replacement algorithm.
3. Clock replacement algorithm.

Indicate when page faults occur.

4.2 Identify which of the following replacement algorithms are stack algorithms:

1. Random replacement algorithm.
2. First-in first-out replacement algorithm.
3. Clock replacement algorithm.
4. Least recently used replacement algorithm.
5. Working set replacement algorithm.
6. Page fault frequency replacement algorithm.

4.3 Suggest how the optimal replacement policy could be implemented given that the memory reference string is known.

4.4 Deduce a sequence of page references for a paging system with eight main memory pages, using the least recently used replacement algorithm, which produces each of the following characteristics:

1. The largest number of page faults.
2. The smallest number of page faults.

4.5 Using one use bit with each page entry, list the pages recorded in the following sequence and hence determine the pages removed using one use bit approximation to the least recently used algorithm:

13, 47, 13, 99, 47, 35, 13, 67, 47, 13, 34, 35, 99, 99, 14, 14, 47, 67

given that there are four pages in the memory partition. The use bits are only read at page fault time, and then scanned in the same order.

Suppose two use bits are provided. The first use bit is set when the page is first referenced. The second use bit is set when the page is referenced again. Deduce an algorithm to remove pages from the partition, and list the pages.

4.6 If the cost of a semiconductor main memory is four times the cost of disk memory per bit, and the total amount of memory required is 25 Mbytes, determine the amount of each type of memory to achieve a total cost per bit of half that of the semiconductor memory.

4.7 A microprocessor generates a 20-bit byte address A19, A18, A17, A16, A15, A14, A13, A12, A11, A10, A9, A8, A7, A6, A5, A4, A3, A2, A1, A0 (A0 being the least significant bit). Design a translation look-aside buffer for the system giving details of the address translation and numbers of bits in address fields, if the following applies. The page size is to be 512 bytes. 256 page addresses are to be handled by the TLB. The groups of virtual addresses below are likely to appear frequently:

Five addresses with A19 the same.
Two addresses with A18 through A0 the same.
Three addresses with A16 through A0 the same.
Four addresses with A15 through A0 the same.
Two addresses with A13 through A0 the same.
Two addresses with A10 through A0 the same.
Two addresses with A9 the same.

Clearly indicate your reasoning. Design for minimum cost.

4.8   In a paging system, the page size is p and a program requires P pages. The last page in the program is 50 per cent full. Each page requires t locations in the main memory page table. Obtain an equation for the total amount of main memory required for the program and page table entry combined. Find the page size to give minimum memory requirements by differentiating the total memory requirement equation with respect to p, and equating the result to zero. Determine a suitable page size for a program of 128 Kbytes given four bytes per page entry.

4.9   Determine the number of locations required in the page tables for a three-level page mapping given that the virtual address has 32 bits divided into a 12-bit directory field, a 10-bit page field and a 10-bit line (offset) field. How many bits are there in the table entries for addresses?

4.10 A cache in a system with virtual memory is addressed with a real address. Both the real addresses and virtual addresses have thirty-two bits and the page size is 512 words. The set size is two. Determine the division of fields in the address to achieve full overlap between the page translation and set selection. Suppose the cache must have only two pages, give a design showing the components and address formats.

4.11 A system has both a virtual memory (paging) and a real address data cache, with the following characteristics:

   40-bit virtual address
   32-bit real address
   16 Kbyte pages
   2-way set associative TLB with 256 entries in total
   4-way set associative data cache with 1024 lines in total

Draw the TLB and data cache, showing the division of bits in the virtual address, real address and the number of bits in the paths between the various component parts of the system. Each line contains one 32-bit word.

4.12 Choose a real computer system or processor with both a cache and virtual memory and identify those methods described in Chapters 3 and 4 which have been employed. Describe how the methods have been implemented (block diagram, etc.) and comment on the design choices made.

4.13 Apply the first fit, best fit and worst fit placement algorithm to insert a 290 byte segment in a 10 Kbyte memory partition which contains segments at locations given in Table 4.2. Show the location of the incoming segment. Repeat, taking into account that no incoming segment will be less than 11 bytes.

Table 4.2 Segment locations and sizes for Problem 4.13

Address	Segment size (bytes)
0	3400
3800	230
4500	630
5590	100
7000	200
7500	550
10000	120

4.14 As a designer of a new paged segmentation memory management system, you are to develop the formats of information stored in the page table and segment tables given that the page size is 512 words, the maximum segment size is 65 536 words and the processor generates a 32-bit address. Making appropriate design decisions, choose and list the sizes of each field in the segment and page table. Memory can be made read-only or execute-only, and four other levels of privileged access are provided (one for the user and three for routines within the operating system).

5 | *Pipelined processor design*

In Chapter 2 we described the basic operations that a processor must perform. We now continue the topic of processor design, by looking at methods of improving the speed of operation of a processor. For the most part, increased speed is achieved by the use of parallelism, that is, by the use of multiple concurrent operations. A very effective way of achieving parallelism within the processor is by the use of pipelining and this chapter concentrates upon the pipeline technique. We will describe how pipelining is applied to instruction processing and include some of the methods of designing pipelines. We will look at how pipelining is used in arithmetic units. Finally we will explore the design of so-called superscalar processors that can execute more than one instruction in one pipeline cycle, by the use of multiple units and pipelines. This chapter could be studied immediately after Chapter 2.

5.1 Overlap and pipelining

5.1.1 Technique

Overlap and the associated concept, *pipelining*, are methods which can be used to increase the speed of operation of the central processor. They are often applied to the internal design of high speed computers, including advanced microprocessors, as a type of multiprocessing. Overlap and pipelining really refer to the same technique, in which a task or operation is divided into a number of subtasks that need to be performed in sequence. Each subtask is performed by its own logical unit, rather than by a single unit which performs all the subtasks. The units are connected together in a serial fashion with the output of one connecting to the input of the next, and all the units operate simultaneously, as shown in Figure 5.1(a). While one unit is performing a subtask on the ith task, the preceding unit in the pipeline is performing its subtask on the $(i + 1)$th task. The operation of pipelines can be illustrated in a diagram known as a *space-time diagram*. In a space-time diagram, the time that each unit operates on each task is illustrated, as shown in Figure 5.1(b).

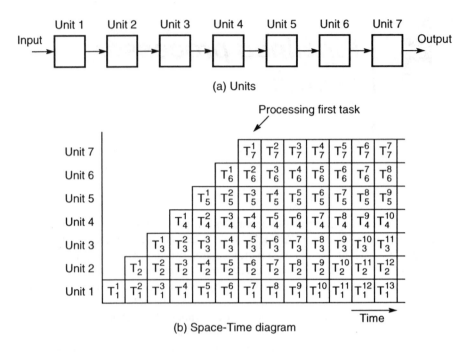

(a) Units

Processing first task

Unit 7						T_7^1	T_7^2	T_7^3	T_7^4	T_7^5	T_7^6	T_7^7	
Unit 6					T_6^1	T_6^2	T_6^3	T_6^4	T_6^5	T_6^6	T_6^7	T_6^8	
Unit 5				T_5^1	T_5^2	T_5^3	T_5^4	T_5^5	T_5^6	T_5^7	T_5^8	T_5^9	
Unit 4			T_4^1	T_4^2	T_4^3	T_4^4	T_4^5	T_4^6	T_4^7	T_4^8	T_4^9	T_4^{10}	
Unit 3		T_3^1	T_3^2	T_3^3	T_3^4	T_3^5	T_3^6	T_3^7	T_3^8	T_3^9	T_3^{10}	T_3^{11}	
Unit 2	T_2^1	T_2^2	T_2^3	T_2^4	T_2^5	T_2^6	T_2^7	T_2^8	T_2^9	T_2^{10}	T_2^{11}	T_2^{12}	
Unit 1	T_1^1	T_1^2	T_1^3	T_1^4	T_1^5	T_1^6	T_1^7	T_1^8	T_1^9	T_1^{10}	T_1^{11}	T_1^{12}	T_1^{13}

Time

(b) Space-Time diagram

Figure 5.1 Pipeline processing ($T_j^i = j$th subtask in the ith task)

The mechanism can be compared to a conveyor belt assembly line in a factory, in which products are in various stages of completion. Each product is assembled in stages as it passes along the assembly line. Similarly, in overlap/pipelining, a task is presented to the first unit. Once the first subtask of this task is completed, the results are presented to the second unit and another task can be presented to the first unit. Results from one subtask are passed to the next unit that are required for the next unit (and subsequent units in the pipeline). A task is completed when the subtasks have been processed by all the units.

Suppose each unit in the pipeline has the same operating time to complete a subtask and that the first task is completed and a series of tasks is presented. The time to perform one complete task is the same as the time for one unit to perform one subtask of the task, rather than the summation of all the unit times. Ideally, each subtask should take the same time, but if this is not the case, the overall processing time will be that of the slowest unit, with the faster units being delayed. It may be advantageous to equalize stage operating times with the insertion of extra delays. We will pursue this technique later.

The term pipelining is often used to describe a system design for achieving a specific computation by splitting the computation into a series of steps, whereas the term overlap is often used to describe a system design with two or more clearly distinct functions performed simultaneously. For example, a floating point arithmetic operation can be divided into a number of distinct pipelined suboperations, which must be performed in sequence to obtain the final floating point result. Conversely, a computer system might perform central processor functions and input/output functions with separate processors – a central processor and an input/output processor operating at the same time. The central processor and input/output processor operations are overlapped.

5.1.2 Pipeline data transfer

Information must be passed from one stage of the pipeline to the next. Two methods of implementing the information transfer in a pipeline can be identified:

1. Asynchronous method.
2. Synchronous method.

These are shown in Figure 5.2. In the asynchronous method, a pair of "handshaking" signals are used between each unit and the next unit – a ready signal and an acknowledge signal. The ready signal informs the next unit that it has finished the present operation and is ready to pass the task and any results onwards. The acknowledge signal is returned when the receiving unit has accepted the task and results. In the synchronous method, one timing signal causes all outputs of units to be transferred to the succeeding units. The timing signal occurs at fixed intervals, taking into account the slowest unit.

The asynchronous method provides the greatest flexibility in stage operating times and naturally should make the pipeline operate at its fastest, limited as always by the slowest

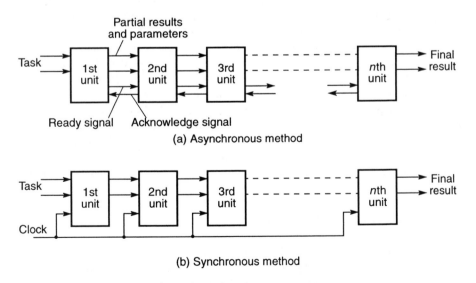

Figure 5.2 Transfer of information between units in a pipeline

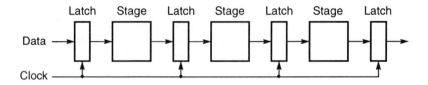

Figure 5.3 Pipeline with staging latches

unit. Though unlikely in most pipeline designs, the asynchronous method would allow stages to alter the operating times with different input operands. The asynchronous method also lends itself to the use of variable length first-in first-out buffers between stages, to smooth the flow of results from one stage to the next. However, most constructed instruction and arithmetic pipelines use the synchronous method. An example of a pipeline that might use asynchronous handshaking is in dataflow systems when nodal instructions are only generated when all their operands are received (see Chapter 10). Other examples include the pipeline structures formed with transputers, as described in Chapter 9.

Instruction and arithmetic pipelines almost always use the synchronous method to reduce logic timing and implementation problems. In the synchronous method, there is a staging latch between each unit and the clock signal activates all the staging latches simultaneously, as shown in Figure 5.3. In all pipelines, the information passed from one stage to the next must be what the subsequent stages require. In the synchronous method, the information is held in staging registers, sited between the stages. The vertical lines in the space-time diagram indicate the times that the contents of the registers are transferred to the next stage.

Pipelines could have been designed without staging latches between pipeline stages and without a synchronizing clock signal – pipeline stages could produce their outputs after natural logic delays, results could percolate through the pipeline from one stage to the next and the final output could be sampled at the same regular frequency as that at which new pipeline inputs are applied. This type of pipeline is called a *maximum-rate pipeline*, as it should result in the maximum speed of operation. Such pipelines are difficult to design because logic delays are not known exactly – the delays vary between devices and depend upon the device interconnections. Testing such pipelines would be a distinct challenge. However, Cray computers do not use staging latches in their pipelines, instead, path delays are equalized.

5.1.3 Performance and cost

Pipelining is present in virtually all computer systems, including microprocessors. It is a form of parallel computation; at any instant more than one task is being performed in parallel (simultaneously). Pipelining is therefore done to increase the speed of operation of the system, although as well as potentially increased speed, it has the advantage of requiring little more logic than a non-pipelined solution in many applications, and sometimes less logic than a high speed non-pipelined solution. An alternative parallel implementation using n replicated units is shown in Figure 5.4. Each unit performs the complete task. The system achieves an equivalent increased speed of operation by applying n tasks simultaneously, one to each of the n units, and producing n results n cycles later. However, complete replication requires much more logic. As circuit densities increase and logic gate costs reduce, complete replication becomes attractive. Replicated parallel systems will be described in later chapters. We can make a general comment that pipelining is much more economical than replication of complete units.

We see from Figure 5.1 that there is a staircase characteristic at the beginning of pipe-lining; there is also a staircase characteristic at the end of a defined number of tasks. If s tasks are presented to an n-stage pipeline, it takes n clock periods before the first task has been completed, and then another $s - 1$ clock periods before all the tasks have been completed. Hence, the number of clock periods necessary is given by $n + (s - 1)$. Suppose a single, homogeneous non-pipelined unit with equivalent function can perform s tasks in sn clock periods. Then the speed-up available in a pipeline can be given by:

$$\text{Speed-up} = \frac{T_1}{T_n} = \frac{sn}{n + (s - 1)}$$

The potential maximum speed-up is n, though this would only be achieved for an infinite stream of tasks and no hold-ups in the pipeline. The assumption that a single homoge-neous unit would take as long as the pipelined system to process one task is also not true. A homogeneous system could be designed to operate faster than the pipelined version.

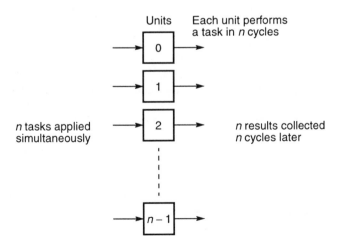

Figure 5.4 Replicated units

There is a certain amount of inefficiency in that only in the steady state of a continuous submission of tasks are all the units operating. Some units are not busy during start-up and ending periods. We can describe the efficiency as:

$$\text{Efficiency} = \frac{\sum_{i=1}^{n} t_i}{n \times (\text{overall operating time})}$$

$$= \frac{s}{n + (s-1)}$$

$$= \frac{\text{Speed-up}}{n}$$

where t_i is time unit i operates. Speed-up and efficiency can be used to characterize pipelines.

Suppose we have two units, A and B, in our pipeline. If each unit requires the same time, we have the timing as shown in Figure 5.5(a). This is the ideal situation. If on the other hand each unit requires a different time to operate depending upon the information passed to the units, we might have the timing shown in Figure 5.5(b). In that case the overall processing time is given by:

$$\text{Processing time} = \sum_{i=1}^{n-1} \text{Max}(T(A_i), T(B_{i-1}))$$

where $T(A_i)$ = time of ith operation in A, and $T(B_i)$ = time of ith operation in B.

Figure 5.5 is applicable for the asynchronous pipeline using a handshaking method between stages. In the synchronous method, we would have to provide sufficient time for the slowest unit to operate. For the most part we would prefer the synchronous method, in which each pipeline stage requires the same time to operate. To achieve this, we will need to equalize the processing times of each unit, maybe by reducing what certain units do and increasing the number of units accordingly. Reducing what each stage does and increasing the number of stages may allow the clock period to be reduced (frequency to be increased). Of course as we increase the number of units, the overhead of passing information from one unit to the next also increases, and a point will be reached when the performance actually decreases if we increase the pipeline length further. Also increasing the pipeline length will exacerbate the problems that occur due to the dependencies between tasks (see next section). Often pipelines are quite short, usually less that twenty stages.

Increasing the length of the pipeline with fixed clock period will increase the *latency* (the time for an instruction to be processed though the pipeline) but not the *throughput* (the number of instructions completing in unit time). The maximum throughput will only

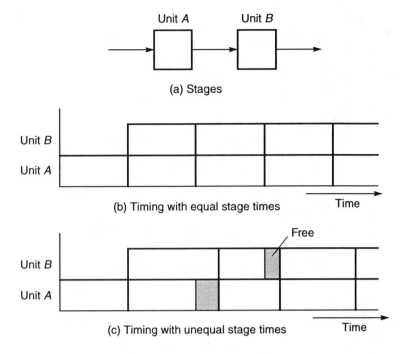

(a) Stages

(b) Timing with equal stage times

(c) Timing with unequal stage times

Figure 5.5 Two stage overlap

depend upon the clock frequency. Pipelines are ideal for situations where latency is not as important as throughput.

Pipelining can be applied to various subunits in a traditional uniprocessor computer and to the overall operation. First, we will consider pipelining applied to overall instruction processing. Later, we shall consider how the arithmetic operations within the execution phase of an instruction can be pipelined. Staging latches are assumed to be present in all of the following.

5.2 Instruction overlap and pipelines

5.2.1 Instruction fetch/execute overlap

The fetch and execute cycles of a processor are often overlapped. Instruction processing requires each instruction to be fetched from memory, decoded, and then executed, in this sequence. In the first instance, we shall assume one fetch cycle fetching a complete instruction and requiring one execute cycle, and no further decomposition. A fetch unit

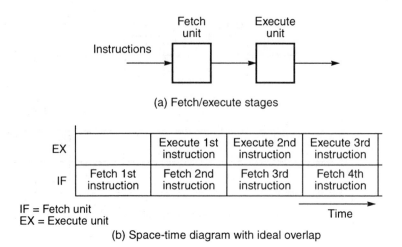

(a) Fetch/execute stages

EX		Execute 1st instruction	Execute 2nd instruction	Execute 3rd instruction
IF	Fetch 1st instruction	Fetch 2nd instruction	Fetch 3rd instruction	Fetch 4th instruction

IF = Fetch unit
EX = Execute unit   Time

(b) Space-time diagram with ideal overlap

Figure 5.6 Fetch unit/execute unit pipeline

fetches an instruction which is passed to an execute unit, as shown in Figure 5.6(a). The execute unit performs the actions to execute the instruction. While the execute unit is executing this instruction, the fetch unit can fetch the next instruction. The space-time diagram of our fetch unit/execute unit pipeline is shown in Figure 5.6(b).

Let us now relate the idea to the actual design presented in Chapter 2. In Chapter 2, we identified the steps required to process an instruction. The pipeline technique is simply one approach to implementing those steps. Those steps performed by the fetch unit are:

```
MAR ← PC
IR ← MDR
PC ← PC + 4
```

The program counter would be accessed by the fetch unit, and could indeed be part of the fetch unit, as shown in Figure 5.7. The MAR and MDR registers are also part of the fetch unit. The execute unit contains all the other components of our design. The output of the fetch unit, i.e., the machine instruction, is passed to the execute unit and loaded into the instruction register, IR, within the execute unit. IR could be the pipeline latch between the fetch unit and execute unit.

The actual steps performed by the execute unit would vary depending upon the instruction fetched. For arithmetic/logic instructions, we have:

```
A ← Rs1;
B ← Rs2
ALUo/p ← A <operation> B
C   ← ALUo/p
```

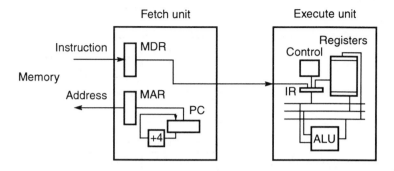

Figure 5.7 Fetch unit and execute unit pipeline

(including the intermediate ALU step). Notice, now we have to include a separate adder in the fetch unit to add 4 to the program counter, rather than use the main ALU, since the ALU is in the execute unit and being used at the same time. Branch and jump instructions can also alter the program counter, and hence there needs to be a path back from the execute unit to the program counter. Branch/jump instructions need special treatment since they can alter the program sequence, and this will be discussed later.

5.2.2 Further overlap

Ideally the stages of the pipeline should require the same time to operate. Clearly the execute unit may operate at a different time to the fetch unit. In particular, it is likely to require more time for complicated instructions, and will dominate the processing time. To reduce this effect, the execute unit could be split into further separate units. A separate instruction decode/operand fetch unit could be provided after the fetch unit, followed by an execute unit as shown in Figure 5.8. This scheme is known as *three-level overlap*. The decode/operand fetch unit is responsible for identifying the instruction, including fetching any operands from registers or memory in order to compute the effective operand address, i.e., for the steps:

        A ← Rs1
        B ← Rs2

in our design. The execute unit performs (for arithmetic/logical instructions):

        ALU$_{o/p}$ ← A <operation> B
        C   ← ALU$_{o/p}$

We could decompose the processor into more pipeline stages to attempt to equalize the unit times. For example, we could have a *four-stage pipeline* having four units, an

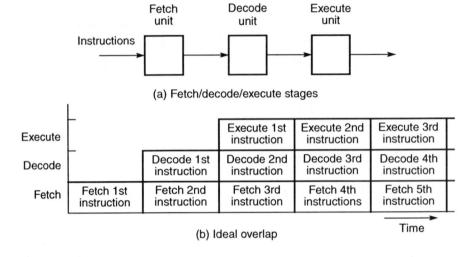

(a) Fetch/decode/execute stages

Execute			Execute 1st instruction	Execute 2nd instruction	Execute 3rd instruction
Decode		Decode 1st instruction	Decode 2nd instruction	Decode 3rd instruction	Decode 4th instruction
Fetch	Fetch 1st instruction	Fetch 2nd instruction	Fetch 3rd instruction	Fetch 4th instructions	Fetch 5th instruction

(b) Ideal overlap   Time

Figure 5.8 Fetch/decode/execute pipeline

instruction fetch unit, an instruction decode/operand fetch unit, an arithmetic/logic execute unit and finally an operand store unit, as shown in Figure 5.9. Now the execute unit performs:

$$ALU_{o/p} \leftarrow A \text{ <operation> } B$$

and the operand store unit performs:

$$C \leftarrow ALU_{o/p}$$

The space-time diagram of this pipeline is shown in Figure 5.10. Here we have simply marked the blocks with the number of the instruction being processed. The information being passed from one stage to the next is that required for receiving stage and subsequent stages. The information is simply passed onwards, together with any results

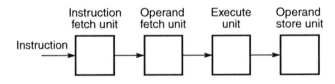

Figure 5.9 Four-stage pipeline

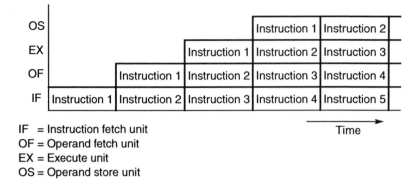

IF   = Instruction fetch unit
OF = Operand fetch unit
EX = Execute unit
OS = Operand store unit

Figure 5.10 Space-time diagram of four-stage pipeline

generated by the stage, in the next cycle. Clearly we could decompose the pipeline further, especially within the execute unit for complex arithmetic operations. We will look into this possibility later.

Notice that space-time diagrams show what each unit is doing at any particular time. Sometimes it is convenient to see the progress of instructions, in an "instruction-time" diagram as shown in Figure 5.11 for the four-stage pipeline. Here we can see clearly when each instruction starts. The diagram shows the same information as the space-time diagram but in a different way. It is also particularly convenient for showing dependencies between instructions at a specific time.

Further instruction processing decomposition can be made. For example, we could have five stages:

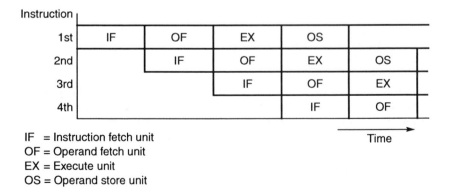

IF   = Instruction fetch unit
OF = Operand fetch unit
EX = Execute unit
OS = Operand store unit

Figure 5.11 Instruction-time diagram of four-stage pipeline

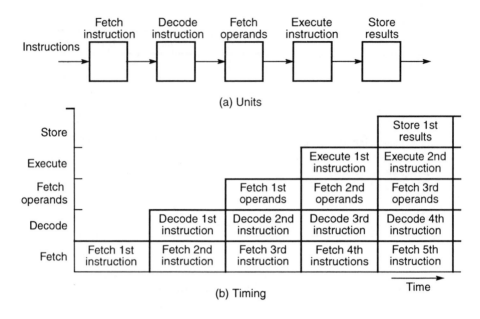

(a) Units

(b) Timing

Figure 5.12   Five-stage instruction pipeline

1. Fetch instruction.
2. Decode instruction.
3. Fetch operand(s).
4. Execute operation (ADD, etc.).
5. Store result.

This is shown in Figure 5.12. Having a separate decode unit and an operand fetch unit is appropriate for a complex instruction set computer (CISC) where the decoding of instructions may be complex. It may not be appropriate for a reduced instruction set computer (RISC) where decoding an instruction may be very simple.

As we divide the processing into more stages and increase the length of the pipeline, we hope to reduce and equalize the stage processing times. However, as we increase the length of the pipeline, more instructions are being processed together. We cannot always process instructions simultaneously in this manner, and the pipeline may have to stop processing instructions for a while. In Section 5.3, we will examine the situations that can cause a pipeline to stop, and methods to avoid having to stop the pipeline.

5.2.3 Pipeline for our RISC processor

Let us briefly look at how our RISC processor could be designed considering first just the arithmetic register-register instructions. In this case a four-stage pipeline is sufficient. The

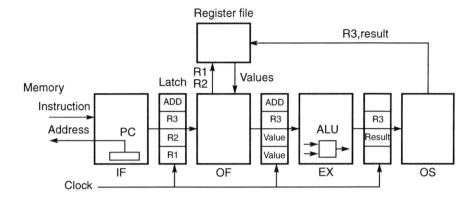

Figure 5.13 Four-stage pipeline with staging latches operating upon register-register instructions

instruction fetch stage will transfer the complete instruction to the operand fetch stage. The operand fetch stage will access the register file to obtain the values of the source operands, which are passed onto the execute stage, together with the opcode and destination fields of the instruction. We could view this as passing the instruction onwards with the source register addresses replaced with the actual values held in the source registers. The execute stage will take the source values and perform the operation as specified by the opcode, and pass onward the result together with the destination register address. The operand store unit will access the register file, using the destination address and pass the result value to the destination register. The arrangement is shown in Figure 5.13. We see that the opcode remains intact until reaching its final destination of the execute unit, and is simply transferred through the intermediate stages. Similarly the destination register field is simply passed through the intermediate stages to reach its final destination of the operand store unit.

By keeping all the information associated with a particular instruction together, it is possible to insert new instructions into the pipeline before previous ones have completed. The observant reader will have noticed that while the nth instruction is writing to the register file, the $(n + 2)$th instruction will be reading from the register file. Clearly this cannot be done to the same register, and is only possible to different registers if the register file has two read ports (for two source operands) and one write port. We did provide this in the centralized design in Chapter 2, though in that design, writing would not be required at the same time as reading.

A popular alternative way of depicting instruction pipelines is to show the instruction and data memories within the stages of the pipeline. This is appropriate especially if these memories are cache memories within the processor (see Chapter 3). An example is shown in Figure 5.14. This does require artistic licence for the data memory being in two places at the same time and we could draw a feedback path from the operand write unit to the

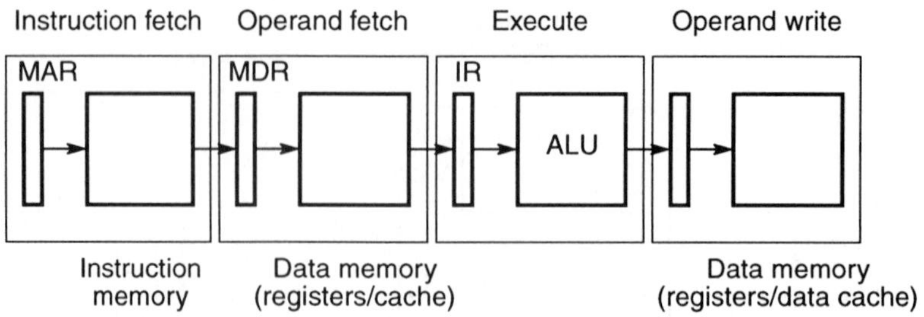

Instruction fetch   Operand fetch   Execute   Operand write

Instruction   Data memory   Data memory
memory   (registers/cache)   (registers/data cache)

Figure 5.14 Alternative way of depicting pipeline showing data register twice

operand fetch unit. (Actually it suggests that the source and destination should not be the same, but of course they may be.) It immediately suggests that the instruction memory and the data memory should be different; this often occurs with cache memory divided in an instruction cache and a data cache.

Our RISC processor is a load/store machine. Accesses are made to memory but only to read memory or to write memory. Hence it is appropriate to have a single pipeline stage for accessing memory. The memory address is computed by register indirect addressing, for both load or store. This suggests the stages:

1. Fetch instruction.
2. Decode/fetch operand from registers.
3. Execute – perform ALU operation or compute effective address.
4. Access memory for writing result or reading memory operand.
5. Write result to register.

Stage 3 is used to compute the effective address for memory access instructions, or to perform arithmetic/logic operations for register-register instructions. Stage 5 is not used for memory write instructions. This pipeline structure is a very common structure for early RISC processors, and is shown in Figure 5.15(a). In a RISC, we do not need arithmetic computations for both the effective address and for arithmetic/logic instructions in one instruction because all arithmetic/logic operations operate upon registers and all memory access instructions are simply load or store. This design illustrates that the pipeline structure is closely connected with the instruction set. It also illustrates a pipeline design in which not all pipeline stages are used for every instruction. Figure 5.15(b) shows the usage of pipeline units for load, store, and arithmetic instructions. Only the load instruction requires all units; arithmetic instructions do not require the memory access unit, and the (memory) store instruction does not require the register store unit. Not using all units does not decrease the throughput. Store instructions simply stop at the end of the fourth cycle and load instructions continue through the fifth cycle.

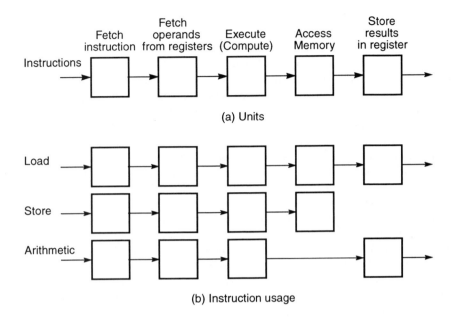

(a) Units

(b) Instruction usage

Figure 5.15   Five-stage instruction pipeline with one stage for accessing memory

5.3 Instruction pipeline hazards

Overlap and pipelining assume there is a sequence of tasks to be performed in one order, with no interaction between tasks other than passing the results of one unit on to the next unit. However, there is interaction between instructions and pipeline units which may require the pipeline to stop (*stall*). We can identify three major causes for breakdown or hesitation of an instruction pipeline (*pipeline hazards*):

1. Resource conflicts.
2. Procedural dependencies (caused notably by branch instructions).
3. Data dependencies.

We will consider these factors separately in the following sections.

5.3.1 Resource conflicts

Resource conflicts occur when a resource such as memory or a functional unit is required by more than one instruction at the same time. Though it may be expensive, in general resource conflicts can always be resolved by duplicating the resource, for example having two memory module ports or two functional units.

A notable resource conflict is the main memory of the system (or the cache if present). For memories with only one read/write port, only one access can be made at any instant. For example, in a five-stage pipeline shown in Figure 5.12 having an instruction fetch unit, an instruction decode unit, an operand fetch unit, execute unit and an operand store unit where both source and destination operands could be in memory, three units might access the memory at the same instant, the instruction fetch unit to fetch an instruction, the operand fetch unit to fetch a source operand, and the operand store unit to store a result in memory. Notice that this can occur even if the instruction set does not have memory-to-memory instructions, as each of the three instructions will be different instructions in the pipeline, the ith instruction is being fetched, the $(i + 2)$th instruction is accessing the source operand, and the $(i + 4)$th instruction is storing the result.

One solution to the problem of reading data operands and writing results at the same time to provide only one pipeline unit for reading data or writing data to memory, as in our five-stage RISC processor pipeline (Figure 5.15). This eliminates data memory conflicts totally as only one instruction at any time can be accessing the data memory. Using only one unit to access memory could not be used with instruction sets having memory-to-memory operations such as the Motorola MC68000 family.

An early method of reducing the problem between fetching instructions and data accesses to memory is to fetch more than one instruction at a time using multiple memory modules or using true memory interleaving (Section 1.3.4). In a two-stage pipeline, the fetch unit could fetch two consecutive instructions simultaneously and then becomes free for two cycles while the execute unit can access the memory as shown Figure 5.16.

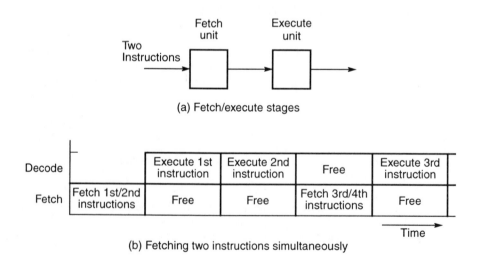

(a) Fetch/execute stages

Decode		Execute 1st instruction	Execute 2nd instruction	Free	Execute 3rd instruction
Fetch	Fetch 1st/2nd instructions	Free	Free	Fetch 3rd/4th instructions	Free

Time

(b) Fetching two instructions simultaneously

Figure 5.16 Fetch/execute overlap

However, none of the units is operating all of the time, and only two instructions are processed in every three cycles. (The method can be extended to further stages; the instruction fetch unit could fetch n instructions simultaneously and be free for n cycles, thereby processing n instructions in $n + 1$ cycles.) Two-way interleaved memory can provide the ideal utilization with the fetch unit fetching one instruction and the execute unit fetching one memory operand in each cycle (assuming only one memory access in the execute cycle). Clearly, memory contention will arise if both the fetch unit and execute unit request the same memory module. An alternative, more common, approach is to provide separate program and data memories, especially at the cache level. Then the fetch unit accesses a different memory to the execute unit.

5.3.2 Procedural dependencies and branch instructions

Although programs are written as a linear sequence, the order of execution may change. Procedural dependencies occur when the execution order is unknown prior to execution of instructions. The most notable cause of procedural dependencies is the branch instruction[1] but there are other causes. For example, CISC instructions may be of variable length, and the length not known until the instruction is partially decoded by the processor. In that case, the location of the next instruction is not known until the length of the previous instruction has been decoded. However let us concentrate upon the most common procedural dependency, namely branch instructions, and more particularly, conditional branch instructions. We shall use the term *target address* as the instruction address given or computed in the branch instruction, i.e. L1 is the target address in the instruction BEQZ R1,L1.

Given no other mechanism, each conditional branch instruction (and the other instructions that follow) could be processed normally in an instruction pipeline. When the branch instruction is completely executed, or at least when the condition can be tested, it would be known which instruction to process next. If this instruction is not the next instruction in the pipeline, all instructions in the pipeline are abandoned and the pipeline cleared. (Hopefully, the abandoned instructions have not altered the state of the processor, i.e., not written to any register, otherwise the changes must be reversed, an expensive operation.) The required instruction is fetched and must be processed through all units in the same way as when the pipeline is first started, and we obtain a space-time diagram such as that shown in Figure 5.17. Unconditional jump instructions have a similar effect, except it may be that the target address can be selected sooner than in a conditional branch instruction.

Typically, 10–20 per cent of instructions in a program are branch instructions and these instructions could reduce the speed of operation significantly. For example, if a five-stage pipeline operated at 10 ns steps, and an instruction which subsequently cleared the pipeline at the end of its execution occurred every ten instructions, the average instruction processing of the ten instructions would be:

---

[1] The term "branch" instructions is used here to include "jump" instructions.

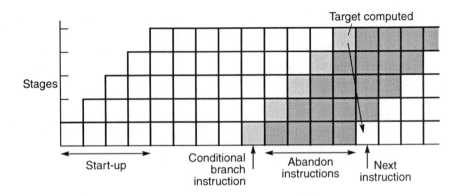

Target computed

Stages

Start-up

Conditional branch instruction

Abandon instructions

Next instruction

Figure 5.17 Effect of conditional branch instruction in a pipeline

$$\frac{9 \times 10 \text{ ns} + 1 \times 50 \text{ ns}}{10} = 14 \text{ ns}$$

i.e. a 40 per cent increase in instruction processing time. The longer the pipeline, the greater the loss in speed due to conditional branch instructions. We have ignored the step-up time of the pipeline, that is, the time to fill the pipeline initially when the system starts executing instructions.

Unconditional branch instructions always cause a change in the sequence. The change is predictable and fixed, but can also affect the pipeline. The fetch unit responsible for fetching instructions takes the value held in the program counter as the address of the next instruction and the program counter is then incremented. Therefore for normal sequential processing, the address of the next instruction is available for the fetch unit immediately the program counter has been incremented, and the fetch unit could keep fetching instructions irrespective of the execution of the instructions. Usually the address of the next instruction even for unconditional branch instructions is not immediately available to the fetch unit. In the case of a relative addressed instruction (as in J L1), the label field of the instruction must be added to the program counter. In the case of a register indirect addressed instruction (as in J [R1]), it must be formed from the contents of the specified register (possibly plus an offset). In any event, the fetch unit does not have the information immediately available and, given no other mechanism, would fetch the next instruction in sequence. It is often assumed that unconditional branch instructions do not cause a serious problem in pipelines. This is not justified with computed effective addresses.

Conditional branch instructions do not always cause a change in the sequence, or even necessarily cause a change in the majority of instances, but this is dependent upon the use of the branch instruction. Conditional branch instructions might typically cause a change 40–60 per cent of the time, on average over a wide range of applications, though in some circumstances the percentage could be much greater or much less. Conditional branch instructions are often used in programs for:

1. Creating repetitive loops of instructions, terminating the loop when a specific condition occurs (loop counter = 0 or arithmetic computational result occurs).
2. To exit a loop if an error condition or other exceptional condition occurs.

The branch usually occurs in 1 when the terminating test is done at the end of the loop (as in DO–WHILE or REPEAT–UNTIL statements), but it does not usually occur in 2 or when the terminating test is done at the beginning of a loop (as in FOR and WHILE statements). Possible uses of conditional branch instructions in loop constructs are FOR, WHILE, and DO–WHILE (in C).

To implement the FOR loop FOR (i=0;i<=100;i++) loop body, we might have:

```
            SUB R4,R4,R4
            ADD R5,R0,100
    L2:     BL  R5,R4,L1            ;Exit if i > 100
                    .
            Loop body
                    .
            ADD R4,R4,1
            J L2
    L1:
```

where i is held in R4. R5 is used to hold the terminating value of i. To implement the WHILE loop WHILE (i==j) loop body, we might have:

```
    L2:     BNE R4,R5,L1
                    .
            Loop body
                    .
            J L2
    L1:
```

where i is held in R4 and j is held in R5. To implement the DO loop body WHILE (i==j), we might have:

```
    L2:             .
            Loop body
                    .
            BEQ R4,R5,L2
```

We can see that a simple change from WHILE to DO–WHILE would change the type of branch instruction. Even the use of conditional branch instructions to detect an error condition may use different branch instructions dependent upon the programmer/compiler. The use is not generally known by the processor.

Strategies exist to reduce the number of times the pipeline breaks down due to conditional branch instructions, using additional hardware, including:

1. Instruction buffers to fetch both possible instructions.
2. Dynamic prediction logic to fetch the most likely next instruction after a branch instruction.
3. Delayed branch instructions.
4. Static prediction.

Instruction buffers

A single first-in first-out instruction buffer is often used in any event to hold instructions fetched from the memory before passing them to the next stage of instruction pipeline. The buffer becomes part of the pipeline as additional delay stages, and extends the length of the pipeline. Extending the pipeline in this way does not decrease the throughput (for a given clock frequency); it only increases the latency. The advantage of a first-in first-out buffer is that it smooths the flow of instructions into the instruction pipeline, especially when the memory is also accessed by the operand fetch unit. It also enables multiple word instructions to be formed. Most recent microprocessors have a pipelined structure with buffers between stages.

The concept of prefetch buffers can be extended to handle the uncertainty of instruction sequences after a branch instruction. Figure 5.18 shows two separate first-in first-out instruction buffers to fetch both possible instruction sequences after a conditional branch instruction. It is assumed that both addresses are available immediately after fetching the branch instruction. Conditional branch instructions cause both buffers to fill with instruc-

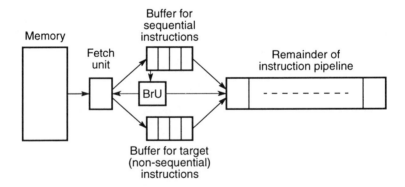

Figure 5.18 Instruction buffers

tions, assumed from an interleaved memory. Decoding and executing the branch instruction to determine the next instruction to be executed begins as soon as the branch instruction is fetched. A separate branch unit (BrU) is shown for this purpose. When the actual next address has been discovered by the branch unit, instructions are taken from the appropriate prefetch buffer and the contents of the other prefetch buffer are discarded. The scheme is sometimes called *multiple prefetching* or *branch bypassing*. Depending upon the detailed timing, the prefetch buffers may hold two to eight instructions. It may be that the prefetch buffer for the non-sequential instructions is smaller than that for the sequential instructions.

Apart for the expense of duplicated hardware, a major disadvantage of multiple prefetching is the problem encountered when more than one conditional branch instruction appears in the instruction stream. With two sequential conditional branch instructions, there are four alternative paths, with three instructions, eight alternative paths and, in general, there are 2^n alternative paths when there are n conditional branch instructions. The number of possible conditional branch instructions to be considered will be given by the number of stages in the pipeline. Of course it is unreasonable to provide a buffer for all alternative paths except for small n.

A technique known as *branch folding* (Lilja, 1988) can be used with a two-stage instruction pipeline having an instruction fetch/decode unit (an I unit) and an instruction execute unit (an E unit). An instruction cache-type buffer is inserted between the I and the E units. Instructions are fetched by the I unit, recognized, and the decoded instructions placed in the instruction buffer, together with the address of the next instruction in an associated field for non-branch instructions. If an unconditional branch instruction is decoded, the next address field of the previous (non-branch) instruction is altered to correspond to the new target location, i.e. the unconditional branch instruction folds into the previous instruction. Conditional branch instructions have two next address fields in the buffer, one for each of the next addresses. The execution unit selects one of the next address paths and the other address is carried through the pipeline with the instruction until the instruction has been fully executed and the branch can be resolved. At that time, either the fetched path is used and the next address carried with the instruction is discarded, or the path of the next address carried with the instruction is used and the pipeline is cleared. The AT&T CRISP processor was the first to use branch folding. The IBM RS 6000 folds many branches which is done by a branch processor.

Another technique is to provide a *loop buffer* which is a small high speed memory for holding instruction loops. Examples can be found in the IBM 360/91, 360/195, Cray 1 and Cray X-MP. Loop buffers are most suitable when a cache is not used.

Prediction logic and branch history

There are various methods of predicting the next address, mainly based upon expected repetitive usage of the branch instruction, though some methods are based upon expected non-repetitive usage. To make a prediction based upon repetitive historical usage, an initial prediction is made when the branch instruction is first encountered. When the true branch instruction target address has been discovered, it is stored in a high speed look-up table, and used if the same instruction at the same address is encountered again. Subsequently, the stored target address will always be the address used on the last occasion. A "stored" bit might be included with each table entry to indicate that a previous prediction has been made. The look-up table can hold various information, the branch tag (the branch instruction address), the branch target address, prediction information, and even the instruction from the branch target address. If the branch instruction is held, this is fetched.

There are variations in the prediction strategy. For example, rather than update the predicted address when it was found to be wrong, allow it to remain until the next occasion and change it then if it is still found to be wrong. This algorithm requires an additional bit stored with each entry to indicate that the previous prediction was correct, but might produce better results. In the extreme, the "run-time execution history" to predict a branch could be based upon the last n executions of the branch. Prediction could also be based upon direction of branch (forward or backward) or branch opcode (Smith, 1981). Notice that it will always be better to choose one path after the branch, if only the next sequential path, rather than simply stop instructions entering the pipeline and wait for the branch to complete because there will be some probability that the path chosen is correct.

The usual form of prediction look-up table is a *branch history table*, also called more accurately a *branch target buffer*, which is implemented in a similar fashion to a cache. A direct mapping scheme could be used, in which target addresses are stored in locations whose addresses are the same as the least significant bits of the addresses of the instructions. The most significant address bits are stored with the target address. We note that, as in the directly mapped data/instruction cache, all branch instructions stored in the cache must have addresses with different least significant bits. Alternatively, a fully associative or a set-associative cache-type table could be employed, as shown in Figure 5.19, when a

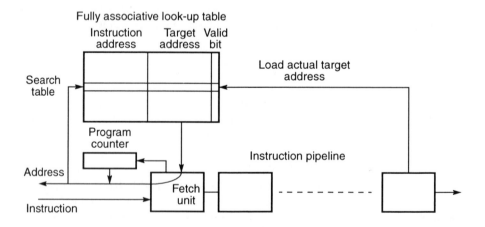

Figure 5.19 Instruction pipeline with branch history table (prediction logic not shown – sequential instructions taken until correct target address loaded)

replacement algorithm is required. In any event, only a limited number of instruction addresses can be stored and at some point we must discard branch information. Though we could use a cache-like LRU replacement algorithm, alternatives are possible; for example, the algorithm could be modified to replace a branch which is least likely to be taken, rather than least likely to be encountered again (assuming that, without any prediction, sequential instructions are fetched).

The branch history table can be designed to be accessed after the decode operation, rather than immediately the instruction is fetched. Then the target address will often be known and hence it is only necessary to store a bit to indicate whether the target address should be taken, rather than the full target address, and the table requires fewer bits. This type of table is called a *decode history table* (Stone, 1987), but it has the disadvantage that the next instruction will have been fetched before the table has been interrogated and so this instruction may have to be discarded.

Branch prediction is possibly in the order of 85–90 per cent with a branch target buffer. They do not require code recompilation or changes in the machine instructions. However they are expensive in hardware, and their effectiveness is affected by context switches. It should be noted that dynamic prediction only works well for branch instructions; other forms of changing the program sequence such as procedural return instructions do not work well here because each return will be to a different location. A separate mechanism can be used for procedural call and return instructions. Wherever a procedural call is made, the return address could be stored in a "prediction stack", a small stack implemented within the processor. Return instructions take addresses from this stack.

Delayed branch instructions

In the delayed branch instruction scheme, branch instructions operate such that the sequence of execution is not altered immediately after the branch instruction is executed (if at all) but after one or more subsequent non-branch instructions, depending upon the design. The subsequent instructions are executed irrespective of the branch outcome. For example, in a two-stage pipeline, a branch instruction might be designed to have an effect after the next instruction, so that this instruction need not be discarded in the pipeline, as shown in Figure 5.20(a). For an n-stage pipeline, the branch instruction could be designed to have an effect after $n - 1$ subsequent instructions, as shown in Figure 5.20(b). Clearly, the instructions after the branch do not affect the branch outcome, and must be such that the computation is still correct by placing the instructions after the branch instruction. It becomes more difficult for the programmer or compiler to find an increasing number of suitable independent instructions to place after a branch instruction. Typically, one instruction can be rearranged to be after the branch instruction in about 70 per cent of occasions, but additional instructions are harder to find.

A one-instruction delayed branch technique has been used extensively in microprogrammed systems at the microinstruction level because microinstructions can often be executed in one cycle and hence can use a two-stage microinstruction fetch/execute pipeline. The one-stage delayed branch instruction also applicable to RISC processors because of their simple instructions and pipeline, and at least it uses one cycle which might be otherwise used. Normally, we might have the sequence:

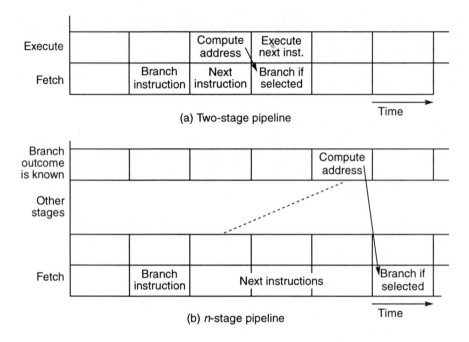

Figure 5.20 Delayed branch technique

```
ADD R3,R4,R5
SUB R2,R2,1
BEQ R2,R0,L1
        .
        .
L1:     .
        .
```

However, the instruction ADD R3,R4,R5, has no influence on whether the branch instruction, BEQ R2,R0,L1, is taken. Using the one-instruction delayed version of the branch instruction, we can move the add instruction to after the branch, i.e.:

```
SUB   R2,R2,1
BEQD  R2,R0,L1
ADD   R3,R4,R5
        .
        .
L1:     .
        .
```

and still have the add instruction execute irrespective of the outcome of the branch instruction, and save one pipeline cycle should the branch be taken which would otherwise be unused.

Delayed versions of branch instructions can be provided in the instruction set or all branches could be designed to act in a delayed fashion. To provide both versions requires one bit allocated in the branch instruction opcode (say 0 for non-delayed version and 1 for delayed version). With all branches automatically delayed, we would use a NOP instruction whenever an instruction could not be found to place after the branch, i.e.:

```
        SUB R2,R2,1
        BEQ R2,R0,L1
        NOP
            .
            .
    L1:     .
            .
```

A compiler can easily insert these NOPs.

A number of refinements have been suggested and implemented to improve the performance of delayed branch instructions. For example, in the *nullification* method for loops, the instruction following a conditional branch instruction at the end of the loop is made to be the instruction at the top of the loop. When the loop is terminated, this instruction is converted into a *no-op*, an instruction with no operation and achieving nothing except an instruction delay.

Static prediction

Static prediction makes the prediction before execution. We could have a very simple hardware prediction which always chooses one way (either always taken, or always not taken). Smith (1981) reports that usually it is slightly more likely (65 per cent to 35 per cent) for a branch to be taken than not taken. However this may be highly dependent upon the applications and compilers.

The compiler knows how a conditional branch is being used in the case of loops and

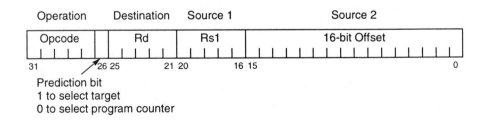

Figure 5.21 Branch instruction format with a prediction bit

compiler inserted error detecting code, and the programmer presumably knows in the case of programmer inserted error detecting code. The compiler/programmer could guide the processor in the choice of the next instruction. This leads to the idea of using a conditional branch instruction which has additional fields to indicate the likely outcome of the branch. For example, a single bit could be provided in the instruction which is a 1 for the fetch unit to select the target address (as soon as it can), and a 0 for the fetch unit to select the next instruction. The instruction might be as shown in Figure 5.21. Here we have effectively created a new set of branch instructions, for example BEQ (select program counter next) and BEQT (select target next). It is then for the compiler/programmer to select the appropriate branch instruction. This technique is particularly attractive for RISC processors where the complexity is taken from the hardware and transferred to the compiler. A static prediction bit is used in the Intel 80960. Reports indicate that one can get 85% accuracy with static bit.

5.3.3 Data dependencies

A data dependency describes the normal situation that the data that instructions use depend upon the data created by other instructions. Instructions depend upon each other in the program and must be executed in a specified order. There are three types of data dependency between instructions, the *true data dependency*, the *antidependency*, and the *output dependency*.

True data dependency

Suppose we have the code sequence:

```
1. ADD R3,R2,R1          ;R3 = R2 + R1
2. SUB R4,R3,1           ;R4 = R3 - 1
```

It would be incorrect to begin reading R3 in instruction 2 before instruction 1 has produced its new value for R3. Hence there is a "data" dependency between instruction 1 and 2. This dependency is called a *true data dependency*. A true data dependency occurs when the value produced by an instruction is required by a subsequent instruction. True data dependencies are also called *read-after-write hazards* because we are reading a value after writing to it. True dependencies are also sometimes known as *flow dependencies* because the dependency is due to the flow of data in the program. In general, they are the most troublesome to resolve in hardware.

Figure 5.22 shows the true data dependency in a four-stage pipeline. Figure 5.22(c) shows how instruction 2 in the pipeline would need to be "stalled" for two cycles while waiting for instruction 1 to complete its register write operation. This is known as a "bubble" in the pipeline. If the two instructions can be separated in the pipeline by independent instructions so that operand reading of one instruction occurs after operand writing of a previous instruction, then the problem of the true dependency can be overcome. Compilers can attempt to reorder the program sequence. (Of course they need

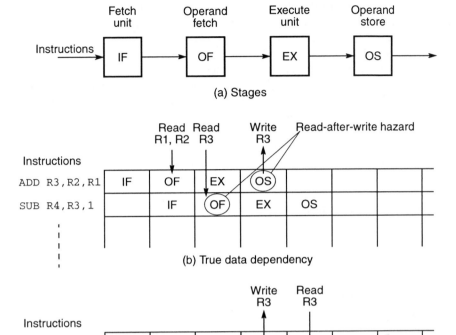

Figure 5.22 True data dependency (Read-after-write hazard)

to know the specific pipeline structure.) However it may not be possible, and we are left with allowing the first instruction to complete before issuing the second instruction from the fetch unit.

Antidependency

Suppose we have the code sequence:

```
1. ADD R3,R2,R1        ; R3 = R2 + R1
2. SUB R2,R3,1         ; R2 = R3 - 1
```

Apart from the true dependency due to R3 being used in both instructions, in this sequence there is another form of dependency. Instruction 2 must not produce its result in R2 before instruction 1 reads R2, otherwise instruction 1 would use the value produced by instruction 2 rather than the previous value of R2. This type of dependency is called an *antidependency* (also called a *write-after-read hazard*) and occurs when an instruction writes to a location which has been read by a previous instruction.

In most pipelines, reading occurs in a stage before writing, so normally if the instructions remain in program order in the pipeline, an antidependency would not be a problem. It becomes a problem if the pipeline structure is such that writing can occur before reading in the pipeline, or the instructions are not processed in program order within the pipeline. The latter situation could occur for example if instructions are allowed to overtake stalled instructions in the pipeline. For example, suppose instruction 1 was stalled because of a resource conflict. Instruction 2 could be allowed to overtake instruction 1 in the pipeline, but then we could have an antidependency (write-after-read hazard). This could also occur with multiple pipelines discussed in Section 5.4.

Output dependency

Suppose we have the code sequence:

```
1. ADD R3,R2,R1        ;R3 = R2 + R1
2. SUB R2,R3,1         ;R2 = R3 - 1
3. ADD R3,R2,R5        ;R3 = R2 + R5
```

Apart from the true and antidependencies previously mentioned, there is a third dependency between instruction 1 and instruction 3. Instruction 1 must produce its result in R3 before instruction 3 produces its result in R3 otherwise instruction 2 might use the wrong value of R2. This type of dependency is called an *output dependency* (also called a *write-after-write hazard*) and occurs when a location is written to by two instructions. Again the dependency would not be significant if all instructions write at the same time in the pipeline and instructions are processed in program order. Actually output dependencies are a form of resource conflict, because the register in question, R3, is accessed by two instructions. The register is being reused and, consequently, the use of another register in the instruction would eliminate the potential problem.

Detecting hazards

Should the programmer know that a pipeline organization exists in the computer used, and also the operation of the pipeline, it may be possible to rewrite some programs to separate data dependencies. Otherwise, when a data dependency does occur, there are two possible strategies:

1. Detect the data dependencies and then hold up the pipeline completely until the dependencies have been resolved (by instructions already in the pipeline being fully executed).
2. Allow all instructions to be fetched into the pipeline but only allow independent

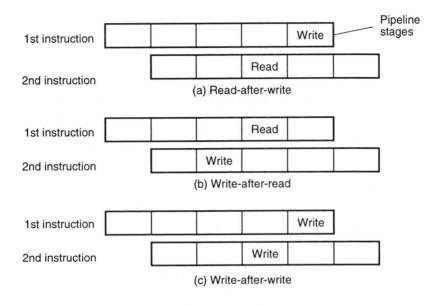

Figure 5.23 Read/write hazards

instructions to proceed to their completion, and delay instructions which are dependent upon other, not yet executed, instructions until these instructions are executed.

Data dependencies can be detected by considering read and write operations on specific locations accessible by the instructions. In terms of two operations, *read* and *write*, operating upon a single location, a *read-after-write* hazard exists if a read operation occurs before a previous write operation has been completed, and hence the read operation would obtain an incorrect value (a value not yet updated). A *write-after-read* hazard exists when a write operation occurs before a previous read operation has had time to complete, and again the read operation would obtain an incorrect value (a prematurely updated value). A *write-after-write* hazard exists if there are two write operations upon a location such that the second write operation in the pipeline completes before the first. Hence the written value will be altered by the first write operation when it completes. *Read-after-read* hazards, in which read operations occur out of order, do not normally cause incorrect results. Figure 5.23 illustrates some of these hazards in terms of an instruction pipeline in which read and write operations are done at various stages.

We can identify a potential hazard between instruction i and instruction j when at least one of the following conditions fails:[2]

---

[2] The three conditions are due to Berstein (1966). We shall use them again in detecting parallelism in Chapter 6.

For read-after-write	$O(i) \cap I(j) = \phi$
For write-after-read	$I(i) \cap O(j) = \phi$
For write-after-write	$O(i) \cap O(j) = \phi$

$O(i)$ indicates the set of (output) locations altered by instruction i; $I(i)$ indicates the set of (input) locations read by instruction i, and ϕ indicates an empty set. Condition code flags must also be included in the hazard detection mechanism. For no hazard, neither of the sets on the left hand side of each condition includes any of the same elements, i.e. all the conditions are satisfied. Clearly these conditions can cover all possible read/write arrangements in the pipeline.

Suppose we have code sequence:

```
1. ADD R3,R2,R1          ;R3 = R2 + R1
2. SUB R5,R1,1           ;R5 = R1 - 1
```

entering the pipeline. Using these conditions, we get: $O(1) = (R3)$, $O(2) = (R5)$, $I(1) = (R1,R2)$, $I(2) = (R1)$. The conditions: $(R3) \cap (R1) = \phi$, $(R2,R1) \cap (R5) = \phi$, $(R3) \cap (R5) = \phi$, are satisfied and there are no hazards.

The method can be extended to cover more than two instructions. The number of hazard conditions to be checked becomes quite large for a long pipeline having many partially completed instructions. For three instructions there are nine conditions that need to be met; for four instructions, 18 conditions, three for each pair of instructions.

Satisfying the conditions are sufficient but not necessary in the mathematical sense. It may be that in a particular pipeline a hazard does not cause a problem. For example, normally all write operations occur in the same pipeline stage, so that a write-after-write hazard will never result in the write operations being out of order (in a single pipeline with instructions kept in order in the pipeline). Similarly a write-after-read hazard may not cause a problem if the stage responsible for a write operation is later in the pipeline than that responsible for a read operation. If fact the only hazard that will cause a problem will be the read-after-write hazard because the stage responsible for a read operation will be before the stage responsible for a write operation. However the other two hazards will also be a problem in pipelines which can be dynamically reconfigured or where there is more than one pipeline (see Section 5.4).

Detecting the hazards at the beginning of the pipeline and stopping the pipeline completely until the hazard has passed is obviously much simpler than only stopping the specific instruction creating the hazard from entering the pipeline, because a satisfactory sequence of operations must be maintained to obtain the desired result (though not necessarily the same order as in the program). Hazard detection must also include any instructions held up at the entrance to the pipeline.

Pipeline interlocks

A relatively simple method of maintaining a proper sequence of read/write operations is to associate a 1-bit tag with each operand register. This tag indicates whether a valid result exists in the register, say 0 for not valid and 1 for valid. A fetched instruction which will write to the register examines the tag and if the tag is 1, it sets the tag to 0 to show that the value will be changed. When the instruction has produced the value, it loads the register and sets the tag bit to 1, letting other instructions have access to the register. Any instruction fetched before the operand tags have been set has to wait. A form of this pipeline interlock technique is used on the Motorola MC88100 RISC microprocessor (Motorola, 1988a). The MC88100 also has delayed branch instructions.

Figure 5.24 shows the mechanism in a four-stage pipeline having registers read only in stage 2 and altered only in stage 4. Figure 5.24 shows a write instruction followed by two read instructions. Suppose the instruction sequence is:

1. ADD R3,R4,4
2. SUB R5,R3,8
3. SUB R6,R3,12

There is a read-after write dependency between instruction 1 and instruction 2 (R3) and a read-after-write dependency between instruction 1 and instruction 3 (again R3). In this case, it is sufficient to reset the valid bit of the R3 register to be altered during stage 2 of instruction 1 in preparation for setting it in stage 4. Both instructions 2 and 3 must examine the valid bit of their source registers prior to reading the contents of the registers, and will hesitate if they cannot proceed.

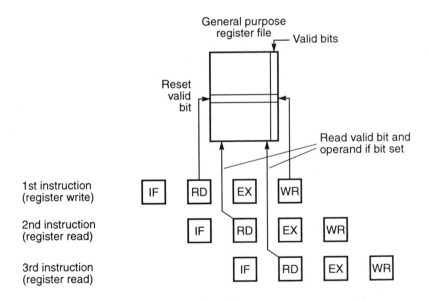

Figure 5.24 Register read/write hazard detection using valid bits (IF, instruction fetch; RD, read operand; EX, execute phase; WR write operand)

The valid bit approach has the potential of detecting all hazards, but write-after-write (output) hazards need special care. For example, suppose the sequence is:

1. `ADD R3,R4,R1`
2. `SUB R3,R4,R2`
3. `SUB R5,R3,R2`

(a very unlikely sequence, but a poor compiler might create such redundant code). There is a write-after-write dependency between instruction 1 and instruction 2. Instruction 1 will reset the valid bit of R3 in preparation to altering its value and move through the pipeline. Instruction 2 immediately behind it would also reset the valid bit of R3 because it too will alter its value, but will find the valid bit already reset. If instruction 2 were to be allowed to continue, instruction 3 immediately behind instruction 2 would only wait for the valid bit to be set, which would first occur when instruction 1 writes to R3. Hence instruction 3 would get the value generated by instruction 1, rather than the value generated by instruction 2 as called for in the program sequence. Hence the proper algorithm would be:

WHILE destination register valid bit = 0 wait.
Set destination register valid bit to 0 and proceed.

Notice that in the four-stage pipeline described, write-after-read hazards do not occur if instruction sequencing is maintained, i.e., if instructions are executed in the order in the program, and if the pipeline is "stalled" by hazards, as in Figure 5.24.

A somewhat more complicated "scoreboard" technique was used in the CDC 6600. The CDC 6600 scoreboard kept a record of the availability of operands and functional units for instructions as they were being processed to allow instructions to proceed as soon as possible and out of sequence if necessary. This is applicable for processors with multiple functional units and pipelines which we shall consider later in Section 5.4. The interested reader should consult Thornton (1970) for details of the CDC 6600 design.

5.3.4 Forwarding

The term *forwarding* refers to the technique of passing the result of one instruction directly to another instruction to eliminate the use of intermediate storage locations. It can be applied at the compiler level to eliminate unnecessary references to memory locations by forwarding values through registers rather than through memory locations. Such forwarding would generally increase the speed of operation, as accesses to processor registers are normally faster than accesses to memory locations. Forwarding can also be applied at the hardware level to eliminate pipeline cycles for reading registers that were updated in a previous pipeline stage. In that case, forwarding eliminates register accesses, by using faster data paths.

Compiler directed forwarding

Let us first look at code changes to eliminate memory accesses. Three types of forwarding can be identified:

1. Store-fetch forwarding.
2. Fetch-fetch forwarding.
3. Store-store overwriting.

Store and fetch refer to writing operands into memory and reading operands from memory respectively. In each case, unnecessary memory references can be eliminated.

In store-fetch forwarding, fetching an operand which has been stored and hence is also held in a processor operand register is eliminated by taking the operand directly from the processor operand register. For example, the code:

```
ST [200],R2              ;Copy contents of R2 register
                         ;into memory location 200
LD R3,[200]              ;Copy contents of memory 200
                         ;to register R3
```

could be reduced to:

```
ST [200],R2
ADD R3,R2,R0
```

which eliminates one memory reference.

In fetch-fetch forwarding, multiple accesses to the same memory location are eliminated by making all accesses to the operand in a processor operand register once it has been read into the register. For example:

```
LD R2,[200]
LD R3,[200]
```

could be reduced to:

```
LD R2,[200]
ADD R3,R2,R0
```

In store-store overwriting, one or more write operations without intermediate operations on the stored information can be eliminated. For example:

```
ST [200],R2
ST [200],R3
```

could be reduced to:

```
ST [200],R3
```

though the last simplification is unlikely in most programs. Rearrangements could be done directly by the compiler/programmer when necessary, or done automatically by the system hardware after it detects the forwarding option, using internal forwarding.

Internal forwarding

Internal forwarding is hardware forwarding implemented by processor registers or data paths not visible to the programmer. It can be applied in an instruction pipeline to eliminate references to general-purpose registers. For example in the code sequence:

```
ADD R3,R2,R0
SUB R4,R3,8
```

the subtract instruction requires the contents of R3, which is generated by the add instruction. The instruction will be stalled in the operand fetch unit waiting for the value of R3 to be come valid. Internal forwarding forwards the value being stored in R3 by the operand store unit directly to the execute unit as shown in Figure 5.25. Without forwarding, the subtract instruction would have to wait for R3 to be updated and then would need to read R3. Though the subtract instruction still needs to be stalled, it is only by one cycle; without forwarding, the stall would be for two cycles.

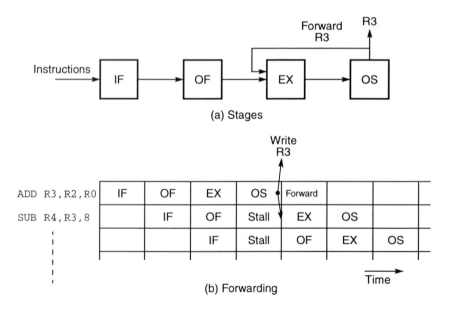

(a) Stages

(b) Forwarding

Figure 5.25 Internal forwarding in a four stage pipeline

Forwarding can be extended to forwarding results to more than one instruction, i.e. in the sequence:

```
ADD  R3,R2,R0
SUB  R4,R3,8
SUB  R5,R3,4
```

both subtract instructions could receive the value held in R3 from the add instruction at the same time. In this pipeline, it is of no advantage to forward to the next instruction even if this instruction requires R3 because the instruction has not yet reached the operand fetch period, and the R3 can be fetched during this period normally. In our five-stage pipeline, we could forward the value of R3 from the memory access unit back to the operand fetch unit and from the operand store unit back to the operand fetch unit, since the value of R3 will be available in the memory access unit.

Forwarding does require considerable extra logic in a pipeline to implement, but is still attractive for boosting the performance of pipelines. RISCs often use internal forwarding in their pipelines. The concept of forwarding can be taken further by recognizing that instructions can execute as soon as the operands they require become available, and not before. Each instruction produces a result which needs to be forwarded to all subsequent instructions that are waiting for this particular result. For example in our sequence of three instructions, we could provide an adder which creates a result for R3, which is forwarded to two subtractors, as shown in Figure 5.26. This idea was developed fully in the IBM 360 Model 91, as reported by Tomasulo (1967). The IBM 360 Model 91 is now only of historical interest and was rapidly superseded by other models with caches (the Model 85 and the Model 195). In Tomasulo internal forwarding, the results generated by an arithmetic unit are passed directly to the input of an arithmetic unit, by matching the destination address carried with the result with the addresses of the units available. Operand pairs are held in buffers at the input of the units. Operations are only executed when a unit receives a full complement of operands, and then new results, which may become new source operands, are generated. It may be that instructions are not executed in the sequence in which they are held in memory, though the final result will be the same. The IBM 360 Model 91 internal forwarding mechanism is similar to dataflow

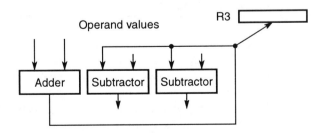

Figure 5.26 Forwarding using multiple functional units

computing described in Chapter 10 and predates the implementation of the latter. A cache could also be regarded as a forwarding scheme which short-circuits the main memory. The complicated forwarding scheme of the Model 91 may not be justified if a cache is present. Indeed, this was the main reason for the demise of the model 91. However, the method has reappeared in superscalar processor designs (see Section 5.4).

5.3.5 Multithreaded processor

We have assumed that the instructions being processed are from one program and that they depend upon the immediately preceding instructions. However, many large computer systems operate in a multiuser environment, switching from one user to another at intervals. Such activities often have a deleterious effect on cache-based systems, as instructions/data for a new program need to be brought into the cache to replace the instructions/data of a previous program. Eventually, the instructions/data of a replaced program will need to be reinstated in the cache.

In contrast, this process could be used to advantage in a pipeline, by interleaving instructions of different programs in the pipeline and by executing one instruction from each program in sequence. This is known as *multistreaming* or a *multithreaded processor*. For example, if there are ten programs to be executed, every tenth instruction would be from the same program. In a ten-stage pipeline, each instruction would be completely independent of the other instructions in the pipeline and no hazard detection for conditional jump instructions or data dependencies would be necessary. The instructions of the ten programs would execute at the maximum pipeline rate of one instruction per cycle. This technique necessitates a complete set of processor registers for each program. For ten programs, ten sets of operand registers are needed, ten program counters, ten memory buffers, and tags are also needed in the instruction to identify the program. In the past, such duplication of registers might have been difficult to justify, but now it may be a reasonable choice, given that the maximum rate is obtained under the special conditions of several time-shared programs and no complicated hazard detection logic is necessary. The scheme may be difficult to expand to more time-shared programs than the number of stages in the pipeline.

5.4 Superscalar processors

A conventional "scalar" processor executes scalar instructions, i.e., instructions operating upon single operands such as integers. A *superscalar* processor is a processor which executes more than one (scalar) instruction concurrently. A limited form of superscalar operation is often present in processors that have integer and floating point instructions. An integer unit is provided for executing integer instructions and a separate floating point unit for executing floating point instructions. Instructions are then sent to the appropriate unit after the decode stage. Then both integer and floating point instructions could be executed simultaneously.

True superscalar operation is achieved by fetching more than one instruction simultaneously, and then executing more than one instruction simultaneously. Given a pipeline structure, a superscalar processor requires more than one pipeline, one pipeline for each instruction to be processed concurrently. Figure 5.27 shows the timing of a superscalar processor having two five-stage pipelines. Each pipeline stage has been effectively "widened" to accommodate two instructions. Now two instructions are fetched and executed simultaneously.[3]

The timing in Figure 5.27 suggests that pairs of instructions would be executed together, and the processor would operate twice as fast as the scalar version. However this cannot always be achieved because instruction sequences may be interdependent. It is often necessary to execute one instruction completely before a subsequent instruction. The key consideration is to identify which instructions are not interdependent and can be executed simultaneously. This consideration is also applicable to single pipeline scalar processors as several instructions are processed within the pipeline, but is much more critical for superscalar processors.

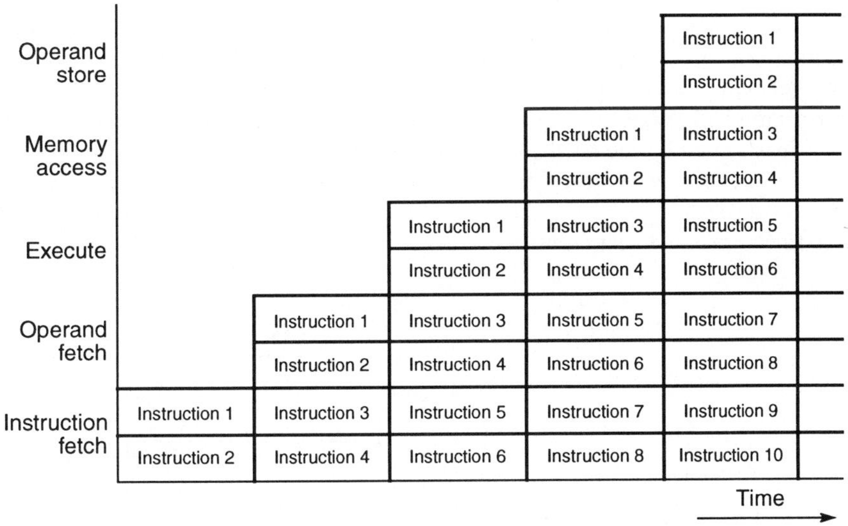

Operand store					Instruction 1
					Instruction 2
Memory access				Instruction 1	Instruction 3
				Instruction 2	Instruction 4
Execute			Instruction 1	Instruction 3	Instruction 5
			Instruction 2	Instruction 4	Instruction 6
Operand fetch		Instruction 1	Instruction 3	Instruction 5	Instruction 7
		Instruction 2	Instruction 4	Instruction 6	Instruction 8
Instruction fetch	Instruction 1	Instruction 3	Instruction 5	Instruction 7	Instruction 9
	Instruction 2	Instruction 4	Instruction 6	Instruction 8	Instruction 10

Time →

Figure 5.27 Superscalar processor timing with two pipelines

[3] An alternative approach is to increase the clock rate so that each basic stage (IF, OF, EX, MEM, OS, above) requires more than one pipeline cycle. Only one instruction enters the pipeline on each cycle. This technique is known as *superpipelining* and can achieve similar performance to a superscalar design but requires a higher clock rate, see Jouppi and Wall (1989) for further details. It is possible to use both superscalar and superpipeline techniques.

One approach to designing a superscalar processor is to simply duplicate the pipelines of a scalar processor, each of which operates semi-independently. This is quite convenient for enhancing an existing scalar processor design and is shown in Figure 5.28. The Intel Pentium has this form of design, with two pipelines, each with its own ALU. Notice that it will always be necessary to fetch more than one instruction in one cycle if we intend to execute more than one instruction in each cycle. Hence the instruction memory will need to be widened to access more than one instruction simultaneously, perhaps simply by having a wider data path and multiple memory modules. Then the instructions fetched would be consecutive instructions in memory. Memory interleaving could be used, but is probably is not justified here as instructions are often sequential.

A more integrated approach can be taken to superscalar pipeline design, as shown in Figure 5.29. A fetch unit fetches more than one instruction which are passed to an operand fetch unit. The instructions are issued to different execute units after operands become available. Instruction buffers are provided to hold instructions waiting for their operands. Each execute unit may have different characteristics and instructions are then sent to an execute unit suitable for the instruction. Notice in branch, load, and store are provided with separate execution units rather than trying to integrate these instructions into a single pipeline as in our five-stage scalar processor design.

We will concentrate upon the form of superscalar design in Figure 5.29. The Intel P6 processor, the successor to the Pentium (Halfhill, 1995) has broadly this form of design, with reservation stations and a reorder buffer (see later for details of these items). In any superscalar design, there are dependencies between instruction which means that certain instructions cannot be executed simultaneously. We identified three types of data dependencies, true data dependency (read-after-write dependency), antidependency (write-after-read dependency), and output dependency (write-after-write dependency). Anti-dependencies may not be a problem in a scalar processor with a single pipeline if instruc-

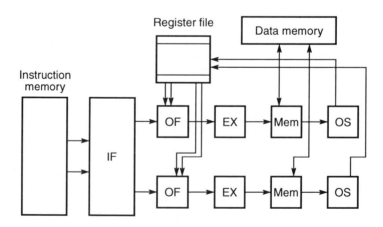

Figure 5.28 Dual pipeline processor

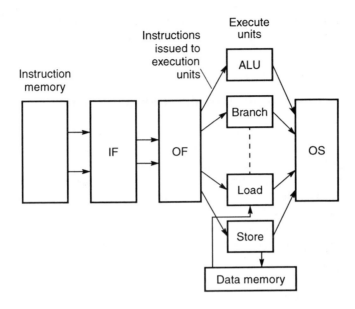

Figure 5.29 Superscalar design with specialized execution units

tions are executed in the order given in the program and write operations always occur after read operations in the pipeline. However they are a problem if the execution sequence is changed, for example by allowing instructions to overtake a stalled instruction. This is known as *out-of-order issue* of instructions. *In-order issue* of instructions describes the situation in which instructions leave the operand fetch unit in program order. Either way, usually instructions may finish execution out-of-order (*out-of-order completion*). *In-order completion* is rarely enforced. For example in the sequence:

```
MUL R1,R2,R3
ADD R4,R5,R6
```

even if we issue the MUL instruction before the ADD instruction, the MUL instruction is likely to require more cycles and will complete after the ADD instruction.

All dependencies are a definite problem in superscalar processors with their multiple pipelines and out-of-order issue/out-of-order completion. Another factor which does not occur in scalar designs but appears in superscalar designs is a resource conflict for a functional unit. Suppose we have the sequence:

```
ADD R1,R2,R3
SUB R4,R5,R6
```

There are no instruction dependencies. However suppose only one ALU is provided, as in

Figure 5.29, and this ALU is responsible for both addition and subtraction. Clearly both ADD and SUB instructions cannot be executed together in such a design. The number of functional units provided will be a compromise between cost and possible resource conflicts.

5.4.1 Implementing out-of-order instruction issue

To show how to deal with out-of-order issue and associated dependencies, consider the representative processor in Figure 5.30. The overall arrangement is similar to our scalar design, except that complete instructions with their operands are passed to functional units. Multiple functional units are provided for superscalar operation. The load and store units access the data memory and contain all the necessary circuitry to implement load and store instructions. We show only one ALU, but more than one could be provided, depending upon the expected usage of the units. Only integer operations are handled in our design. Additional units and registers could be provided for floating point operations.

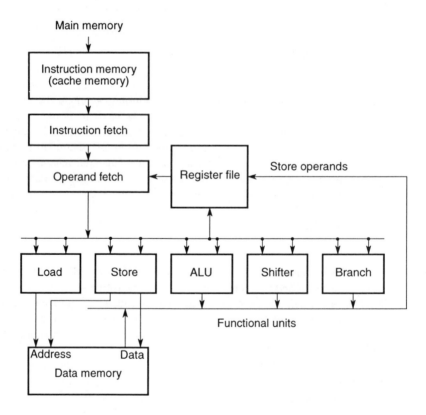

Figure 5.30 Superscalar (integer) processor model

Typically, however, floating point instructions use a separate floating point register file and may be completely distinct from the integer unit.

To achieve out-of-order issue, an instruction buffer called an *instruction window* is used. The instruction window is placed between the fetch and execute stages and is used to hold instructions waiting to be executed. Instructions are issued from the window whenever it is possible to execute the instructions, which occurs when the operands the instruction needs are available and the functional unit required for the operation is free. The instruction window can be implemented in two ways:

1. Centralized or
2. Distributed.

5.4.2 Centralized instruction window

Figure 5.31 shows the position of a centralized instruction window. A centralized instruction window holds all pending instructions irrespective of their type. When an instruction has its operands and can be issued, it is routed to the appropriate functional unit for execution. More than one bus is provided to allow the issue of multiple instructions. The centralized instruction window mechanism could be controlled using valid bits as described in Section 5.3.3. Instructions are fetched and loaded into the instruction window. Required operands are fetched from the register file. If an operand is not available (not yet updated by a previous instruction), the valid bit will be reset. In that case, the register identifier is stored in the instruction window in place of the operand value. Hence the instruction window will hold instructions with operands or register identifiers as shown in Figure 5.32. Only when an instruction has all its operands can it be released to the appropriate functional unit for execution. When an instruction does update a register value, the instruction window must also be accessed and any matching register identifiers replaced by operand values. Thus updating the register file and instruction window occurs simultaneously. The instruction window must be implemented using content addressable memory. In our example, instructions 1, 2, 3, and 5 each have one of their source operand values, but have to wait for the other one. Instruction 4 has both its operand values and can be issued from the instruction window.

More than one instruction may be ready after a value has been updated, and all ready instructions should be issued if possible. The centralized instruction window must also select an appropriate functional unit if there are more than one, and logic is required for this.

When an instruction has been issued from the instruction window, the entry is deallocated and can be used for an incoming instruction. However program order must be maintained. In the *dispatch stack* version of the instruction window, existing instruction window entries are moved down filling empty entries and new instructions entered at the top of the window. In the *register update unit* version of the instruction window, the instruction window also operates a first-in first-out queue but with all entries moved down including empty entries. This has somewhat simpler logic.

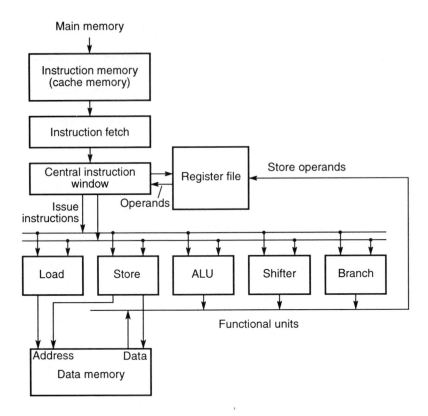

Figure 5.31 Superscalar processor with centralized instruction window

Instruction	Opcode	Destination register	Operand 1	Operand 1 register	Operand 2	Operand 2 register
1	Operation	ID	Operand value			ID
2	Operation	ID	Operand value			ID
3	Operation	ID		ID	Operand value	ID
4	Operation	ID	Operand value		Operand value	
5	Operation	ID		ID	Operand value	ID

Figure 5.32 Instruction window contents

5.4.3 Distributed instruction window

In the distributed instruction window approach, the instruction buffers called *reservation stations* are placed at the front of each functional unit. Decoded instructions are routed to the appropriate reservation station and subsequently issued to the function unit when all the required operands are received at the reservation station, and the function unit is free. Figure 5.33 shows the positions of the distributed instruction window approach. Now when the register file is updated, the reservation stations are accessed and any register identifiers replaced with operand values.

The number of instructions that are independent and could be issued simultaneously will vary within a program and between programs. Typically it might average about 2–3 instructions with occasionally 5–6 or even more being possible at times. The instruction window mechanism must be able to support multiple issue. This is generally easier to do with the distributed instruction window than with a centralized instruction window as the distributed buffers can be loaded at a lower rate than the potential instruction issuance.

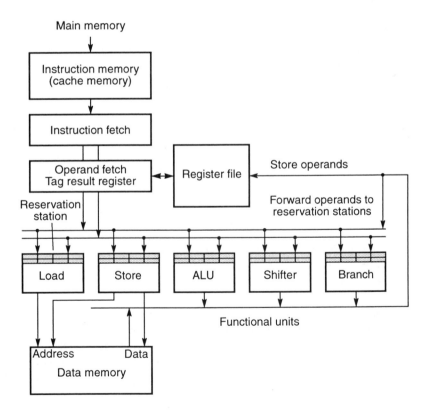

Figure 5.33 Reservation stations (without renaming, see later)

The connections between a centralized window and functional units would require a much higher bandwidth than using the distributed instruction window. However a centralized instruction window is more efficient storage as the locations can be used for any type of instruction.

The size of each reservation station does not need to be the same. Each functional unit could have a different size of reservation station depending upon the expected number of decoded instructions for it (say as determined by simulation studies). Reservation stations with two or three entries are typically sufficient. Each reservation could issue one instruction to its function unit simultaneously. If more than one instruction is ready in one reservation station, then they are executed in the sequence loaded (though this does not matter if all dependencies have been resolved).

In the mechanism so far described, the register window only allows one pending update to a given register. Instructions with output dependencies must be stalled during decode. The instruction window mechanism alone simply deals with out-of-order issue of instructions. Now let us look at how to deal with instruction dependencies.

5.4.4 Register renaming

Antidependencies and output dependencies are caused essentially by reusing storage locations, i.e., they are resource conflicts. As mentioned, resource conflicts in general can be reduced by duplicating the resource. Consequently the effects of these dependencies can be reduced by duplicating the storage locations. Assuming the dependencies are caused by writing to registers, we can duplicate registers.

Suppose we have the sequence:

```
ADD R1,R2,R4          ;R1 = R2 + R4
ADD R2,R1,1           ;R2 = R1 + 1
ADD R1,R4,R5          ;R1 = R4 + R5
```

which has several dependencies. (It also has a resource conflict if there is only one adder.) By introducing new registers, R1* and R2*, we have:

```
ADD R1,R2,R4          ;R1 = R2 + R4
ADD R2*,R1,1          ;R2* = R1 + 1
ADD R1*,R4,R5         ;R1* = R4 + R5
```

eliminating the antidependency and output dependency. Clearly we cannot keep creating new registers throughout the program. In any event, it would be undesirable to have a very large number of registers within the processor from an implementation point of view (increased hardware, complexity of handling interrupts, etc.) A solution is to rename existing registers temporarily. R1 might be temporarily be called R1a, R1b, R1c ... as R1 is being reused in the program, and similarly for other registers, i.e.

```
ADD R1a,R2a,R4a
```

```
ADD R2b,R1a,1
ADD R1b,R4,R5
```

This is known as *register renaming*. Register renaming can remove both antidependencies and output dependencies, and is implemented in hardware. New register instances are created and destroyed when there are no outstanding references to the stored values.

5.4.5 Reorder buffer

Register renaming can be achieved with a *reorder buffer*. A reorder buffer is a first-in, first-out queue with entries that are dynamically allocated to instruction register results. The reorder buffer is placed as shown in Figure 5.34. A centralized or distributed instruction window would also be present. Figure 5.34 shows a distributed instruction window.

When an instruction which writes to a register is decoded, it is allocated an entry at the top of the queue. (Instructions which do not write to a register do not need an entry in the

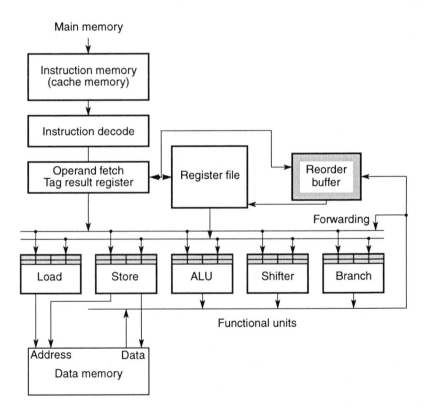

Figure 5.34 Reorder buffer with reservation stations

reorder buffer because there are no output or antidependencies.) Instruction results are written to the reorder buffer entry. When the entry reaches the bottom of the queue, and the value has been written, it is transferred to the register file. If the value has not been written by this time, the queue does not advance until the value has been written. Since the reorder buffer allocates entries to registers, register identification numbers must be stored in entries which are used in an associative look-up using content addressable memory. There may be more than one entry corresponding to a specific register, e.g., R1a, R1b, R1c, etc. A unique tag is generated for each entry and this is entered if the value for the register has not been computed. These tags identify uncomputed values. Hence the entries in the reorder buffer might look like Figure 5.35.

When an instruction is decoded and source register operands are required, a look-up is performed on the reorder buffer. If no matching register is found, then the register file is accessed. If an entry is found in the reorder buffer, either the value is read if present and loaded into the reservation station, or the tag is read and loaded into the reservation station. When a result is written to the reorder buffer replacing tags, at the same time tags are also replaced by values in the reservation stations. For this to occur, the result tags are carried through the functional units and passed with the results to both the reservation stations and the reorder buffer. A similar operation would occur with a centralized instruction window. In this case, the tags in the centralized window are replaced with results. The general algorithm for processing instructions is shown in Figure 5.36.

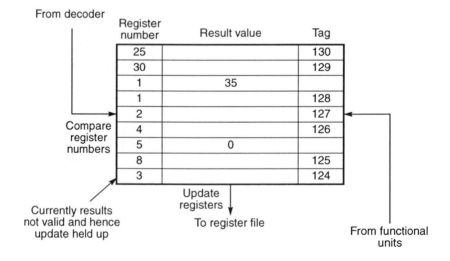

Figure 5.35 Reorder buffer organization

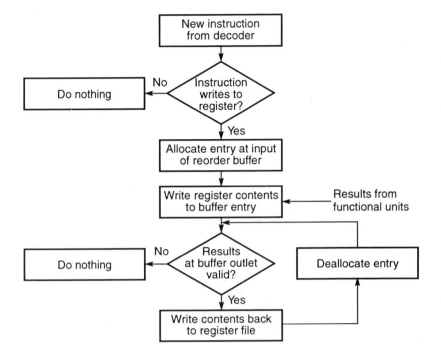

Figure 5.36 Reorder buffer update algorithm

5.5 Interrupt handling

One of the most perplexing parts of design processor is how to handle hardware inter-rupts. The term *interrupt* is the name given to a mechanism whereby the processor can stop executing its current program and respond to an event. This event could be within the processor or external to the processor. The term *exception* is sometimes also used to describe all types of the interrupts (notably by Motorola). More useful though is to use the term exception to describe an exceptional condition occurring with the program such as arithmetic overflow, and reserve the term interrupt to describe an asynchronous external event not directly related to the current program. External interrupts use at least two signals, an interrupt request signal from the interface/device requesting a response, and an interrupt acknowledge signal from the processor to the requesting interface/device, generate by the processor when it is ready to respond to the interrupt request. The external interrupt (request) signal may be generated at any time and is not externally syn-chronized with the internal clock of the processor. The processor may be executing a machine instruction, and generally cannot respond until at least this instruction has been completed. Therein is our problem for a pipelined processor; more than one instruction will be in the process of being executed at any instant, and we would rather not have to wait until all instructions within the pipeline have executed before responding to the interrupt – because interrupts are generally used to get a response to important time-critical events.

Interrupts can be handled as *precise interrupts* or *imprecise interrupts*. For a precise interrupt, sufficient information must to stored to enable the processor to restart at the exact point where it was interrupted. The processor state to be saved includes the contents of the registers, the program counter, condition register, index registers, and that portion of the main memory being used for data. If instructions are being issued and executed out-of-order, implementing precise interrupts is very costly. It may be that some if not all instructions in the pipeline have to be allowed to complete, thereby introducing significant latency in responding to an interrupt. For an imprecise interrupt, not all information is stored to enable the processor to restart exactly where it was interrupted. It may be that both precise and imprecise interrupts are supported.

A number of potential interrupt implementations have being suggested. Hwu and Patt (1987) proposed using checkpoints which divide the instruction stream into sections to reduce the cost of restoring the processor state. Some other methods are given in Smith and Pleszkum (1988). Torng and Day (1993) use a centralized instruction window in their proposed precise interrupt mechanism. A treatment of interrupt in complex processors is outside the scope of this book. Walker and Cragon (1995) provides a good overview of designs.

5.6 Arithmetic pipelines

5.6.1 General

In the previous sections we considered the arithmetic units as single entities. In fact, arithmetic operations of the execute phase could be decomposed further into several separate operations. We will briefly consider how arithmetic operations might be pipelined in the following sections. Pipelined arithmetic units are used for the following reasons:

1. Increased performance should a series of similar computations be encountered.
2. Reduced logic compared to non-pipelined designs in some cases.
3. Multifunction units might be possible.

When a pipeline is continuously supplied with tasks, it will provide results on every cycle even if each computation requires several pipeline stages. Consequently if a processor has to perform a series of similar computations which are heavy pipelined (with several pipeline stages) it will produce results at a higher rate. Of course, we usually do not expect a general-purpose processor to be, say, continuously doing addition. However there are applications which require a series of identical operations, notably vector and matrix operations where a element of array may be operated upon in a similar way. Since such applications are very important, a special type of computer called a *vector computer* or *vector processor* has been developed to be efficient for vector and array operations. Such processors are heavily pipelined. We will review these processors later in Section 5.7.

Reduced logic can be achieved by reusing pipeline stages, so that intermediate results pass back to a previous pipeline stage rather than to a new pipeline stage. Such pipelines are called *feedback pipelines*. A feedback pipeline will have reduced performance over an equivalent non-feedback pipeline because new tasks cannot be inserted into the pipeline on every cycle; a previous task may have been fed back and be using a pipeline stage again. The general motive for designing feedback pipelines is reduction in hardware, compared to a non-feedback pipeline. New inputs cannot be applied to a feedback pipeline (at least not when the feedback is to the input) until previous results have been generated and consumed, and hence this type of pipeline does not necessarily increase throughput, and externally the unit may not be regarded as a pipeline. We will use the term *linear pipeline* to describe a pipeline without feedback paths.

Multifunction arithmetic pipelines can be designed with internal paths that can be reconfigured statically to produce different overall arithmetic functions, or can be reconfigured dynamically to produce different arithmetic functions on successive input operands. In a dynamic pipeline, different functions are associated with sets of operands as they are applied to the entrance of the pipeline. The pipeline does not need to be cleared of existing partial results when a different function is selected and the execution of previous functions can continue unaffected. Multifunction pipelines have not been used much in practice because of the complicated logic required, but they should increase the performance of a single pipeline in scalar processors. Multifunction pipelines do not seem to have an advantage in vector computers, as these computers often perform the same operation on a series of elements fed into the pipeline.

First we will give a couple of examples, and then describe pipeline control algorithms.

5.6.2 Floating point pipelines

Floating point is the name given to the internal representation of "real" numbers in a high level language (a number which may have a fractional part and may be raised to a power). In fact some languages, notably C, use the reserved word FLOAT for such numbers. For example, we might declare Pi in the C language as:

```
FLOAT Pi = 3.142
```

Given that we have such numbers, there must be an internal binary representation. Normal integer representation is insufficient. Also we would prefer a processor designed to be capable of processing the internal representation at high speed.

Each floating point number is represented by a mantissa and exponent, given by:

$$\text{number} = \text{mantissa} \times \text{base}^{\text{exponent}}$$

where the base of the number system is 2 for internal binary representation[4] and 10 for external representation in programs. Internally the number is stored in a register or memory location, usually 32 bits or 64 bits long. (The IEEE has set standards to make it easier to interchange information.) Two's complement representation is not used for either the mantissa or the exponent for implementation reasons. The sign of the number, a positive mantissa, and exponent are stored in separate fields.

Numbers are also usually stored in a *normalized* form in which the most significant digit of the (positive) mantissa is made to be non-zero (i.e. 1 for a base of 2) and the exponent adjusted accordingly, to obtain the greatest possible precision of the number (the greatest number of significant digits in the mantissa). In fact, the most significant bit is not stored because it is always 1. The stored mantissa is normally a fraction, i.e. the binary point is to the immediate left of the stored mantissa.

A biased exponent representation is used for the exponent such that the stored exponent is always positive, even when representing a negative exponent. In the 2's complement representation, the range of numbers is from -2^{n-1} through $+2^{n-1} - 1$ where there are n bits in the number. In the biased exponent system, the stored exponent = actual 2's complement exponent + bias. To make the range positive, the bias could be -2^{n-1}. In the IEEE standard, the bias is $2^{n-1} - 1$. The actual exponents -2^{n-1} and $-2^{n-1} + 1$ are not used to represent normalized numbers so the bias changes the actual range of the exponent to a stored positive range from 1 through $2^n - 2$. The stored exponent 0 with a mantissa of zero is used to represent zero and the stored exponent $2^n - 1$ is used to indicate "not-a-number". The biased exponent representation makes it easier to implement the comparison of exponents which is necessary in floating point addition (not in floating point multiplication).

Floating point arithmetic is particularly suitable for pipeline implementation as a sequence of steps can be readily identified. It is perhaps the commonly quoted example for pipeline implementation. Even in a non-pipelined computer system, floating point arithmetic would normally be computed as a series of steps (whereas fixed point arithmetic might be computed in one step.) Usually a separate ALU is provided for floating point arithmetic. Floating point instructions would be routed to the floating point unit. Since floating point instructions usually use dedicated floating point registers, it is common to provide a completely separate internal structure for floating point operations, with separate internal buses and register files.

A typical floating point instruction would be:

```
FADD FR1,FR2,FR3
```

where the registers FR2 and FR3 hold floating point numbers and the register FR1 will hold the floating point result of adding FR2 and FR3. The addition of two normalized

---

[4] Internally, the base could also be a power of 2, for example 16, but this is not used much today.

floating point numbers, represented by the mantissa/exponent pairs, m_1e_1 and m_2e_2, requires a number of sequential steps, for example:

1. Subtract exponents e_1, e_2, and generate the difference $e_1 - e_2$.
2. Interchange mantissa m_1 and m_2, if $e_1 - e_2$ is negative and make the difference positive. Otherwise no action is performed in this step.
3. Shift mantissa m_2 by $e_1 - e_2$ places right.
4. Add mantissas to produce result mantissa replacing m_2.
    (Subtract for floating point subtraction)
5. Normalize result as follows. If mantissa greater than 1, shift one place right and add 1 to exponent. If mantissa less than 0.5, shift mantissa left until leftmost digit = 1 and subtract number of shifts from exponent. If mantissa = 0, load special zero pattern into exponent. Otherwise do nothing. Check for underflow (number too small to be represented) or overflow (number too large to be represented) and in such cases generate the appropriate actions.

Figure 5.37 shows the floating point pipeline. Some steps might be divided further, and any group of sequential steps in a pipeline can be formed into one step.

Floating point multiplication is conceptually easier, having the steps:

1. Add exponents e_1 and e_2.
2. Multiply mantissa m_1 and m_2.
3. Normalize if necessary.
4. Round mantissa to a single length result.
5. Renormalization if necessary (rounding may increase mantissa one digit which necessitates renormalization).

The mantissa multiplication operation would typically be divided into two or more stages (perhaps iterative stages with feedback) which would make floating point multiplication a longer process than floating point addition. It is possible to combine floating point multiplication with addition, as the exponent addition of the floating point multiplication and the exponent subtraction of floating point addition could both be performed with a parallel adder. Also, both operations require normalization. A floating point multiply/

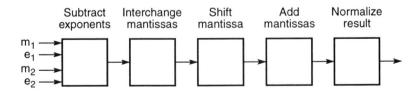

Figure 5.37 Floating point pipeline

divide unit can be designed as a feedback pipeline by internally feeding back partial product results until the final result is obtained.

5.6.3 Fixed point arithmetic pipelines

Often fixed point (integer) arithmetic units are not heavily pipelined, but let us look at how they could be pipelined, as a precursor to formal techniques on pipeline design. The conventional method of adding two integers (fixed point numbers) is to use a parallel adder consisting of cascaded full adder circuits. Suppose the two numbers to be added together have digits $A_{n-1} \ldots A_0$ and $B_{n-1} \ldots B_0$. There are n full adders in the parallel adder. Each full adder adds two binary digits, A_j and B_j, together with a "carry-in" from the previous addition, C_{i-1}, to produce a sum digit, S_i, and a "carryout" digit, C_i, as shown in Figure 5.38(a). One pipelined version of the parallel adder is shown in Figure 5.38(b). Here, the n full adders have been separated into different pipeline stages.

A multifunction version of the parallel adder pipeline giving both addition and subtraction can be achieved easily. Subtraction, A − B, can be performed in a parallel adder by complementing the B digits and setting the carry-in digit to the first stage to 1 (rather than to 0 for addition), assuming 2's complement representation. Hence, one of each pair of digits passed on to the adjacent stage needs to be complemented and this operation can be incorporated into the pipeline stage. The adder/subtractor pipeline could be static. In this case, the complementing operation occurs on the appropriate bits of each pair of operands applied to the pipeline as they pass through the pipeline. Alternatively, the adder/subtractor pipeline could be dynamic, and the complementing operation performed upon specific operands. These operands could be identified by attaching a tag to them; the tag is passed from one stage to the next with the operands. Additional functions could be incorporated, for example, single operand increment and decrement. Multiplication and division might be better performed in a separate unit, though it is possible to design a multifunction pipeline incorporating all of the basic arithmetic operations.

The previous addition pipeline is based upon a parallel adder in which the carry signal "ripples" from one pipeline stage to another. In a non-pipelined version, the speed of operation is limited by the time it takes for the carry to ripple through all the full adders. (This is also true in the pipelined version, but other additions can be started while the process takes place.) A well-known method of reducing ripple time is to predict the carry signals at each full adder by using *carry-look-ahead* logic rather than waiting for each to be generated by adjacent full adders. Such prediction logic can also be pipelined. The full details of carry-look-ahead adders can be found in many logic design books including Wilkinson (1992c).

There are also various ways to perform multiplication. Most of these are suitable for arrangement as a pipeline as they involve a series of additions, each of which can be done in a pipeline stage. The conventional method to implement multiplication is a shift-and-add process using a parallel adder to successively add A to an accumulating sum when the appropriate bit of B is 1. Hence, one pipeline solution would be to unfold the iterative process and have n stages, each consisting of a parallel adder.

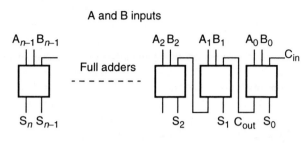

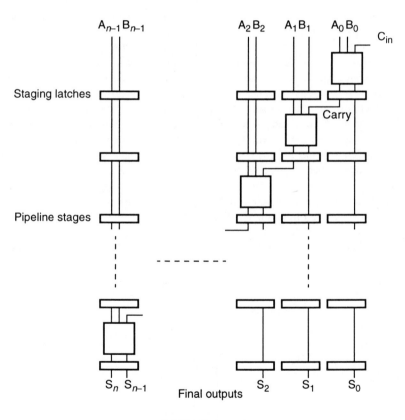

(a) Parallel adder

(b) Pipeline version

Figure 5.38 Pipelined parallel adder

5.6.4 Reservation tables and feedback pipelines

The reservation table is central to pipeline designs. A *reservation table* is a two-dimensional diagram showing pipeline stages and their usage over time, i.e. a space-time diagram for the pipeline. Time is divided into equal time periods, normally equivalent to the clock periods in a synchronous pipeline. If a pipeline stage is used during a particular time period, an X is placed in the reservation table time slot. The reservation table is used to illustrate the operation of a pipeline and also used in the design of pipeline control algorithms. A reservation table of a five-stage linear pipeline is shown in Figure 5.39. In this particular case, each of the five stages operate for one time period, and in sequence. It is possible to have stages operate for more than one time period, which would be shown with Xs in adjacent columns of one row. More than one X in one row, not necessarily adjacent columns, could also indicate that a stage is used more than once in a feedback configuration. A reservation table with more than one X in a column would indicate that more than one stage is operating simultaneously on the same or different tasks. Operating on the same task would indicate parallel processing, while operating on different tasks would generally indicate some form of feedback in the pipeline.

The pipelined parallel adder in Figure 5.38 is a linear pipeline. It could be reconfigured as a feedback pipeline by reusing some of the full adders. There are many possibilities. Figure 5.40 shows one. Here two 8-bit numbers are added together using the technique of one full adder for each pair of bits. There are four full adders instead of eight. After stages 1, 2, 3 and 4 have processed the least significant four bits, results are passed back to the second stage, and the second, third, and fourth full adders are used again, but now to process the 5th, 6th and 7th bits of the number. Finally stage 4 is used again to process the 8th bit of the number. Figure 5.40(b) shows the corresponding reservation table.

A reservation table describes the actions performed by the pipeline during each time period. A single function pipeline has only one set of actions and hence would have one reservation table; a multifunction pipeline would have one reservation table for each function of the pipeline. In a static multifunction pipeline, only one function can be selected for all entering tasks until the whole pipeline is reconfigured for a new function,

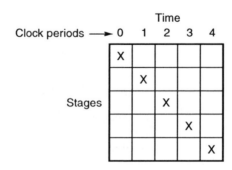

Figure 5.39 Reservation table of a five-stage linear pipeline

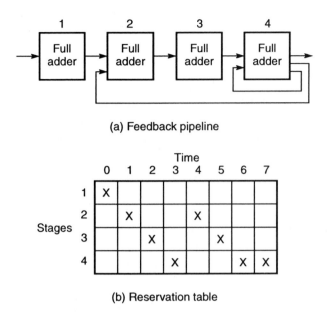

(a) Feedback pipeline

(b) Reservation table

Figure 5.40 Pipelined parallel adder with feedback

and only one of the reservation tables is of interest at any instant corresponding to overall function selected. In a dynamic multifunction pipeline, different overall functions can be performed on entering data, and all of the reservation tables of functions selected need to be considered as a set.

Pipelines generally operate in synchronism with a common clock signal and each time slot would be related to this clock period, the boundary between two adjacent slots normally corresponding to clocking the data from one pipeline stage to the next stage. Note though, that the reservation table does not show the specific paths taken by information from one stage to another, and it is possible for two different pipelines to have the same reservation table.

The reservation table does help determine whether a new task can be applied after the last task has been processed by the first stage. Each time the pipeline is called upon to process a new task is an *initiation*. Pipelines may not be able to accept initiations at the start of every period. A *collision* occurs when two or more initiations attempt to use the same stage in the pipeline at the same time.

Consider, for example, the reservation table of a static pipeline shown in Figure 5.41. This table has adjacent Xs in rows. Two consecutive initiations would cause a collision at slots 1–2. Here, the stage is still busy with the first initiation when the second reaches the input of the stage. Such collisions need to be avoided by delaying the progress of the second initiation through this particular pipeline until one cycle later. A potential collision can be identified by noting the distance in time slots between Xs in each row of

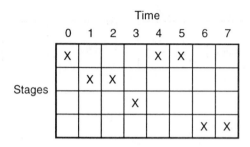

Figure 5.41 Reservation table with collision

the reservation table. Two adjacent Xs have a "distance" of 1 and indicate that two initiations cannot be applied in successive cycles. A distance of 2 would indicate that two initiations could be separated by an extra cycle.

A *collision vector* is used to describe the potential collisions and is defined for a given reservation table in the following way:

Collision vector $C = C_{n-1}C_{n-2} \ldots C_2C_1C_0$

where there are n time slots in the reservation table. $C_i = 1$ if a collision would occur with an initiation i cycles after an initiation (taking into account all existing tasks in the pipeline), otherwise $C_i = 0$. We note that C_0 will always be 1, as two simultaneous initiations would always collide. Hence, sometimes C_0 is omitted from the collision vector. C_n and subsequent bits are always 0, as initiations so separated would never collide. All previous initiations would have passed through the pipeline completely.

The *initial collision vector* is the collision vector after the first initiation is presented to the pipeline. To compute this it is only necessary to consider the distance between all pairs of Xs in each row of the reservation table. The distances between all pairs in the reservation table shown in Figure 5.41 are (5, 4, 1, 0) and the initial collision vector is 110011 (including C_0).

5.6.5 Pipeline scheduling and control

Now let us consider the situations when a pipeline should not accept new initiations on every cycle because a collision would occur sometime during the processing of the task. The pipeline needs a control or scheduling mechanism to determine when new initiations can be accepted without a collision occurring.

Latency is the term used to describe the number of clock periods between two initiations. The *average latency* is the average number of clock periods between initiations generally over a specific repeating cycle of initiations. The *forbidden latency set* contains those latencies which cause collisions, e.g. (5, 4, 1, 0) previously. This set is also represented in the collision vector. The smallest average latency considering all the possible sequences of tasks (initiation cycles) is called the *minimum average latency* (MAL). Depending upon the design criteria, the optimum scheduling strategy might be one which produces the minimum average latency.

The following scheduling strategy is due to Davidson (1971). A pipeline can be considered in a particular state; it changes from one state to another as a result of accepted initiations. A diagram of linked states becomes a state diagram. Each state in the state diagram is identified by the collision vector (sometimes called a *status vector* in the state diagram) which indicates whether a new initiation may be made to the pipeline. The initial state vector of an empty pipeline before any initiations have been made is 00 … 00, since no collision can occur with the first initiation. After the first initiation has been taken, the collision vector becomes the initial collision vector and C_1 in the collision vector will define whether another initiation is allowed in the next cycle.

First the collision vector is shifted one place right and 0 is entered into the left side. If $C_0 = 1$, indicating that an initiation is not allowed, the pipeline is now in another state defined by the shifted collision vector. If $C_0 = 0$, indicating that an initiation is allowed, there are two possible new states – one when the initiation is not taken, which is the same as when $C_0 = 1$, and one when the initiation is taken. If the initiation is taken, the initial collision vector is bit-wise logically ORed with the shifted collision vector to produce a new collision vector. This logical ORing of the shifted collision vector with the initial collision vector incorporates into the collision vector the effect of the new initiation and its effect on potential collisions.

Figure 5.42 illustrates the algorithm for computing the collision vector for a pipeline when initiations may or may not be taken. It immediately leads to a possible scheduling algorithm. After shifting the collision vector, if $C_0 = 0$, an initiation is taken and a new collision vector is computed by logically ORing operations. The strategy of always taking the opportunity of submitting an initiation to the pipeline when it is known that a collision will not occur, i.e. choosing the minimum latency on every suitable occasion, is called a *greedy strategy*. Unfortunately, a greedy strategy will not necessarily result in the minimum average latency (an optimum strategy), though it normally comes fairly close to the optimum strategy, and is particularly easy to implement.

The state diagram for the collision vector 110011 (the reservation table in Figure 5.41) is shown in Figure 5.43. All possible states are included, whether or not an initiation is taken. Clearly such state diagrams could become very large.

The state diagram can be reduced to only showing changes in state when an initiation is taken. The various possible cycles of initiations can be easily located from this *modified* (or *reduced*) *state diagram*. The modified state diagram is shown in Figure 5.44. The number beside each arc indicates the number of cycles necessary to reach a state. We can identify possible closed *simple cycles* (cycles in which a state is only visited once during the cycle), as given by 3, 3, 3, 3, …, 2, 6, 2, 6, …, 3, 6, 3, 6, …, and 6, 6, 6, 6, …. These simple cycles would be written as (3), (2, 6), (3, 6), and (6).

There is usually more than one greedy cycle if the starting point for a cycle can be other than the initial state. In Figure 4.22, the greedy cycles are (2, 6) starting at the initial state 110011 and (3) starting at 110111. The average latency of any greedy (simple) cycle is less than or equal to the number of 1s in the initial collision vector (see Kogge, 1981).

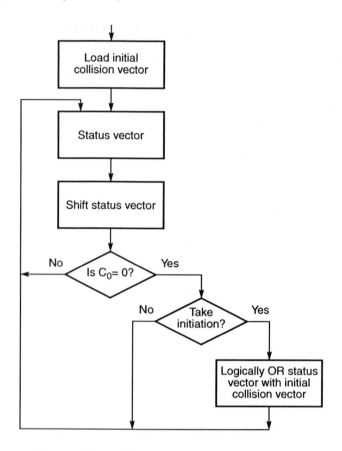

Figure 5.42 Davidson's pipeline control algorithm

More complex cycles exist, in which states are visited more than once. However it has been shown (see Kogge (1981) for proof) that for any complex cycle with a given average latency, there is at least one simple cycle with an average latency no greater than this latency. In searching for an optimum strategy there is no need to consider complex cycles, as a simple cycle exists with the same or better latency, assuming the criterion is minimum latency.

The minimum average latency is always equal to or greater than the maximum number of Xs in the rows of the reservation table. This condition gives us the lower bound on latency and can be deduced as follows: let the maximum number of Xs in a reservation table row be n_{max}, which equals the number of times the most used stage is used by one initiation. Given t time slots in the reservation station, the maximum possible number of initiations is limited by the most used stage which, of course, can be used by one initiation at a time. Hence the maximum number of initiations = t/n_{max}. The minimum latency = $t/$(maximum number of initiation) = n_{max}.

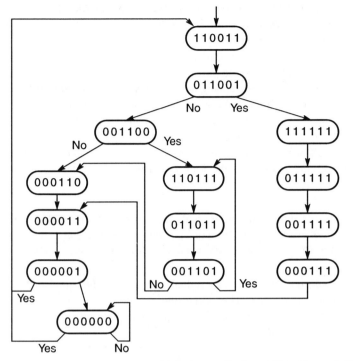

Yes/No refers to "Is $C_0 = 0$?" in Figure 5.42

Figure 5.43　State diagram for collision vector 110011

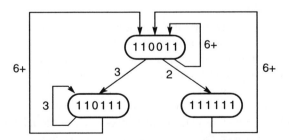

Figure 5.44　Modified state diagram (6+ = 6 or more cycles to reach state)

We now have the conditions: maximum number of Xs in row ≤ minimum average latency (MAL) ≤ greedy cycle average latency ≤ number of initial collision vector 1s, giving upper and lower bounds on the MAL.

A given pipeline design may not provide the required latency. A method of reducing the latency is to insert delays into the pipeline to expand the reservation table and reduce the chances of a collision. In general, any fixed latency equal to or greater than the lower bound can be achieved with the addition of delays, though it may never be possible to achieve a particular cycle of unequal latencies. Mathematical methods exist to determine whether a particular cycle could be achieved (see Kogge, 1981).

Assuming that all operations (Xs) shown in the reservation table depend upon previously marked operations, we have the following algorithm to identify where to place delays to obtain a latency of n cycles:

1. Starting with the first X in the original reservation table, enter the X in a revised table and mark every n cycles from this position to indicate that these positions have been reserved for the initiations every n cycles. Mark with, say, an F (for forbidden).

2. Repeat for subsequent Xs in the original reservation table until an X falls on an entered forbidden F mark. Then delay the X one or more positions until a free position is found for it. Re-mark delayed positions with a D. Delay all subsequent Xs by the same amount.

All Ds in the reservation table indicate where delays must be generated in the pipeline.

Figure 5.45(a) shows a reservation table with a collision vector 11011. There is one simple cycle (2, 5) giving an MAL of 3.5. However, the lower bound (number of Xs in any row) is 2. The previous algorithm is performed for a cycle of 2 in Figure 5.45(b). Only one delay is necessary in Figure 5.45(b). This delay consists of a stage in the pipeline which simply holds the information for one cycle as it passes from one stage to the next. It can be implemented using only one extra stage latch. Multiple delays between processing stages, had they been required, might be best implemented using a dual port memory in which different locations can be read and written simultaneously, as shown in Figure 5.46. Locations read are those which were written n cycles previously, when an n-cycle delay was required.

The algorithm described assumes that Xs must be maintained in the same order as in the original reservation table. It may be that certain stages could be executed before others, though the relationship between the stages is not shown in the reservation table. In that case, it would not be necessary to delay all subsequent Xs, only those which depended upon the delayed stage.

Apart from having a strategy for accepting initiations, pipeline control logic is necessary to control the flow of data between stages. A flexible method of control is by microprogramming, in which the specific actions are encoded in a control memory. This method can be extended so that the specific actions are encoded in words which pass from one stage to the next with the data.

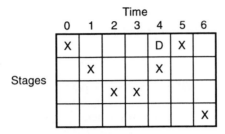

(a) Original reservation table

(b) Reservation table with delay added

Figure 5.45 Adding delays to reduce latency

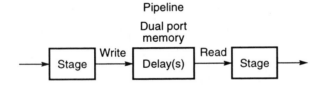

Figure 5.46 Using dual port memory for delay

5.7 Pipelining in vector computers

We conclude this chapter with some remarks on the design of large, very high speed *vector computers*, these being a very successful application of pipelining, which can take advantage of arithmetic pipelines. Apart from normal "scalar" instructions operating upon one or two single element operands, vector computers have instructions which can operate on strings of numbers formed as one-dimensional arrays (vectors). Vectors can

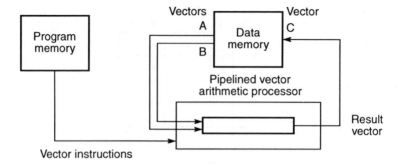

Figure 5.47 Pipelined vector processing

contain either all integers or all floating point numbers. A vector computer might handle sixty-four element vectors. One operation can be specified on all the elements of vectors in a single instruction. Various vector instructions are possible, notably arithmetic/logic operation requiring one or two vectors, or one scalar and one vector producing a vector result, and an arithmetic/logic operation on all the elements of one vector to produce a scalar result. *Vector processors* can also be designed to attach to scalar computers to increase their performance on vector computations. *Supercomputers* normally have vector capability.

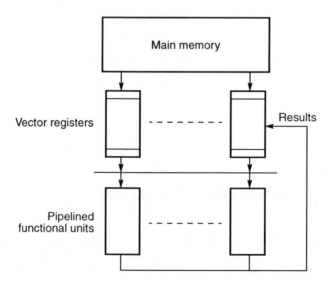

Figure 5.48 Multiple functional units

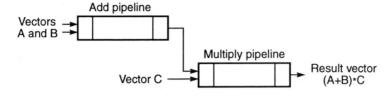

Figure 5.49 Chaining

Vector computers can be register-to-register type, which use a large number of processor registers to hold the vectors (e.g. Cray 1, 2, X-MP, Y-MP computers) or memory-to-memory type, which use main memory locations to hold the vectors (e.g. Cyber 205). Most systems use vector registers. In either case, the general architecture is broadly as shown in Figure 5.47, where the data elements are held in main memory or processor registers. As in all stored program computers described, instructions are read from a program memory by a processor. The vector processor accepts elements from one or two vectors and produces a stream of result elements.

Most large, high speed computer systems have more than one functional unit to perform arithmetical and logical operations. For example, in a vector computer, separate scalar and vector arithmetical functional units can be provided, as can different functional units for addition/subtraction and multiplication/division. Functional units can be pipelined and fed with operands before previous results have been generated if there are no hazard conditions. Figure 5.48 shows multiple functional units using vector registers to hold vector operands, as in Cray computers; scalar register would also exist. The units take operands from vector registers and return results to the vector registers. Each vector register holds the elements of one vector, and individual elements are fed to the appropriate functional unit in succession.

Typically, a series of vector instructions will be received by the processor. To increase the speed of operation, the results of one functional unit pipeline can be fed into the input of another pipeline, as shown in Figure 5.49. This technique is known as *chaining* and overlaps pipeline operations to eliminate the "drain" time of the first pipeline. More than two pipelines can be chained when available. Details of vector pipelining and chaining in large vector processor systems can be found in Cheng (1989).

PROBLEMS

5.1 Derive an expression for the minimum clock period in a ten-stage synchronous pipeline in terms of the stage operating time, t_{stage}, stage latch set-up time, t_{set-up} and the clock propagation time from one stage to the next, t_{cprop}, assuming that the clock passes from one stage to the next stage.

5.2   A microprocessor has two internal units, an instruction fetch unit and an instruction execute unit, with fetch/execute overlap. Compute the overall processing time of eight sequential instructions, in each of the following cases.

1. $T(F_i) = T(E_i) = 100$ ns for $i = 1$ to 8
2. $T(F_i) = 50$ ns, $T(E_i) = 100$ ns for $i = 1$ to 8
3. $T(F_i) = 100$ ns, $T(E_i) = 50, 75, 125, 100, 75$ and 50 ns for $i = 1, 2, 3, 4, 5, 6, 7$ and 8 respectively.

where $T(F_i)$ is the time to fetch the ith instruction and $T(E_i)$ is the time to execute the ith instruction.

5.3 A computer system has a three-stage pipeline consisting of an instruction fetch unit, an instruction decode unit and an instruction execute unit. Determine the time to execute twenty sequential instructions using two-way interleaved memory if all three units access memory simultaneously. Draw the timing diagram for maximum concurrency given four-way interleaved memory.

5.4 A microprocessor has five pipelined internal units, an instruction fetch unit (IF), an instruction decode unit (ID), an operand fetch unit (OF), an operation execute unit (OE) and a result operand store unit (OS). Different instructions require particular units to operate for the periods shown in Table 5.1 (in cycles, one cycle = 100 ns).

Table 5.1 Pipeline unit operating times for instructions in Problem 5.4

Instruction	T(IF)	T(ID)	T(OF)	T(OE)	T(OS)
Load memory to register	1	1	1	0	0
Load register to register	1	1	0	1	0
Store register to memory	1	1	0	0	1
Add/subtract memory to register	1	1	1	1	0

Compute the overall processing time of sequential instructions, in each of the following cases.

```
1.    LD  R1,100[R0]
      LD  R2,200[R0]
      LD  R3,300[R0]
      LD  R4,400[R0]

2.    LD  R1,100[R0]
      LD  R2,200[R0]
```

```
ADD R2,R2,R1
ST 200[R0],R1
```

5.5   Given that an instruction pipeline has five units, as described in Problem 5.4, deduce the times required for each unit to process the following instructions:

```
LD R1,102[R0]
ADD R2,R1,R1
SUB R2,R3,R4
ADD R3,R3,1
ST 102[R0],R3
```

Identify three types of instructions in which $T(OF) = T(OE) = T(OS) = 0$ ns.

5.6   What is the average instruction processing time of a five-stage instruction pipeline if conditional branch instructions occur as follows: third instruction, ninth instruction, tenth instruction, twenty-fourth instruction, twenty-seventh instruction, given that there are thirty-six instructions to process? Assume that the pipeline must be cleared after a branch instruction has been decoded.

5.7   A two-address processor has a three-stage pipeline consisting of an instruction fetch/decode unit, and operand fetch unit, and an instruction execute/write unit. Hazards are detected by a single scoreboard bit associated with each operand register. The scoreboard bits are set during the instruction fetch/decode stage, and reset during the instruction execute stage. In-order issue is practiced. Determine the delays that occur within the pipeline as instructions are processed when the following sequence is fetched.

```
        MOV CX,5     ;CX = 5
L1:     ADD AX,CX    ;AX = AX + CX
        DEC CX       ;CX = CX - 1
        JNZ L1       ;Jump to L1 if not zero
```

Draw a space-time diagram showing the progression of instructions through the pipeline.

5.8   Identify potential data dependency hazards in the following code:

```
LD R1,100[R0]
ADD R1,R2,R1
ADD R3,R3,1
ST 100[R0],R1
ST 200[R0],R2
ADD R3,R2,R1
```

given a five-stage instruction pipeline. Suppose that hazards are recognized using scoreboard bits (valid bits). Determine the sequence in which the instructions are processed.

5.9   A serial adder has been created by using three full adders with feedback as shown in Figure 5.50. The inner loop, A, is first traversed once before results continue though the pipeline. The outer loop, B, is then traversed once without including loop A. Derive a reservation table. Draw the state diagram, and simplify the diagram into a reduced state diagram. List the simple cycles. Can the lower bound for the minimum average latency (MAL) be obtained without delays?

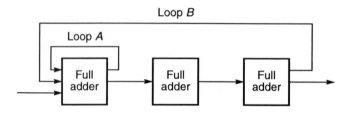

Figure 5.50 Pipeline for Problem 5.9

5.10 Design a dynamic arithmetic pipeline which performs fixed point (integer) addition or subtraction.

5.11 Design an arithmetic pipeline which performs shift-and-add unsigned integer multiplication.

5.12 Design a static multifunction pipeline which will perform floating point addition or floating point multiplication.

5.13 Draw the reservation table for the pipeline shown in Figure 5.51, and draw an alternative pipeline which has the same reservation table.

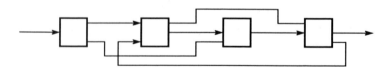

Figure 5.51 Pipeline for Problem 5.13

5.14 Determine the initial collision vector for the reservation table shown in Figure 5.52. Derive the state diagram and simplify the diagram into a reduced state diagram. List the simple cycles, and give the minimum average latency (MAL).

Stages	Time 0	1	2	3	4	5	6
	X						
		X		X		X	
			X		X		
							X

Figure 5.52 Reservation table for Problem 5.14

5.15 For the reservation table shown in Figure 5.53, introduce delays to obtain the cycle (3), i.e. an initiation every third cycle.

Stages	Time 0	1	2	3	4	5	6
	X	X		X			
			X			X	
				X		X	
					X		X

Figure 5.53 Reservation table for Problem 5.15

Shared memory multiprocessor systems

CHAPTER 6
Multiprocessor systems and programming

This chapter identifies various types of multiprocessor systems and outlines their operation. How the system will be programmed is closely related to the specific architecture, and similarly the design of architecture is affected by programing issues. It is not possible to separate the two and we introduce both multiprocessor architectures and programming in this chapter. We will outline the basic software techniques applicable to general-purpose multiprocessors, in preparation for further study of general-purpose multiprocessor architectures in subsequent chapters. Sample code will be given; however, programing multiprocessors is an extensive topic outside the scope of this architecture book. The reader will be referred to further reading to continue the study.

6.1 General

In previous chapters, we considered methods of improving the performance of single processor computer systems. Now we will consider the extension of the stored program computer concept to systems having more than one processor. Such systems are called *multiprocessor systems*. Each processor usually executes different programs simultaneously, but could execute the same instructions depending upon the type of system. The principal motive behind developing multiprocessor systems is to increase the speed of operation. (There are sometimes other motives, such as fault tolerance and matching the application.) It seems apparent that increased speed should result when more than one processor operates simultaneously. The best possible increase in speed would be proportional to the number of processors, and would occur when all the processors are operating simultaneously all the time on the application and there is no additional computation or data transfer, or resource contention, involved in the multiprocessor implementation. Such an increase in speed is rarely achieved in practice because it is rarely possible to get all the processors doing useful work on a single problem at the same time and there is normally a substantial overhead in the communication between processors. However, considerable speed-up can be achieved. The terms *parallelism* and *concurrency* are used to describe the simultaneous operation of multiple processors (and hence *parallel pro-*

gramming, parallel computers, concurrent programming); the term parallelism is occasionally restricted to processors all executing the same code, though we will not make that distinction here.

There is a continual demand for greater computational speed than is possible with available computer systems. General areas which require great computational speed include modeling, simulation and prediction, which often need repetitive calculations on large amounts of data to give valid results. Commonly quoted application examples include weather forecasting, economic forecasting and aerodynamic simulation for aircraft and space vehicles. Computer design also requires modeling and extensive calculations to simulate the systems and VLSI integrated circuits prior to manufacture. As the VLSI circuits become more complex, it takes increasingly more time to simulate them; a simulation which takes two weeks to reach a solution is usually unacceptable in a manufacturing environment. The time needs to be short enough for the designer to work effectively. Certain applications have specific target times. For example, two days for forecasting the weather the next day would make the prediction useless.

It is also human nature to develop applications which extend existing abilities of systems, and require more computational power and speed than presently available. Recent applications such as virtual reality require considerable computational power to achieve results in an acceptable time. Even home computers with their CD-ROM drives require significant computational power. We have seen in previous chapters how a scalar processor can be extended into superscalar operation and at least one manufacturer (Intel) has turned to superscalar versions of their scalar processors (Intel's superscalar Pentium version of the 486). Superscalar processors could be designed to execute many instructions concurrently – however traditional programming with a single computational thread rarely has *instruction level parallelism* (the number of independent instructions that could be executed together) greater than 3 or 4.

There has been a debate on whether one fast processor would be faster and more cost-effective than a system with more than one slower but less expensive processor. Most manufacturers of large computer systems in the 1970s chose to develop pipelined single processor systems with the fastest technology available if the highest speeds were required. Sometimes these processors were designed or extended to operate upon vectors as well as scalars, to improve the performance with vectors. These systems often used emitter-coupled logic (ECL) gates and interconnection delays significantly affected the overall speed operation. Prototype multiprocessor research machines designed and constructed during the 1970s were based upon much slower microprocessor devices although these systems generally did not demonstrate that multiple slower devices could be harnessed together to be faster and more cost-effective than ECL-based high speed single processor systems. However, in the 1980s, even manufacturers of the fastest computer systems had to develop multiprocessor versions of their single processor systems, e.g., the four-processor Cray 2 system. It is now apparent that multiple processors must be used to obtain improvements in speed even though the difficulties of using more than one processor on a single problem have not been resolved.

Research into multiprocessor architectures continues, with each plan calling for more processors – sometimes for thousands of processors – and in the research community there have been conferences which will only accept papers describing results concerned with no less than a thousand processors. The main software aspect is how to use the processors together on a single problem. Competitions have even been organized to find the greatest possible speed-up over a single processor solution. The main architectural problem for large scale multiprocessors is how to interconnect the processors in a feasible manner. This topic is examined in Chapter 8.

Multiprocessor systems are also designed to gain fault tolerance, i.e., to be able to continue operating in the presence of hardware (and possibly software) faults. Hardware fault tolerance is achieved by the addition of circuits that are not necessary for normal operation but that enable the system to continue if faults occur. The number of faults that can be present is limited and dependent upon the system design. Specific applications exist in which computer systems must continue operating for as long as possible or over an initial time period. For example, the computer system in an aircraft must continue working while operating the aircraft, and a faulty system could lead to loss of life. In the commercial field, computer breakdown could lead to financial loss. Manufacturing plants controlled by computers need to exhibit fault tolerance if possible, sometimes for safety, sometimes to avoid financial loss. Fault tolerance is also extremely important in the military areas (missile control, etc.).

6.2 Multiprocessor classification

6.2.1 Flynn's classification

A normal single processor stored program computer (von Neumann computer) generates a single stream of instructions which acts upon single data items. Flynn (1966) called this type of computer a *single instruction stream-single data stream* (SISD) computer. In a general purpose multiprocessor system, one instruction stream is generated for each processor. Each instruction acts upon different data. Flynn called this type of computer a *multiple instruction stream-multiple data stream* (MIMD) computer. Apart from these two extremes, it is possible (and there are some advantages in doing so) to design a computer in which a single instruction stream is generated by a single control unit, and the instructions are broadcast to more than one processor. Each processor executes the same instruction, but using different data. The data items form a vector and the instructions act upon the complete vector in one instruction cycle. Flynn called this type of computer a *single instruction stream-multiple data stream* (SIMD) computer. This type of computer has been developed because there is a number of important applications which mostly operate upon arrays of data. For example most computer simulations of physical systems (from molecular systems to weather forecasting) start with large arrays of data points which must be manipulated. Having a system which will perform similar operations of data points at the same time will be both efficient in hardware and relatively simple to program. The program simply consists of a single sequence of instructions operating on the array of data points together with normal control structures (IF, FOR etc.). The fourth combination, *multiple instruction stream-single data stream* (MISD) computer does not exist, unless one specifically classifies pipelined architectures in this group, or possibly some fault tolerant systems. Flynn's classifications are shown in Figure 6.1. The SIMD computer has an array of processing elements, one for each element in the vectors being processed, and hence is also called an *array computer.*

The original stored program computer has the SISD form, with instructions operating sequentially upon integers, and later upon floating point numbers. The use of pipelining

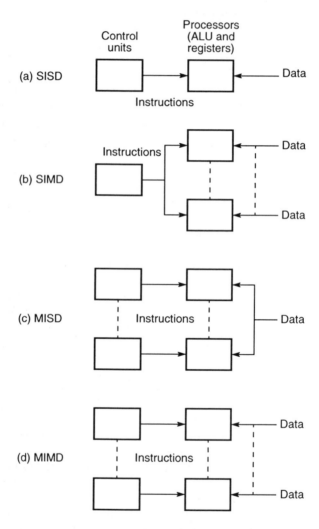

Figure 6.1 Flynn's classification (1966)

in the stored program computer does not really alter the general classification as a single instruction stream still exists and operates upon a single data stream. The SISD classification does not define the type of data items to be processed. Some large scale vector computers operate upon vectors as well as scalars (integers or floating point numbers) where a vector is a one-dimensional array of scalar elements, using the pipelining principle to process the series of elements. We shall classify such pipelined vector computers as SISD. The SIMD computer also processes vectors. Hence, there are two types of vector computer, one using the pipeline technique and one using an SIMD array of processing elements.

It is possible to have combined systems; for example a MSIMD system (multiple single instruction stream-multiple data stream computer) consists of more than one SIMD system each controlled separately.

6.2.2 Other classifications

Flynn's classifications are now very old and several other attempts have been made to classify computer systems. Feng (1972) classified systems in terms of number of bits and number of words that can be processed simultaneously, given as a tuple (bits, words). Classifications have been also proposed by Reddi and Feurstel (1976), Händler (1977), Skillicorn (1988) and Dasgupta (1990). However, as none of these classifications has been as widely used as Flynn's classifications, we shall use the latter. Classifications play a part in the study of computer architectures by cataloging existing systems and exposing architectures perhaps not yet developed.

6.3 Array computers

6.3.1 General architecture

In an array (SIMD) computer, a program memory holds the sequence of instructions to be executed and a centralized control unit extracts each instruction from the program memory in the same way as a normal von Neumann stored program (SISD) computer – by using a program counter. As in a simple SISD computer, one instruction is generally executed in its entirety, followed by the next instruction, etc. The instructions in the instruction set comprise a set of normal single processor instructions, such as integer arithmetical/logical instruction control instructions and jump/branch instructions, which are executed directly by the control unit, i.e. the control unit has the ability to perform arithmetical and control processor functions. There is also a group of instructions, especially vector instructions, which are not executed by the control unit but by the array of processing elements. These instructions are recognized by the control unit which broadcast the instructions to the processing elements for execution. Each processing element performs the operation defined upon data stored in data memory connected directly or indirectly to the processing elements. The data memory may be local to each

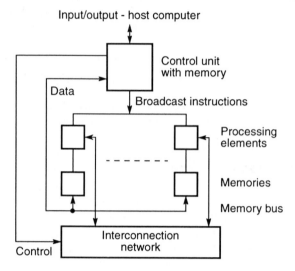

(a) System with local memory

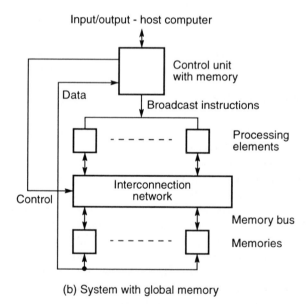

(b) System with global memory

Figure 6.2 SIMD architectures

processing element or it may be global memory connected to the processing elements through an interconnection network. The two possible schemes are shown in Figure 6.2. Suitable interconnection networks are presented in Chapter 7.

A key feature of the systems is that all processing elements operate in lock step fashion, all starting and finishing together. Each processing element has local addressable registers and the ability to perform arithmetical and logical operations upon a different data element which would be part of a vector or an array. A typical vector instruction might be ADD A,D, where A is an array of accumulators and D is a data array. The ith accumulator of A is in the ith processing element. The ith processing element adds the ith data item of array D to the ith accumulator of A. In the architecture shown in Figure 6.2(a), it is necessary for the ith data item to be in the local memory of the ith processing element before the instruction can be executed correctly.

Branch instructions (conditional and unconditional) are executed by the control unit. In a single processor system, the conditions for the jump instructions are related to the result after an arithmetic/logical operation. The condition might be zero result, positive or negative result, etc. Individual flags in a condition code register indicate specific conditions and others may be inferred by combining conditions (i.e. positive or zero). In an array computer with n processing elements, there can be n identical arithmetical/logical operations taking place simultaneously with n different accumulator registers (one in each processing element).

Typically, in an array computer we might like to perform a computation for those results that exhibit a particular condition, and perhaps a different computation for those results that exhibit the converse condition. This situation and other situations are handled by providing a vector of condition flags for each condition, with one bit for each processing element. This vector of condition code flags might be transferable to a control unit register under program control and then recognized by jump instructions. Masking operations on this register will identify the processing elements in which the condition is present and subsequent actions can be selected as appropriate. Specific control unit instructions can be provided for recognizing, for example, the most significant 1 in the register. A specific broadcast instruction is provided to load the register with the conditions prevailing in the processing elements. Conditional jump instructions might jump on the condition that all, any, or none of the bits are 1.

A masking mechanism is also introduced to inhibit selected processing elements from responding to the broadcast instructions. A mask is generated by specific instructions. Processing elements are given individual address index registers to modify the address of the data element to be accessed. Hence, it is possible to access rows, columns or every alternative element by each processing element modifying its index register. Each processing element can have more than one index register, additional data registers, a status/condition code register and other registers.

6.3.2 Features of some array computers

In this section we will highlight particular features of some array computers.

Illiac IV

The Illiac IV has historical importance, being the first major attempt at constructing an array computer. The Illiac IV computer system (Bouknight *et al.*, 1972) was developed in the late 1960s by the University of Illinois (hence Illinois Array Computer) and constructed by the Burroughs Corporation in 1972. The general architecture corresponds to the type shown in Figure 6.2(a), though the interconnection network paths are limited. The original design called for four quadrants of sixty-four processing elements (256 processing elements in all) but only one quadrant of sixty-four processing elements was finally constructed because of economic reasons and schedule delays. Each element can communicate directly with four neighboring processing elements using direct links between processing elements in an 8×8 matrix pattern as shown in Figure 6.3. The processing elements are numbered 0 to 63, so that the ith processing element can communicate directly with the $(i-1)$th, $(i+1)$th, $(i-8)$th and the $(i+8)$th processing elements. This restricted interconnection scheme can achieve any processing element connection, if not to neighboring processing elements then via intermediate processing elements. A maximum of six intermediate processing elements is necessary (seven communication steps), but most applications require less than the worst case communication overhead.

A particular feature of the system is that the control unit does not have a separate program memory described in the general scheme. Instead, the memory of the processing elements is used in an interleaved fashion, i.e. the first addressed location is in the local

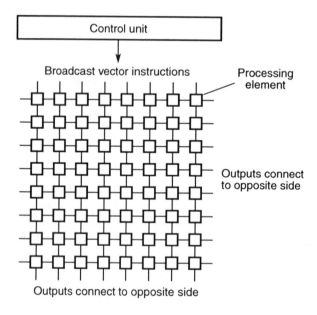

Figure 6.3 Array SIMD computer using nearest neighbor connections

memory of the first processing element, the second addressed location is in the local memory of the second processing element, and so on, with every sixty-fourth location in one processing element memory. Eight 64-bit words can be transferred simultaneously from the processing element memories to the control unit using a 512-bit bus between the processing elements and the control unit. Each processing element has local memory consisting of 2048 × 64-bit words. The control unit connects to all of the processing elements via a common data bus to pass instructions to the processing elements, and to all of the local memories through a common control bus to obtain program instructions.

The sixty-four processing elements operate in lock step fashion and receive broadcast instructions for a control unit as described previously with scalar instructions executed by the control unit. Control unit operations can overlap processing element operations. Each instruction has a fixed length of thirty-two bits and sixteen instructions are taken into an instruction buffer within the control unit simultaneously. The instruction buffer can hold sixty-four 64-bit words (128 instructions) and when execution has reached halfway through the block of instructions fetched, the next block is prefetched, replacing the oldest block. The control unit also has a 64-word data buffer (data cache) which can be loaded from the processing element memories, 512 bits at a time, and a 64-bit ALU, a program counter and four accumulators. Instructions for the processing elements (the vector and associated instructions) have their effective address calculated, using a 24-bit address adder, before passing on to the processing elements. Each processing element can perform 64-bit floating point, 32-bit floating point, 64-bit unsigned integer or 8-bit unsigned integer arithmetic.

Burroughs' Scientific Processor

The Burroughs' Scientific Processor (BSP) was developed in the mid-1970s as an attempt to construct a commercial SIMD array computer after Burroughs' involvement in the Illiac IV, though this project was abandoned and no systems were marketed. The BSP system employs architecture of the type shown in Figure 6.2(b).

A particular feature of the BSP is the use of seventeen memory modules with sixteen arithmetic processing elements. Only sixteen of the seventeen memory modules can connect to the processing elements at any instant. Two full crossbar switch interconnection networks (see Figure 6.7) are used to make the connection between the arithmetic processing elements and memory modules. An "output" interconnection network is used for transfers from the sixteen processing elements to sixteen memories and an "input" interconnection network is used for transfers from the memories to the processing elements. The use of seventeen modules rather than a number which is a power of two is a unique feature of the system. The technique allows contention-free communication between the arithmetic processing elements and memory modules for most types of accesses to arrays stored in the memory modules. Only when the accesses are to elements separated by seventeen consecutively addressed locations, or a multiple of seventeen, is there memory conflict, as then the elements are inserted in the same memory module.

Spreading array elements across memory modules to avoid contention is also done in MIMD systems; a standard parallel programming technique is to spread an $n \times n$ matrix across $n + 1$ memory modules (see Rettberg and Thomas, 1986).

GF-11

The GF-11 is an array computer system developed by IBM in the early 1980s as a research vehicle primarily for numerical calculations of some of the predictions in quantum chromodynamics, a proposed theory of particles which participate in nuclear interactions (Beetem, Denneau and Weingarten, 1987). The architecture is of the type shown in Figure 6.2(a) with full interconnectivity provided between processing elements (as opposed to the limited nearest neighbor connections of the Illiac IV). There are 576 arithmetic processors, each capable of achieving 20 Mflops (million floating point operations per second). Each processor has separate fixed point and floating point units. The floating point unit has two multiply and two arithmetic units capable of addition, subtraction, computing absolute values and fixed/floating point conversion. There are three levels of local memory provided with each processor, a 12.5 ns cycle-time 256 word register file, a 50 ns cycle-time 16 Kword static memory and a 512 Kword dynamic memory arranged in two banks and providing one access every 200 ns (one word = 32 bits). The control unit broadcasts 180-bit microcode words to the processors at a 50 ns rate. The controller microcode memory consists of 512×200-bit words. A host computer connects to the control unit.

A three-stage interconnection network, which allows all permutations of connections between the 576 processors, is used. The basic switching cell is a 9-bit wide (including parity) 24×24 crossbar switch, and each stage has twenty-four cells. Three stages call for seventy-two cells. (See Chapter 8 for more details of multistage interconnection networks.)

The GF-11 system has a definite goal; to reduce the time it takes to perform some particularly time-consuming calculations which typically require 1×10^{17} arithmetic operations. At 20 Mflops, the calculation would take 150 years; at 10 Gflops the calculation takes four months.

Concluding comments

SIMD array vector computers have a long history, with the Illiac IV a landmark in the development of the idea which can be traced back to the late 1950s. After the Illiac IV, a few subsequent systems were constructed and refined the basic concept. None of the systems were developed into commercial products and commercial computer manufacturers have been less than enthusiastic about the idea, preferring to keep to traditional SISD systems, enhanced by vector instructions using pipelining. (Some people do refer to pipelined systems as a form of SIMD.)

6.3.3 Bit-organized array computers

The array computers so far described use processing elements which operate upon binary words (*word-organized* or *word-slice array computers*); it is possible to design an array computer in which the processing elements operate upon one bit, or possibly a few bits, of a word each. Such *bit-organized* or *bit-slice array computers* have particular applications in image processing. Picture elements (*pixels*) of the images are represented by an array of bits, and commonly the same Boolean operation needs to be performed upon each picture element simultaneously at great speed. Alternatively, bit-organized array computers might be designed such that processing elements can be linked together to process a selected word size in much the same way as bit-slice microprocessors are linked together to create processors operating upon words.

Examples of bit-organized array computers include the CLIP computer, developed in the mid-1970s at University College, London, for visual applications, the DAP (Distributed Array Processor) also developed in the mid-1970s by ICL, for general array computations, and the MPP (Massively Parallel Processor) (Batcher, 1980) developed by Goodyear Aerospace in the early 1980s. The MPP is really a massively parallel processor system having 16 384 bit-slice microprocessors arranged as a 128 × 128 array. The connection machine (Hillis, 1985) also comes under the bit-organized array computer classification.

BLITZEN project

The BLITZEN project (Blevins *et al.*, 1988) developed a system similar to the MPP using VLSI technology. Each array chip in the BLITZEN system has 128 processors, each with 1K-bit local static memory and with processors locally interconnected using an X-grid interconnection network, as shown in Figure 6.4. (The MPP used the north-south-east-west nearest neighbor network). In the X-network, the crossover point of the diagonal paths are joined together. The network provides north, south, east, west and diagonal

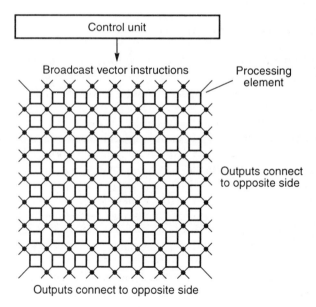

Figure 6.4 Array SIMD computer using X-network

transfers but only with all transfers in the same direction at any instant. For example, suppose a north direction is required. Each processing element can send information on the north-east diagonal path and accept information on the south-east diagonal path. For SIMD operations, all transfers in one step are in the same direction.

We will not investigate these systems further, and will leave array and vector computers to concentrate on MIMD computer systems. The reader is directed to the references quoted for further information on array computers.

6.4 General purpose (MIMD) multiprocessor systems

6.4.1 Architectures

In a general purpose MIMD computer system, a number of independent processors operate upon separate data concurrently. Hence each processor has its own program memory or has access to program memory. Similarly, each processor has its own data memory or access to data memory. Clearly there needs to be a mechanism to load the program and data memories and a mechanism for passing information between processors as they work on some problem. There are several possible architectures for general purpose MIMD multiprocessor systems. First, we can divide the multiprocessor systems into two types:

1. Shared memory multiprocessor systems.
2. Message-passing multiprocessor systems (without shared memory).

Shared memory multiprocessors use the centralized memory for holding data and communication purposes. Given that each processor must connect to program memory and data memory, most (fully) shared memory architectures can be represented by a set of processors, perhaps with local memory, connecting to one or more shared memory modules as shown in Figure 6.5. This is occasionally referred to as a "dance-hall architecture" as the processors are on one side of the network and the memories on the other side. We shall see there are many variations of interconnection networks, not all dance-halls. However, shared memory means that all processors have access to a common memory space. Hence location 100 (say) could be accessed by any processor. In any shared memory multiprocessor system, cache memory may be incorporated into the system. Cache memory creates significant complications into the design. We shall consider caches in shared memory multiprocessors in Chapter 7, Section 7.8. Also virtual memory may be incorporated into the system so that each processor must first translate a virtual address into a real address before passing the request to the memories.

A *message-passing multiprocessor* uses direct links to pass data between processors/processing elements and only have local memory (memory with each processor not directly accessible by other processors). A message-passing multiprocessor can be represented by Figure 6.6. Message-passing multiprocessors are sometimes called *multicom-*

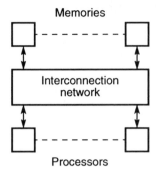

Figure 6.5 Shared memory multiprocessor model

*puter*s because each processor/memory pair can be a separate computer. There are various possible direct link (*static*) interconnection networks for message-passing multiprocessor systems. A very restricted static interconnection network, but a particularly suitable scheme for VLSI fabrication, is to connect processors directly to their nearest neighbors, perhaps to other processors, in a two-dimensional array of processors. There are many other possible static interconnection networks. A major aspect of a message-passing multiprocessor system is how to map programs or processes onto individual processors and how to pass data that must be accessed by individual processors. Generally shared memory multiprocessors are easier to program and more flexible, but do not scale as well (not as easy to enlarge). Part III concentrates upon message-passing multiprocessor systems. In Part II, we concentrate upon shared memory multiprocessor systems.

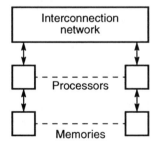

Figure 6.6 Message-passing multiprocessor model

6.4.2 Shared memory multiprocessor systems

In a shared memory multiprocessor system, different interconnection networks lead to systems with one of two characteristics:

1. Shared memory architecture with a uniform memory access (UMA).
2. Distributed shared memory architecture with non-uniform memory access (NUMA).

A third possibility exists, using only cache memory. This is known as a cache-only memory architecture (COMA).

Shared memory with a uniform memory access (UMA)

The uniform memory architecture is the direct implementation of the shared memory principle – a centralized shared memory is provided which is accessible by all processors via an interconnection network such that the path length and access time are about the same for all processors to all memory locations, just as a normal single processor system provides for equal access time to any main memory location. Uniform memory architectures can be described as consisting of a set of processors, perhaps with local cache memory connecting to one or more shared memory modules, as shown in Figure 6.5. If there is equal access to peripherals, the system is called a *symmetric multiprocessor*, otherwise it is an *asymmetric multiprocessor*.

Some UMA interconnection methods are shown in Figure 6.7. The single bus system (Figure 6.7(a)) is particularly convenient as a multiprocessor extension to a normal single processor microprocessor system, or other computer systems. In a single bus system with more than one processor attached to the bus, individual processors can access any of the memory modules attached to the bus, though only one data or instruction transfer can occur on the bus at any instant. The single bus system has been taken up by microprocessor manufacturers for multiple processor operation, and there are several standard buses which can support more than one microprocessor.

The multiple bus multiprocessor architecture shown in Figure 6.7(b) is a direct extension of the single bus architecture but with more than one bus connecting to all of the processors, memory modules and input/output interfaces. Processors can use any free bus to make a connection to a memory, but only B such connections can be made simultaneously, given B buses. Arbitration logic is necessary to resolve simultaneous requests, first to select up to one request for each memory module and then to select up to B of those requests to use the buses.

In the crossbar switch system (Figure 6.7(c)), a direct path is made between each processor and each memory module using one electronic bus switch to interconnect the processor and memory module. Each bus switch connects the set of processor bus signals, perhaps between forty and eighty signals, to a memory module. The crossbar architecture eliminates bus contention completely, though not memory contention, and can allow processors and memory to operate at their maximum speed.

The multiport memory architecture, as shown in Figure 6.7(d), uses one multiport memory connecting to all the processors. Multiport memory is designed to enable more

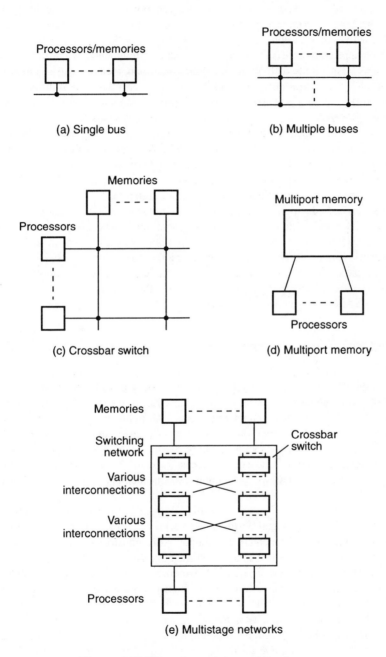

Figure 6.7 Shared memory architectures

than one memory location to be accessed simultaneously, in this case by different processors. If there are, say, sixteen processors, sixteen ports would be provided into the memory, one port for each processor. Though large multiport memory could be designed, the design is too complex and expensive and consequently "pseudomultiport" memory is used, which appears to access more than one location simultaneously but in fact accesses the locations sequentially at high speed. Pseudomultiport memory can be implemented using normal single-port high speed random access memory with the addition of arbitration logic at the memory/processor interface to allow processors to use the memory on a first-come first-served basis. Using normal memory components, it is necessary for the memory to operate substantially faster than the processors. To service N simultaneous requests, the memory would need to operate at least N times faster than when servicing a single request. The multiport architecture with pseudomultiport memory can be considered as a variation of the crossbar switch architecture, with each column of crossbar switches moved to be close to the associated memory module.

The cost and complexity of the crossbar switch grows as $O(N^2)$ where there are N processors and memory modules. Hence, the crossbar interconnection network would be unsuitable for large numbers of processors and memory modules. In such cases, a multistage network (Figure 6.7(e)) can be used to reduce the number of switches. In such networks, a path is established through more than one switching element in an array of switching elements. Most multistage networks have three or more stages and each path requires one switch element at each stage.

Distributed shared memory with non-uniform memory access (NUMA)

In the distributed shared memory system, shared memory modules are distributed among the processors so that each processor has attached a part of the total shared memory of the system. Again each processor could (and would normally have) cache memory. It is important to note that the memory has a single address space so that any processor could access any memory location directly by using its (real) address. Once we distribute the memory modules around the system, the access time to modules will depend upon the distance to the processor, i.e., we have a non-uniform memory access (time) architecture (NUMA).

A NUMA system will essentially be created by the use of a network in which the path length is longer for more distant destinations. Various networks are possible which have this characteristic, most of which are based upon a tree construction. Figure 6.8(a) shows the basic tree network as applied to a shared memory system. Here each processor has a memory which it can reach directly. All the memory in the system is reachable, but a processor must make a request through the network to make a connection to other memories. The network is made of switches which route the request to the desired memory. The route will be up until a downward path can be made, and then downwards. The path length will be a logarithmic function of the distance between the source and the destination. The primary motive for designing such a system is to aid scalability, as the tree can be extended relatively easily. Also some parallel algorithms have a tree structure

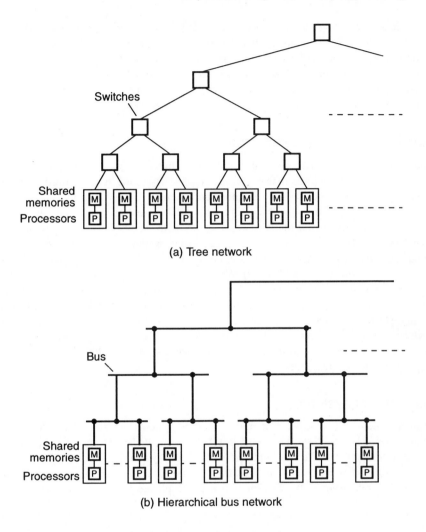

(a) Tree network

(b) Hierarchical bus network

Figure 6.8 NUMA networks

and these algorithms may map onto a tree network efficiently. Even if the algorithm does not have tree structure, many parallel algorithms have a locality in their communication/ memory reference patterns – or can be designed with this is locality. Since the tree network favors locality of reference, algorithms with locality of reference will operate efficiently on the tree. A variation of the tree structure is the hierarchical bus structure shown in Figure 6.8(b). Here requests are first routed along the local bus and to higher level buses as needed to reach the destination. The hierarchical ring network is similar but with the buses replaced by paths formed as rings. The Kendall Square Research KRS1 had a hierarchical ring structure but with a COMA model (see next section). Other examples of NUMA networks include the reflective network (Chapter 8). Introducing separate cache memory with each processor into a system effectively creates non-uniform access. With non-uniform access, it is necessary to consider how best to distribute data and code for individual processors. It is almost a necessity that truly scalable systems employ a NUMA network.

Cache-only memory architecture (COMA)

Apart from the shared memory with a uniform memory access (UMA) and the shared memory with a non-uniform memory access (NUMA) architectures, a third possibility has been proposed, the cache-only memory architecture (COMA). In the COMA, each processor has a part of the shared memory, as in NUMA, but each part consists of cache memory, i.e., all the shared memory consists of cache memory. Therefore some of the cache memory could have data not being requested by the attached processor. COMA should cause data to migrate to the processor requesting it, just as in any multiprocessor having cache memory. It could be expensive to provide all memory as cache memory. Hagwersen, Landin and Haridi (1992) describe a COMA system having only some of the memory as true cache memory and the rest as normal memory which they call attraction memory. (Data is attracted to the attraction memory closest to the processor requesting it.) Other examples of COMA architectures include the Kendall Square Research KSR1 computer, and Swedish Institute of Computer Science's DDM system. Figure 6.9 shows the general COMA arrangement.

Fault tolerant systems

We mentioned in Section 6.1 that multiprocessor systems are sometimes designed to obtain increased reliability. The reliability of a system can be increased by adding redundant components. We can duplicate parts at the system level (extra systems), gate level (extra gates) or component level (extra transistors, etc.). To be able to detect failures and continue operating in the face of faults, the duplicate parts need to repeat actions

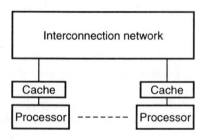

Figure 6.9 Cache-only memory architecture

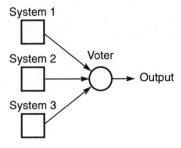

Figure 6.10 Triplicated system with a voter

performed by other parts, and some type of combining operating is performed which disregards the faulty actions. Alternatively, error detecting codes could be used; this requires extra gates.

One arrangement for system redundancy is to use three systems together with a voter circuit which examines the outputs of the systems, as shown in Figure 6.10. Each system performs the same computations. If all three systems are working, the corresponding outputs will be the same. If only two of the three systems are working, the voter chooses the two identical outputs. If more than one system is not working, the system fails. The probability that the system will operate is given by $P_s = P^3 + 3P^2(1 - P)$, i.e., the probability of all three systems operating or three combinations of two systems working and one not working. The triplicated system reliability is greater than for a single system during an initial operating period, but becomes less reliable later if the reliability decreases with time (see Problem 6.4). It is assumed that there is negligible probability of two faulty systems producing the same output, and that the voter will not fail. The concept can be extended to handle two faulty systems using five systems.

6.5 Potential for increased speed

To achieve an improvement in speed of operation through the use of parallelism, it is necessary to be able to divide the computation into tasks or processes which can be executed simultaneously. We might use a different computational algorithm with a multiprocessor rather than with a uniprocessor system, as it may not always be the best strategy simply to take an existing sequential computation and find the parts which can be executed simultaneously. Hence, a direct comparison is somewhat complicated by the algorithms chosen for each system. However, let us ignore this point for now. Suppose that a computation can be divided, at least partially, into concurrent tasks for execution on a multiprocessor system. A measure of relative performance between a multiprocessor system and a single processor system is the *speed-up factor*, S(n), defined as:

$$S(n) = \frac{\text{Execution time using one processor (uniprocessor system)}}{\text{Execution time using a multiprocessor with } n \text{ processors}}$$

which gives the increase in speed in using a multiprocessor. The (system) *efficiency*, E, is defined as:

$$E = \frac{S(n)}{n} \times 100\%$$

which gives how much processors are being used on the computation. If E = 50 per cent, the processors are being used half the time on the actual computation, on average. The maximum efficiency of 100 per cent occurs when all the processors are being used on the computation and the speed-up factor, $S(n)$, would be n.

There are various possible divisions of processes onto processors depending upon the computation, and different divisions lead to different speed-up factors. Also, any communication overhead between processors should be taken into account. Again, there are various possible communication overheads, from exhaustive communication between all processors to very limited communication between processors. The communication overhead is normally an increasing function of the number of processors. Here we will investigate some idealized situations. We shall use the term process to describe a contained computation performed by a processor; a processor may be scheduled to execute more than one process.

Equal duration process

The computation might be such that it can be divided into equal duration processes, with one process mapped onto one processor. This ideal situation would lead to the maximum speed-up of n, given n processors. The speed-up factor becomes:

$$S(n) = \frac{t}{t/n} = n$$

where t is the time on a single processor. Normally there would be communication between the processors. Suppose there is a communication overhead such that each process communicates once with one other process, but concurrently, as in a linear pipeline. The communications all occur simultaneously and thus appear as only one communication, as shown in Figure 6.11. Then the speed-up would be:

$$S(n) = \frac{t}{t/n + ct/n} = \frac{n}{1 + c}$$

where c is the fractional increase in the process time which is taken up by communication between a pair of processes. If $c = 1$ then the time taken to communicate between

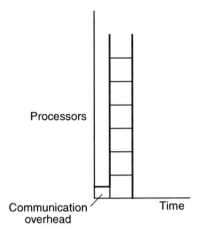

Processors

Communication
overhead

Time

Figure 6.11 Equal duration tasks

processes is the same as the process time, $S(n) = n/2$, a reduction to half the speed-up.

In more general situations, the communication time will be a function of the number of processes and the communications cannot be fully overlapped.

Parallel computation with a serial section

It is reasonable to expect that some part of a computation cannot be divided at all into concurrent processes and must be performed serially. For example, the computation might be divided as shown in Figure 6.12. During some period, perhaps an initialization period or period before concurrent processes are being set up, only one processor is doing useful work and, for the rest of the computation, all of the available processors (n processors) are operating on the problem, i.e. the remaining part of the computation has been divided into n equal processes.

If the fraction of the computation that cannot be divided into concurrent tasks is f, and no overhead incurs when the computation is divided into concurrent parts, the time to perform the computation with n processors is given by $ft + (1 - f)t/n$ and the speed-up factor is given by:

$$S(n) = \frac{t}{ft + (1 - f)t/n} = \frac{n}{1 + (n - 1)f}$$

This equation is known as *Amdahl's law*. Figure 6.13 shows $S(n)$ plotted against number of processors and plotted against f. We see that indeed a speed improvement is indicated, but the fraction of the computation that is executed by concurrent processes needs to be a substantial fraction of the overall computation if a significant increase in speed is to be

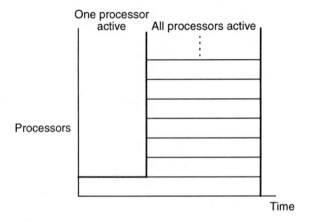

Figure 6.12 Parallel computation with serial section

achieved. The point made in Amdahl's law is that even with an infinite number of processors, the maximum speed-up is limited to $1/f$. For example, with only 5 per cent of the computation being serial, the maximum speed-up is 20, irrespective of the number of processors.

In fact, the situation could be worse. There will certainly be an additional computation to start the parallel section and general communication overhead between processes. In the general case, when the communication overhead is some function of n, say $tf_c(n)$, we have the speed-up given by:

$$S(n) = \frac{n}{1 + (1 - f)n + nf_c(n)}$$

In practice we would expect computations to use a variable number of processors, as illustrated in Figure 6.14.

Optimum division of processes

We need to know whether utilizing all the available processors and dividing the work equally among processors is the best strategy, or whether an alternative strategy is better. Stone (1987) investigated this point and developed equations for different communication overheads, finding that the overhead eventually dominates, after which it is better not even to spread the processes among all the processors, but to let only one processor do the work, i.e., a single processor system becomes faster than a multiprocessor system. In our equations, this point is reached when the denominator of the speed-up equations equals or exceeds n, making $S(n)$ equal or less than one. Stone confirms that if dividing the process is best, spreading the processes equally among processors is best (assuming

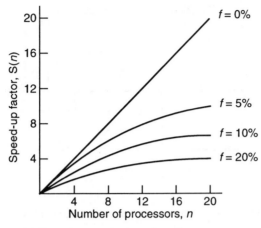

(a) Speed-up against number of processors

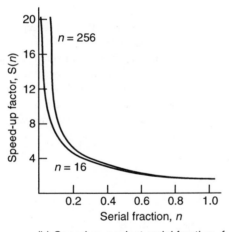

(b) Speed-up against serial fraction, *f*

Figure 6.13 Speed-up factor

that the number of processes will divide exactly into the number of processors).

Speed-up estimates

It was once speculated that the speed-up is given by $\log_2 n$ (Minsky's conjecture). Lea (1986) used the term *applied parallelism* for the parallelism achieved on a particular system given the restricted parallelism processing capability of the system, and suggested that the applied parallelism is typically $\log_2 n$. He used the term *natural parallelism* for

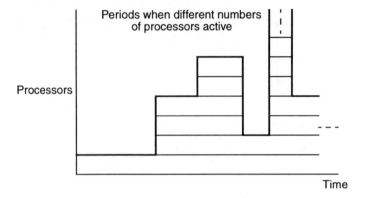

Figure 6.14 Parallel computation with variable processor usage

the potential in a program for simultaneous execution of independent processes and suggested that the natural parallelism is $n/\log_2 n$.

Hwang and Briggs (1984) presented the following derivation for speed-up being less than or equal to $n/\log_e n$. Suppose at some instant i processors are active and sharing the work equally with a load $1/i$ (seconds). Let the probability that i processors are active simultaneously be $P_i = 1/n$ where there are n processors. There is an equal chance of each number of processors ($i = 1, 2, 3 \ldots n$) being active. The (normalized) overall processing time on the multiprocessor is given by:

$$T_n = \frac{1}{n} \sum_{i=1}^{n} \frac{1}{i}$$

The speed-up factor is given by:

$$S(n) = \frac{1}{\dfrac{1}{n} \displaystyle\sum_{i=1}^{n} \frac{1}{i}} \le \frac{n}{\log_e n} \le \frac{n}{\log_2 n}$$

Figure 6.15 shows the speed-up estimates. If these values could not be improved upon in practice they would lead to the conclusion that multiprocessors give poor speed-up on large numbers of processors! The challenge is to disprove this statement in practical situations and with specific multiprocessor designs. In fact, some studies have achieved nearly perfect speed-up. For example, a 256-processor Butterfly multiprocessor system has achieved a speed-up of 230 on a range of numerical calculations (Rettberg and Thomas, 1986), whereas $n/\log_2 n$ gives a value of 32.

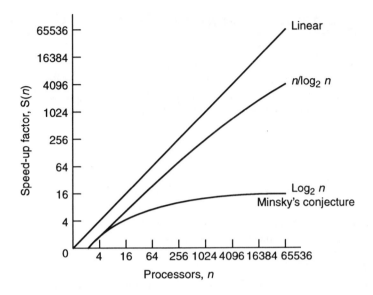

Figure 6.15 Speed-up factor estimates

Scalability

Scalability is a rather imprecise term used to indicate a design which allows the system to be increased in size and in doing so obtains increased performance. Of course we would want all multiprocessor systems to be scalable, but this will depend heavily upon the architecture of the system. Usually as we add processors to a system, the interconnection network must be expanded. Greater communication delays and contention results and the system efficiency, E, reduces. The underlying goal of most multiprocessor designs is to achieve scalability, and this is reflected in the multitude of interconnection networks which have been devised.

The scalability requirement can be relaxed by saying that increased performance only needs to be achieved with a larger problem size. For example, multiplication of 64×64 matrices might be performed on a 64 processor system in a time t, and multiplication of 256×256 matrices might be performed on a 256 processor system in time t in a (very) scalable system. This can be captured in a *scale up function*, $f(n)$, which is the actual execution time for n processors when n is increased proportionally to the size of the problem. This function indicates how well more processors can be employed with an increasing problem size. Ideally $f(n) = k$ where k is a constant. Scalability and the scale-up function are dependent upon the parallel algorithm being used. We need to use scalable parallel algorithms, algorithms in which the number of computational steps preferably increase faster than communication steps as the size of the problem increases.

6.6 Programming multiprocessor systems

In this section, we will review key aspects of using shared memory multiprocessor systems in so far as it impacts upon the architecture. Further details including the specific algorithms suitable for multiprocessors can be found in specialized texts such as JáJá (1992) and Leighton (1992). Further details of programming techniques can be found in Lester (1993) and Quinn (1994).

6.6.1 Concurrent processes

A *process* or *task* is a computation performed by a processor with defined sets of inputs and outputs (results). A process could be one machine instruction, but is much more likely to be a group of machine instructions executed in sequence. The size of a process and its input/output requirements have a profound effect on the performance of the system. A graphical representation of concurrent processes may be made, as shown in Figure 6.16.

Some computations might immediately suggest a solution involving concurrent processes. Such computations also tend to suggest specialized system architectures, for example, arrays of processors for visual applications. Here we will start with a computation which has been specified in a sequential manner; a transformation is then necessary to obtain a parallel computation. Transformations can be achieved in one of two principal ways:

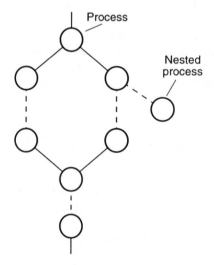

Figure 6.16 Parallel and serial processes

1. By a compiler recognizing potential parallel parts and performing a restructuring algorithm, i.e., *implicit parallelism.*

2. By the programmer recognizing and specifying the parts which are to be executed in parallel, i.e., *explicit parallelism.*

A third method is to have a hardware structure which finds the parallelism when it exists. The dataflow technique, considered in Chapter 10, has this property.

In implicit parallelism, a *parallelizing compiler* accepts a high level language source program and makes translations and code restructuring to create independent code which can be executed concurrently. There are various recognition algorithms and strategies that can be applied and incorporated into a parallelizing compiler apart from the methods outlined previously. Information can be found in Padua, Kuck and Lawrie (1980) and Padua and Wolfe (1986). Some parallelizing compilers are designed to translate code into parallel form for vector computers. Padua and Wolfe use the term *concurrentizing* for code translation to create multiprocessor computations.

In both explicit parallelism and implicit parallelism, it is necessary to establish which parts can be executed together. Generally a *dependency analysis* has to be performed either by the compiler or by the programmer. It is most usual not to rely on a compiler exclusively. Rather the programmer must identify some parallelism. The area where compiler detected implicit parallelism has been most successful is in vector computers, where the computation revolve around processing elements of arrays. In shared memory multiprocessor systems, the programmer has to do a great deal of work to expose parallelism in a program. Let us first describe typical high level language constructs for actually specifying concurrent parts in a program. Then we will look at dependency analysis.

6.6.2 Constructs for specifying parallelism

Several constructs have been proposed to define the parallel processes within a programming language. We will describe typical constructs:

Constructs for FORTRAN-like languages

Perhaps the first example of programming language structures to specify parallelism is the FORK-JOIN group of statements, introduced by Conway (1963). (Conway refers to earlier work and it appears that the idea was known before 1960.) FORK-JOIN constructs have been applied as extensions to FORTRAN and, much more recently, to the UNIX operating system. In the original FORK-JOIN construct, a FORK statement generates one new path for a concurrent process and the concurrent processes use JOIN statements at their ends. When both JOIN statements have been reached, processing continues in a sequential fashion. For more concurrent processes, additional FORK statements are necessary either in sequence or at the head of the spawned processes to create further concurrent processes. The FORK-JOIN constructs are shown nested in Figure 6.17. Each spawned process requires a JOIN statement at its end which brings together

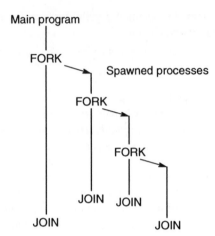

Figure 6.17 FORK-JOIN construct

the concurrent processes to a single terminating point. Only when all concurrent processes have completed can the subsequent statements be executed, and typically a counter is used to keep a record of processes not completed.

The FORK statement has the general form:

```
FORK A,J,N
```

where A is a label indicating the beginning of the spawned process and J identifies a counter which is set to the value N. If N is omitted, the counter is incremented. If J is also omitted, a counter is not involved in the operation. The counter is used to indicate the number of concurrent processes which have not finished.

The JOIN statement has the general form:

```
JOIN J,B
```

where J identifies a counter which is decremented. If the counter contents then become zero, the statement specified by the label B is executed. B can be omitted, in which case the statement at the next location is executed. If the counter contents are not zero, the processor executing the JOIN statement is released.

The JOIN statement has three sequential operations. First, a counter has to be decremented. Next, the value held in the counter must be examined and finally, associated processing is either terminated or continued, dependent upon the value of the counter (not zero or zero). It is important that JOIN statements operate on the counter separately; if more than one JOIN statement were to operate on a counter simultaneously, there would be instances when incorrect program sequences would subsequently be followed. Hence, the decrement and test operations of JOIN statements must be made "indivisible" by, for example, the use of indivisible test and set machine instructions or "locked" instruction sequences (see Section 6.6.4). There are also instances when FORK and JOIN statements must not operate upon the same counter simultaneously.

There are variations to the FORK-JOIN syntax described. FORK statements can be defined as spawning a number of processes, rather than only one additional process. These processes are identified by a list of parameters, for example:

```
FORK L1, L2, L3 ... Ln
```

generates n separate processes. The first process has the label L1 at its start, the second L2 and so on. The CREATE construct creates a new instance of a subroutine which is executed on a separate processor. A simple example of using CREATE is to add together the elements of a 1000 element array by dividing the summation into 10 routines, each adding up 100 elements, as in the following:

```
          DO 100 J = 1,9
          CREATE ('SUM',ACC(J),A(I),100)
          I = I + 100
100       CONTINUE
          CALL SUM (ACC(10),A(I),100)
          JOIN
          CALL SUM (SUM,ACC,10)
                .
                .
                .

          END


          SUBROUTINE SUM (ACC,A,N)
          DIMENSION A(100)
          ACC = 0.0
          DO 10 I = 1,N
          ACC = ACC + A(I)
10        CONTINUE
          RETURN
          END
```

Nine instances of the subroutine SUM are created, in addition to one instance in the main program before the JOIN construct. Each instance uses a separate global accumulator, ACC(1), ACC(2), ACC(10). After the JOIN, the main program adds together the results held in the accumulators to produce the final result in SUM. Further examples of the CREATE construct are given in Karp (1987).

Other constructs have been proposed to specify n identical processes or similar processes, for example DOPAR-DOEND:

```
        DOPAR L1, i = 1,10,1
            statements
  L1:    PAREND
```

generates ten identical sequences. The parameters 1,10,1 are initial value, final value and step value of a variable *i*. Successive values are used in a different process. The construct can be compared to the FORTRAN DO-CONTINUE construct.

Constructs for block structured languages

The FORK-JOIN constructs have their origins at the time of the FORTRAN sequential programming language, which employs labels to identify the start of new program sequences selected by GOTO statements. Such methods have generally lost favor and block structured languages are now preferred, at least in the academic community. Parallel programming structures can be introduced into block structured languages such as Pascal and C.[1] For example, a PARBEGIN ... PAREND construct (or COBEGIN ... COEND construct) can identify a group of statements which are to be executed simultaneously in Pascal-derived parallel languages, as shown below:

```
PARBEGIN
  S1;
  S2;
   .
   .
  Sn
PAREND
```

In languages derived from C/C++, we might find:

```
par {
  S1;
  S2;
   .
   .
  Sn;
}
```

In both cases, the statements S1, S2 ... Sn are specified as executed simultaneously. Each statement could be a block of statements and hence a set of "multi-statement" processes can be specified as being executed simultaneously. Single statement processes might incur an unacceptable communication overhead, though the construct allows this possibility. The par { ... } construction can be found in CC++ (Foster, 1995).

---

[1] According to Kernighan and Ritchie (1988), C is not block structured in the sense of Pascal as functions cannot be declared within other functions.

An earlier example of this approach can be found in ALGOL-68. The order of execution of statements (or compound statements) separated by a comma instead of a semicolon was not defined, i.e. the statements would be executed in any order in a single processor system, and could be executed simultaneously in a multiprocessor system.

The PARFOR construct, found in concurrent versions of Pascal and C/C++, generates a number of separate processes as specified in the construct of the form (derived from C++):

```
parfor (int i = 0; i < n; i++) {
  S1;
  S2;
  .
  .
  Sm
}
```

which generates *n* processes each consisting of the statements S1, S2 ... Sm. Each process uses a different value of *i*. For example:

```
parfor (int i = 0; i < 5; i++)
  a[i] = 0;
```

clears a[0], a[1], a[2], a[3] and a[4] to zero concurrently. The parfor construct can be found in CC++ (Foster, 1995). Examples of the similar FORALL construct for the C language are given in Terrano, Dunn and Peters (1989). The equivalent in FORTRAN is DOALL, e.g.:

```
DOALL n = 1 TO 5
    .
    .
END DOALL
```

In fact as FORTRAN was very widely used in engineering computations, it has been carried over to parallel computer applications.

Using system calls

As an alternative to having a specially designed parallel languages, a normal sequential language, say C, could be used together with system calls to achieve process creation and sharing data. Operating systems such as UNIX are based upon the notion of a process. On a single processor system, the processor has to be time-shared between active processes, switching from one process to another at regular intervals. On a multiprocessor, there is an opportunity to execute processes truly concurrently. UNIX provides system calls to create processes, and it is possible to use these facilities to write parallel programs. Brawer (1989) describes how this can be done in detail. (Of course we would not get an increased execution speed on a single processor; actually the speed would reduce because of the overhead of creating the processes, and for time-sharing the processor.) Two forms of process are generally available, the original UNIX *heavyweight process*, and the *lightweight process* (or *thread*) which naturally share memory address space and hence can be created with a much lower overhead. The UNIX (heavyweight process) system calls correspond to FORK and JOIN. Using normal languages with embedded system calls in the programs is particularly convenient for message passing multiprocessors which are described in Chapter 9.

6.6.3 Dependency analysis

One of the key issues in parallel programming is identifying which processes could be executed together. This is a prelude to rearranging programs to achieve the maximum parallelism. Processes cannot be executed together because of some dependency between them. The process of finding the dependencies in a program is called *dependence analysis*.

Bernstein's conditions

Bernstein (1966) established a set of conditions which are sufficient to determine whether two processes can be executed in parallel. These conditions, which we will reduce to a simple form here, relate to memory locations used by the processes (usually statements). Generally, these memory locations would be used to hold variables which are to be altered or read during the executing of the processes or statements. Let us define two sets of memory locations, I (input) and O (output), such that:

I_j is the set of memory locations read by a process P_i.
O_i is the set of memory locations altered by a process P_j.

For two processes P_1 and P_2 to be executed simultaneously, the input to process P_1 must not be the output of P_2, and the input of P_2 must not be the output of P_1, i.e.:

$$I_1 \cap O_2 = \phi$$
$$I_2 \cap O_1 = \phi$$

where ϕ is an empty set. The output of each process must also be different, i.e.:

$$O_1 \cap O_2 = \phi$$

We will refer to the three conditions as Bernstein's conditions. We used exactly the same conditions to detect dependencies in pipelines in Chapter 5. The condition $I_2 \cap O_1 = \phi$ corresponds to true dependencies (read-after-write hazards) where instruction 2 follows instruction 1. The condition $I_1 \cap O_2 = \phi$ corresponds to antidependencies (write-after-read hazards). The condition $O_1 \cap O_2 = \phi$ corresponds to output dependencies (write-after-write hazards).

We should mention in passing that Bernstein differentiated between read-only operations, write-only operations, read then write operations and write then read-only operations. He also included the set read by the process after the two processes considered for parallelization, which led to the third condition being $I_3 \cap O_2 \cap O_1 = \phi$. As noted by Baer (1980), the third condition reduces to $O_1 \cap O_2 = \phi$ for high level language statements.

If the three conditions are all satisfied, the two statements can be executed concurrently. The conditions can be applied to processes of any complexity. A process can be a single statement, when it can be determined whether the two statements can be executed simultaneously. I_i corresponds to the variables on the right hand side of the statements and O_j corresponds to the variables on the left hand side of the statements.

Example: Suppose the two statements are (in C):

```
a = x + y;
b = x + z;
```

we have:

$$I_1 = (x, y)$$
$$I_2 = (x, z)$$
$$O_1 = (a)$$
$$O_2 = (b)$$

and the conditions:

$$I_1 \cap O_2 = \phi$$
$$I_2 \cap O_1 = \phi$$
$$O_1 \cap O_2 = \phi$$

are satisfied. Hence the statements $a = x + y$, $b = x + z$ can be executed simultaneously. Suppose the statements are:

```
a = x + y;
b = a + b;
```

Then $I_2 \cap O_1 \neq \phi$ and the two statements cannot be executed simultaneously.

The technique can be extended to processes involving more than two statements. Then, the set of inputs and outputs to each process, rather than each statement, is considered. The technique can also be used to determine whether several statements can be executed in parallel. In this case, the conditions are:

$$I_i \cap O_j = \phi$$
$$I_j \cap O_i = \phi$$

$$O_i \cap O_j = \phi$$

for all i, j (excluding $i = j$).

Example:

```
a = x + y;
b = x * z;
c = y - x;
```

Here $I_1 = (x, y)$, $I_2 = (x, z)$, $I_3 = (y, x)$, $O_1 = (a)$, $O_2 = (b)$ and $O_3 = (c)$. All the conditions:

$$
\begin{array}{lll}
I_1 \cap O_2 = \phi & I_1 \cap O_3 = \phi & I_2 \cap O_3 = \phi \\
I_2 \cap O_1 = \phi & I_3 \cap O_1 = \phi & I_3 \cap O_2 = \phi \\
O_1 \cap O_2 = \phi & I_1 \cap O_3 = \phi & I_2 \cap O_3 = \phi
\end{array}
$$

are satisfied and hence the three statements can be executed simultaneously (or in any order).

Some dependencies only exist if the computation follows a particular path (a *procedural dependency*) whereas others always exist. For example, not all instructions after a branch (IF statement) are dependent upon the branch outcome. In:

```
if (a == 0) {
  b = 5;
  c = d + 8;
}
b = c;
```

the statement b = c is not dependent upon the outcome of the IF statement because it will always be executed, and is not strictly procedurally dependent. Hence both statements could be executed together. The other statements are dependent upon the branch outcome and are procedurally dependent.

Berstein's conditions can be easily automated in a compiler, and could conceivably be used by programmer. The conditions are completely general and do not use any special characteristics of the computation in finding the parallelism. However, some common programming constructs have a natural parallelism which a compiler or the programmer can take utilize, in particular program loops.

Parallelism in loops

Parallelism can be found in high level language loops. For example the C loop:

```
for (i = 1; i <= 20; i++)
  a[i] = b[i];
```

could be expanded to:

```
a[1]  = b[1];
a[2]  = b[2];
a[3]  = b[3];
    .
    .
a[19] = b[19];
a[20] = b[20];
```

Given twenty processors, these statements could all be executed in parallel (Bernstein's conditions being satisfied).

The above case is the ideal case as there are no dependencies between any of the statements. However there may be dependencies within an iteration of a loop which will not prevent different iterations of the loop to be executed in parallel, though will necessitate the statements in one iteration to be executed in order. A dependency which is between loop iterations is called a *loop-carried* dependency, while a dependency which is not dependent of loop iterations is called *loop-independent*. For example in:

```
for (i = 1; i <= 8; i++) {
  a[i] = a[i+3];
  b[i] = a[i] + 2;
}
```

The first statement in the loop body has a loop-carried antidependency, while the second is a loop-independent dependency. The number of iterations between two instructions having the loop-carried antidependency is usually a constant, i.e. 3 above, though it need not be. It could be a computed value. Loop-independent and loop-carried dependencies could be true dependencies, antidependencies or output dependencies. Loop-carried dependencies occurring in nested loops may depend upon the "level" of the iteration.

Loop-carried dependencies can sometimes to handled by decomposing the loop into more than one loop which are dependent of each other. For example the C loop:

```
for (i = 3; i <= 20; i++)
  a[i] = a[i-2] + 4;
```

computes:

```
a[3]  = a[1] + 4;
a[4]  = a[2] + 4;
a[5]  = a[3] + 4;
    .
    .
a[19] = a[17] + 4;
```

```
a[20] = a[18] + 4;
```

Hence a[5] can only be computed after a[3], a[6] after a[4] and so on. The computation can be split into two independent sequences (partitions):

```
a[3]  = a[1]  + 4;        a[4]  = a[2]  + 4;
a[5]  = a[3]  + 4;        a[6]  = a[4]  + 4;
a[17] = a[15] + 4;        a[18] = a[16] + 4;
a[19] = a[17] + 4;
```

or written as two FOR loops:

```
i = 3;
for (j = 1; j <= 9; j++) {
  i = i + 2;
  a[i] = a[i-2] + 4;
}
```

and

```
i = 4;
for (j = 1; j <= 8; j++) {
  i = i + 2;
  a[i] = a[i-2] + 4;
}
```

Each loop can be executed by a separate processor in a multiprocessor system. The approach can be applied to generate a number of partitions, dependent upon the references within the body of the loop.

Dependencies require explicit synchronization to ensure that statements are not executed before all required values have been computed. Dependencies of a computation can be illustrated by a *directed acyclic graph* (DAG) where the nodes represent tasks and the directed edges represent precedence constraints. If a dependence edge is transitive, there is an alternative path from the source node of that dependence to the destination node through a sequence of other nodes (Krothapalli and Sadayappan, 1991). This is significant because if there is an alternative path, it is not necessary to provide synchronization for that dependency. Krothapalli and Sadayappan (and other workers) have developed ways to remove redundant dependency edges in the graph in these cases.

Dependencies in loops can be described using a form of DAG called an *iteration space dependence graph* (ISDG). In this graph, each node corresponds to one iteration of the loop, and the edges show dependencies between iterations. Suppose we have the loop:

```
for (i = 2; i <= 10; i++)
  a[i] = a[i-4] + a[i+6]
```

True dependencies

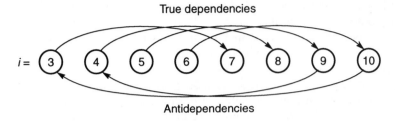

Antidependencies

Figure 6.18 Iteration dependency graph

There is a (true) dependency between iteration i and iteration $i + 4$. There is also an anti-dependency between iteration i and iteration $i + 6$. These dependencies are shown by edges in the iteration dependence graph in Figure 6.18.

Nested loops require the nodes to be identified by all the indices of the loop counters. A dependence from iteration i to iteration k is redundant at node i if and only if:

1. There exists a sequence of iterations $i_1, i_2, \ldots, i_j$, such that $j > 0$ and there is a dependence from i_m to i_{m+1} for $1 \leq m < j$, and

2. There is a dependence from iteration i to iteration i_1 and from iteration i_j to iteration k.

Such conditions can be found by search processes (Krothapalli and Sadayappan, 1991). There are also software tools for identifying and showing dependencies, e.g. the Parascope editor for parallel Fortran programs.

Studying the parallel execution of FOR/DO loops has a long history and we give only an overview. Early works include Lamport (1974). In this section we have assumed that there are no architectural constraints in accessing array elements from memory. It may be that shared memory is divided into modules and only one location in each module can be accessed simultaneously. If such constraints exist, the layout of data in the memory becomes important.

6.6.4 Critical sections

Suppose we have obtained, by either explicit or implicit parallelism, a set of processes that are to be executed simultaneously. A number of questions arise. First, we need a mechanism for processes to communicate and pass data, even if this only occurs when a process terminates. Coupled with this, we need a mechanism to ensure that communication takes place at the correct time, i.e. we need a synchronization mechanism. A synchronization mechanism is also required to terminate processes, as we have seen in the JOIN construct. If processes are to access common variables (memory locations) or interact in some other way, we need to ensure that incorrect data is not formed while two or more processes attempt to alter variables.

A process typically accesses a shared resource from time to time. The shared resource might be physical, such as an input/output device or a database contained within shared memory, and may accept data from, or provide data to, the process. More than one process might wish to access the same resource from time to time.

A mechanism for ensuring that only one process accesses a particular resource at a time is to establish sections of code involving the resource as so-called *critical sections* and arrange that only one such critical section is executed at a time, i.e. *mutual exclusion* exists. The first process to reach a critical section for a particular resource executes the critical section ("enters the critical section") and prevents all other processes from executing a critical section for the same resource by some as yet undefined mechanism. Once the process finishes the critical section, another process is allowed to enter it for the same resource.

Locks

The simplest mechanism for ensuring mutual exclusion of critical sections is by the use of a *lock*. A lock is a 1-bit variable which is set to 1 to indicate that a process has entered the critical section and reset to 0 to indicate that no process is in the critical section, the last process having left the critical section. The lock operates like a door lock. A process coming to the "door" of a critical section and finding it open may enter the critical section, locking the door to prevent other processes entering. Once the process has finished the critical section, it unlocks the door and leaves.

Suppose that a process reaches a lock which is set, indicating that the process is excluded from the critical section. It now has to wait until it is allowed to enter the critical section. The process might need to examine the lock bit continually in a tight loop, for example, equivalent to:

```
while (lock == 1) skip;    /* Skip means no operation */
lock = 1;                  /* enter critical section */

   Critical Section

lock = 0;                  /* leave critical section */
```

Such locks are called *spin locks* and the mechanism is called *busy waiting*. Busy waiting is inefficient of processors as no useful work is being done while waiting for the lock, though this is a common approach with locks.

Other computations could be done in place of `skip`. In some cases it may be possible to deschedule the process from the processor and schedule another process while waiting for a lock to open, though this in itself incurs an overhead in saving and reading process information. If more than one process is busy waiting for a lock to be reset, and the lock opens, a mechanism might be necessary to choose the best or highest priority process to enter the critical section, rather than let this be resolved by indeterminate busy waiting. Such a mechanism is incorporated into the semaphore operation (see Section 6.6.3).

It is important that more than one process does not set the lock (open the door) and enter the critical section simultaneously, or that one process finds the lock reset (door open) but before it can set it (close the door) another process also finds the door open and enters the critical section. Hence the actions of examining whether a lock is set and of setting it must be done as one "uninterruptable" operation, and one during which no other process can operate upon the lock. This exclusion mechanism is generally implemented in hardware by having special indivisible machine instructions which perform the complete operation sequence. Most recent microprocessors have such indivisible machine instructions.

Intel 8086 family lock prefix/signal

The Intel 8086 family implements a lock operation by providing a special 1-byte LOCK instruction which prevents the next instruction from being interrupted by other bus trans-actions. Only certain instructions are allowable to be locked after a LOCK. The LOCK instruction causes a LOCK signal to be generated for the duration of the LOCK instruction and the next instruction, whatever type of instruction this may be. The LOCK signal is used with external logic to inhibit bus transactions of other processors. If a bus request is received by the processor, the request is recorded internally but not honored until after the LOCK instruction and the next instruction.

The lock operation preceding a critical section could be implemented in 8086 assembly language as follows:

```
L2:   MOV CX,FFFFH    ;Set up value to load into lock
      LOCK            ;Make next instruction indivisible
      XCHG Lock,CX    ;Set lock
      JCXZ L1         ;Start critical section if
                      ;lock not originally set
      JMP L2          ;Wait for lock to open
L1:                   ;Critical section
```

In this sequence, XCHG Lock,CX exchanges the contents of memory location Lock and register CX. The exchange instruction takes two bus cycles to complete. Without the LOCK prefix, the exchange operation could be interrupted between bus cycles in a multi-processor system, and lead to an incorrect result.

Motorola MC68000 Test and Set instruction

The original MC68000 microprocessor had one indivisible instruction, the TAS instruc-tion (test and set an operand), having the format:

```
TAS effective address
```

where effective address identifies a byte location using any of the MC68000 "data alterable addressing" modes (Motorola, 1984). There are two sequential operations, "test" and "set". First, the value read from the addressed location is "tested" for positive/ negative and zero, i.e. the N (negative) and Z (zero) flags in the condition code register are set according to the value in the location. The Z flag is set when the bit is zero and the N flag is set when the whole number held is negative. Next, the most significant bit of the addressed location is set, irrespective of the previous test, i.e. whether or not the bit was 1, it is set to 1 during the TAS instruction. The addressed location is read, modified as necessary and the result written in one indivisible read-modify-write bus cycle. A lock operation before a critical section could be encoded using a TAS instruction in MC68000 assembly language as:

```
L1: TAS Flag
    BMI L1        ;Repeat if lock already set (negative)
```

The MC68000 also has a *test a bit and set* instruction (BSET) which is not indivisible and could not be used alone as a lock operation. An indivisible compare and swap (CAS) instruction was introduced into the MC68000 family starting with the 32-bit MC68020 and continued with MC68030 and MC68040 processors. Compare and swap can be used to maintain linked lists in a multiprocessor environment. Most processors have some form of indivisible instruction.

Though indivisible instructions simplify the locks, locks with mutual exclusion can be implemented without indivisible TAS instructions. For example, one apparent solution is given below using two variables a and b:

Process 1

```
a = 0;
 Non-critical section
a = 1;
while (b == 1) skip;
 Critical section
a = 0;
 Non-critical section
```

Process 2

```
b = 0;
 Non-critical section
b = 1;
while (a == 1) skip;
 Critical section
b = 0;
 Non-critical section
```

However, this scheme can easily be deadlocked. In *deadlock*, the processes cannot proceed as each process is waiting for others to proceed. The code will deadlock when both a and b are set to 1 and tested simultaneously. Skip could be replaced with code to avoid this type of deadlock.

The solution is still susceptible to both Process 1 and Process 2 entering the critical section together if the sequence of instructions is not executed as specified in the program, which is possible in some systems. We have seen, in Chapter 5, for example, that some pipelined systems might change the order of execution. Memory contention and delays might also change the order of execution, if queued requests for memory are not executed in the order presented to the memory. The effect of such changes of execution was first highlighted by Lamport (1979) who used code similar to that given for

Process 1 and Process 2 to elucidate a solution, namely that the following conditions must prevail:

1. Each processor issues memory requests in the order specified by its program.
2. Memory requests from all processors issued to an individual memory location are serviced from a single first-in first-out queue (in the order in which they are presented to the memory).

In fact, it is only necessary for memory requests to be serviced in the order that they are made in the program, but in practice that always means that the two separate Lamport conditions are satisfied.

To eliminate the busy waiting deadlock condition and maintain at most one process in the critical section at a time, a third variable, p, can be introduced into the code as below:

Process 1	Process 2
`a = 0;`	`b = 0;`
Non-critical section	Non-critical section
`a = 1;`	`B = 1;`
`p = 2;`	`P = 1;`
`while((b==1)&&(P==2)) skip;`	`while((a==1)&&(P==1)) skip;`
Critical section	Critical section
`a = 0;`	`b = 0;`
Non-critical section	Non-critical section

Irrespective of whether any of the instructions of one process are separated by instructions of the other process, p can only be set to Process 1 or Process 2 and hence the conditional loop will resolve the conflict and one process will be chosen to enter its critical section. It does not matter whether both conditional loops are performed simultaneously or are interleaved, though it is assumed that only one process can access a variable at a time (read or write), which is true for normal computer memory. Also, assuming that each critical section executes in a finite time, both processes will eventually have the opportunity to enter their critical sections (i.e. the algorithm is fair to both processes). It is left as an exercise to determine whether Lamport's conditions must still be satisfied.

6.6.5 Semaphores

Dijkstra (1968) devised the concept of a *semaphore* which is a positive integer (including zero) operated upon by two operations named **P** and **V**. The **P** operation on a semaphore, s, written as **P**(s), waits until s is greater than zero and then decrements s by one and allows the process to continue. The **V** operation increments s by one. The **P** and **V** operations are performed indivisibly. (The letter **P** is from the Dutch word "passeren" meaning to pass, and the letter **V** is from the Dutch word "vrijgeven" meaning to release.)

268   Shared memory multiprocessor systems

A mechanism for activating waiting processes is also implicit in the **P** and **V** operations, though the exact algorithm is not specified; the algorithm is expected to be fair. Delayed processes should be activated eventually, commonly in the order in which they are delayed. Processes delayed by **P**(s) are kept in abeyance until released by a **V**(s) on the same semaphore. Processes might be delayed using a spin lock (busy waiting) or more likely by descheduling processes from processors and allocating in its place a process which is ready.

Mutual exclusion of critical sections of more than one process accessing the same resource can be achieved with one semaphore having the value 0 or 1 (a *binary semaphore*) which acts as a lock variable, but the **P** and **V** operations include a process scheduling mechanism. The semaphore is initialized to 1, indicating that no process is in its critical section associated with the semaphore. Each mutually exclusive critical section is preceded by a **P**(s) and terminated with a **V**(s) on the same semaphore, i.e.:

Process 1	Process 2	Process 3 ...
Non-critical section	Non-critical section	Non-critical section
P(s)	**P**(s)	**P**(s)
Critical section	Critical section	Critical section
V(s)	**V**(s)	**V**(s)
Non-critical section	Non-critical section	Non-critical section

Any process might reach its **P**(s) operation first (or more than one process may reach it simultaneously). The first process to reach its **P**(s) operation, or to be accepted, will set the semaphore to 0, inhibiting the other processes from proceeding past their **P**(s) operations, but any process reaching its **P**(s) operation will be recorded in a first-in first-out queue. The accepted process executes its critical section. When the process reaches its **V**(s) operation, it sets the semaphore s to 1 and allows one of the processes waiting to proceed into its critical section.

A general semaphore (or counting semaphore) can take on positive values other than zero and one. Such semaphores provide, for example, a means of recording the number of "resource units" available or used. Consider the action of a "producer" of data linked to a "consumer" of data through a first-in first-out buffer. The buffer would normally be implemented as a circular buffer in memory, using a pointer to indicate the front of the queue and a different pointer to indicate the back of the queue. The locations currently not holding valid data are those locations between the front and back pointer, in the clockwise direction, not including the locations pointed at by each pointer. The locations holding valid items to be taken by the consumer are those locations between the front and back pointer in the counterclockwise direction, including the locations pointed at by each pointer.

Loading the queue and taking items from the queue must be indivisible and separate operations. Two counting semaphores can be used, one called empty, to indicate the number of empty locations in the complete circular queue, and one called full, to indicate the number of data items in the queue ready for the consumer. When the queue is full, full

= n, the total number of locations in the queue, and empty = 0. When the queue is empty, the initial condition, full = 0 and empty = n. The two semaphores can be used as shown below:

Producer	Consumer

Produce data message
P(empty)   **P**(full)
Load buffer   Take next message from queue
V(full)   **V**(empty)

Notice that the **P** and **V** operations surrounding each critical section do not operate on the same semaphore as in the previous example of a mutually exclusive critical section.

When the producer has a message for the queue, it performs a **P**(empty) operation. If empty = 0, indicating that there are no empty locations, the process is delayed until empty $\neq$ 0, indicating that there is at least one free location. Then the empty semaphore is decremented, indicating that one of the free locations is to be used and the producer enters its critical section to load the buffer using the back pointer of the queue, updating the back pointer accordingly. On leaving the critical section, a **V**(full) is performed, which increments the full semaphore to show that one location has been filled.

When the consumer wants to take the next message from the queue, it performs a **P**(full) operation which delays the process if full = 0, i.e. if there are no messages in the queue. When full $\neq$ 0, i.e. when there is at least one message in the queue, full is decremented to indicate that one message is to be taken from the queue. The consumer then enters its critical section to take the next message from the queue, using the front pointer and updating this pointer accordingly. On leaving the critical section, a **V**(empty) is performed which increments the empty semaphore to show that one more location is free.

The previous example can be extended to more than one buffer between a producer and a consumer, and with more than two processes. An important factor is to avoid deadlock (sometimes called a *deadly embrace*) which prevents processes from ever proceeding. Deadlock can occur with two processes when one requires a resource held by the other, and this process requires a resource held by the first process, as shown in Figure 6.19(a). In this figure, each process has acquired one of the resources. Both processes are delayed and unless one process releases a resource wanted by the other process, neither process will ever proceed. Deadlock can also occur in a circular fashion, as shown in Figure 6.19(b), with several processes having a resource wanted by another. Process P_1 requires resource R_2, which is held by P_2, process P_2 requires resource R_3, which is held by process P_3, and so on, with process P_n requiring resource R_1 held by P_1, thus forming a deadlock situation. Given a set of processes having various resource requests, a circular path between any group indicates a potential deadlock situation. Deadlock cannot occur if all processes hold at most only one resource and release this resource in a finite time. Deadlock can be eliminated between two processes accessing more than one resource if both processes make requests first for one resource and then for the other.

It is widely recognized that semaphores, though capable of implementing most critical

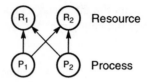

(a) Two-process deadlock

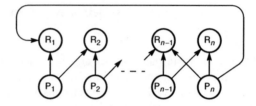

(b) *n*-process deadlock

Figure 6.19 Deadlock (deadly embrace)

section applications, are open to human errors in use. For example, for every **P** operation on a particular semaphore, there must be a corresponding **V** operation on the same semaphore. Omission of a **P** or **V** operation, or misnaming the semaphore, would create havoc. The semaphore mechanism is a very low level mechanism programmed into processes.

Semaphores combine two distinct purposes; first, they achieve mutual exclusion of critical sections and second, they achieve synchronization of processes. Mutual exclusion is concerned with making sure that only one process accesses a particular resource. The separate action of making sure that processes are delayed until another process has finished with the resource has been called *condition synchronization*, which leads to a *conditional critical section*, proposed independently by Hoare and by Brinch Hansen (see Andrews and Schneider (1983) for details). Another technique is to use a *monitor* (Hoare, 1974), a suite of procedures which provides the only method to access a shared resource. Reading and writing can only be done by using a monitor procedure and only one process can use a monitor procedure at any instant. If a process requests a monitor procedure while another process is using one, the requesting process is suspended and placed on a queue. When the active process has finished using the monitor, the first process in the queue (if any) is allowed to use a monitor procedure (see Grimsdale, 1984). A study of these techniques is beyond the scope of this book.

PROBLEMS

6.1   Suggest two advantages of MIMD multiprocessors and two advantages of SIMD multiprocessors.

6.2   Suggest two advantages of shared memory MIMD multiprocessor systems and two advantages of message-passing MIMD multiprocessors.

6.3   How many systems are necessary to survive any four systems failing in a fault tolerant system with a voter?

6.4   Determine when a triplicated system becomes less reliable than a single system, given that the reliability of a single system is given by $e^{\lambda \text{-} t}$. λ is the failure rate.

6.5   Identify unique features of each of the following array computers:

1. Illiac IV.
2. BSP.
3. GF-11.
4. Blitzen.

6.6   Determine the execution time to add together all elements of a 33×33 element array in each of the following multiprocessor systems:

1. An MIMD computer system with sixty-four independent processors accessing a shared memory through an interconnection network.

2. An SIMD computer system with sixty-four processors connected through a north-south-east-west nearest neighbor connection network. The processors only have local memory.

3. As 2 but with sixteen processors.

4. An SIMD system having sixty-four processors connected to shared memory through an interconnection network.

One addition takes t_a sec. Make and state any necessary assumptions.

6.7   Show a suitable path taken between two nodes which are the maximum distance apart in the Illiac IV system (with an 8×8 mesh nearest neighbor network). Develop a routing algorithm to establish a path between any two nodes. Repeat assuming that paths can only be left to right or top to bottom (in Figure 6.3).

6.8 Develop an equation for the speed-up factor of a multiprocessor system given that each processor communicates with four other processors but simultaneous communications are not allowed.

6.9 In a multiprocessor system, the time each processor executes a critical section is given by t_c Prove that the total execution time is given by:

$$T_p = fT_1 + (1-f)T_1/p + t_c$$

and hence prove that the best case time becomes:

$$T_p = fT_1 + t_c + \max((1-f)T_1/p, (p-1)t_c)$$

where T_1 is the total execution time with one processor, p is the number of processors in the system and f is the fraction of the operations which must be performed sequentially. Differentiate the first expression to obtain the number of processors for the minimum execution time. Assume that a sufficient number of processors is always available for any program.

6.10 Using Bernstein's conditions, identify the statements that can be executed simultaneously in the following:

```
a = d*e;
d = a*e;
e = a*d;
b = a*b;
e = e+1;
```

Are there any statements that can be executed simultaneously and are not identified by Bernstein's conditions? Is it possible for such statements to be present?

6.11 Separate the following Pascal nested loop into independent loops which can be executed on different processors simultaneously:

```
FOR i := 2 TO 12 DO
FOR j := 1 To 10 DO
 X[i] : = X [i + j] x [i];
```

6.12 Deduce what the following parallel code achieves (given in two versions, one "C-like" and one "Pascal-like"):

C-like:

```
PARFOR (i = 1, j = 1; i <= 10; i++, j++) {
 pixel[i][j] = (pixel[i][j+1] + pixel[i+1][j]
```

```
    + pixel[i][j-1] + pixel[i-1][j])/4;
}
```

Pascal-like:

```
j := 1;
PARFOR i = 1 TO 10 DO
BEGIN
 j := i;
 pixel[i,j] := (pixel[i,j+1] + pixel[i+1,j]
  + pixel[i,j-1] + pixel[i-1,j])/4
END
```

In what aspect is the Pascal version inefficient?

6.13 Identify the conditions (if any) which lead to deadlock or incorrect operation in the code for a lock using the three shared variables A, B and P (Section 6.6.4).

7 | *Bus-based multiprocessor systems*

This chapter will consider the use of buses to interconnect processors to form a multiprocessor. The use of a single bus is particularly attractive for microprocessor systems, and can be practical for a multiprocessor with a small number of processors (typically less than six). We also consider multiple buses, including the full crossbar switch in which one bus is provided for each processor, and variations of the multiple bus network. Other forms of interconnection networks are considered in Chapter 8. We consider caches in shared memory multiprocessor systems at the end of this chapter.

7.1 Sharing a bus

7.1.1 General

Microprocessor systems with one processor normally use a bus to interconnect the processor, memory modules and input/output units. This method serves well for transferring instructions from the memory to the processor and for transferring data operands to or from the memory. A single bus can be used in a multiprocessor system for interconnecting all the processors with the memory modules and input/output units, as shown in Figure 7.1. Clearly, only one transfer can take place on the bus at any instant; however, it is practical and has been adopted by microprocessor manufacturers.

In a single bus multiprocessor system, all memory modules connecting to the bus become a single memory, available to all processors through the bus. Processors make requests to bus arbitration circuitry for the bus, and only one processor is allowed to use the bus at a time. This processor can access any memory module and the performance is unaffected by the selection of the memory module. Processors compete for the use of the bus and a mechanism must be incorporated into the system to select one processor at a time to use the bus. When more than one processor wishes to use the bus, *bus contention* occurs.

A single bus can only improve processing speed if each processor attached to it has times when it does not use the bus. If each processor requires the bus continuously, no

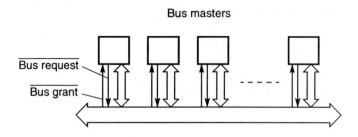

Figure 7.1 Time-shared bus system

increase in speed will result, because only one processor will be active and all the other processors will be waiting for the bus. Most processors have times when they do not require the bus, though processors without local memory require the bus perhaps 50–80 per cent of the time. If a processor requires the bus 50 per cent of the time, two processors could use it alternately, giving a potential increase of speed of 100 per cent over a single processor system.

A synchronous system could achieve this speed. For example, the Motorola MC6800 8-bit microprocessor operated on a two phase clock system with equal times in each phase. Memory references are only made during one phase. Hence, two processors could be arranged to operate on memory in opposite phases, and no bus arbitration circuitry would be required. If the processors each required the bus $1/n$ of the time, then n processors could use the bus in an interleaved manner, resulting in an n-fold increase in speed. If further similar processors were added, no further increase in speed would result. Below maximum utilization of the bus there is a linear increase in speed, while at the point the bus is fully utilized, no increase in speed results as further processors are added.

Synchronizing memory references is rather unusual and not applicable to more recent microprocessors; microprocessors have times when they use the bus, which change depending upon the instructions. For an asynchronous multiprocessor system where processors have to compete for the bus, processors will sometimes need to wait for the bus to be given to them, and the speed-up becomes less than in a synchronous system. A mathematical analysis is given in Section 7.3. It is rare for it to be worthwhile to attach more than 5 processors to a single bus.

Processors are usually provided with local cache-holding instructions and data which will reduce the number of requests for memory attached to the bus and reduce bus contention. First, though, let us discuss the various mechanisms for transferring control of the bus from one processor to another. Processors, or any other device that can control the bus, will be called bus masters. The processor controlling the bus at any instant will be called the current bus master. Bus masters wishing to use the bus and making a request for it will be called requesting bus masters.

7.1.2 Bus request and grant signals

There are two principal signals used in the transfer of control of the bus from one bus master to another, namely the *bus request* signal and the *bus grant* signal. Other signals are usually also present and the signals are variously entitled depending upon the system designer or microprocessor manufacturer. Transfer of the control of the bus from one bus master to another uses a handshaking mechanism. The bus master wishing to use the bus makes a request to the current bus master by activating the bus request signal. The current bus master releases the bus some time later, and passes back a bus grant signal to the requesting bus master, as shown in Figure 7.2(a). The exact timing is system dependent. Figure 7.2(b) shows one possible timing using the two signals described. Bus request causes, in due course, bus grant to be returned. When bus grant is received, bus request is deactivated, which causes bus grant to be deactivated. Bus control signals are often active-low, meaning that the quiescent state is 1 and that 0 indicates action. Such signals

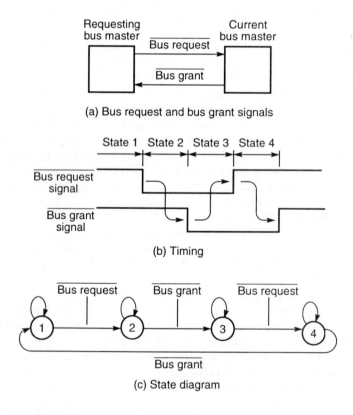

(a) Bus request and bus grant signals

(b) Timing

(c) State diagram

Figure 7.2 Bus request/grant mechanism

are shown with a bar over their name. We shall use the word "activated" to indicate action.

Buses can be classified as either *synchronous* or *asynchronous*. For all bus transactions in the synchronous bus, the time for each transaction is known in advance, and is taken into account by the source device in accepting information and generating further signals. In the asynchronous bus, the source device does not know how long it will take for the destination to respond. The destination replies with an acknowledgement signal when ready. When applied to transferring control of the bus, the asynchronous method involves not only a request signal from the requesting bus master and a grant signal from the current bus master, but also a further *grant acknowledge* signal from the current bus master acknowledging the grant signal.

The two signal handshake system is often augmented with a *bus busy* signal, which indicates whether the bus is being used. It may be that an *acknowledge* signal, rather than a grant signal, is returned from the current bus master to the requesting bus master after the request has been received. The current bus master then releases the bus busy line when it eventually releases the bus, and this action indicates that the requesting master can take over the bus, as shown in Figure 7.3.

Microprocessors designed for multiprocessor operation have request/acknowledge/grant signals at the pin-outs although, when there are more than two processors in the system, additional logic may be necessary to resolve multiple requests for particular mechanisms.

7.1.3 Multiple bus requests

It is necessary for the current bus master to decide whether to accept a particular request and to decide between multiple simultaneous requests, should these occur. In both cases, the decision is normally made on the basis of the perceived priority of the incoming requests, in much the same way as deciding whether to accept an interrupt signal in a normal single processor microprocessor system. Individual bus masters are assigned a priority level, with higher priority level masters being able to take over the bus from lower priority bus masters. The priority level may be fixed by making specific connections in a priority mechanism (i.e. static priority/fixed priority) or, less commonly, altered by hardware which alters the priority according to some algorithm (dynamic priority).

Arbitration can generally be:

1. Parallel arbitration.
2. Serial arbitration.

In parallel arbitration, the bus request signals enter the arbitration logic separately and separate bus grant signals are generated. In serial arbitration, a signal is passed from one bus master to another, to establish which requesting bus master, if any, is of higher priority than the current bus master. The serial configuration is often called a *daisy chain* mechanism.

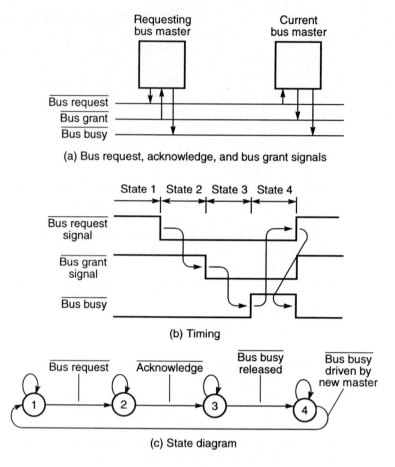

(a) Bus request, acknowledge, and bus grant signals

(b) Timing

(c) State diagram

Figure 7.3 Bus request/acknowledge/busy mechanism

Arbitration can also use:

1. Centralized arbitration.
2. Decentralized arbitration.

In centralized arbitration, the request signals, either directly or indirectly, reach one central location for resolution and the appropriate grant signal is generated from this point back to the bus masters. In decentralized arbitration, the signals are not resolved at one point – the decision to generate a grant/acknowledge signal may be made at various places, normally at the processor sites. Decentralized arbitration often (but not always) has the potential for fault tolerance, whereas the centralized arbitration is always susceptible to point failures. Parallel and serial arbitration can either be centralized or decentralized, though the centralized forms are most common.

7.2 Priority mechanism

7.2.1 Parallel priority

The general centralized parallel priority mechanism is shown in Figure 7.4. Each bus master can generate a bus request signal which enters the centralized arbitration logic (arbiter). One of the requests is accepted and a corresponding grant signal is returned to the bus master. A bus busy signal is provided; this is activated by the bus master using the bus. A bus master may use the bus when it receives a grant signal and the bus is free, as indicated by the bus busy line being inactive. While a bus master is using the bus, it must maintain its request and bus busy signals active. Should a higher priority bus master make a request, the arbitration logic recognizes the higher priority master and removes the grant from the current bus master. It also provides a grant signal to the higher priority requesting bus master, but this bus master cannot take over the bus until the current bus master has released it. The current bus master recognizes that it has lost its grant signal from the arbitration logic, but it will usually not be able to release the bus immediately if it is in the process of making a bus transfer. When a suitable occasion has been reached, the current bus master releases the bus and the bus busy line, which signals to the requesting master that it can take over the bus.

Notice that it is necessary to provide a bus busy signal because bus masters are incapable of releasing the bus immediately when they lose their grant signal. Hence we have a three signal system. There are various priority algorithms which can be imple-

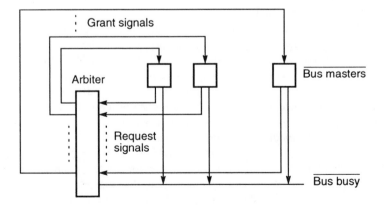

Figure 7.4 Centralized parallel arbitration

mented by the arbitration logic to select a requesting bus master, all implemented in hardware as opposed to software because of the required high speed of operation. We have already identified static and dynamic priority. In the first instance, let us consider static priority.

In static (fixed) priority, requests always have the same priority. For example, suppose that there were eight bus masters 0, 1, 2, 3, 4, 5, 6 and 7 with eight request signals REQ0, REQ1, REQ2, REQ3, REQ4, REQ5, REQ6 and REQ7, and eight associated grant signals GRANT0, GRANT1, GRANT2, GRANT3, GRANT4, GRANT5, GRANT6 and GRANT7. Bus master 7 could be assigned the highest priority, with the other bus masters assigned decreasing priority such that bus master 0 has the lowest priority. If the current master is bus master 3, any of the bus masters 7, 6, 5 and 4 could take over the bus from the current master, but bus masters 2, 1 and 0 could not. In fact, bus master 0 could only use the bus when it was not being used and would be expected to release it to any other bus master wishing to use it.

Static priority is relatively simple to implement. For eight request inputs and eight "prioritized" grant signals, the Boolean equations to satisfy are:

```
GRANT7 = REQ7
GRANT6 = REQ7.REQ6
GRANT5 = REQ7.REQ6.REQ5
GRANT4 = REQ7.REQ6.REQ5.REQ4
GRANT3 = REQ7.REQ6.REQ5.REQ4.REQ3
GRANT2 = REQ7.REQ6.REQ5.REQ4.REQ3.REQ2
GRANT1 = REQ7.REQ6.REQ5.REQ4.REQ3.REQ2.REQ1
GRANT0 = REQ7.REQ6.REQ5.REQ4.REQ3.REQ2.REQ1.REQ0
```

which could be implemented as shown in Figure 7.5. This arrangement could be extended for any number of bus masters and standard logic components are available to provide static priority (for example the SN74278 4-bit cascadable priority component (Texas Instruments, 1984) which also has flip-flops to store requests).

Static priority circuit devices can generally be cascaded to provide further inputs and outputs, as shown in Figure 7.6. In this figure, each priority circuit has an enable input, EI, which must be activated to generate any output, and an enable output, EO, which is generated when any priority request output is active. When a request is received by a priority circuit, the outputs of the lower priority circuits are disabled. Hence, after all requests have been applied and sufficient time has elapsed for all logic levels to be established, only the highest priority grant signal will be generated. The previous Boolean equations can easily be modified to incorporate enable signals.

The speed of operation of cascaded priority arbiters is proportional to the number of circuits cascaded. Clearly, the method is unsuitable for a large number of requests. To improve the speed of operation of systems with more than one arbiter, two-level, parallel bus arbitration can be used, as shown in Figure 7.7. Groups of requests are resolved by a first level of arbiters and a second level arbiter selects the highest priority first level arbiter. For larger systems, the arrangement can be extended to further levels.

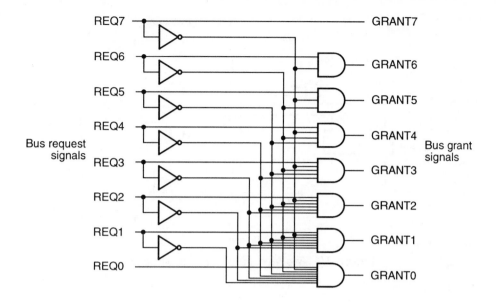

Figure 7.5 Parallel arbitration logic

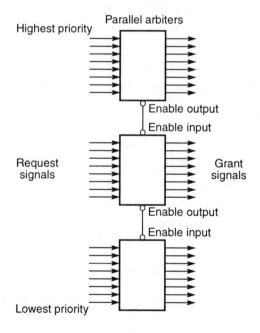

Figure 7.6 Cascaded arbiters

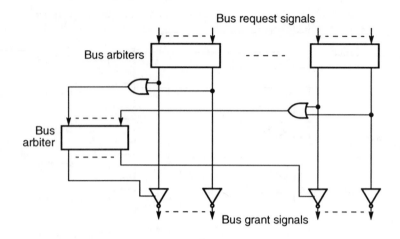

Figure 7.7 Two-level parallel bus arbitration

Decentralized parallel priority

In the decentralized parallel priority mechanism, one arbiter is used at each processor site, as shown in Figure 7.8, to produce the grant signal for that processor, rather than a single arbiter producing all grant signals. All the request signals need to pass along the bus to all the arbiters, but individual processor grant signals do not need to pass to other processors. Each processor will use a different arbiter request input and corresponding arbiter grant output. An implementation might use wire links for the output of a standard arbiter part, as shown in Figure 7.8. Alternatively, the arbiter function could be imple-

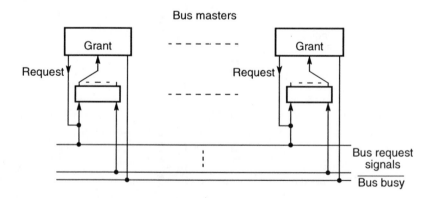

Figure 7.8 Decentralized parallel arbitration

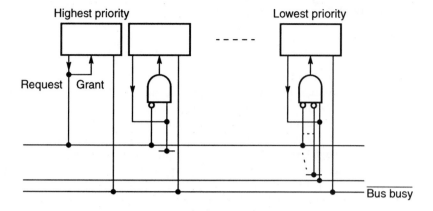

Figure 7.9 Decentralized parallel arbitration using gates

mented from the basic Boolean equations given earlier for parallel priority logic, as shown in Figure 7.9. In this case, the total arbitration logic of the system would be the same as the centralized parallel priority mechanism.

The decentralized parallel priority mechanism is potentially more reliable than the centralized parallel priority, as a failure of one arbiter should only affect the associated processor. An additional mechanism would be necessary to identify faulty arbiters (or processors), perhaps using a time-out signal. However, certain arbiter and processor faults could affect the complete system. For example, if an arbiter erroneously produced a grant signal which was not associated with the highest priority request, the processor would attempt to control the bus, perhaps at the same time as another processor. This particular fault could also occur on a centralized system.

An advantage of decentralized parallel priority is that it requires fewer signals on the bus. It does not require grant signals on the bus. Also, in a multi-board system with individual processors on separate boards, a special arbiter board is not necessary. All processor boards can use the same design.

Dynamic priority in parallel priority

The implementation of the parallel priority mechanisms so far described assigns a fixed priority to individual bus masters. More complex logic, which assigns different priorities depending upon conditions present in the system, can be provided at the arbitration sites. The general aim is to obtain more equitable use of the bus, especially for systems in which no single processor should dominate the use of the bus. Various algorithms can be identified, notably:

1. Simple rotating priority.
2. Acceptance-dependent rotating priority.

3. Random priority.
4. Equal priority.
5. Least recently used (LRU) algorithm.

After each arbitration cycle in *simple rotating priority*, all priority levels are reduced one place, with the lowest priority processor taking the highest priority. In *acceptance-dependent rotating priority* (usually called *rotating priority*), the processor whose request has just been accepted takes on the lowest priority and the others take on linearly increasing priority. Both forms of rotating policies give all processors a chance of having their request accepted, though the request-dependent rotating policy is most common. In *random priority*, after each arbitration cycle, the priority levels are distributed in a random order, say by a pseudorandom number generator. In *equal priority*, when two or more requests are made to the arbiter, there is an equal chance of any one request being accepted. Equal priority is applicable to asynchronous systems in which requests are processed by the arbiter as soon as they are generated by processors operating independently. If two or more requests occur simultaneously, the arbiter circuit resolves the conflict. In the *least recently used algorithm* the highest priority is given to the bus master which has not used the bus for the longest time. This algorithm could also be implemented in logic.

In the (acceptance-dependent) rotating priority algorithm, all possible requests can be thought of as sequential entries in a circular list, as shown in Figure 7.10, for a sixteen bus master system. A pointer indicates the last request accepted. The bus master associated with this request becomes of the lowest priority after being serviced. The next entry has the highest priority and subsequent requests in the list are of decreasing priority. Hence, once a request has been accepted, all other requests become of greater priority. When further requests are received, the highest priority request is accepted, the pointer adjusted to this request and a further request from this master becomes the lowest priority request. For example, the list shown in Figure 7.10(a) shows the allocation of sixteen devices after request 3 has been received and is serviced. In Figure 7.10(b) request number 6 has been received and the pointer is moved accordingly.

Rotating priority has been used in interrupt controllers, for example the Advanced Micro Devices Am9519, and in many ways the interrupt mechanism is similar to the bus control mechanism but uses interrupt request and acknowledge/grant signals rather than bus request and acknowledge/grant signals. Various features in the Am9519 device can be preprogrammed, including a fixed priority or rotating priority and particular responses to interrupts. Features such as mask registers to lock out specific requests are not normally found in bus arbitration systems. Rotating priority can also be performed in the serial priority mechanism (see Section 7.2.2).

There are some techniques which assign priority according to some fixed strategy: these are not strictly dynamic, in so far as the assignment does not necessarily change after each request is serviced. We can identify two such algorithms:

1. Queueing (first-come first-served) algorithm.
2. Fixed time slice algorithm.

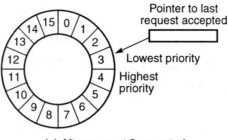

(a) After request 3 accepted

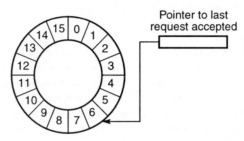

(b) After request 6 accepted

Figure 7.10 Rotating priority algorithm

The queueing (*first-come first-served*) algorithm is sometimes used in analytical studies of bus contention and assumes a queue of requests at the beginning of an arbitration cycle. The request accepted is the first request in the queue, i.e. the first request received. This algorithm poses problems in implementation and is not normally found in microprocessor systems. In the *fixed time slice algorithm*, each bus master is allocated one period in a bus arbitration sequence. Each bus master can only use the bus during its allocated period, and need not use the bus on every occasion. This is suitable for systems in which the bus transfers are synchronized with a clock signal.

7.2.2 Serial priority

The characteristic feature of serial priority mechanisms is the use of a signal which passes from one bus master to another, in the form of a *daisy chain*, to establish whether a request has the highest priority and hence can be accepted. There are three general types, depending upon the signal which is daisy chained:

1. Daisy chained grant signal.
2. Daisy chained request signal.
3. Daisy chained enable signal.

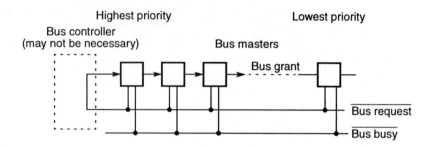

Figure 7.11 Centralized serial priority arbitration with daisy chained grant signal

The *daisy chained grant mechanism* is the most common. In this mechanism, the bus requests from bus masters pass along a common (wired-OR) request line, as shown in Figure 7.11. A bus busy signal is also common and, when active, indicates that the bus is being used by a bus master. When one or more bus masters make a request, the requests are routed to the beginning of the daisy chain, sometimes through a special bus controller and sometimes by direct connection to the highest priority master. The signal is then passed from one bus master to the next until the highest priority requesting bus master is found. This bus master prevents the signal passing any further along the daisy chain and prepares to take over the bus.

In the *daisy chained request mechanism*, as shown in Figure 7.12, the daisy chain connection is again from the highest priority bus master through to the lowest priority bus master, but with the request signal being routed along the daisy chain. Each requesting bus master generates a bus request signal which is passed along the daisy chain, eventually reaching the current bus master. This bus master is of lower priority than any of the requesting bus masters to the left of it, and hence will honor the request by generating a common (wired-OR) bus acknowledge/grant signal. All requesting bus masters notice this signal but only the one which has a request pending and does not have a request present at its daisy chain input responds, as it must be the highest priority requesting bus

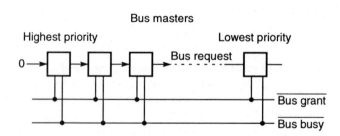

Figure 7.12 Centralized serial priority arbitration with daisy chained request signal

master. Other requesting bus masters have an opportunity to compete for the bus in future bus arbitration cycles.

In the *daisy chained enable mechanism*, both the bus request and bus acknowledge/ grant signals are common (wired-OR) signals and an additional enable signal is daisy chained. When a bus master makes a request it disables the daisy chained enable output, indicating to lower priority bus masters that a higher priority bus master has presented a request. The common request signal is routed to a bus controller, which generates a common (wired-OR) bus acknowledge signal to all bus masters. The highest priority requesting bus master will have its enable input activated and this condition will allow it to take over the bus. The daisy chained enable system was used in single processor Z-80 systems for organizing interrupts from input/output interfaces.

In all types of daisy chain mechanisms, a key point is that the mechanism must be such that a requesting bus master cannot take over the bus until it has been freed. A bus controller can be designed to issue an acknowledge/grant signal only when the bus is free. If there is no bus controller, there are two possible mechanisms, namely:

1. Bus masters are not allowed to make a request until the bus is free.
2. Bus masters are allowed to make a request at any time but are not allowed to take over the bus until the bus is free (and after receipt of a grant signal).

In 1, after the grant signal comes via the daisy chain, the bus master can take over the bus immediately. In 2, the bus master must wait until the bus is free. When the bus is taken over, the bus busy line is activated.

A strategy must be devised for terminating the control of the bus. One strategy would be to allow a bus master only one bus cycle and to make it compete with other bus masters for subsequent bus cycles. Alternatively, bus masters could be forced off the bus by higher priority requests (and perhaps requested to terminate by lower priority bus masters).

Decentralized serial priority

Though the daisy chain distributes the arbitration among the bus master sites, the daisy chain signal originates at one point and subsequently passes along the daisy chain. Hence the daisy chain methods so far described are categorized as centralized priority. The daisy chain grant method can be modified to be a decentralized mechanism by making the current bus master generate the daisy chain grant signal and arranging a circular connection, as shown in Figure 7.13. The daisy chain signal now originates at different points each time control is transferred from one bus master to another, which leads to a rotating priority. The current bus master has the lowest priority for the next bus arbitration. The bus master immediately to the right of the current bus master has the highest priority and bus masters further along the daisy chain have decreasing priority.

When a bus master has control of the bus, it generates a grant signal which is passed to the adjacent bus master. The signal is passed through bus masters that do not have a request pending. Whenever a bus master makes a request, and has a grant input signal active, it inhibits the grant signal from continuing along the daisy chain. However, it

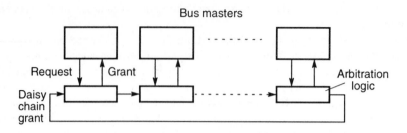

Figure 7.13 Rotating daisy chain

cannot take over the bus until the current bus master releases the bus (assuming a bus master is using the bus). When the current bus master finds that it has lost its daisy chained grant, it must release the bus at the earliest opportunity and release a common bus busy line. Then the requesting master can take over the bus. When more than one bus master makes a request for the bus, the requesting bus master nearest the current bus master in the clockwise direction is first to inhibit the daisy chain grant signal and claim the bus.

An implementation of the *rotating daisy chain* mechanism typically requires one flip-flop at each bus master to indicate that it was the last to use the bus or that it is currently using the bus. One design is given by Nelson and Refai (1984). Flip-flops are usually activated by a centralized clock signal, and request signals should not change at about the time of the activating clock transition or the circuit might enter a metastable state for a short period (with an output voltage not at a binary level).

Finally, note that though the mechanism is decentralized, it still suffers from single point failures. If one of the arbitration circuits fails to pass on the grant signal, the complete system will eventually fail as the daisy chain signal propagates.

Combined serial-parallel

The serial priority mechanism is physically easy to expand though the speed of operation is reduced as the daisy chain length increases. The parallel priority mechanism is faster but requires extra bus lines. The parallel mechanism cannot be expanded easily in a parallel fashion beyond the original design since it is dependent upon the number of lines available on the bus for request and acknowledge/grant signals, and the arbitration logic. Typically eight or sixteen bus masters can be handled with a parallel priority mechanism.

The parallel priority mechanism can be expanded by daisy chaining each request or grant signal, thus combining the serial and parallel techniques. An arrangement is shown in Figure 7.14. Here the bus request signals pass to the parallel arbitration circuit as before. However, these signals are wired-OR types and several bus masters may use each line. The grant signals are daisy chained for each master using the same request line, so that the requesting master can be selected. The operation is as follows: the requesting master produces a bus request signal. If accepted by the priority logic, the corresponding grant signal is generated. This signal passes down the daisy chain until it reaches the

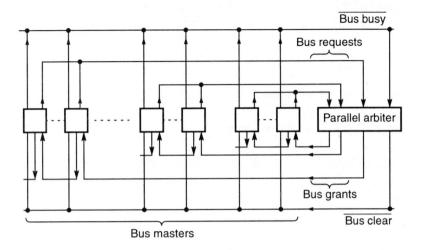

Figure 7.14 Parallel arbiter with daisy chained grant signals

requesting master. At the same time, an additional common *bus clear* signal is generated by the priority logic and sent to all the bus masters. On receiving this signal the current master will release the bus at the earliest possible moment, indicating this by releasing the bus busy signal. The new master will then take over the bus.

The parallel and serial mechanisms are in fact two extremes of implementing the same Boolean equations for arbitration given in Section 7.2.1. From these equations, we can obtain the equations implemented at each bus master site in a daisy chain grant system. Defining INn as the nth daisy chain input and OUTn as the nth daisy chain output, which are true if no higher priority request is present, then:

```
INn-1   = OUTn
OUTn    = REQn.INn

GRANT7 = REQ7
OUT7    = IN6 = REQ7

GRANT6 = REQ7.REQ6 = IN6.REQ6
OUT6    = IN5 = REQ7.REQ6 = IN6.REQ6

GRANT5 = REQ7.REQ6.REQ5 = IN5.REQ5
OUT5    = IN4 = REQ7.REQ6.REQ5 = IN5.REQ5

GRANT4 = REQ7.REQ6.REQ5.REQ4 = IN6.REQ4
OUT4    = IN3 = REQ7.REQ6.REQ5.REQ4 = IN6.REQ4
```

```
GRANT3 = REQ7.REQ6.REQ5.REQ4.REQ3 = IN3.REQ3
OUT3   = IN2 = REQ7.REQ6.REQ5.REQ4.REQ3 = IN3.REQ3

GRANT2 = REQ7.REQ6.REQ5.REQ4.REQ3.REQ2 = IN2.REQ2
OUT2   = IN1 = REQ7.REQ6.REQ5.REQ4.REQ3.REQ2 = IN2.REQ2

GRANT1 = REQ7.REQ6.REQ5.REQ4.REQ3.REQ2.REQ1 = IN1.REQ1

OUT1   = IN0 = REQ7.REQ6.REQ5.REQ4.REQ3.REQ2.REQ1
       = IN1.REQ1
GRANT0 = REQ7.REQ6.REQ5.REQ4.REQ3.REQ2.REQ1.REQ0
       = IN0.REQ0
```

Alternatively, we could have grouped two grant circuits together to get:

```
GRANT7 = REQ7
GRANT6 = REQ7.REQ6
OUT7/6 = IN5/4 = REQ7.REQ6

GRANT5 = REQ7.REQ6.REQ5 = IN5/6.REQ5
GRANT4 = REQ7.REQ6.REQ5.REQ4 = IN5/6.REQ5.REQ4
OUT5/4 = IN3/2 = REQ7.REQ6.REQ5.REQ4 = IN5/6.REQ5.REQ4

GRANT3 = REQ7.REQ6.REQ5.REQ4.REQ3 = IN3/2.REQ3
GRANT2 = REQ7.REQ6.REQ5.REQ4.REQ3.REQ2 = IN3/2.REQ3.REQ2
OUT3/2 = IN1/0 = REQ7.REQ6.REQ5.REQ4.REQ3.REQ2
       = IN3/2.REQ3.REQ2

GRANT1 = REQ7.REQ6.REQ5.REQ4.REQ3.REQ2.REQ1 = IN1/0.REQ1
GRANT0 = REQ7.REQ6.REQ5.REQ4.REQ3.REQ2.REQ1.REQ0
       = IN1/0.REQ1.REQ0
```

Similarly, groups of four arbitration circuits can be created with a daisy chain signal between them, i.e.:

```
GRANT7 = REQ7
GRANT6 = REQ7.REQ6
GRANT5 = REQ7.REQ6.REQ5
GRANT4 = REQ7.REQ6.REQ5.REQ4
OUT7-4 = IN3-0 = REQ7.REQ6.REQ5.REQ4

GRANT3 = REQ7.REQ6.REQ5.REQ4.REQ3 = IN3-0.REQ3
GRANT2 = REQ7.REQ6.REQ5.REQ4.REQ3.REQ2 = IN3-0.REQ3.REQ2
GRANT1 = REQ7.REQ6.REQ5.REQ4.REQ3.REQ2.REQ1
       = IN3-0.REQ3.REQ2.REQ1
```

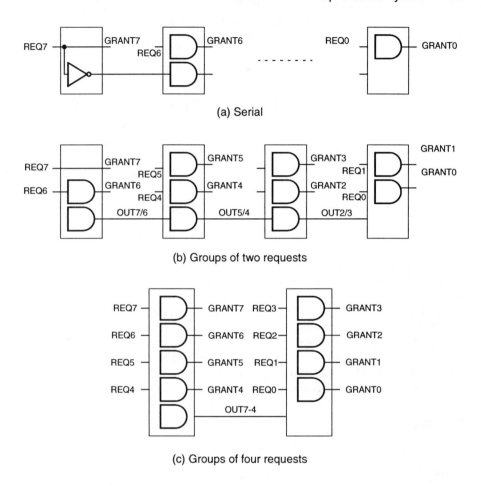

(a) Serial

(b) Groups of two requests

(c) Groups of four requests

Figure 7.15 Serial-parallel arbitration logic

$$GRANT0 = \overline{\overline{REQ7}.\overline{REQ6}.\overline{REQ5}.\overline{REQ4}.\overline{REQ3}.\overline{REQ2}.\overline{REQ1}.REQ0}$$
$$= IN3-0.\overline{REQ3}.\overline{REQ2}.\overline{REQ1}.REQ0$$

Figure 7.15 shows implementations for a purely serial approach, arbiters with groups of two request inputs and arbiters with groups of four request inputs.

7.2.3 Polling

In polling mechanisms, rather than the bus masters issuing requests whenever they wish to take over control of the bus and a bus controller deciding which request to accept, a

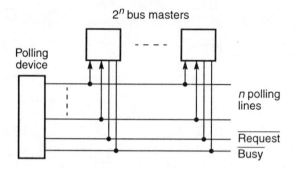

Figure 7.16 Centralized polling arrangement

bus controller asks bus masters whether they have a request pending. Such polling can be centralized, with one bus controller issuing request inquiries, or decentralized, with several bus controllers.

The mechanism generally uses special polling lines between the bus controller(s) and the bus masters to effect the inquiry. Given 2^n bus masters, 2^n lines could be provided, one for each bus master, and one activated at a time to inquire whether the bus master has a request pending. Alternatively, to reduce the number of polling lines, a binary encoded polling address could be issued on the polling lines and then only n lines would be necessary. In addition, there are bus request and busy lines.

Centralized polling

A centralized polling mechanism is shown in Figure 7.16. The bus controller asks each bus master in turn whether it has a bus request pending, by issuing each bus master polling address on the n polling lines. If a bus master has a request pending when its address is issued, it responds by activating the common request line. The controller then allows the bus master to use the bus. The bus master addresses can be sequenced in numerical order or according to a dynamic priority algorithm. The former can be implemented using a counter which is temporarily halted from sequencing by the bus busy line.

Decentralized polling

A decentralized polling arrangement is shown in Figure 7.17. Each bus master has a bus controller consisting of an address decoder and an address generator. First, at the beginning of the polling sequence, an address is generated which is recognized by a controller. If the associated processor has a request outstanding, it may now use the bus. On completion, the bus controller generates the address of the next processor in the sequence and the process is repeated. It is usually necessary to have a handshaking system as shown in Figure 7.17, consisting of a request signal generated by the address generator and an acknowledge signal generated by the address decoder.

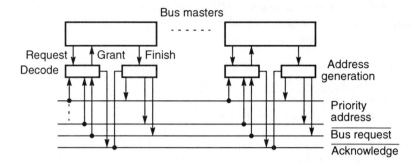

Figure 7.17 Decentralized polling arrangement

Decentralized polling, as described, is not resilient to single point failures, i.e. if a bus controller fails to provide the next polling address, the whole system fails. However, a time-out mechanism could be incorporated such that if a bus controller fails to respond in a given time period, the next bus controller takes over.

Software polling

Although all the priority mechanisms presented are implemented in hardware to obtain high speed of operation, polling lends itself to a software approach. The arbitration algorithms could be implemented in software, using processor-based bus controllers if the speed of operation is sufficient. For example, the bus controller(s) in the polling mechanism could store the next polling addresses, and these could be modified if a bus master is taken out of service. A degree of fault tolerance or the ability to reconfigure the system could be built into a polling mechanism. For example, each bus master could be designed to respond on a common "I'm here" line when polled. No response could be taken as a fault at the bus master, or a sign that the bus master had been removed from service. However, such mechanisms are more appropriate for systems in which the shared bus is used to pass relatively long messages between computers, or message-passing systems.

7.3 Performance of single bus network

In this section, we will present an analysis of the single bus network and the arbitration function. The methods will be continued for multiple bus systems later and for other interconnection networks in Chapter 8.

7.3.1 Methods and assumptions

One of the key factors in any interconnection network is the bandwidth, BW, which is the average number of requests accepted in a bus cycle. Bandwidth gives the performance of the system under bus contention conditions. Bandwidth and other performance figures can be found by one of four basic techniques:

1. Using analytical probability techniques.
2. Using analytical Markov queuing techniques.
3. By simulation.
4. By measuring an actual system performance.

Simplifying assumptions are often made for techniques 1 and 2 to develop a closed form solution, which is then usually compared to simulations. Measurements on an actual system can confirm or contradict analytical and simulation studies for one particular configuration. We shall only consider probabilistic techniques. The principal assumptions made for the probabilistic analysis are as follows:

1. The system is synchronous and processor requests are only generated at the beginning of a bus cycle.
2. All processor requests are random and independent of each other.
3. Requests which are not accepted are rejected, and requests generated in the next cycle are independent of rejected requests generated in previous cycles.

If bus requests are generated during a cycle, they are only considered at the beginning of the next cycle. Arbitration actions are only taken at the beginning of each bus cycle. Asynchronous operation, in which requests can occur and be acted upon at any time, can be modeled by reducing the cycle time to that required to arbitrate asynchronous requests. In practice, most bus-based multiprocessor systems respond to bus requests only at the beginning of bus cycles, or sometimes only at the beginning of instruction cycles. Instruction cycles would generally be of variable time, but virtually all published probabilistic analyses assume a fixed bus cycle.

Assumption 2 ignores the characteristic that programs normally exhibit referential locality for both data and instruction references. However, requests from different processors are normally independent. A crossbar switch system can be used to implement an interleaved memory system and some bandwidth analysis is done in the context of interleaved memory. Low order interleaving would generally ensure that references are spread across all memory modules, and though not truly in a random order, it would be closer to the random request assumption.

According to assumption 3, rejected requests are ignored and not queued for the next cycle. This assumption is not generally true. Normally when a processor request is rejected in one cycle, the same request will be resubmitted in the next cycle. However, the assumption substantially simplifies the analysis and makes very little difference to the results.

Though it is possible to incorporate memory read, write and arbitration times into the probabilistic analysis, we will refrain from adding this complexity. Markov queuing techniques take into account the fact that rejected requests are usually resubmitted in subsequent cycles.

7.3.2 Bandwidth and execution time

Suppose requests for memory are generated randomly and the probability that a processor makes a request for memory is r. The probability that the processor does not make a request is given by $1 - r$. The probability that no processors make a request for memory is given by $(1 - r)^p$ where there are p processors. The probability that one or more processors make a request is given by $1 - (1 - r)^p$. Since only one request can be accepted at a time in a single bus system, the average number of requests accepted in each arbitration cycle (the bandwidth, BW) is given by:

$$BW = 1 - (1 - r)^p$$

which is plotted in Figure 7.18. We see that at a high request rate, the bus soon saturates.

If a request is not accepted, it would normally be resubmitted until satisfied, and the request rate, r, would increase to an adjusted request rate, say a. Figure 7.19 shows the execution time, T, of one processor with all requests accepted, and the execution time, T', with some requests blocked and resubmitted on subsequent cycles (Yen *et al.*, 1982). Since the number of cycles without requests is the same in both cases, we have:

$$T'(1 - a) = T(1 - r)$$

Let P_a be the probability that a request will be accepted with the adjusted request rate, a, and BW_a be the bandwidth. With a fair arbitration policy, each request will have the same

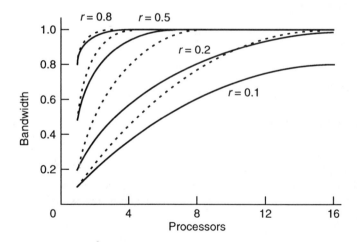

Figure 7.18 Bandwidth of a single bus system (· · · using rate adjusted equations)

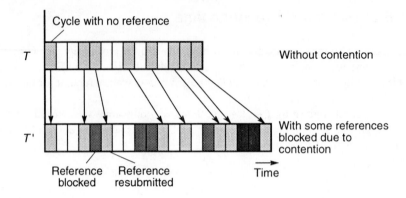

Figure 7.19 Memory references without contention and with contention

probability of being accepted and hence P_a is given by:

$$P_a = \frac{BW_a}{pa} = \frac{1 - (1 - a)^p}{pa}$$

The number of requests before a request is accepted (including the accepted request) = $1/P_a$. Hence, we have:

$$T' = ((1 - r) + r/P_a)T$$

and then:

$$a = \frac{1}{1 + P_a(1/r - 1)}$$

Here the request rate with the presence of resubmissions is given in terms of the original request rate and the acceptance probability at the rate a. The equations for P_a and a can be solved by iteration.

On a single processor system, the execution time would be Tp. If all requests were accepted, the time on the multiprocessor would be T and the speed-up factor would be p. In the presence of bus contention and resubmitted requests, the execution time is T' and the speed-up factor is given by:

$$\text{Speed-up factor} = \frac{Tp}{T'} = \frac{p}{r/P_a + (1 - r)}$$

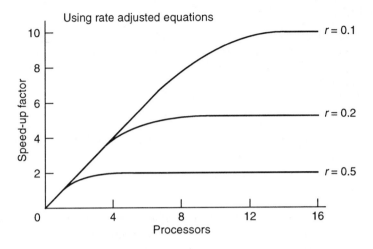

Figure 7.20 Speed-up factor of a single bus system

Figure 7.20 shows the speed-up factor using iteration to compute P_a. We see that the speed-up is almost linear until saturation sets in. The maximum speed-up is given by $1/r$. For example, if $r = 0.1$ (10 per cent) the maximum speed-up is 10, irrespective of the number of processors. With $r = 0.1$ and with ten processors, the speed-up is 9. Note that the derivation uses random requests; in practice the sequence may not be random.

7.3.3 Access time

From the number of requests before a request is accepted being given by $1/P_i$, we obtain the time before a rejected request from the ith processor is finally accepted (the *access time*) as:

$$T_i = \frac{(1 - P_i)}{P_i}$$

where P_i is the probability that processor i successfully accesses the bus, that is, the probability that a submitted request is accepted. (An alternative derivation is given in Hwang and Briggs, 1984.) If a request is immediately accepted in the first arbitration cycle (i.e. $P_j = 1$), the access time is zero. The access time is measured in arbitration cycles. The probability that a processor successfully accesses the bus will depend upon the arbitration policy, and the initial request rate, r.

Fair priority

The probability, P_i, for a fair priority giving equal chance to all processors was given by P_a previously, i.e. $P_i = (1 - (1 - r)^p)/pr$ or, if the adjusted rate is used, $P_i = (1 - (1 - a)^p)/pa$. Figure 7.21 shows the access time against number of processors using the adjusted rate equations with iteration.

Fixed priority

Ignoring resubmitted requests, the probability, P_i, for fixed priority (e.g. daisy chain arbitration) would seem to be given by:

$$P_i = (1 - r)^{i - 1}$$

which is the probability that none of the processors with higher priority than processor i makes a request. The lower processor number corresponds to the higher priority. (Processor i has priority i and processor $i - 1$ is the next higher priority processor.) Resubmitted requests have a very significant effect on the computed access time with fixed priority. The previous equation is invalid for $a = r$. Unfortunately it is very difficult to incorporate an adjusted request rate into the equations as the probability of an individual processor not making a request is dependent upon other processors (see Wilkinson (1992a) for a solution). Computer simulation can be performed to obtain the most accurate results.

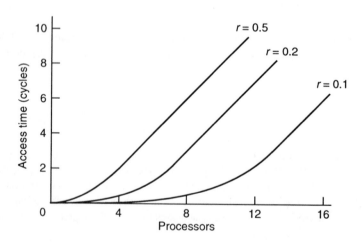

Figure 7.21 Access time of a single bus system

7.4 System and local buses

We noted in Section 7.1 that a single bus cannot be used for all processor-memory transactions with more than a few processors and we can see the bus saturation in the previous
analysis. The addition of a cache or local memory to each processor would reduce the bus
traffic. This idea results in each processor having a local bus for local memory and
input/output, and a system bus for communication between local buses and to a shared
memory, as shown in Figure 7.22. Bus arbitration is still necessary at the system bus level
and possibly also at the local bus level. This architecture is quite common when using a
standard bus for the system bus such as the IEEE 896 Future+ bus. Then the local bus is
simply the bus created by the processor signals available. Manufacturers provide special
chips implementing the local/system bus interface for specific processors and system
buses.

A local/system bus interface circuitry connects the local and system buses together.
Memory addresses are divided into system addresses referring to memory on the system
bus, and local memory addresses referring to memory on the local bus. No local bus arbitration is required if there is only one processor on the local bus, but generally system bus
arbitration logic is necessary to resolve multiple system bus requests to select one
processor to use the system bus. When a processor issues a memory address, decode logic
identifies the bus. Input/output addresses could be in local or system space, depending
upon the design.

Since blocks of memory locations generally need to be transferred from the system
memory to the local memory before being used, it is advantageous to provide a direct
path between the system bus and the local memory using two-port memory. Two-port
memory can be accessed by one of two buses, sometimes simultaneously. Small two-port
memory with simultaneous access characteristics are available, but in any event two-port
memory can be created (though without simultaneous access characteristics) using
normal random access memory components and memory arbitration logic to select one of

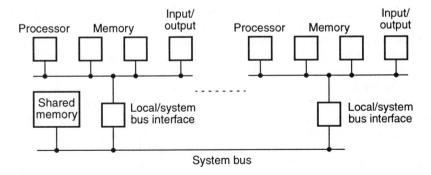

Figure 7.22 Multiple microprocessor system with local buses and system bus

potentially two requests for the memory. In effect, the bus arbitration logic is replaced by similar memory arbitration logic. Care needs to be taken to ensure data consistency in the two-port memory using critical section locks (see Chapter 6). Most recent microprocessors have facilities for local and system buses, either built into the processors or contained in the bus controller interfaces.

The local bus could, of course, carry more than one processor if suitably designed. More commonly, it carries *coprocessors* and DMA devices which are allowed to use the local bus, though overall control is always returned to the processor. Coprocessors are devices designed to enhance the capabilities of the central processor and operate in cooperation with the central processor. For example, an arithmetic coprocessor enhances the arithmetical ability of the central processor by providing additional arithmetical operations, such as floating point and high precision fixed point addition, subtraction, compare, multiplication and division operations. Arithmetic coprocessors also include floating point trigonometric functions such as sine, cosine and tangent, inverse functions, logarithms and square roots. The coprocessor can perform designed operations at the same time as the central processor is performing other duties. Basic floating point instructions are now often incorporated into the processor chip.

7.5 Crossbar switch multiprocessor systems

7.5.1 Architecture

In the crossbar switch system, processors and memories are interconnected through an array of switches with one electronic crossbar switch for each processor/memory connection. All permutations of processor-memory connections are possible simultaneously, though of course only one processor may use each memory at any instant. The number of switches required is $p \times m$ where there are p processors and m memory modules.

Each path between the processors and memories normally consists of a full bus carrying data, address and control signals, and each crossbar switch provides one simultaneous switchable connection. Hence the switch may handle perhaps 100–200 lines if it is to be connected between each processor and each memory. The address lines need only be sufficient to identify the location within the selected memory module. Additional addressing is necessary to select the memory module. The memory module address is used to select the crossbar switch. Each processor bus entering the crossbar network contains all the necessary signals to access the memory modules, and would include all the data lines, sufficient address lines and memory transfer control signals. The switch network can also be implemented using multiport memory. In effect, then, all of the switches in one column of the crossbar are moved to be within one memory module. The number of switches in a crossbar network becomes excessive and impractical for large systems. However the crossbar is suitable for small systems, perhaps with up to twenty processors and memories.

7.5.2 Modes of operation and examples

There are two basic modes of operation for crossbar switch architectures, namely:

1. Master-slave architecture.
2. Architecture without a central control processor.

Each has distinct hardware requirements.

In the master-slave approach, one processor is assigned as the master processor and all the other processors are slave processors. All crossbar switches are controlled by the master processor, as shown in Figure 7.23. The operating system for this architecture could also operate on a master-slave principle, possibly with the whole operating system on the master processor. Alternatively, the central part of the operating system could be on the master processor, with some dedicated routines passed over to slave processors which must report back to the master processor. The slave processors are available for independent user programs. In any event, only the master processor can reconfigure the network connections, and slave processors executing user programs must request a reconfiguration through the master processor. The master-slave approach is certainly the simplest, both for hardware and software design.

In the crossbar switch system without central control, each processor controls the switches on its processor bus and arbitration logic resolves conflicts. Processors make independent requests for memory modules. Each memory module/bus has its own arbitration logic and requests for that memory module are directed to the corresponding

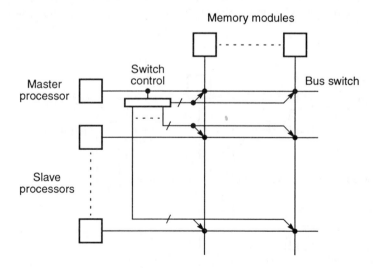

Figure 7.23 Crossbar switch system with central control (master-slave)

memory arbitration logic. Up to one request will be accepted for each memory module, and other requests are held back for subsequent arbitration cycles. Arbitration is effected by one arbiter for each memory module receiving requests for that module, as shown in Figure 7.24.

Perhaps the first example of a crossbar switch multiple processor system (certainly the first commercial example) was the Burroughs D-825 four processor/sixteen memory module crossbar switch system introduced in 1962 for military applications. Subsequently, commercial crossbar switch systems have occasionally appeared, usually with small numbers of processors. There is at least one commercial example of a master-slave architecture, the IP-1 (International Parallel Machines Inc.). The basic configuration of the IP-1 has nine processors, one a master processor, with eight crossbar switch memory modules. The system can be expanded to thirty-three processors. The crossbar switch memory operates like multiport memory. There has been at least one small master-slave architecture research project (Wilkinson and Abachi, 1983).

A significant, influential and extensively quoted but now obsolete crossbar switch system without central control called the C.mmp (Computer.multiminiprocessor) was designed and constructed in the early 1970s at Carnegie-Mellon University (Wulf and Harbison, 1978). C.mmp employed sixteen PDP 11 computer systems, each with local memory, connected to a sixteen memory module. In 1978, at the end of the main investigation, the five original PDP 11s were PDP 11/20s and the eleven introduced in 1974 to complete the system were the faster PDP 11/40s. There were 3 Mbytes of memory in total (32 Mbytes possible). The total hardware cost of $600 000 was divided into $300 000 for the processors, $200 000 for the shared memory and $100 000 for the crossbar switch. Apart from the crossbar switch communication paths between the processors and memory, a communication path was established between the processors using an interprocessor (IP) bus. Input/output devices and backing memory were connected to specific processors. As C.mmp employed the approach without central control, any

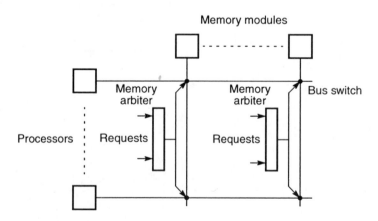

Figure 7.24 Crossbar switch system without central control

processor could execute any part of the operating system at any time. Shared data structures were accessed by only one process at a time, using one of two general mechanisms, either fast simple binary locks for small data structures, or semaphores with a descheduling and queuing mechanism for larger data structures. A widely reported disadvantage of the C.mmp, as constructed with PDP-11s, is the small user address space allowed by the 16-bit addresses.

The crossbar switch architecture without central control has been used more recently, for example the S1 multiprocessor system developed for the United States Navy. The S1 also has sixteen processors connected to sixteen memory modules through a 16×16 crossbar switch. However, the processors are specially designed very high speed ECL (emitter-coupled logic) processors.

In a crossbar system, input/output devices and backing memory can be associated with particular processors, as in the C.mmp and S1. Alternatively, they can be made accessible to all processors by interconnecting them to the processors via the same crossbar switch network as the memory modules; the crossbar switch would then need to be made larger. Input/output devices and backing memory could also be connected to the processors via a separate crossbar switch.

There are a number of possible variations in the arrangement of a crossbar switch network. For example, Hwang *et al.* (1989) proposed the *orthogonal multiprocessor* using a network in which processors have switches to one of two orthogonal buses in the crossbar network. At any instant, the processors can all connect to the vertical or horizontal buses. Each memory module needs to access only two buses. Hwang develops several algorithms for this system. Various memory access patterns are allowed. Overlapping connectivity networks including crossbar versions, are considered in Section 7.7.1.

7.5.3 Bandwidth of crossbar switch

In a crossbar switch, contention appears for memory buses but not for processor buses, because only one processor uses each processor bus but more than one processor might compete for a memory module and its memory bus. In the multiple bus system, to be considered later, both system bus contention and memory contention can limit the performance. In the crossbar switch, we are concerned with the probability that more than one request is made for a memory module as, in such cases, only one of the multiple requests can be serviced, and the other requests must be rejected.

First, let us assume that all processors make a request for some memory module during each bus cycle. Taking a small numerical example, with two processors and three memories, Table 7.1 lists the possible requests. Notice that there are nine combinations of two requests taken from three possible requests. The average bandwidth is given by the average number of requests that can be accepted. Fifteen requests can be accepted and the average bandwidth is given as $15/9 = 1.67$. Memory contention occurs when both processors request the same memory module. For our two processor/three memory system, we see that processor 1 makes a request for memory 1 three times, memory 2 three times and memory 3 three times, and similarly for processor 2. Hence there is a 1/3 chance of requesting a particular memory.

Table 7.1 Processor requests with two processors and three memories

Memory requests Processors		Number of requests accepted	Memory contention
P_1	P_2		
1	1	1	YES
1	2	2	NO
1	3	2	NO
2	1	2	NO
2	2	1	YES
2	3	2	NO
3	1	2	NO
3	2	2	NO
3	3	1	YES

Now let us develop a general expression for bandwidth, given p processors and m memory modules. We have the following probabilities: The probability that a processor P_j makes a request for a particular memory module M_j is $1/m$ for any i and j (as there is equal probability that any memory module is requested by a processor). The probability that a processor, P_j, does not make a request for that memory module, M_j, is $1 - 1/m$. The probability that no processor makes a request for the memory module is given by $(1 - 1/m)^p$. The probability that one or more processors make a request for memory module M_j (i.e. the memory module has at least one request) is $(1 - (1 - 1/m)^p)$. Hence the crossbar switch bandwidth, i.e. the number of memory modules with at least one request, is given by:

$$BW = m(1 - (1 - 1/m)^p)$$

The bandwidth function increases with p and m and is asymptotically linear for either p or m, given a constant p/m ratio (Baer, 1980). Alternative explanations and derivations of bandwidth exist, perhaps the first being in the context of interleaved memory (Hellerman, 1966). An early derivation for the bandwidth can be found in Ravi (1972), also in the context of interleaved memory.

The crossbar switch bandwidth can be derived for the situation in which processors do not always generate a request during each bus cycle, for example, in a system having local memory attached to the processors. Let r be the probability that a processor makes a request. Then the probability that a processor makes a request for a memory module, M_j = r/m. For a simple derivation, this term can be substituted into the previous derivation to

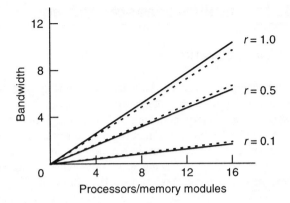

Figure 7.25 Bandwidth of crossbar switch network (—— analysis, · · · simulation)

get the bandwidth as:

$$BW = m(1 - r/m)^p$$

Patel (1981) offers an alternative derivation for the bandwidth with requests not necessarily always generated.

Figure 7.25 shows the bandwidth function. Simulation results (Lang *et al.*, 1982; Wilkinson, 1989) are also shown using a random number generator to specify the requests and with blocked requests resubmitted on subsequent cycles. For a request rate of 1, the bandwidth equation derived will give a value higher than that found in simulation and in practice, because rejected requests which are resubmitted in the next cycle will generally lead to more contention. At request rates of less than 1, the simulation results can give a higher bandwidth than analysis because there is then an opportunity for blocked requests to be satisfied later, when some other processors do not make requests.

The probability that an arbitrary request is accepted is given by:

$$P_a = \frac{BW}{rp} = (m/rp)(1 - (1 - r/m)^p)$$

and the expected wait time for a request to be accepted is $(1/P_a - 1)t_c$ where t_c is the bus cycle time.

7.6 Multiple bus multiprocessor systems

7.6.1 Multiple bus networks

The crossbar switch network is expensive, while the single bus network has poor performance for a large number of processors. We can extend the single bus system to one with b buses, p processors and m memory modules, as shown in Figure 7.26(a), in which no more than one processor can use one bus simultaneously. Each bus is dedicated to a particular processor for the duration of a bus transaction. Each processor and memory module connects to each of the buses using electronic switches (normally three-state gates). A connection between two components is made, with two connections to the same bus. We will refer to processors and memory modules only. (Memory and I/O interfaces can be considered as similar components for basic bus transactions.) Processor-memory module transfers can use any free bus, and up to b requests for different memory modules can be serviced simultaneously using b buses. A two-stage arbitration process is necessary, as shown in Figure 7.26(b). In the first phase, processors make requests for individual memory modules using one arbiter for each memory module, and up to one request for each memory module is accepted (as only one request can be serviced for each

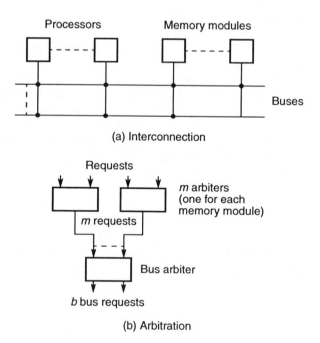

(a) Interconnection

(b) Arbitration

Figure 7.26 Multiple bus system

module). There might be up to m requests accepted during this phase, with m memory modules. In the second phase, up to b of the requests accepted in the first phase are finally accepted and allocated to the b buses using a bus arbiter. If m is less than b, not all the buses are used. Blocked requests need to be honored later.

Clearly, bus contention will be less than in a single bus system, and will reduce as the number of buses increases; the complexity of the system then increases. Though extensive analytical studies have been done to determine the performance characteristics of multiple bus systems, few systems have been constructed for increased speed. Apart from such applications, multiple bus systems (especially those with two or three buses) have been used in fault tolerant systems. A single bus system collapses completely if the bus is made inoperative (perhaps through a bus driver short-circuited to a supply line).

Variations of the multiple bus system have been suggested. For example, not all the memory modules need to be connected to all the buses. Memory modules can be grouped together, making connections to some of the buses, as shown in Figure 7.27. Multilevel multiple bus systems can be created in which multiple bus systems connect to other multiple bus systems, either in a tree configuration or other hierarchical, symmetrical or non-symmetrical configurations.

Lang *et al.* (1983) showed that some switches in a multiple bus system can be removed (up to 25 per cent) while still maintaining the same connectivity and throughput (bandwidth). In particular, Lang showed that a single "rhombic" multiple bus system can be designed with the same connectivity of a full multiple bus network and no reduction in performance whatever when:

1. $p - b + 1 \leq m_i \leq m$
2. $p + m + 1 - b - m_i \leq p_i \leq p$

where m_i memory modules and p_i processors are connected to bus i. Lang also showed that the minimum switch configuration can be achieved by keeping the processor connections complete and minimizing the memory module connections. We shall use Lang's observations later in overlapping multiple bus networks (Section 7.7.2).

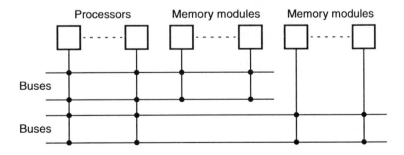

Figure 7.27 Partial multiple bus system

7.6.2 Bandwidth of multiple bus systems

In the multiple bus system, processors and memory modules connect to a set of b buses, and the bandwidth will depend upon both memory contention and bus contention. Only a maximum of b requests can be serviced in one bus cycle, and then only if the b requests are for different memory modules. We noted that servicing a memory request can be regarded as a two stage process. First, up to m memory requests must be selected from all the requests. This mechanism has already been analyzed in the crossbar switch system as it is the only selection process. We found that the probability that a memory has at least one request is $(1 - r/m)^p = q$ (say). Second, of all the different memory requests received, only b requests can be serviced, due to the limitation of b buses. The probability that exactly i different memory modules are requested during one bus cycle is given in Mudge *et al.* (1984) (see also Goyal and Agerwala, 1984):

$$f(i) = \binom{p}{i} q^i (1 - q)^{p - i}$$

where $\binom{p}{i}$ is the binomial coefficient. The overall bandwidth is given by:

$$BW = \sum_{b-1}^{p} bf(i) + \sum_{i=1}^{i=b} if(i)$$

The first term relates to b or more different requests being made and all b buses being in use, and the second term relates to fewer than b different requests being made and fewer than b buses being used. Figure 7.28 shows the bandwidth function and also simulation results (Lang *et al.*, 1982). As with the crossbar switch for a request rate of 1, the simulation bandwidth is slightly less than the analytical value, but for request rates of less than 1, the analytical values are less than the simulation values, as then there is more opportunity for rejected requests to be accepted in later cycles.

In the analysis we have assumed that rejected requests are discarded and do not influence the bandwidth. In Section 7.3.1, we presented a method of computing the effect of rejected requests being resubmitted by adjusting the request rate. This method can be applied to multiple bus (and crossbar switch) networks to obtain a more accurate value for the bandwidth. However, the method assumes that the rejected requests will be resubmitted to a memory module selected at random rather than to the same memory module as would normally happen. This does not matter in the case of the single bus system with a single path to all memory modules, but has an effect in the case of multiple buses and crossbar switches. However, the method does bring the results closer to actual values from simulation.

Some work has been done to incorporate priority into the arbitration function (see Liu and Jou, 1987) and to have a "favorite" memory module for each processor which is more likely to be selected (see Bhuyan, 1985) and to characterize the reliability (see Das and

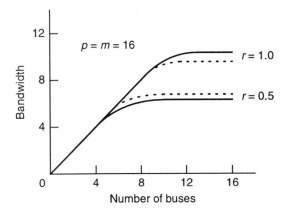

Figure 7.28 Bandwidth of multiple bus system (⎯⎯ analysis, ···· simulation)

Bhuyan, 1985). An early example of the use of Markov chain model is given by Bhandarkar (1975). Markov models are used by Irani and Önyüksel (1984) and Holliday and Vernon (1987). Actual measurements and simulation are used to compare analytical models, for example as in Baskett and Smith (1976).

7.7 Overlapping connectivity networks

In this section we will introduce a new class of networks called *overlapping connectivity networks* developed over a series of papers by this author (Wilkinson, 1989, 1990a, 1991a, 1991b, 1992b, 1993; Wilkinson and Farmer, 1994). Overlapping connectivity networks have the characteristic that each processor can connect directly to a group of memory modules and processors, and to other groups through intermediate processors. Adjacent interconnection groups include some of the same memories and processors. The networks are attractive, especially for a very large number of processors which cannot be provided with full connectivity but need to operate with simultaneous requests to locally shared memory or by communication between processors. There are many suitable application areas having localized request patterns, including engineering computations using arrays/matrices, simulation of most physical systems, and image processing.

Overlapping connectivity networks can be based upon buses or on multistage interconnection networks. We will consider implementations using buses here and implementations using multistage interconnection networks in Chapter 8.

7.7.1 Overlapping crossbar switch networks

Two forms of an overlapping connectivity "rhombic" crossbar switch network are shown in Figure 7.29. In Figure 7.29(a) each memory module has two ports, and processors can access whichever side the processor buses connect. The buses form rings by connecting one edge in the figure to the opposite edge, and the network expands to any size. With four buses, as shown in the figure, processor P_i can connect to memory modules M_{i-3}, M_{i-2}, M_{i-1} M_i, M_{i+1}, M_{i+2}, M_{i+3} and M_{i+4} using one of the two ports on each memory, for all i where M_i is the memory to the immediate left of processor P_j. Hence, each processor has an overlapping range of eight memory modules. In the general case of b vertical and b horizontal buses in each group, processor P_i can connect to memory modules, M_{i-b+1} ... M_{i-1}, M_i, M_{i+1} ... M_{i+b}, i.e. $2b$ memory modules. Connections from processor to memory modules are made with one crossbar switch. Since two memories are accessed via each bus, there will be bus contention as well as memory contention. The

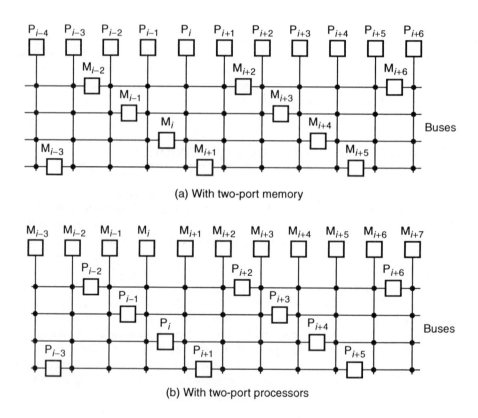

(a) With two-port memory

(b) With two-port processors

Figure 7.29 Crossbar switch with overlapping connectivity
Reprinted with permission from *IEEE Transactions on Computers*, June 1992

bus contention could be removed by providing separate buses for the memory modules to the right and left of processors, but this would double the number of switches and buses. We shall assume only one bus providing access to two memory modules and separate memory addresses used to differentiate between the memory modules.

Let the total number of processors and memory modules in the system be P and M respectively, and the number of processors and memory modules in each section be p and m respectively. Mb switches are needed in the cascaded networks compared to MP in a crossbar switch (M^2 in a square switch).

In Figure 7.29(b), single port memory modules are used, together with processors having access to two buses. With four buses, as shown in the figure, all processors can connect to four memory modules on each side of the processor, or to $2b$ memory modules when there are b buses. There are $2b - 2$ memory modules common to two adjacent sets of reachable elements, as in Figure 7.29(a). Note that not all requests can be honored because the corresponding bus may be used to honor another request to a different memory module, i.e. the system has bus contention because two processors share each bus. The bus arbitration might operate by memory module arbiters independently choosing a request from those pending, and when two requests which require the same bus are chosen, only one is accepted. Ideally, the arbitration circuitry should consider all requests pending before making any selection of requests, so that alternative selections can be made to avoid bus contention when possible.

Bandwidth

The bandwidth of the networks in Figure 7.29 with one stage (i.e. a single stage "rhombic" crossbar switch network with circular bus connections) can be derived in a

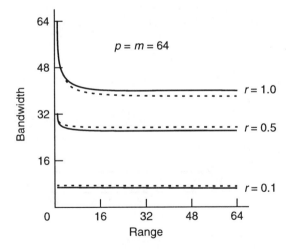

Figure 7.30 Bandwidth of single stage rhombic crossbar network
(· · · analysis, —— simulation)

similar fashion to a full crossbar switch network and leads to:

$$BW = M(1 - (1 - r/m)^m)$$

where M is the total number of memory modules, m is the number of memory modules reached by each processor, and there are the same number of processors as memories. Figure 7.30 shows the bandwidth function plotted against a range of requests for a single stage network, and simulation results when rejected requests are resubmitted until satisfied.

The bandwidth of the unidirectional cascaded rhombic crossbar network can be derived approximately by deducing the probability that a request has been issued for a memory in an immediate group, rm say, and by substituting rm for r in the previous equation. Suppose that each processor generates an output request from either an internal program

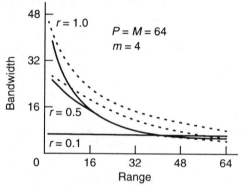

(a) Bandwidth against range of requests

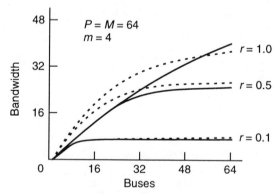

(b) Bandwidth against number of buses

Figure 7.31 Bandwidth of cascaded rhombic crossbar network
($\cdots$ simulation, — analysis)

queue or from an input buffer holding requests passed on from adjacent processors, and that the program queue has priority over the input buffer. As a first approximation, we can consider the program queue from the nearest processor, and then if no program requests are present, the program queue from the next processor in the previous cycle is passed forward, then the next processor in the cycle before. This leads to:

$$r_m = r/g + (1 - r)r/g + (1 - r)^2 r/g \ldots (1 - r)^g r/g$$

$$= (1 - (1 - r)^g)/g$$

and hence:

$$\text{BW} = M(1 - (1 - (1 - r)^g)/gm)^m$$

where requests from each processor extend over g groups of memories. This equation ignores queuing, but has been found to compare reasonably well with simulation results of the network. Figure 7.31(a) and (b) show the bandwidth of the cascaded network against range and against number of buses respectively. Simulation results are also shown. A more accurate analysis can be found in (Wilkinson, 1993).

The overlapping connectivity crossbar switch network can be expanded into two or higher dimensional networks. A two-dimensional network is shown in Figure 7.32. The

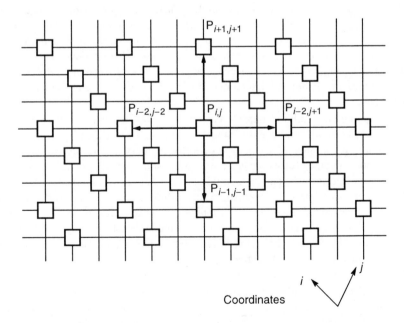

Figure 7.32 Two-dimensional network with overlapping connectivity

processors (or processing elements) are identified by the tuple (i, j) along the two diagonals. Each processor in Figure 7.32 can reach twelve other processors with an overlapping connectivity. $P_{i,j}$ can reach $P_{i-1,j-1}$, $P_{i,j-1}$, $P_{i+1,j-1}$, $P_{i+2,j-1}$, $P_{i-2,j}$, $P_{i-1,j}$, $P_{i+1,j}$, $P_{i+2,j+1}$, $P_{i-2,j+1}$, $P_{i-1,j+1}$, $P_{i,j+1}$, $P_{i+1,j+1}$, via horizontal and vertical buses. The network can be expanded to provide more processors within each group. In the general case, if each bus has c switching elements, $4c + 4$ processors can be reached by any processor (with edges wrapping round). The switch points could be three-state switches providing left, right and crossover paths. However, two-state switches providing crossover and either right or left turn are sufficient. By always crossing over or making one a right turn (say), a path will be established between two processors.

7.7.2 Overlapping multiple bus networks

Figure 7.33 shows two overlapping bus configurations. In Figure 7.33(a) there are four buses with four processors connecting to the buses. As in all multiple bus systems, two connections need to be made for each path. Under these circumstances, with four buses, processor P_i can connect to a group of processing elements to the immediate left, P_{i-3}, P_{i-2} and P_{i-1}, and to the immediate right, P_{i+1}, P_{i+2} and P_{i+3}, for all i. P_{i-3} can be reached through one bus, P_{i-2} can be reached through two buses, P_{i-1} through three buses, P_{i+1} through three buses, P_{i+2} through two buses and P_{i+3} through one bus, for all i. As the processor to be reached is further away, there are fewer buses available and consequently less likelihood of reaching the processor. In the general case, processor P_i can connect to processors $P_{i-b+1} \ldots P_{i-1}$, $P_{i+1} \ldots P_{i+b-1}$ or $2(b-1)$ other processors. There are $b-1$ buses available to connect processors P_{i-1} and P_{i+1} and a linearly decreasing number of buses for more distant processors, which is an appropriate characteristic. The network as described is appropriate to interconnect processors with local memory. Global memory could be incorporated into the interconnection network by replacing some processors with memory modules.

An overlapping connectivity multiple bus network with fewer buses than elements in each group and both processors and memory modules is presented in Figure 7.33(b). The processors are fully connected to the buses and the memory is partially connected to the buses. (Memory modules fully connected and processors partially connected is also possible.) Since each group of memory modules connect to two adjacent sets of buses, these modules can be shared between adjacent groups of processors. The network can be considered as composed of a number of rhombic crossbar switches, cascaded together, similar to Lang's simplification (Section 8.1). A suitable rhombic configuration would be eight processors completely connected to eight buses and sixteen memory modules connecting to the buses in a rhombic pattern.

In Figure 7.33(b), the memory modules form the Lang rhombic pattern but are divided by processors which are fully connected to the buses. Hence, the same connectivity is possible between the processors and memory modules on both sides of the processors (given suitable b and m to satisfy Lang's conditions). If we ignore contention arising when requests from adjacent rhombic groups are made to the same shared memory

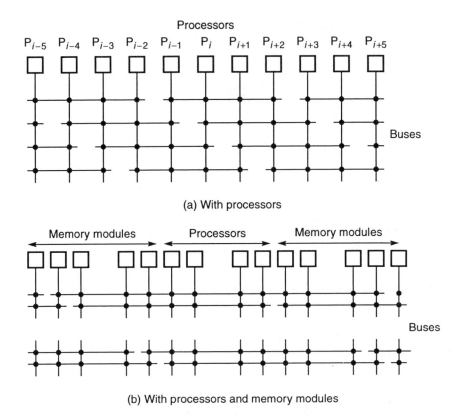

(a) With processors

(b) With processors and memory modules

Figure 7.33 Multiple bus network with overlapping connectivity
Reprinted with permission from *IEEE Transactions on Computers*, June 1992

module, the bandwidth can be derived from the bandwidth of a fully connected multiple bus system.

7.7.3 Generalized arrays

Overlapping connectivity networks using buses can be represented as cellular array of processors, memories and bus switches. This generalization leads to a large family of alternative networks (Wilkinson, 1993). Figure 7.34 shows a general cell design for a one-dimensional array. The horizontal buses correspond to the buses in the previous over-lapping connectivity networks. Vertical buses connect the processors and memories to the horizontal buses using switches. A switch can be provided for a direct connection between the processor and memory to eliminate the need for using the main buses for local requests. Not all switches are implemented depending upon the network being con-

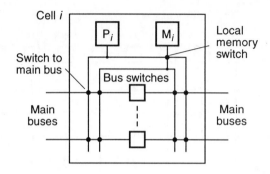

Figure 7.34 Generalized cell design
Reprinted with permission from *IEEE Transactions on Computers*, June 1992

figurated. Bus arbitration can be provided locally within each cell rather than using centralized bus arbitration. The general cell design naturally suits VLSI design. Figure 7.35 shows various network configurations using the cell design. Figure 7.35(a) shows the network with all the switches in place. Figure 7.35(b) is a form of multiple bus network with bus switches between pairs of processors and memories. Figure 7.35(c) corresponds to an overlapping connectivity multiple bus network with processors and memories placed alternately along the network. Figure 7.35(d) corresponds to the overlapping connectivity crossbar switch network with two-port memory, which is achieved by having a switch on both side of the main bus switch to the memory. However requests generated by a processor to be routed to the left may need to pass through a bus switch. This can be eliminated by having an extra switch in place as shown in Figure 7.35(e). Figure 7.35(f) corresponds to the overlapping connectivity crossbar switch network with two-port processors. Again extra switches could be in place. Figure 7.35(g) corresponds to an overlapping connectivity multibus network where processors and memories are placed alternately along the network and bus switches are staggered at sites between pairs of processors and memories. This is similar to the overlapping connectivity network of Figure 7.33 except that each processor can connect to one bus rather than all buses. There is in fact little performance difference between any of these networks (see Wilkinson, 1992c).

7.8 Caches in multiprocessor systems

In this section we consider caches in shared memory multiprocessor systems, whatever form of interconnection network is used. Bus-based systems will be considered in detail.

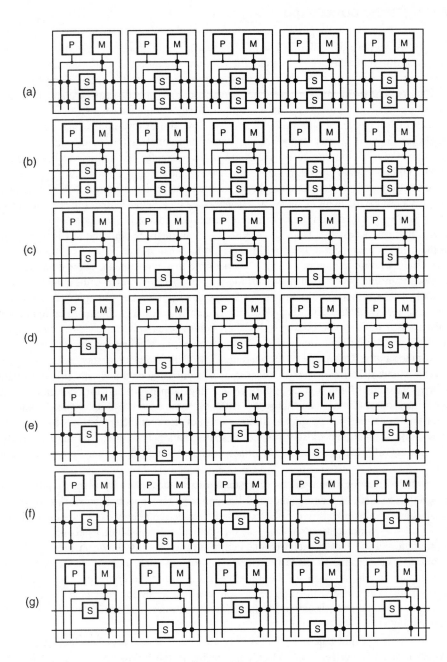

Figure 7.35 Generalized cell networks
Reprinted with permission from *IEEE Transactions on Computers*, June 1992

7.8.1 Cache coherence

Caches, as we have described in Part I, are used in single processor systems to alleviate the speed differential between the main memory and the processor, a differential which is widening as techniques such as superscalar operation increase the speed of operation of processors. The differential in speeds of processors and shared memory also exists in a shared memory multiprocessor, and it is quite natural to apply caches to a shared memory multiprocessor system. Using cache memory is a natural extension of using a cache in a single processor. However, there are significant additional factors to consider in using cache memory in a multiprocessor environment, in particular maintaining accurate copies of data in the multiple caches in the system. In a single processor system with a cache, it is generally necessary to maintain the data in the cache the same as that in the main memory because the main memory may be accessed by an input/output processor directly and would expect to obtain the most recent values. Of course if the processor is the only device that can access the data, the copy in the main memory could be left inconsistent, or the data not even held in the main memory at all when in the cache. In a multiprocessor system with more than one cache, it is possible that copies of the same data are held in more than one cache. Hence in addition to inconsistency between the main memory and the caches, there could be inconsistency between caches. In all cases, reading different copies of the same data does not generally cause a problem. A complication only exists if individual processors alter their copies of data, because shared data copies should generally be kept identical for correct operation. Maintaining the data in all the caches the same is known as *cache coherence*. The phase *cache consistency* is also used.

Why would different processors wish to access the same data and why this must data be kept the same? First of course, the parallel algorithm might call for operations to be performed on different data items by different processors. For example, a sorting algorithm might call for swapping different pairs of items at different times by different processors. Second, and closely related to shared data access, a shared item might be accessed by different processors to maintain synchronization (locks and semaphore variables).

All shared memory multiprocessor systems can be described by a set of processors connecting to a set of memory modules through an interconnection network – different systems are characterized by the choice of interconnection network (single bus, multiple bus, multistage interconnection network, hierarchical interconnection network, etc.) An appropriate place for each cache is attached to a processor, as shown in Figure 7.36. It would also be possible to place the caches in front of each memory module, but this arrangement would not decrease the interconnection traffic and contention, and would in effect share each cache with those processors wanting accessing data held in the corresponding main memory. In addition, the delay of the interconnection network would be included in the cache access time.

As we have seen in Chapter 3, there may be two levels of caches, a first level within the processor and a larger second level external cache. In the following we assume that the caches are external second level caches. If the first and second caches are maintained such that all the items in the first level is contained in the second level and the values are

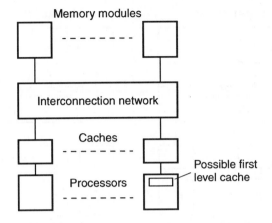

Figure 7.36 Shared memory multiprocessor system with caches

kept the same, then maintaining cache coherence between the second level caches in the system should be sufficient.

7.8.2 Write policy

Write-through is not sufficient, or even necessary, for maintaining cache coherence, as more than one processor writing-through the cache does not keep all the values the same and up to date. Figure 7.37 shows the effect of write-through. Initially a shared variable, x, is stored in the shared memory. Suppose processor 0 reads variable x. A copy of x moves into the cache of processor 0. Suppose processor 1 now reads variable x. A copy of x moves into the cache of processor 1 and the situation is as Figure 7.37(a). Now suppose processor 1 writes to location x. We obtain Figure 7.37(b). After write-through, we obtain Figure 7.37(c) and still inconsistency between caches. Now even though the main memory and the cache of processor 1 are consistent, the cache of processor 0 still has the old value for x.

There are two solutions to this situation, either:

1. Invalidate copy in the cache of processor 0, or
2. Update copy in the cache of processor 0

both of which require access to the cache of processor 0 as shown in Figure 7.37(d). Invalidation of the copy of x held in the cache of processor 0 is done by resetting the valid bit associated with x in the cache. Now processor 0 must access the main memory if it references x again, to bring a new copy of x back into its cache. If copies existed in caches apart from the cache of processor 1, these copies would also need to be invalidated. The alternative to invalidation would be to update all cached copies with the new

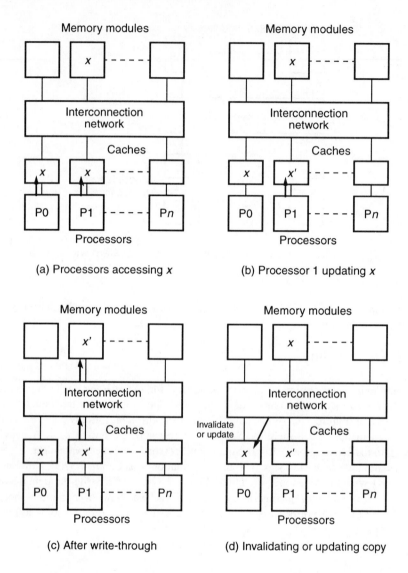

Figure 7.37 Inconsistency with write through policy copy

value of x. This option is not usually implemented because of the overhead of the update. In any event, it may be not completely necessary because not all processors may access the location again. With invalidation, write back may be practiced rather than write-through to reduce the memory traffic. Then there is only one valid copy in one cache, and one processor has *ownership* of this copy.

There are numerous variations of invalidate and update protocols developed in the research community, see Flynn (1995) for further details. We will review one protocol, MESI used with bus-based microprocessor systems, and directory methods used also with other types of interconnection networks later.

False sharing in multiprocessors with caches

In all protocols, access to one location in the line of a cache is considered access to the line. *False sharing* is the term used to describe the situation when more than one processor accesses different parts of a line but not the actual data items. False sharing can result in significant reduction in performance because, in maintaining cache coherence, the smallest unit considered is the line. False sharing can be reduced by distributing the data into different lines if sharing is expected. This would be a task for the compiler, and requires both knowledge of the use of the data and the architectural arrangements of the caches.

Ordering of references

Usually we would expect that when a processor reads a shared variable, it obtains the value produced by the most recent write to the shared variable, irrespective of the processor that did the write operation. This is known as *strict consistency*. We always assume that instructions are executed in program order.[1] Given more than one program executed by separate processors, we generally also assume that the overall effect of the parallel programs is not changed by any arbitrary interleaving of instruction execution in time. This assumption is know as *sequential consistency* (Lamport, 1979). Most shared memory multiprocessor systems and their caches conform to the sequential consistency model, and most parallel programming languages have this implicit assumption. With additional constraints on the programming, it is possible to relax these consistency assumptions and potentially improve the performance of the system. Since access to shared data items is usually controlled through critical sections and other synchronization constructs, it is reasonable to insist on using such constructs for accessing shared data. Only the access to shared variables (locks and semaphore variables) need be sequentially consistent if we force access to all other shared variables through critical sections. This is known as *weak ordering* (Dubois, Scheurich and Briggs, 1988[2]; Adve and Hill, 1990). In weak ordering, accesses to global synchronization variables are sequentially consistent. No access to a synchronization variable is issued before all previous global data accesses have been performed, and no access to global data is issued before a previous access to a synchronization variable has been performed.

---

[1] This restriction is relaxed within a superscalar processor for internal functions or read/write operations on internal registers – with significant hardware complexity to detect data dependencies. Detecting data dependencies on data stored externally in main/cache memory is impractical – hence our assumption is reasonable and not restrictive.

[2] See this reference for a formal definition of *strong ordering* which is similar to sequential consistency.

It is necessary to ensure that during any cache coherence protocol (invalidate or update) processors are not allowed to access locations before coherence has been established, i.e. sequential consistency must be maintained.

7.8.3 Methods of achieving cache coherence

Several possibilities exist to maintain *cache coherence*, in particular:

1. Shared caches.
2. Non-cacheable items.
3. Broadcast write mechanisms.
4. Snoop bus mechanism.
5. Directory methods.

Clearly, a single *shared* cache shared by all processors with the appropriate controls would maintain cache coherence. Also, a shared cache might be feasible for DMA devices accessing the cache directly rather than relying on a write policy. However, with several processors the performance of the system would seriously degrade, due to contention, and a shared cache is not a viable option.

Non-cacheable items

Cache coherence problems only occur on data that can be altered. Such writable data could be maintained only in the shared main memory and not placed in the cache at all (i.e. *non-cacheable* items). It is difficult to make arbitrary memory locations non-cacheable, but it is easy to provide hardware to completely disable a specific cache. It is also possible to make a specific cache line non-cacheable. When the processor accesses a line and gets a miss, the data word is accessed in main memory but the line is not brought into the cache. Of course this approach would cause all locations in the main memory having the same index in the cache to be non-cacheable. Non-cacheable items are probably best done at the virtual memory translation stage, by having specific pages non-cacheable.

Since writing usually only applies to data, caches can be separated into a code cache and data cache as we have seen in Chapter 3. Our cache coherence problems really only need to deal with data, ignoring the possibility of self-modifying code – which unfortunately could not be ignored by Intel in developing compatible upgrades in their 8086 family. Motorola with their MC68000 was in a better position when they clearly separated data addressing and code addressing modes and introduced a *data (alterable) addressing* mode, but still software problems have occurred with the MC68040 (Feldman and Retter, 1994). Note that code need not be self-modifying to cause problem; simply interleaving code and data so that both could exist in the same cache line creates the same situation.

Broadcast writes

In *broadcast writes*, every cache write request is also sent to all other caches in the system. Such broadcast writes interrogate the caches to discover whether each cache holds the information being altered. The copy is then either updated (*update* write) or invalidated (*invalidate* write) by resetting the valid bit associated with the line as described earlier. The use of invalidating words is generally preferable. In any event, significant additional memory transactions occur with the broadcast method, though it has been implemented on large computer systems.

Snoop bus mechanism

Though broadcast methods would be expensive to implement with a multistage interconnection network, there is one interconnection network which can achieve broadcast fairly efficiently, namely the single bus network found in many microprocessor systems. In the *snoop bus* mechanism, a bus watcher unit with each processor/cache observes the transactions on the bus and in particular monitors all memory write operations. Figure 7.38 shows the general hardware arrangement. If a location in main memory is altered and a copy exists in the cache, the snoop bus controller invalidates the cache copy by resetting the corresponding valid bit in the cache. This action requires the unit to have access not only to the valid bits in the cache, but also to the tags in the cache, or copies of the cache tags, in order to compare the main memory address tag with the cache tag. Alternatively, the cache line with the same index as the main memory location can be invalidated, whether or not the tags correspond. The unit then does not need to access the tags, though access to the valid bits is still necessary. However, the unit might mark as invalid a cache line which does not correspond to an altered main memory word, because the cache location with the same index as the main memory location would be invalidated, irrespective of the values of the tags.

In the snoop bus protocol, sufficient time must elapse for the signals to stabilize along the bus. This might require several bus propagation delays along the bus as the signals settle down. With increasing processor clock frequencies, the bus propagation delay times become more significant, and ultimately limit the speed of the cache coherence protocols.

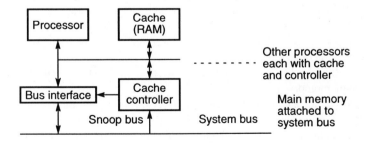

Figure 7.38 Cache with snoop bus controller

Mathematical performance analysis of seven different multiprocessor cache coherence techniques for single bus systems is given by Yang, Bhuyan and Liu (1989). Perhaps the most popular snoop protocol with microprocessor manufacturers is the four-state MESI (Modified/Exclusive/Shared/Invalid) invalidate protocol, which is based upon Goodman's write-once 4-state protocol (Goodman, 1983). The MESI protocol can be found in the internal data cache of Intel Pentium, the second level Pentium cache controller, the Intel 82490 (Intel, 1994c), the Intel i860 processor (Intel, 1992b), and Motorola MC88200 cache controller (Motorola, 1988b), among others. One version of the MESI protocol has a "write-once" transition. We will describe the protocol without this transition as applied to a multiprocessor situation. The variation with the write-once transition is also appropriate for a single processor system to maintain first and second level caches consistent.

In the MESI protocol, each line in the cache can be in one of four states:

1. Modified (exclusive) – The line is only in this cache and has been modified (written) with respect to memory. Copies do not exist in other caches *or in memory*.
2. Exclusive (unmodified) – The line is only in this cache and has not being modified. It is consistent with memory. Other copies do not exist in other caches.
3. Shared (unmodified) – This line potentially exists in other caches. It is consistent with memory. To stay in this state, access to line can only be for reading.
4. Invalid – This line has been invalidated and does not contain valid data.

Two bits can be associated with each line to indicate the state of the line. The modified (exclusive) and exclusive (unmodified) states are used to indicate that the processor has the only copy of the cache line. In the modified (exclusive) state, the processor has altered the contents of the line from that kept in the main memory and hence a valid copy does not even exist in the main memory. It will be necessary to write back the line before any other cache can use the line. Lines enter the invalid state by being invalidated by other processors, i.e. this is an invalidate protocol.

A transition from one state to another state will depend upon the current state, whether the processor is reading the line or writing to the line, a hit or miss occurs, and whether access is to a shared line. The major transitions are shown in the state diagram in Figure 7.39 assuming fetch-on write is practiced. Two types of transition are indicated, those initiated by the local processor, and those initiated by a remote processor's activity on the bus when a shared line is accessed.

Suppose a processor makes a read request for a line not in the cache (read miss). The request will be broadcast along the bus. If no other cache holds a copy of the line, no complaints will be forthcoming from remote processors (actually their snoop bus controllers). The main memory will be accessed to load the line into the cache and the line enters the exclusive state. If a copy of the line did exist elsewhere, a response would be obtained from a remote processor indicating access to a shared line. The line would enter the shared state, and all other copies of the line will enter the shared state irrespective of their initial state (modified, exclusive, or shared).

If the processor had made a write request for a line not in the cache (write miss), the line has to be read from the main memory and modified before loading into the cache. (It

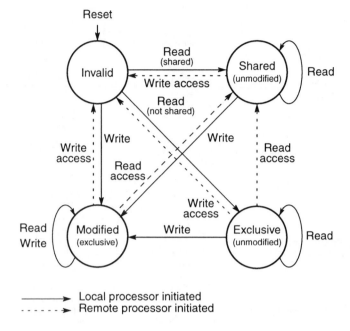

Reset

Read
(shared)

Invalid

Shared
(unmodified)

Read

Write access

Read
(not shared)

Write

Write

Write
access

Read
access

Read
access

Write
access

Read
Write

Modified
(exclusive)

Write

Exclusive
(unmodified)

Read

Local processor initiated
Remote processor initiated

Figure 7.39 MESI protocol – major transitions without write-once

may be that only part of the line is altered, say a single byte.) Before the processor can load the line, it has to establish that the main memory holds a valid copy, which it may not because a copy may exist in a remote cache in the modified state. A generated sequence called "read with intent to modify, RWITM" is made. If a copy of the line does exist in another cache in the modified state, a remote processor will interrupt the RWITM sequence and write the line back to the main memory. The state of the remote copy will be changed to the invalid state. Then the the RWITM sequence can resume and memory accessed again to obtain the updated line. The final state of the line is the modified state in which no other copy exists even in the main memory. If a copy of the line had existed in another cache but not in the modified state, this copy is simply invalidated and the memory access can continue immediately.

All read hits do not alter the state of the line. If a processor makes a write reference to an existing line in its shared state, it will broadcast the request on the bus to inform the other caches, update its line, and change the state of the line to the modified state. All other existing copies will enter the invalid state. If a processor makes a write reference to a line in its exclusive state, all it needs to do is update the line and change its state to the modified state since there are no other copies of the line.

Figure 7.40 shows a typical sequence of events between two processors, 1 and 2, making requests for a location x. (Access to any location in a line in the cache is considered access to the whole line and it does not matter which location in the line is accessed;

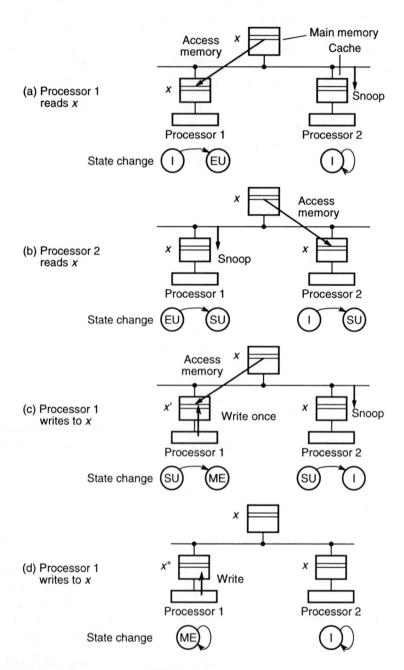

Figure 7.40 A sequence of MESI protocol state changes (I = Invalid, SU = Shared – unmodified, EU = Exclusive – unmodified, ME = Modified – exclusive)

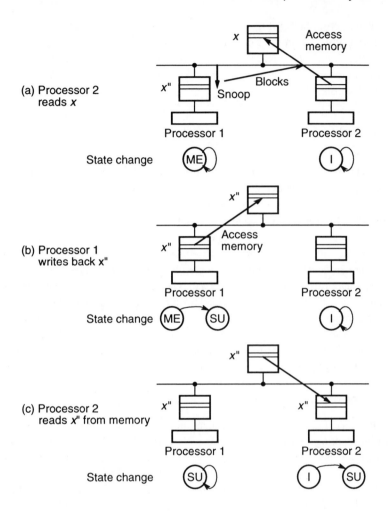

Figure 7.41 MESI protocol state changes from exclusive ownership to shared

the effects are the same.)

Figure 7.41 illustrates the steps when processor 2 tries to read location line x''. It obtains a read miss, and attempts to access the main memory. Processor 1 is snooping the bus and recognizes the access to a location which it has exclusive ownership, and blocks processor 2's read operation. Then it writes x'' back to the main memory and releases processor 2 to retry accessing the main memory. Processor 2 now obtains x'' which it loads into its cache. The state of both cache lines changes to shared state.

In the write-once version of the MESI protocol, the state transitions are slightly different to that described in Figure 7.39. All read misses cause a change to the shared state. The next write hit on the line causes a change to the exclusive state (the so-called write-once transition). The next write hit causes a change to the modified state. Full details of this protocol can be found in the description of the Motorola MC88200 cache controller (Motorola, 1988b).

Directory methods

Directory methods are particularly suitable for shared memory multiprocessor systems with multistage or hierarchical interconnection networks where broadcast mechanisms would be expensive to implement. A directory is a list of entries identifying cached copies of shared memory locations. The directory is used after a processor writes to a cached location, to invalidate (or update) copies in other caches.

The shared memory directory has one entry for each shared memory location that can be cached. Each entry has pointers to cached locations (lines). Pointers to the processors/caches are sufficient. In addition, a single bit is provided with each entry to indicate whether the location is "dirty" or "clean", i.e. whether the location has been modified or not. We share call this bit D (= 1 if dirty). This bit will be used to establish whether any processor can write to the location. Bits are attached to the lines in the caches indicating whether the processor has permission to write to the line (generally whether the line is shared or not). There are three main ways of implementing the directory, the full directory, limited directories, and chained directories:

1.   A full directory

In a full directory, the directory is centralized in the main memory, and provides for the capability of pointing to all caches. Hence with n processors, there would be n pointers for each entry. This can be implemented efficiently with a single bit for each processor. Each bit is set to a 1 if the corresponding cache has a copy of the data, otherwise the bit is a 0. Figure 7.42 shows a full directory. In this figure, a copy of location x is held in each cache. Each line in the caches is provided with two "state" bits, a *valid bit* which is set to a 1 if the information in the cache is valid, and a *private bit* which is set to a 1 if the processor is allowed to write to the line.

Suppose processor 2 writes to location x. At this time, processor 2 does not have permission to write to this location. A request to memory is made to write to this location, and processor 2 waits for permission to proceed. An invalidate signal is issued to all caches holding copies of x. Each cache receiving this invalidate signal sets the corresponding valid bit to 0, and sends back an acknowledgement signal to the memory. After the acknowledgement signals are received, the memory module sets the dirty bit to 1, and sends a signal to processor 2 giving it permission to write to location x. At that time, processor 2 may proceed to write to location x in the cache (and write-through to the memory assuming write-through is implemented). This protocol ensures sequential consistency.

Main memory

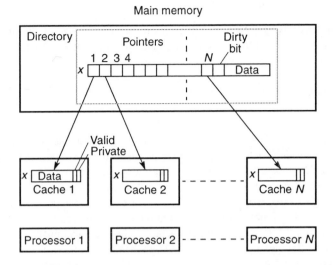

Figure 7.42 Shared memory cache protocol using a full directory

2.   Limited directories

A significant problem with the full directory method is the overhead of the directory entries. Each location needs an extra $N + 1$ bits for N processors, and hence the complexity grows linearly with increasing system size. The full directory method allows all shared memory locations to have copies in all caches. However it is quite unlikely that all caches would need a copy of every cached location. It is more likely that only a few copies actually exist at any instant. In the limited directory method, only a fixed number of caches may have copies of any particular location, say n copies. Therefore only n pointers are provided in the directory where $n < N$. Now each pointer must uniquely identify a cache, and $\log_2 N$ bits will be needed for each pointer rather than a single bit, $n \log_2 N$ bits are needed for each entry rather than N bits. Moreover, the limited directory will scale much better than the full directory because the size of the directory grows less than linearly with increasing system size, for any constant value of n.

When more than n copies are requested, a decision has to be made as to which copies are to be maintained, and which are to be invalidated. Pointers are altered to point to those copies which are to be maintained, "evicting" other copies.

Choosing the value for n is analogous to selecting the working set in a paging system. We want a value for n which captures a sufficient number of copies for application programs to execute efficiently. Preferably some mechanism should be in place to cope with more than n copies. One method is to use a broadcast mechanism to invalidate copies when more than n copies are requested. This would be suitable for networks which can support broadcast mechanisms. The reader is directed to Agarwal *et al.* (1988) for more details for such mechanisms.

3. Chained directories

The chained directory approach also attempts to reduce the size of the directory. In the chained directory, a linked list is used to hold the directory entries. Two possibilities exist for implementing the linked list:

    a. Single linked list.
    b. Double linked list.

A single linked list is shown in Figure 7.43. Here the shared memory directory pointer points to one copy in a cache. A pointer here points to the next copy of the location. The last location in the linked list is terminated with a special symbol. The chained directory allows N copies of a location to be maintained. Whenever a new copy is called for, the linked list must be broken and pointers altered. For example, suppose processor 5 wishes keep a copy of x. The pointer from the shared memory is altered to point to cache 5, and the pointer in cache 5 is set to point to cache 2. The memory must send the pointer to cache 2 to cache 5, together with the data. Only when the whole structure has been established, will processor 5 be allowed to access location x. If a processor writes to a location, an invalidate signal must be sent down the chained path. The chain must also be altered when a location is removed from a cache. A double linked list maintains both backward and forward pointers which enables a location to be inserted and deleted more efficiently although it requires more pointers.

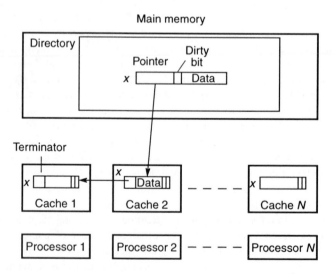

Figure 7.43 Shared memory cache protocol using a chained directory

Apart from hardware solutions to cache coherence, software approaches are possible. The reader is directed to Cheong and Veidenbaum (1990) for further details. We should mention that a shared memory multiprocessor system also is likely to have a paging mechanism, and multiple TLBs (translation look-aside buffers). These are essentially cache memories and need to be maintained consistent. The reader is directed in the first instance to Teller (1990) for details of how multiple TLBs can be maintained consistent.

PROBLEMS

7.1 Prove that the maximum speed-up of a multiprocessor system having n processors, in which each processor uses the bus for the fraction m of every cycle, is given by m.

7.2 Identify the relative advantages of the synchronous bus and the asynchronous bus.

7.3 Identify the relative advantages of parallel arbitration and serial arbitration.

7.4 Identify the relative advantages of centralized arbitration and decentralized arbitration.

7.5 Identify the relative advantages of the daisy chain grant arbitration mechanism and the daisy chain request arbitration mechanism. Which would you choose for a new microprocessor? Why?

7.6 A 3-to-8 line priority encoder is a logic component which accepts eight request inputs and produces a 3-bit number identifying the highest priority input request using fixed priority. A 3-to-8 line decoder accepts a 3-bit number and activates one of its eight outputs, as identified by the input number. Show how these components could be used to implement parallel arbitration. Derive the Boolean expressions for each component and show that these equations correspond to the parallel arbitration expressions given in the text.

7.7 Design a parallel arbitration system using three levels of parallel arbiter parts and determine the arbitration time of the system.

7.8 Suppose a rotating daisy chain priority circuit has the following signals:

BR	Bus request from bus master
BG	Bus grant to bus master

BRIN   Bus grant daisy chain input
BROUT   Bus grant daisy chain output

and contains one J-K flip-flop whose output, BMAST (bus master), indicates that the master is the current bus master. Draw a state table showing the eight different states of the circuit. Derive the Boolean expressions for the flip-flop inputs, and for BROUT. (See Nelson and Refai (1984) for solution.)

7.9 For any microprocessor that you know, develop the Boolean expressions and logic required to generate bus request and grant signals for both local and global (system) buses. The local bus addresses are 0 to 65535 and the global bus addresses are from 65536 onwards.

7.10 Derive Boolean expressions to implement a daisy chain mechanism having three processors at each arbitration site.

7.11 Derive an expression for the arbitration time of a combined serial parallel arbitration mechanism having m processors, using one n-input parallel arbiter. (m is greater than n.)

7.12 What is the access time for the highest and next highest priority processor in a system using daisy chain priority, given that the request rate is 0.25?

7.13 Suppose a new arithmetic coprocessor can have eight arithmetic operations. List those operations you would choose in the coprocessor. Justify.

7.14 Suggest relative advantages of the crossbar switch system with central control and the crossbar switch system without central control.

7.15 Design a 16×16 crossbar switch multiprocessor system using microprocessors (any type) for the master-slave mode of operation. Give details at the block diagram level of the major components.

7.16 Repeat the design in Problem 7.15 for a system without central control.

7.17 Derive an expression for the probability that i requests are made for a particular memory, given that the probability that a request made by one processor is r and there are m memories. (Clue: look at the Bernoulli formula.) Using this expression, derive the general expression for the bandwidth of a $p \times m$ crossbar switch system.

7.18 Derive an expression for the bandwidth of a crossbar switch system, given that each processor has an equal probability of making a request for any memory or of not making a request at all.

7.19 Design an 8-bus multiple bus multiprocessor system using microprocessors (any type) for a system without a master processor. Give details at the block diagram level of the major components.

7.20 Suggest how a multiple bus system could be designed for a master/slave operation. Are there any advantages of such systems?

7.21 Derive an expression for a multiple bus system in which the bus arbitration is performed before the memory arbitration. Show that this arrangement leads to a lower bandwidth than the normal method of having memory arbitration before the bus arbitration.

7.22 Figure 7.44 shows a combined crossbar switch/shared bus system without central control. There are P processors and M memory modules in the system with p processors sharing each horizontal bus. Show that the bandwidth of the system is given by:

$$ \mathrm{BW} = M\left(1 - \left(1 - \frac{1 - (1 - r)^p}{M}\right)^{P/p}\right) $$

7.23 Work through the state transitions in the MESI protocol for each of the following sequences (two processors, P1 and P2):

(a) P1 reads x, P2 reads x, P2 write to x, P1 reads x, P2 reads x.

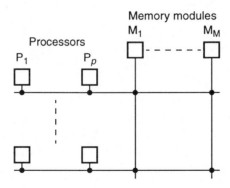

Figure 7.44 System for Problem 7.22

(b) P1 writes to x, P2 reads x, P2 reads x, P1 reads x, P2 writes to x.

(c) P1 writes to x, P2 writes to x, P2 writes to x, P1 writes to x, P2 writes to x.

8 | *Interconnection networks*

In Chapter 7, we considered buses to interconnect processors and memories in a shared memory multiprocessor system. The single bus, in particular, is unsuitable for interconnecting a large number of components, though variations of bus networks such as hierarchical structures are more suitable. In this chapter, we will consider other forms of interconnection networks applicable to connecting a large number of processors together, notably multistage interconnection networks and limited connectivity static interconnection networks. These networks are also applicable to message-passing multicomputers described in Chapter 9

8.1 Dynamic interconnection networks

8.1.1 General

In a *dynamic interconnection network*, the connection between two nodes (processors, processor/memory) is made by electronic switches such that some (or all) of the switch settings are changed to make different node to node connections. For ease of discussion, we will refer to inputs and outputs, implying that the transfer is unidirectional; in practice most networks can be made bidirectional to enable bidirectional communication between processors on one side of the network, and memory on the other side. (Of course, the whole network could be replicated, with input and outputs transposed.)

Principal performance figures of merit for networks include the number of switches in the network, the allowable permutation, the bandwidth (the average number of requests accepted in unit time), the latency (the time to send a request completely through the network), and the path length (the number of physical links/switches that a request must pass through from the source to the destination).

Networks sometimes allow simultaneous connections between all combinations of input and outputs; such networks are called non-blocking networks. Non-blocking networks are *strictly non-blocking* if a new interconnection between an arbitrary unused input and an arbitrary unused output can always be made, irrespective of existing connections, without disturbing the existing paths. Some non-blocking networks may require paths to be routed according to a prescribed routing algorithm to allow new input/output connections to be made without disturbing existing interconnections; such non-blocking networks are called *wide-sense non-blocking networks*. Many networks are formulated to reduce the number of switches and do not allow all combinations of input/output connections simultaneously; such networks are called *blocking networks*. A network is *rearrangeable* if any blocked input/output connection path can be re-established by altering the internal switches to reroute paths and free the blockage.

Most interconnection networks we discuss in this chapter have several intermediate links and switches that must be setup between a source and a destination (processor and memory in this context). Such networks can be designed to operate in two basic modes:

1. Circuit switched mode.
2. Packet switched mode.

In the *circuit switched* mode, a path is established between a source and a destination and maintained for the duration of the data transfer. None of the links within the whole path is available to other requests until the transfer has been completed and the links released. This mode is analogous to a public telephone system, in which a path is established between two telephones during dialing, and the path is maintained for the duration of the telephone call. It is also the most natural way to use interconnection networks with a shared memory multiprocessor as a path needs to be established between a processor and a memory to allow a data transfer between the two.

In the *packet switched* mode, request "packets" are created each holding data and a destination address. (Usually the identity of the source is also needed.) Request packets are routed from one switching cell in the network to the next cell along links between the cells. Each link is released after the request packet has passed through the link, and a packet may be stored at a cell before being routed forward. This is analogous to the mail service where letters are written, placed in envelopes ("packets"), addressed, and sent from one person to another by way of intermediate postal offices.

The packet switched mode corresponds to the way computers communicate across a computer network. To use this mode in a shared memory system, a packet must be send back the processor by the memory after it receives a request for reading data. This might be done by a separate network connecting the memories to the processors. The packet switched mode has the potential for much greater capacity for handling requests, as many requests could be in the network at any instant. However, the latency for a request to navigate through the network might be significantly longer. We will look more at variations of the packet switched mode which can reduce this latency in Chapter 9 when considering message-passing multicomputers.

In general, the switches are grouped into switching stages which may have one (or more) input capable of connecting to one (or more) output. Dynamic networks can be classified as:

1. Single stage.

2. Multistage.

In a single stage network, information being routed passes through one switching stage from input to output. In a multistage network, information is routed through more than one switching stage from input to output. Multistage networks generally have fewer internal switches, but are often blocking. Some networks have non-blocking characteristics for certain input/output combinations, which may be useful in particular applications.

8.1.2 Single stage networks

A fundamental example of a dynamic single stage network is the crossbar switch network analyzed previously, in which the stage consists of $n \times m$ switches (n input nodes, m output nodes) and each switch allows one node to node connection. This network is non-blocking and has the minimum delay through the network compared to other networks, as only one switch is involved in any path. The number of switches increases as $O(nm)$ (or $O(n^2)$ for a square network) and becomes impractical for large systems. We shall see that the non-blocking nature of the crossbar switch network can be preserved in the multistage Clos network and with substantially fewer switches for large systems. However, the single stage crossbar switch network is still a reasonable choice for a small system. The complete connectivity and flexibility of the crossbar is a distinct advantage over multistage blocking networks for small systems. The term "crossbar" stems from the historical use of mechanical switches in old telephone exchanges.

8.1.3 Multistage networks

Multistage networks can be divided into two types:

1. Crossbar switch-based networks.
2. Cell-based networks.

crossbar switch-based networks use switching elements consisting of crossbar switches, and hence multistage crossbar switch networks employ more than one crossbar switch network within a larger network. Cell-based networks usually employ switching elements with only two inputs and two outputs, and hence could be regarded as a subset of the crossbar switch network, though the 2×2 switching elements in some cell-based networks are not full crossbar switches. Instead they have limited interconnections.

Multistage crossbar switch-based networks – Clos networks

In 1953 Clos showed that a multistage crossbar switch network using three or more stages could give the full non-blocking characteristic of a single stage crossbar switch with fewer switches for larger networks. This work was done originally in the context of telephone exchanges, but has direct application to computer networks, especially when the non-blocking characteristic is particularly important.

A general *three-stage Clos network* is shown in Figure 8.1, having r_1 input stage crossbar switches, m middle stage crossbar switches and r_2 output stage crossbar switches. Each crossbar switch in the first stage has n_1 inputs and m outputs, with one output to each middle stage crossbar switch. The crossbar switches in the middle stage have r_1 inputs, matching the number of input stage crossbar switches, and r_2 outputs, with one output to each output stage crossbar switch. The crossbar switches in the final stage have m inputs, matching the number of middle stage crossbar switches, and n_2 outputs. Hence the numbers n_1, n_2, r_1, r_2 and m completely define the network. The number of inputs, N, is given by $r_1 n_1$ and the number of outputs, M, is given by $r_2 n_2$.

Clearly, any one network input has a path to any network output. Whether the network is non-blocking will depend upon the number of middle stages. Clos showed that the network is non-blocking if the number of crossbar elements in the middle stage, m, satisfies:

$$m \geq n_2 + n_1 - 1$$

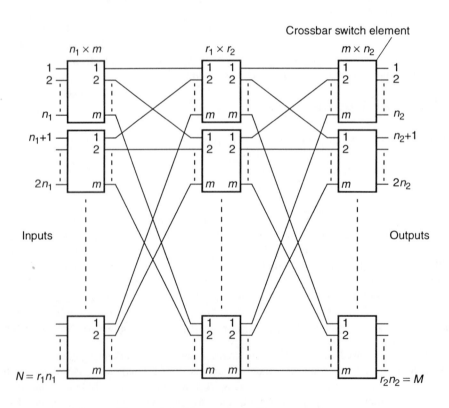

Figure 8.1 Three-stage Clos network

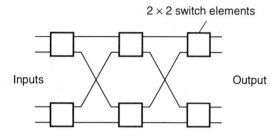

2 × 2 switch elements

Inputs   Output

Figure 8.2 Three-stage Benes network

For a network with the same number of inputs as outputs, the number of input/outputs = $r_1 n_1 = r_2 n_2$. If $n_1 = n_2$, the middle stages are square crossbar switches and the non-blocking criterion reduces to:

$$m \geq 2n - 1$$

Clos derived the number of switches in a square three-stage Clos network with input and output networks of the same size, as:

$$\text{Number of switches} = (2n - 1)\left(2N + \frac{N^2}{n^2}\right)$$

resulting in fewer switches than a single stage crossbar switch when N is greater than about twenty-five for a square network (Broomell and Heath, 1983). It has been shown that a Clos network is rearrangeable if $m \geq n_2$, otherwise the network becomes blocking.

Clos networks can be created with five stages by replacing each switching element in the middle row with a three-stage Clos network. Similarly seven, nine, eleven stages, etc. can be created by further replacement. The *Benes network* is a special case of the Clos network with 2 × 2 crossbar switch elements. A three-stage Benes network is shown in Figure 8.2. Benes networks could also be classified as cell-based networks.

Cell-based networks

The switching element (or cell) in cell-based networks typically has two inputs and two outputs. A full crossbar switch 2 × 2 network cell has twelve different useful input/output connections (states). Three further 2 × 2 network patterns exist, one connecting the inputs together, leaving the outputs free, one connecting the outputs together, leaving the inputs free, and one connecting the inputs together and the outputs together; there is no input/output connection. A final state has no interconnections. Four binary control signals would be necessary to specify the states of a 2 × 2 network.

Some, if not most, cell-based networks employ 2 × 2 cells which do not have all possible states. The two state (straight through or exchange) 2×2 network is the most common. In practice, once a path is chosen for one of the inputs – either the upper or the lower output – there is only one possible path allowed for the other input (which will be the upper output if the lower output has been taken, or the lower output if the upper output has been taken). Hence, the straight through/exchange states are sufficient and only one binary signal need be present to select which state should exist at any instant.

Most cell-based networks are highly blocking, which can be evidenced by the fact that if there are s switching cells, each with two states, there are only 2^s different states in the complete network. However, with, say, p input/outputs, there are $p!$ different combinations of input/output connections and usually $p!$ is much larger than 2^s.

Each stage of cells can be interconnected in various ways. The *baseline network* (Feng, 1981) shown in Figure 8.3 is one example of a network with a very convenient self-routing algorithm (*destination tag algorithm*) in which successive bits of the destination address control successive stages of the network. Each stage of the baseline network divides the routing range into two. The first stage splits the route into two paths, one to the lower half of the network outputs and one to the upper half. Hence, the most significant bit of the destination address can be used to route the inputs to either the upper half of the second stage, when the bit is 0, or to the lower half if the bit is 1. The second stage splits the route into the upper quarter or second quarter if the upper half of the outputs has been selected, or to the third quarter or lower quarter if the lower half has been selected. The second most significant bit is used to select which quarter, once the most significant bit selection has been made. This process is repeated for subsequent stages if present. For eight inputs and outputs, there would be three stages, for sixteen inputs and outputs there would be four stages, and so on. The least significant bit controls the last stage. Such self-routing networks suggest packet switching data transmission.

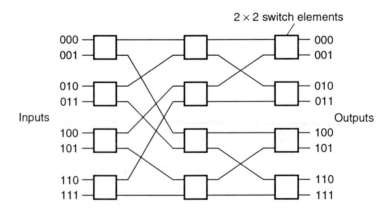

Figure 8.3 8×8 baseline network

Shuffle interconnection pattern

The perfect shuffle pattern finds wide application in multistage networks, and can also lead to destination tag self-routing networks. Originally, the perfect shuffle was developed by Pease, in 1968, for calculating the fast Fourier transform (Broomell and Heath, 1983), and was later developed for other interconnection applications by Stone and others. The input to output permutation of the (two-) perfect shuffle network is based upon shuffling a pack of cards by dividing the pack into two equal parts which are slid together with the cards from each half of the pack interleaved. The perfect shuffle network takes the first half of the inputs and interleaves the second half such that the first half of inputs pass to odd numbered outputs and the second half to even numbered outputs. For example, with eight inputs, the first half of the inputs consists of 0, 1, 2 and 3 and the second half of 4, 5, 6 and 7. Input 0 passes to output 0, input 1 to output 2, input 2 to output 4, input 3 to output 6, input 4 to output 1, input 5 to output 3, input 6 to output 5 and input 7 to output 7.

Given that the input/output addresses have the form $a_{n-1}a_{n-2} \ldots a_1 a_0$, the perfect shuffle performs the following transformation:

$$\text{Shuffle } (a_{n-1}a_{n-2} \ldots a_1 a_0) = a_{n-2} \ldots a_1 a_0 a_{n-1}$$

i.e. the address bits are cyclically shifted one place left. The inverse perfect shuffle cyclically shifts the address bits one place right.

To make all possible interconnections with the shuffle pattern, a *recirculating network* can be created by recirculating the outputs back to the inputs until the required connection is made. Exchange "boxes" are introduced; these selectively swap pairs of inputs, as shown in Figure 8.4 (*shuffle exchange network*). Each exchange box has two inputs and two outputs. There are two selectable transfer patterns, one when both inputs pass to the two corresponding outputs, and one when each input passes to the other output (i.e. the inputs are transposed). The exchange boxes transform the address bits by complementing the least significant bit, i.e.:

$$\text{Exchange } (a_{n-1}a_{n-2} \ldots a_1 a_0) = a_{n-1}a_{n-2} \ldots a_1 \overline{a_0}$$

For example, 6 (110) passes over to 7 (111) and 7 passes over to 6. The interconnection function is given by a number of shuffle exchange functions. Any input can be transferred to any output by repeated passes through the network. For example, to make a connection from 0 (000) to 6 (110) would require two passes, one pass to exchange to 1 (001) and shuffle to 2 (010), and one pass to exchange to 3 (011) and shuffle to 6 (110). A maximum of n recirculations are necessary to obtain all permutations.

Multistage perfect shuffle networks – Omega network

Rather than recirculate the paths, perfect shuffle exchange networks can be cascaded to become the *Omega network*, as shown in Figure 8.5. The network (like the baseline network) has the particular feature of the very simple destination tag self-routing algo-

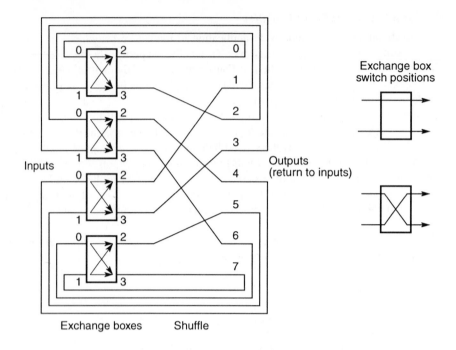

Exchange box
switch positions

Inputs

Outputs
(return to inputs)

Exchange boxes   Shuffle

Figure 8.4 Shuffle exchange network

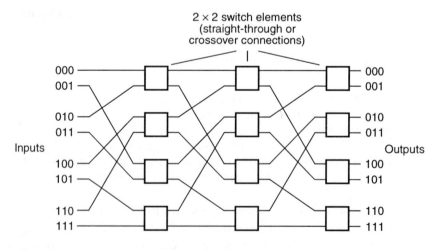

2 × 2 switch elements
(straight-through or
crossover connections)

Inputs

Outputs

Figure 8.5 Omega network

rithm. Each switching cell requires one control signal to select either the upper cell output or the lower cell output (0 specifying the upper output and 1 specifying the lower). The most significant bit of the address of the required destination is used to control the first stage cell; if this is 0 the upper output is selected, and if it is 1, the lower output is selected. The next most significant bit of the destination address is used to select the cell output of the next stage, and so on until the final output has been selected.

The cells used need to be able to select either the upper or the lower output and a 2×2 straight through/exchange cell is sufficient. The Omega network was proposed for array processing applications with four-state cells (straight through/exchange/broadcast upper/broadcast lower). The Omega network is highly blocking, though one path can always be made from any input to any output in a free network. The *indirect binary n-cube network*, which is similar to the Omega network, was proposed for processor to processor interconnections using only two-state cells. (The *direct* binary n-cube is a static network with links between particular nodes and is also called a hypercube, see Section 8.2.3.) The indirect binary n-cube and Omega networks were found to be functionally equivalent by a simple address translation. Switching networks are deemed equivalent if they produce the same permutations of input/output connections irrespective of their internal connections or actual input/output address numbering system.

Generalized self-routing networks

The self-routing networks such as Omega, baseline and indirect binary n-cube networks can be extended to use numbering system bases other than two and a generalized q-shuffle. In terms of cards, the q-shuffle takes qr cards and divides the cards into q piles of r cards. Then one card from each pile is taken in turn to create a shuffled pile.

The *Delta network* (Patel, 1981) is a generalization using a numbering base which can be other than 2 throughout. This network connects a^n inputs to b^n outputs through n stages of $a \times b$ crossbar switches. (Omega, baseline and indirect n-cube networks use $a = b = 2$.) The destination address is specified in base b numbers and the destination tag self-routing algorithm applies. Each destination digit has a value from 0 to $b - 1$ and selects one of b outputs of the $a \times b$ crossbar element. An example of a Delta network is shown in Figure 8.6. Notice that in the Delta network, the inputs are not shuffled as in the Omega network. This does not alter the routing algorithm since only the destination is significant, not the source. It also does not affect the performance with random request patterns. It may affect the performance for particular combinations of source to destination request patterns, the input shuffle altering the allowable simultaneous input/output permutations.

In Figure 8.6, the stage to stage link pattern is a four-shuffle. The destination tag self-routing networks have been further generalized into the *generalized shuffle network* (GSN) (Bhuyan and Agrawal, 1983). The GSN uses a shuffle network pattern constructed from arbitrary number system radices. An example is shown in Figure 8.7. Different radices can be used at each stage.

Note that now the basic 2×2 cell is not necessarily employed. Some studies have indicated that better performance/cost might be achieved by, for example, using 4×4 networks. In all destination tag routing networks (baseline, Omega, n-cube, and all

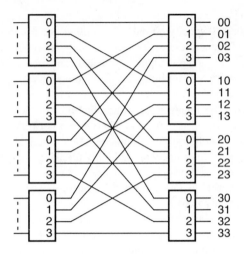

Figure 8.6 Delta network (base-4)

networks that come under generalized networks) there can be only one route from each input to each output. Hence the networks are not resilient to cell failures. Extra stages can be introduced, as shown in Figure 8.8 to provide more than one path from input to output. This method has been studied by Raghavendra and Varma (1986).

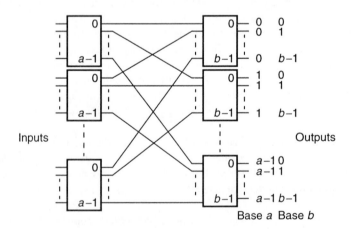

Figure 8.7 Generalized shuffle network stage

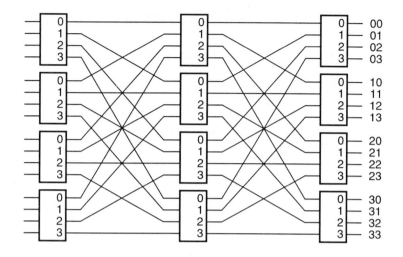

Figure 8.8 Extra stage Delta network

Arbitrary sized networks

The binary shuffle-exchange network (using 2×2 cells) can be constructed with any even number of inputs, not necessarily $N = 2^n$ since the shuffle pattern can be applied to any even number. A pack of cards can be shuffled irrespective of the number of cards. In a shuffle-exchange network, an even number is necessary so that there are no unconnected outputs. However 2×2 cells are desirable because of low cost. Also 2×2 cells have potential in optical systems. Not being restricted to powers of 2 is convenient, especially for larger networks. Padmanabhan (1991) has developed a distributed tag-based control algorithm as follows:

When N is not a power of two, the tag is a function of both the source and destination addresses. To set up a path between input i and output j, the control, tag is:

$$T_1 = (j + 2Mi) \bmod N$$

where $N = p + q$, $p = 2^n$ and $0 < q \le p$. If $T_1 + N < 2p$, then a second control tag exists given by:

$$T_2 = T_1 + N$$

If there are two paths, these paths use different links (proof in Padmanabhan, 1991). Hence there may be innate fault tolerance possibilities in the network. Each bit of T_1 or T_2 is used to control one cell as in a normal shuffle-exchange network.

8.1.4 Bandwidth of multistage networks

In Chapter 7, we derived the bandwidth of a single crossbar switch as:

$$BW = m(1 - r/m)^p$$

It follows that for a multistage network composed of stages of $a \times b$ crossbar switches (Delta, GSN etc.) the number of requests that are accepted and passed on to the next stage is given by:

$$b(1 - (1 - r_0/b)^a)$$

where r_0 is the request rate at the input of the first stage. The number of requests on any one of the b output lines of the first stage is given by:

$$r_1 = 1 - (1 - r_0/b)^a$$

These requests become the input to the next stage, and hence the number of requests at the output of the second stage is given by:

$$r_2 = 1 - (1 - r_1/b)^a$$

Hence the number of requests passed on to the output of the final stage can be found by recursively evaluating the function:

$$r_i = 1 - (1 - r_{i-1}/b)^a$$

for $i = 1$ to n, where n is the number of stages in the network, and $r_0 = r$. The bandwidth is given by:

$$BW = b^n r_n$$

as there are b^n outputs in all; there are a^n inputs. The probability that a request will be accepted is given by:

$$P_A = \frac{b^n r_n}{a_n r}$$

The derivation given is due to Patel (1981) in connection with Delta networks. Figure 8.9 shows the bandwidth and probability of acceptance of an Omega network compared to a single stage $N \times N$ crossbar switch network, where $N = 2^n$. (The Omega network can be considered here the same as a Delta network with $a = b = 2$.)

Note that the number of stages in the $2^n \times 2^n$ multistage network is $\log_2 N$ and this can be significant for a large system, e.g. for $N = 4096$, there are twelve stages.

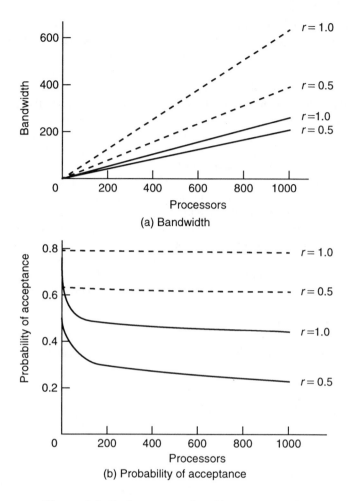

Figure 8.9 Performance of multistage networks
(— Omega, - - - full crossbar switch)

8.1.5 Hot spots

Though memory references in a shared memory multiprocessor might be spread across a number of memory locations, some locations may experience a disproportionate number of references, especially when used to store locks and synchronization variables. These shared locations have been called *hot spots* by Pfister and Norton (1985). When a multistage interconnection network is used between the memory and processors, some paths between processors and memories are shared. Accesses to shared information can cause widespread contention in the network, as the contention at one stage of the network can affect previous stages. Consider a multistage network with request queues at the input of each stage. A hot spot in memory occurs and the last stage request queue fills up. Next, requests entering the inputs of the stage become blocked and the queues at this stage fill up. Then requests at the inputs of previous stages become blocked and the queues fill up, and so on, if there are more stages. This effect is known as *tree saturation* and also blocks requests not even aimed for the hot spot. The whole network can be affected.

Pfister and Norton (1985) present the following analysis to highlight the effect of hot spots. Suppose there are N processors and N shared memory modules, and the memory request rate is r. Let the fraction of these requests which are for hot spots be h. Then the number of hot-spot requests directed to the hot-spot memory is Nrh. The number of remaining non-hot-spot requests directed to the memory module is $Nr(1 - h)/N = r(1 - h)$ assuming that these requests are uniformly distributed among all memory modules. The total number of requests for the memory module is $Nrh + r(1 - h) = r(h(N - 1) + 1)$. The asymptotically maximum number of requests that can be accepted by one memory module is 1. Hence the asymptotically maximum number of accepted requests is $r/r(h(N - 1) + 1) = 1/(h(N - 1) + 1)$. Hence the maximum bandwidth is given by:

$$BW = N/(h(N - 1) + 1)$$

This equation is plotted in Figure 8.10. We see that even a small fraction of hot-spot

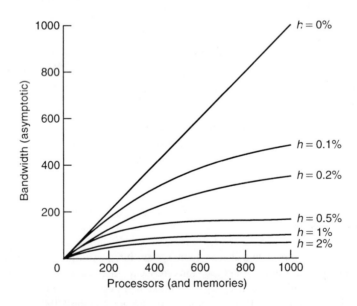

Figure 8.10 Asymptotic bandwidth in presence of hot spots

requests can have a profound effect on the bandwidth. For example, with $h = 0.1$ per cent, the bandwidth is reduced to 500 with 1000 processors. The request rate, r, has no effect on the bandwidth, and for large numbers of processors (P), the bandwidth tends to $1/h$. For example, when $h = 1$ per cent, the bandwidth is limited to 100 irrespective of the number of processors.

Two approaches have been suggested to alleviate the effects of hot spots, namely:

1. Software combining trees.
2. Hardware combining circuits.

In the software approach, operations on a single variable are broken down into operations which are performed separately so as to distribute and reduce the hot spots. The operations are arranged in a tree-like manner and results are passed along the tree to the root. Further information on the software approach can be found in Yew, Tzeng and Lawrie (1987).

In the hardware approach, circuits are incorporated into the network to recognize requests for shared locations and to combine the data access. In one relatively simple hardware combining network, read accesses to the same shared memory location are recognized at the switching cells and the requests combined to produce one read request to the memory module. The returning data is directed through the network to all required destinations.

Since shared variables are often used as synchronization variables, synchronization operations can be combined. The *fetch-and-add operation* suggested by Gottlieb *et al.* (1983) for combining networks returns the original value of a stored variable and adds a constant to the variable as specified as an operand. The addition is performed by a cell within the network. When more than one such operation is presented to the network, the network recognizes the operations and performs additions, leaving the memory to return the original value through the network and be presented with one final store operation. The network will modify the value returned to give each processor a value it would have received if the operations were performed serially.

An example of fetch-and-add operations in a multistage network is shown in Figure 8.11. Three fetch-and-add operations are received from three processors to operate upon memory location M:

Processor 1   f-&-a M,+x
Processor 2   f-&-a M,+y
Processor 3   f-&-a M,+z

Suppose the original value stored in M is w. As requests are routed through the network, individual cells perform additions and store one of the increments internally. In Figure 8.11, the first two requests are routed through the same cell and x and y are added together to be passed forward, to be added to the z from the third operation. The result, $x + y + z$, is presented to the memory and added to the stored value, giving $w + x + y + z$ stored in the memory. The original value, w, is passed back through the network. At the

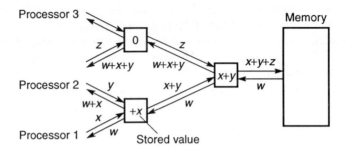

Figure 8.11 Fetch-and-add operations in a multistage network

first cell encountered, $x + y$ had been stored and this is added to the w to give $w + x + y$, which is routed towards processor 3, and w is routed towards processors 1 and 2. In this cell, x had been stored, and is added to the w to give $w + x$, which is routed to processor 2, and w is routed to processor 1. Hence the three processors receive w, $w + x$ and $w + x + y$ respectively, which are the values they might have received had the operations been performed separately (actually the values if the operations were in the order: first processor 1, then processor 2 and then processor 3).

The significance of the fetch-and-add operation is that it provides a way of satisfying the *serialization principle* (modeling effect of simultaneous accesses by an unspecified but acceptable sequential order). It allows various parallel programming constructs to be implemented including semaphores and barriers (see Almasi and Gottlieb, 1994). For example, a barrier could be implemented with:

```
f-&-a x,1;
while (x < N) skip;
```

where x is initialized to zero. If the barrier variable, x, is to be reused in another barrier, a reusable barrier (as might be necessary if there were many barriers in the program), the code must be modified (see again Almasi and Gottlieb, 1994). Fetch-and-add can also be used to control the issuance of work to processors, as each processor will receive a unique value. To implement the FOR loop:

```
parfor (n = 1; n <= 100; n++) {
    code using n
}
```

so that each processor returns to the next iteration when free, Hwang (1993) gives the following code which is executed by each processor:

```
f-&-a n,1;
while (n ≤ 100) {
```

```
code using n;
    f-&-a n,1;        /* get next available n */
}
```

Fetch-and-add operations are implemented on the NYU Ultracomputer. However it requires additional hardware in the switches, and is applicable only to systems with multistage interconnection networks. It cannot be readily implemented using other inter-connection structures.

8.1.6   Overlapping connectivity multistage interconnection networks

We introduced in Chapter 7 the concept of overlapping connectivity where each processor has a range of nearby memories that it can reach and the ranges overlap. The overlapping characteristic can be created in multistage networks. Figure 8.12 shows one example (Wilkinson, 1992b). In this design, the stage-to-stage connection links provide either a connection to the cell directly below or staggered by a distance of 2^i at stage i (1, 2, 4, 8 etc.) The staggered layout of the link connecting to the cell directly below is to reduce the number of link crossovers and is not otherwise significant. The edge connections of the

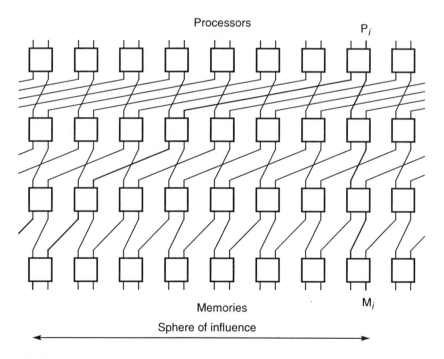

Figure 8.12 Overlapping connectivity multistage interconnection network

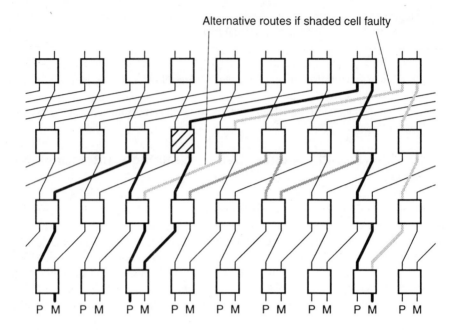

Figure 8.13 Reflective interconnection network

Reprinted from *Computers & Electrical Engineering*, copyright 1994, page 291, with kind permission from Elsevier Science Ltd., The Boulevard, Langford Lane, Kidlington, OX5 1GB, UK

network wrap around. Each stride taken between two cells contributes a binary weighted distance to the total distance.

The network can be made one-sided so that both processors and memories connect to the same side of the network as shown in Figure 8.13 (*reflective interconnection networks*; Wilkinson and Farmer, 1994). In this case, the switching cells have three states as shown in Figure 8.14. The path between a processor and a memory requires a path up

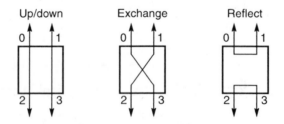

Figure 8.14 States of switching cells

Reprinted from *Computers & Electrical Engineering*, copyright 1994, page 291, with kind permission from Elsevier Science Ltd., The Boulevard, Langford Lane, Kidlington, OX5 1GB, UK

to a "reflection" point and then downwards. The left route in Figure 8.13 requires a distance of 2 to be covered which could be achieved with one stride of 2^1. The right route requires a distance of 6 to be covered which could be achieved with two strides 2^1 and 2^2. There are many alternative routes, some of which are shown in Figure 8.13, which leads to significant fault tolerance. In general the equation:

$$\sum(\text{all upward strides taken to the right}) - \sum(\text{all downward strides taken to the left}) = d$$

has to be satisfied, where d is the distance between the processor and memory. Reflective networks with separate links in each direction, called *double reflective networks* here, eliminate completely any deadlock which can occur with single bidirectional links between switching cells.

Figure 8.15 shows typical comparative simulation results using the synchronous circuit-switch mode of operation with requests being made to destinations to one side of the source selected randomly within the range, R (256 processors and 256 memories) (Wilkinson and Farmer, 1994). In a completely synchronous mode, the operation is divided into major cycles. Each major cycle is composed of a number of minor cycles. Processor requests are only considered by the network at the beginning of each major cycle. Requests are routed from one cell to the next in the path in each minor cycle. In a purely asynchronous mode, some form of handshaking mechanism used for establishing a path through the network from one cell to the next, and a processor can make a request at any time. In any event, most systems would synchronize the signals locally with a high speed clock.

In Figure 8.15(a), we see the effects of increasing the range, R, on the bandwidth, for a number of common networks, the crossbar, 8-stage Omega, 8-stage 2×2 Delta network and 8-stage reflective networks. The Omega and 2×2 Delta networks are essentially similar networks except for the interconnection patterns to the first stage (see Figure 8.5 and Figure 8.6). Both use the destination tag routing algorithm and would only have different performance for specific request patterns. In fact they have different performance here. The Delta network never achieves a bandwidth greater than half the maximum bandwidth because adjacent processors must use the same link initially for adjacent memories. In Figure 8.15(b), we see the effects of increasing range on the path length. All double sided networks, such as the Omega and Delta networks have a constant path length given by the number of stages. In contrast, the path length of reflective networks is almost proportional to the separation of source and destination (see Problem 8.10 for the theoretical path length).

As illustrated in Figure 8.13 and in the equation given previously, the reflective networks have many different routes for individual requests. These routes can be used to avoid contention in the network when more than one request requires the same link/cell, and also can be used to avoid faulty links and switching cells, to provide resilience to faults. One important result in Wilkinson and Farmer (1994) is that regardless of the distance between a processor and a memory (excluding a local memory) there always exists at least two disjoint single reflective routes, and these are identified. (A single reflective route has only one point at which the path reflects downwards.) *Disjoint routes*

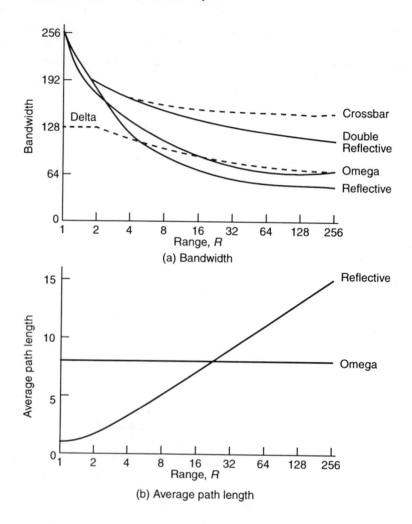

Figure 8.15 Performance of reflective network - circuit switched mode

Reprinted from *Computers & Electrical Engineering*, copyright 1994, page 295, with kind permission from Elsevier Science Ltd., The Boulevard, Langford Lane, Kidlington, OX5 1GB, UK

have no common links. It is advantageous to identify disjoint routes. Then if a route is blocked because a fault exists in the route, the request can be launched again from the source along the disjoint route without having to identify the location of the fault.

Figure 8.16 shows representative results for the double reflective network under fault conditions. Here requests can be made across the full request range. A dynamic re-routing algorithm is used to find alterative routes through the network should a path be

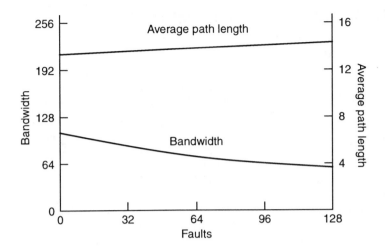

Figure 8.16 Performance of double reflective network with faults

Reprinted from *Computers & Electrical Engineering*, copyright 1994, page 306, with kind permission
from Elsevier Science Ltd., The Boulevard, Langford Lane, Kidlington, OX5 1GB, UK

unavailable. The routing algorithm used to obtain results is as follows. Each switching
cell is given a column address. Suppose the switching cell having column address C
receives a request to route. The destination address, D, is subtracted from C, to obtain the
remaining distance in the right direction, $R = r_{n-1} \ldots r_1 r_0$. The distance to the left, $L =
l_{n-1} \ldots l_1 l_0$, is given by $N - R$ where there are N processors/memories. The dynamic
routing algorithm is given by:

```
IF L ≥ 2^j {              /* insufficient height to reach destination by left/down */
                          /* go right/up */
    IF R ≤ L {            /* best route to the right */
      IF r_j = 1 take line 1
      ELSE take line 0
    } ELSE take line 0    /* best route to the left */
} ELSE                    /* best route is to the left */
    IF l_{j-1} = 1 take line 2
    ELSE take line 3
```

where the lines around the switch cell are numbered as in Figure 8.14. The reader is
referred to Wilkinson and Farmer (1994) for more details of the theoretical results and
performance of reflective networks in various circuit switched and packet switched
modes, with and without faults, and the routing algorithms.

8.2 Static interconnection networks

8.2.1 General

Static interconnection networks are those which allow only direct fixed paths between two processing elements (nodes). Each path could be unidirectional or bidirectional. In the following, we will generally assume links capable of bidirectional transfers when counting the number of links. The number of links would, of course, be double if separate links were needed for each direction of transfer. Static interconnection networks would be particularly suitable for regular processor-processor interconnections, i.e. in which all the nodes are processors and processors could process incoming data or pass the data on to other processors. We will find that static networks are used in message-passing multiprocessors/multicomputers described in Chapter 9. However, static networks can also be used for shared memory systems. In that case, the memory is physically distributed with the processors and direct links connect the processor-memory pairs as shown in Figure 8.17. To maintain the shared memory concept, the memories must have a single address space. Either circuit switching or packet switching could be used. If circuit switching, a path is established through the crossbar switches in each node from the source to the destination. If packet switching, generally buffers would need to be provided within each node to hold the packets. We will refer again in Chapter 9 to the static networks described here.

In general, the number of links in a static interconnection network when each element has the same number of links is given by (number of nodes) × (number of links of a node)/2, the factor of 1/2 due to each path being used in two nodes.

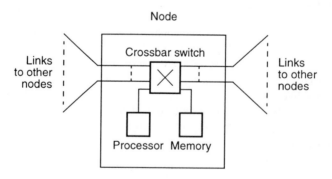

Figure 8.17 Processor-memory node

8.2.2 Exhaustive static interconnections

In *exhaustive* or *completely connected networks*, all nodes have paths to every other node. Hence n nodes could be exhaustively interconnected with $n - 1$ paths from each node to the other $n - 1$ node. There are $n(n - 1)/2$ paths in all. If each direction of transfer involves a separate path, there are $n(n - 1)$ paths. Exhaustive interconnection has application for small n. For example, a set of four microprocessors could reasonably be exhaustively interconnected using three parallel or serial ports attached to each microprocessor. All four processors could send information simultaneously to other processors without contention. The absence of contention makes static exhaustive interconnections particularly attractive, when compared to the non-exhaustive shared path connection schemes to be described. However, as n increases, the number of interconnections clearly becomes impractical for economic and engineering reasons.

8.2.3 Limited static interconnections

Interconnections could be limited to, say, a group of the neighboring nodes; there are numerous possibilities. Here we will give some common examples.

Linear array and ring structures

A one-dimensional *linear array* has connections limited to the nearest two neighbors and can be formed into a *ring* structure by connecting the free ends as shown in Figure 8.18. The interconnection might be unidirectional, in which case the former creates a linear pipeline structure; alternatively the links might be bidirectional. In either case, such arrays might be applicable to certain computations. Each node requires two links, one to each neighboring node, and hence an n node array requires n links. In the *chordal ring* network, shown in dotted lines, each node connects to its neighbors as in the ring, but also to one node three nodes apart. There are now three links on each node and $3n/2$ paths in all.

Two-dimensional arrays

A two-dimensional array or *near-neighbor mesh* can be created by having each node in a

Ring

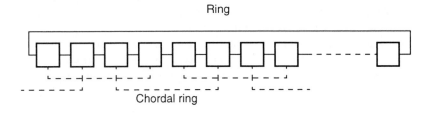

Chordal ring

Figure 8.18 Linear array

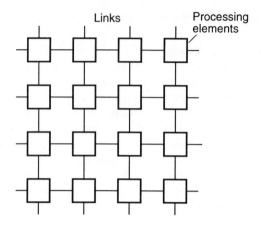

Figure 8.19 Two-dimensional array

two-dimensional array connect to all its four nearest neighbors, as shown in Figure 8.19. The free ends might circulate back to the opposite sides. Now each node has four links and there are $2n$ links in all. This particular network is popular with VLSI structure because of the ease of layout and expandability. The network can be *folded*, that is, rows are interleaved and columns are interleaved so that the wraparound connections simply turn back through the network rather than have to stretch from one edge to the opposite edge.

An array is often formed with wraparound connections (torus) to reduce the maximum distance between a source and destination node by about factor of two. However then we have long connections from one side of the array to the oppose side of the array, which would have to be broken if the array were to be expanded. A solution to this problem is to "fold" the array. In a folded array, nodes are laid out in an interleaved fashion as shown in Figure 8.20.

Meshes are usually with wraparound connections to reduce the maximum distance between nodes by approximately half, since the route from one node to another can be to the left or right and up or down. Variations include having wraparound connections connect to nodes with some offset distance, this creating diagonal wraparound connections, i.e. the *Midimew networks* (minimum distance mesh with wraparound links, Beivide, Herrada, Balcázar and Arruabarrena (1991).

The two-dimensional array can be given extra diagonal links. For example, one, two, three or all four diagonal links can be put in place, allowing connections to diagonally adjacent nodes. Each node has eight links and the network has $4n$ links. In Figure 8.21, each node has six links and there are $3n$ links in the network.

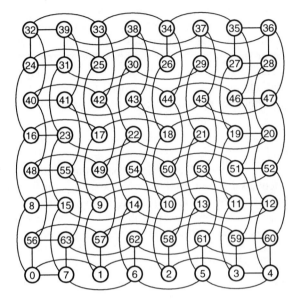

Figure 8.20 Folded mesh

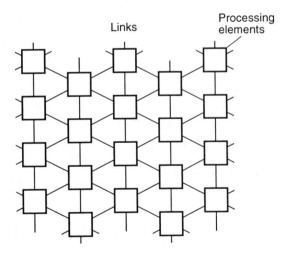

Figure 8.21 Hexagonal configuration

Star network

The star connection has one node into which all other nodes connect. There are $n - 1$ links in all, i.e. the number of links grows proportional to n, which is generally the best one could hope for, and any two nodes can be reached in two paths. However, the central node must pass on all transfers to required destinations and substantial contention or bottleneck might occur in high traffic. Also, should the central node fail, the whole system would fail. This might be the case in other networks if additional mechanisms were not incorporated into the system to route around faulty nodes but, given alternative routes, fault tolerance should be possible. Duplicated star networks would give additional routes.

Tree networks

The *binary tree* network is shown in Figure 8.22. Apart from the root node, each node has three links and the network fans out from the root node. At the first level below the root node there are two nodes. At the next level there are four nodes, and at the jth level below the root node there are $2j - 1$ nodes (counting the root node as level 0). The number of nodes in the system down to the jth level is:

$$n = N(j) = 1 + 2 + 2^2 + 2^3 \ldots 2^j$$
$$= \frac{(2^j - 1)}{(2 - 1)}$$
$$= 2^j - 1$$

and the number of levels $j = \log_2(n + 1)$. This network requires $n - 1$ links. (The easiest way to prove this expression is to note that every additional node except the root node adds one link.)

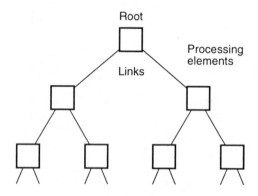

Figure 8.22 Tree structure

The tree network need not be based upon the base two. In an m-ary tree, each node connects to m nodes beneath it and one from above. The number of nodes in this system down to the jth level is:

$$n = N(j) = 1 + m + m^2 + m^3 \dots m^j$$
$$= \frac{(m^j - 1)}{(m - 1)}$$

and the number of levels $j = \log_m(n + 1)$. Again, the network requires $n - 1$ links, but fewer intermediate nodes are needed to connect nodes as the value of m is increased.

The binary and general m-ary tree networks are somewhat similar to the star network in terms of routing through combining nodes. The root node is needed to route from one side of the tree to the other. Intermediate nodes are needed to route between nodes which are not directly connected. This usually means travelling from the source node up the tree until a common node in both paths from the route node is reached and then down to the destination node.

The tree is particularly convenient for divide and conquer algorithms. The average distance grows logarithmically with size of the network. However under uniform request patterns, the communication traffic increases towards the root, which can be a bottleneck. In the *fat tree network* (Leiserson, 1985), the number of the links (channels) is progressively increased towards the root. In the *binary fat tree*, we simply add links in parallel as required between levels of a binary tree, and increase the number of links towards the root. Leiserson developed the *universal fat tree* where the links grow exponentially. Alternatively a fat tree can be based upon an m-ary tree. The Thinking Machine's Connection Machine CM5 uses a 4-ary fat tree (Hwang, 1993).

The networks so far described are generally regular in that the structure is symmetrical. In irregular networks, the symmetry is lost in either the horizontal or vertical directions, or in both directions. An irregular network can be formed, for example, by removing existing links from a regular network or inserting extra links. The binary tree network is only regular if all nodal sites are occupied, i.e. the tree has 1 node, 3 nodes, 7 nodes, 15 nodes, 31 nodes, etc.

Hypertree networks

In the *hypertree network* (Goodman and Séquin, 1981) specific additional links are put in place directly between nodes to reduce the "average distance" between nodes. (The average distance is the average number of links that must be used to connect two nodes, see Section 8.2.5.) Each node is given a binary address starting at the root node as node 1, the two nodes below it as nodes 2 and 3, with nodes 4, 5, 6 and 7 immediately below nodes 2 and 3. Node 2 connects to nodes 4 and 5. Node 3 connects to nodes 6 and 7, and so on. The additional links of the hypertree connect nodes whose binary addresses differ by only one bit (a Hamming distance of one). Notice that the hypertree network is not regular.

Cube networks

In the *3-cube network*, each node connects to its neighbors in three dimensions, as shown in Figure 8.23. Each node can be assigned an address which differs from adjacent nodes by one bit. This characteristic can be extended for higher dimension *n*-cubes, with each node connecting to all nodes whose addresses differ in one bit position for each dimension. For example, in a 5-cube, node number 11101 connects to 11100, 11111, 11001, 10101 and 01101. The number of bits in the nodal address is the same as the number of dimensions. *N*-cube structures, particularly higher dimensional *n*-cubes, are commonly called *hypercube networks*. The *generalized hypercube* (Bhuyan and Agrawal, 1984) can use nodal address radices other than 2, but still uses the characteristic that addresses of interconnected nodes differ in each digit position.

The (binary) hypercube is an important interconnection network; it has been shown to be suitable for a very wide range of applications. Meshes can be embedded into a hypercube by numbering the edges of the mesh in Gray code. In Chapter 9, we will describe message-passing multiprocessor systems using hypercube networks. An *n*-dimensional hypercube consists of two $n-1$ dimensional hypercubes with *n*th dimension links between them. Figure 8.24 shows a four dimensional hypercube drawn as two 3-dimensional hypercubes with connections between them. In a practical system the network must be laid out in one or possibly two dimensions. A six-dimensional hypercube is shown in Figure 8.25 laid out in one plane. Hypercube connections could be made in one backplane, as shown in Figure 8.26 for a three-dimensional hypercube.

Numerous other networks have been proposed, though in most cases they have not been used to a significant extent. In the *cube connected cycles network*, 2^k nodes divided into $2^{k-r} \times 2^r$ nodes are connected such that 2^r nodes form a group at the vertices of a (2^{k-r})-cube network. Each group of 2^r nodes is connected in a loop, with one connected to each of the two neighboring nodes and also one link to a corresponding node in another dimension.

Though we have described direct link static networks in terms of communicating nodes, the links could be buses. A possibility is to have multiple buses which can extend through to other nodes. This can, for example, be applied to a mesh network or a

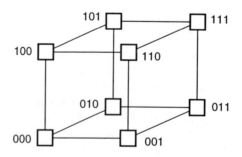

Figure 8.23 Three-dimensional hypercube

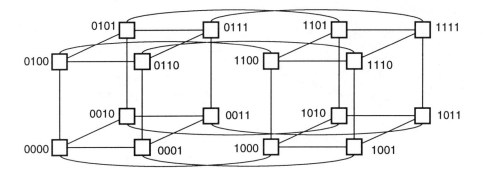

Figure 8.24 Four-dimensional hypercube

hypercube network. In a *spanning bus hypercube network*, each node connects to one bus in each dimension of the network. For a two-dimensional network, nodes connect to two buses or two sets of buses that stretch in each of the two dimensions. For a three-dimensional network, each node connects to three buses.

8.2.4 Altering the number of links between nodes

Obviously if we add links to an interconnection network, the performance will improve because the network congestion is reduced (depending upon the actual network traffic). Assuming that we wish to keep the network interconnection pattern regular, there are two

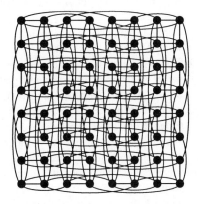

Figure 8.25 Six-dimensional hypercube laid out in one plane

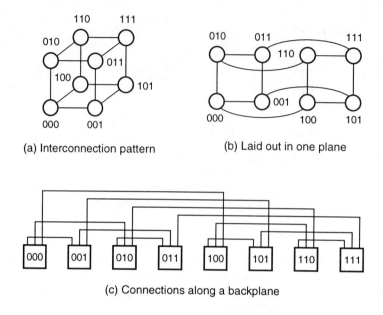

(a) Interconnection pattern

(b) Laid out in one plane

(c) Connections along a backplane

Figure 8.26 Three-dimensional hypercube

basic ways that extra links can be added to the network:

1. Duplicating links between nodes throughout, i.e. having parallel links between nodes. For example, there could be four separate communication links between all nodes. This in effect replaces the links with a higher bandwidth link.
2. Adding a single link between selected pairs of nodes in some regular way.

Method 1 could be easily applied to any static or dynamic network. Figure 8.27 shows the effects of having such parallel links in mesh and hypercube networks (obtained by simulation (Wilkinson, 1990b)). In Figure 8.27(a), the hypercube and two-dimensional mesh are compared using packet switching (which would generally be appropriate for message-passing systems, see Chapter 9). There are 256 nodes. The request rate, R, is 100 per cent (a request on every cycle from each processor) and 50 per cent (one request in every two cycles on average from each processor). Here we see that significant improvement can be achieved simply by increasing the number of parallel links from one to two. Four parallel links are needed in the mesh to achieve the bandwidth of a hypercube with one link between nodes. Increasing the number of links further does not have a significant effect at 50 per cent request rates. It is interesting to see that a mesh network with four parallel links between nodes has about the same bandwidth as a hypercube with one link, yet the mesh will be much easier to lay out in practice.

In Figure 8.27(b), the performance of a circuit switched mesh is presented, showing the

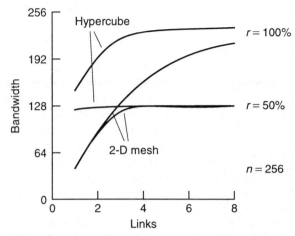

(a) Bandwidth of mesh and hypercube networks with packet switching

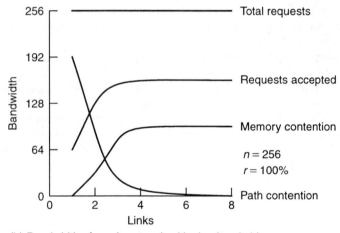

(b) Bandwidth of mesh network with circuit switching

Figure 8.27 Increasing the number of parallel links in mesh and hypercube networks

average number of requests accepted, the average number blocked by path contention (due to links being used by another requests), the average number of requests blocked by memory contention (because memory was being used for another request when the request reached the memory). Again two links improve the bandwidth significantly, and further links increase the bandwidth, though with diminishing returns.

There have been many proposals for adding extra links to networks in some regular manner in order to improve the network performance. The hypercube network has attracted much attention for this treatment. Several people have independently discovered that simply swapping the destination node of certain links leads to dramatic improvements without increasing the number of links. Such modified hypercubes have been called *twisted hypercubes*, or *crossed hypercubes*. Perhaps the first to make this proposal were Hilberts, Koopman and van de Snepscheut (1987). Others, including Efe (1991, 1992), proposed the crossed cube network, a hypercube network with one or more links changed in this fashion, and showed that the diameter of the resultant "cross" hypercube is $\lceil n + 1)/2 \rceil$ for an *n*-dimensional hypercube (almost half that of a normal hypercube). A three-dimensional hypercube only requires one pair of links to be crossed as shown in Figure 8.28. Higher dimensional hypercubes require further links to crossed. This idea was extended by Das, Mukhopadhyaya and Sinha (1994) to twisting many links. They demonstrated that by adding 8 extra links, the diameter of an *n*-cube ($n \geq 4$) could be reduced by 2 and by adding 16 extra links the diameter could be reduced by 3 ($n \geq 6$), and other reductions were proved using either twisting of links or by adding bridge links. Extra links can be added in many ways. An *n*-dimensional folded hypercube (El-Amawy and Latifi, 1991) is an *n*-dimensional hypercube with extra lines between two nodes that are Hamming distance *n* apart. In 1991, Estahanian, Ni and Sagan proved rather startlingly that by exchanging *any* two independent links in a hypercube, its diameter decreases by one.

Just as increasing the number of links will improve the performance at a cost, reducing the number of links will decrease the performance but will also reduce the cost. An example of a hypercube network with reduced links is a hypercube laid out in one plane with the longer links deleted. The resultant network is somewhat similar to overlapping connectivity networks. Other possibilities include constructing hypercubes with a number of nodes which is not a power of two, either intentionally or because one or more nodes have become faulty. These hypercubes are usually called *incomplete hypercubes* (Katseff, 1988). One form of incomplete hypercube consists of two interconnected complete hypercubes of size 2^n and 2^k ($1 \leq k \leq n$) (Tzeng and Chen, 1994).

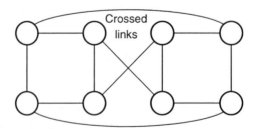

Figure 8.28 Three-dimensional hypercube with crossed links

8.2.5 Evaluation of static networks

Clearly, there are numerous variations in limited interconnections, some of which suit particular computations. With limited interconnections, some transfers will require data to pass through intermediate nodes to reach the destination node. Whatever the limited connection network devised, there must be a means of locating the shortest route from the source to the destination. A routing algorithm which is easy and fast to implement is preferable.

Request paths

A critical factor in evaluating any interconnection network is the number of links between two nodes. The number of intermediate nodes/links is of interest because this gives the overall delay and the collision potential. The *average distance* is defined as (Agrawal *et al.*, 1986):

$$\text{Average distance} = \frac{\displaystyle\sum_{d=0}^{\text{Max}} dN_d}{N-1}$$

where N_d is the number of nodes separated by d links. Max is the maximum distance necessary to interconnect two nodes (not the maximum distance as this would be infinity) and N is the number of nodes. For any particular network, interconnection paths for all combinations of nodal connections would need to be computed, which is not always an easy task. Notice that the average distance formulae may not be the actual average distance in an application.

Number of links

Another factor of interest is the number of links emanating from each node, as this gives the node complexity. The number of links is usually fairly obvious from the network definition. With an increased number of links, the average distance is shorter; the two are interrelated. A *normalized average distance* is defined as:

Normalized average distance = Average distance × Links/node

which gives an indication of network performance taking into account its complexity. The *message density* has been defined as:

$$\text{Message density} = \frac{\text{Average distance} \times \text{Number of nodes}}{\text{Total number of links}}$$

In a limited static interconnection network, distant nodes can be reached by passing requests from a source node (processor) through intermediate nodes (called "levels"). Links to four neighbors reach $4(2i - 1)$ nodes at the ith level from the node. For hexagonal groups (Figure 8.21), there are $6i$ nodes at the ith level, i.e. the number of nodes at each level increases proportionally, and the number of nodes that can be reached, n, is given by:

$$n = \sum_{i=1}^{L} 6i = 3L(L + 1)$$

where L is the number of levels. In the hexagonal configuration, every node at each level can be reached by one path from the previous level (this is not true for the square configuration). The average number of levels to reach a node, and hence the average number of requests in the system for each initial nodal request, is given by:

$$\text{Average number of levels} = \sum_{i=1}^{L} \frac{6i^2}{n}$$

To place an upper bound on the number of simultaneous requests in the system, requests from one processor to another can be passed on through a fixed number of nodes.

Bisection width

The (channel) *bisection width* is the number of links (channels) that must be cut to divide a network into two equal parts. For example the bisection width of an n-dimensional hypercube is n since removing one link from each node can separate the hypercube into two $(n - 1)$-dimensional hypercubes. The bisection width is useful in determining the complexity of laying out a network on a VLSI chip. The *wire bisection width* is the actual number of wires that have to be cut.

Fault tolerance

A static network has a fault diameter of d_f if its diameter increases to d_f as a result of f processor failures. For an n-cube (hypercube) $d_n = $ infinity (worst case), $d_{n-1} = n + 1$ (Krishnamoorthy and Krishnamurthy, 1987). The term *node disjoint* is used to indicate that there are no common nodes in path and the term *edge disjoint* to indicate that there are no common links in path. As we have mentioned with reflective networks, disjoint paths (with disjoint edges or nodes) are useful to know, so that a completely different route can be selected.

Bandwidth of static networks

We have seen that the performance of dynamic networks is often characterized by their bandwidth and also probability of acceptance. The bandwidth and the probability of acceptance metric can be carried over to static networks, though this is rarely done. One example of a direct binary *n*-cube (hypercube) is given in Abraham and Padmanabhan (1989). We can make the following general analysis for any static network.

Suppose that each node has *input requests* and can generate *output requests* either by passing input requests onwards or from some internal program (*internal requests*). Let the probability that a node can generate an internal request for another node be *r*. The requested node might be one directly connected to it or it might be one which can be reached through intermediate nodes. In the latter case, the request must be presented to the intermediate nodes as external requests, but these nodes might also have internally generated requests and only one request can be generated from a node, irrespective of how many requests are present. There could be at most one internal request and as many external requests as there are links into the node. Let r_{out} be the probability that a node generates a request (either internally or passes on an external request) and r_{in} be the probability that a node receives an external request. Some external requests will be for the node and only a percentage, say *A*, will be passed onwards to another node. Incorporating *A*, we get:

$$r_{out} = r + Ar_{in}(1 - r)$$

and the bandwidth given by:

$$BW = (1 - A)r_{in}N$$

where there are *N* nodes. The value for *A* will depend upon the network.

The probability that an external request is received by node *i* from node *j* will depend upon the number of nodes that node *j* can request, i.e. the number of nodes connected directly to node *j*, and the probability is given by r_{out}/n, where *n* nodes connect directly to node *j* and all links are used. We shall assume that all nodes have the same number of links to other nodes and, for now, all are used. The probability that node *j* has not requested node *i* is given by $(1 - r_{out}/n)$. The probability that no node has requested node *i* is given by $(1 - r_{out}/n)^n$. The probability that node *i* has one or more external requests at its inputs is given by:

$$r_{in} = 1 - (1 - r_{out}/n)^n$$

The probability that a node generates a request in terms of the probability of an internal request and the number of nodes directly connected (and communicating) to the node is given by:

$$r_{out} = r + A(1 - r)(1 - (1 - r_{out}/n)^n)$$

which is a recursive formula which converges by repeated application. A suitable initial value for r_{out} is *r*, r_{out} being some value in excess of *r*.

The derivation assumes that an external request from node *j* to node *i* could be sent through node i and back to node j, which generally does not occur, i.e. an external request passing through node i can only be sent to $n - 1$ nodes at most, and more likely only to nodes at the next level in the sphere of influence (up to two nodes in the hexagonal configuration) whereas internal requests will generally have an equal probability of requesting any of the nodes connected.

PROBLEMS

8.1   Design a non-blocking Clos network for sixty-four processors and sixty-four memories.

8.2   Identify relative advantages of multistage networks and single stage networks.

8.3   Ascertain all input/output combinations in an 8×8 single stage recirculating shuffle exchange network which require the maximum number of passes through the network.

8.4   How many stages of a multistage Omega network are necessary to interconnect 900 processors and 800 memories? What is the bandwidth when the request rate is 40 per cent? Make a comparison with a single stage crossbar switch network.

8.5   Design the logic necessary with each cell in an 8×8 Omega network for self-routing.

8.6   Determine whether it is possible to connect input i to output i in an 8×8 Omega network for all i simultaneously.

8.7   Show that a three-stage indirect binary n-cube network and a three-stage Omega network are functionally equivalent.

8.8   Draw a MIN using 2×2 cells for connecting 12 processors to 12 memories with no spare inputs or outputs.

8.9   Illustrate the flow of information in a three-stage multistage network with fetch-and-add operations, given that four processors execute the following:

Processor 1	f-&-a 120,9
Processor 2	f-&-a 120,8
Processor 3	f-&-a 120,7
Processor 4	f-&-a 120,6

8.10 Prove the following for the reflective interconnection network:

(a) Number of stages necessary to establish a path between any source and any destination using the basic direct routing algorithm (a single reflective point, and a straight downward path) is:

$$s = \left\lceil \log_2\left(\frac{N-1}{2} + 1\right) \right\rceil + 1 \qquad \text{if } N \text{ is odd}$$

$$s = \left\lceil \log_2\left(\frac{N}{2} + 1\right) \right\rceil + 1 \qquad \text{if } N \text{ is even}$$

(b) The average path length is given by:

$$\text{Average path length} = \frac{1 + \sum_{i=1}^{\log_2 R} 2^{i-1}(2i+1)}{R}$$

if paths can only be to the right (unidirectional routing), and is:

$$\text{Average path length} = \frac{1 + \sum_{i=0}^{\log_2 r} 2^i(2i+1)}{R}$$

if paths can be either to the left or right (bidirectional routing) where $R = 2r + 1$. $N =$ number of processors/memories. $R =$ the range of requests.

8.11 Derive the average distance between two nodes in a three-dimensional hypercube.

8.12 Demonstrate how each of the following structures can be implemented on a hypercube network:

1. Binary tree structure.
2. Mesh network.

8.13 Derive an expression for the number of nodes that can be reached in a north-south-east-west nearest neighbor mesh network at the Lth level from the node.

PART III

Multiprocessor systems without shared memory

9 | *Message-passing multiprocessor systems*

This chapter concentrates upon the design of multiprocessor systems which do not use global memory; instead each processor has local memory and will communicate with other processors via messages, usually through direct links between processors. Such systems are called *message-passing multiprocessors* and are particularly suitable when there is a large number of processors.

9.1 General

9.1.1 Architecture

The shared memory multiprocessors described in the previous chapters have some distinct disadvantages, notably:

1. They do not easily expand to accommodate large numbers of processors.
2. Synchronization techniques are necessary to control access to shared variables.
3. Memory contention can significantly reduce the speed of the system.

Other difficulties can arise in shared memory systems. For example, data coherence must be maintained between caches holding shared variables. Shared memory is, however, a natural extension of a single processor system. Code and data can be placed in the shared memory to be accessed by individual processors.

An alternative multiprocessor system to the shared memory system which totally eliminates the problems cited, is to have only local memory and remove all shared memory from the system. Code for each processor is loaded into the local memory and any required data is stored locally. Programs are still partitioned into separate parts, as in a shared memory system, and these parts are executed concurrently by individual processors. When processors need to access information from other processors, or to send information to other processors, they communicate by sending messages, usually along direct communication links. Data words are not stored globally in the system; if more than one processor requires the data, it must be duplicated and sent to all requesting processors.

The basic architecture of the message-passing multiprocessor system is shown in Figure 9.1. The message-passing multiprocessor consists of nodes, which are normally connected by direct links to a few other nodes. Each node consists of an instruction processor with local memory and input/output communication channels. The system is usually controlled by a host computer, which loads the local memories and accepts results from the nodes. For communication purposes, the host can be considered simply as another node, though the communication between the instruction processor nodes and the host will be slower if it uses a single globally shared channel (for example an Ethernet channel). There are no global memory locations. The local memory of each nodal processor can only be accessed by that processor and the local memory addresses only refer to the specific local memory. Each local memory may use the same addresses. Since each node is a self-contained computer, message-passing multiprocessors are sometimes called *message-passing multicomputers*.

The number of nodes could be as small as sixteen (or less), or as large as several thousand (or more). However, the message-passing architecture gains its greatest advantage over shared memory systems for large numbers of processors. For small multi-processor systems, the shared memory system probably has better performance and greater flexibility. The number of physical links between nodes is usually between four and eight. A principal advantage of the message-passing architecture is that it is readily scalable and has low cost for large systems. It suits VLSI construction, with one or more nodes fabricated on one chip, or a few chips, depending upon the amount of local memory provided.

Each node executes one or more *processes*. A process often consists of sequential code, as would be found on a normal von Neumann computer. If there is more than one process mapped onto one nodal processor, one process is executed at a time. A process may be

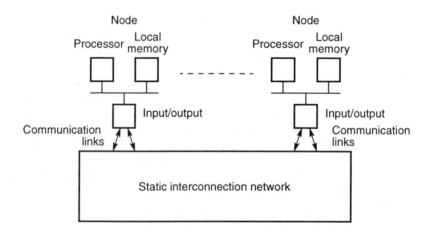

Figure 9.1 Message-passing multiprocessor architecture

descheduled when it is waiting for messages to be sent or received, and in the meantime another process started. Messages can be passed between processes on one processor using internal channels. Messages between processes in different processors are passed through external channels using physical communication links between processors. We will use the term *link* to refer to a physical communication path between a pair of processors. *Channel* refers to a named communication path either between processes in one processor or between processes on different processors.

Ideally, the process and the processor which will execute the process are regarded as completely separate entities, even at this level. The application problem is described as a set of communicating processes which is then mapped onto the physical structure of processors. A knowledge of the physical structure and composition of the nodes is necessary to plan an efficient computation.

The size of a process is determined by the programmer and can be described by its *granularity*, which can be informally described by the ratio:

$$\text{Granularity} = \frac{\text{Computation time}}{\text{Communication time}}$$

or the terms:

1. Coarse granularity.
2. Medium granularity.
3. Fine granularity.

In coarse granularity, each process contains a large number of sequential instructions and takes a substantial time to execute. In fine granularity, a process might consist of a few instructions, even one instruction; medium granularity describes the middle ground. As the granularity is reduced, the process communication overhead generally increases. It is particularly desirable to reduce the communication overhead because of the significant time taken by a nodal communication. Message-passing multiprocessors usually employ medium/coarse granularity; fine granularity is possible and is found in dataflow systems. (Dataflow is described in Chapter 10.) A fine grain message-passing system has been developed by Athas and Seitz (1988) after pioneering work by Seitz on medium grain message-passing designs, which will be described later. For fine grain computing, the overhead of message passing can be reduced by mapping several processes onto one node and switching from one process to another when a process is held up by message passing. The process granularity is sometimes related to the amount of memory provided at each node. Medium granularity may require megabytes of local memory whereas fine granularity may require tens of kilobytes of local memory. Fine grain systems may have a much larger number of nodes than medium grain systems.

Process scheduling is usually *reactive* – processes are allowed to proceed until halted by message communication. Then the process is descheduled and another process is executed, i.e. processes are message-driven in their execution. Processes do not commonly migrate from one node to another at run time; they will be assigned to particular nodes statically before the program is executed. The programmer makes the selection of nodes. A disadvantage of static assignment is that the proper load sharing, in which work is fairly distributed among available processors, may be unclear before the programs are executed. Consideration has to be given to spreading code/data across available local memory given limited local memory.

Each node in a message-passing system typically has a copy of an operating system kernel held in read-only memory. This will schedule processes within a node and perform the message-passing operations at run time. The message-passing routing operations should have hardware support, and should preferably be done completely in hardware. Hardware support for scheduling operations is also desirable. The whole system would normally be controlled by a host computer system.

There are disadvantages to message-passing multiprocessors. Code and data have to be physically transferred to the local memory of each node prior to execution, and this action can constitute a significant overhead. Similarly, results need to be transferred from nodes to the host system. Clearly the computation to be performed needs to be reasonably long to lessen the loading overhead. Similarly, the application program should be computational intensive, not input/output or message-passing intensive. Code cannot be shared. If processes are to execute the same code, which often happens, the code has to be replicated in each node and sufficient local memory has to be provided for this purpose. Data words are difficult to share; the data would need to be passed to all requesting nodes, which would give problems of incoherence. Message-passing architectures are generally less flexible than shared memory architectures. For example, shared memory multiprocessors could emulate message passing by using shared locations to hold messages, whereas message-passing multiprocessors are very inefficient in emulating shared memory multiprocessor operations. Both shared memory and message-passing architectures could in theory perform single instruction stream-multiple data stream (SIMD) computing, though the message-passing architecture would be least suitable and would normally be limited to multiple instruction stream multiple data stream (MIMD) computing.

9.1.2 Communication paths

Networks

Regular static direct link networks which give local or nearest neighbor connections (as described in Chapter 8) are generally used for large message-passing systems, rather than indirect dynamic multistage networks. Some small dedicated or embedded applications might use direct links to certain nodes chosen to suit the message transfers of the application. Routing a message to a destination not directly connected requires the message to be routed through intermediate nodes.

A network which has received particular attention for message-passing multiprocessors is the direct binary hypercube, described in Section 8.2.3. The direct binary hypercube network has good interconnection patterns suitable for a wide range of applications, and expands reasonably well. Nearest neighbor two-dimensional and three-dimensional mesh networks are also candidates for message-passing systems, especially for large systems, and have become more popular than hypercubes, partly because they are easier to implement on a VLSI chip and to expand. Also many applications are naturally two-dimensional and three-dimensional in nature; a simulation of a physical system is often modeled by 2-D and 3-D arrays of data.

Key issues in network design are the link *bandwidth* and network *latency.* The bandwidth is the number of bits that can be transmitted in unit time, given as bits/sec. The nodal links could be unidirectional or bidirectional. They could transfer the information one bit at a time (bit-serial) or several bits at a time. Complete words could be transmitted simultaneously. Bit-serial lines are often used, especially in large systems, to reduce the number of lines in each link. For coarse grain computations, message passing should be infrequent and the bit-serial transmission may have sufficient bandwidth. The network latency, the time to complete a message transfer, has two components; first there is a path set-up time, which is proportional to the number of nodes in the path; second is the actual transmission time, which is proportional to the size of the message for a fixed link bandwidth. The link bandwidth should be about the same as memory bandwidth. A greater bandwidth often cannot be utilized by the node, especially since the message will normally have to be stored in memory.

Information transfer

As we have mentioned in Chapter 8, there are two general classifications for getting the information from the source to the destination:

1. Circuit switched network.
2. Packet switched network.

In a circuit switched network, first the path is established between the source and destination through all the required intermediate nodes, and all the links are reserved. The information is then sent through the network. Afterwards the links are released. No buffering is necessary at each node. Circuit switching produces the minimum latency and delay in transferring the information. The principal disadvantage of circuit switching is that the links are completely dedicated for the information transfer and pure circuit switching is rarely done in large message-passing systems. Some form of packet switching is more common. In packet switching, the information (message) is divided into packets and packets are transferred from node to node. Links are only reserved for the time required to transfer the packet from one node to the next node, and become available for other packets afterwards. Buffers are necessary inside the nodes to the hold packets before transferring onwards to the next node, and remain the buffers if blocked from moving forward to the next node. The packets may be blocked from proceeding by previous packets not being accepted, and would then become queued, until the buffers become full and eventually the blockage would extend back to the source process. The order in which packets are sent to a particular process should normally be maintained, even when packets are allowed to take different routes to the destination. Of course, constraining the route to be the same for all packets between two processes simplifies maintaining packet order.

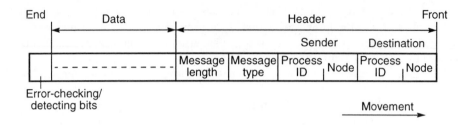

Figure 9.2 Packet format

Packets can use a similar format to computer network message-passing. Each process is given an identification number (process ID) which is used in the message-passing scheme. Packets consist of a header and the data; Figure 9.2 shows a typical format of a packet. Because more than one process might be mapped onto a node, the process ID has two parts, one part identifying the node and one part the process within the node. The nodal part (physical address) of the ID is used to route the packet to the destination node. The message type enables different messages/packets along the same link to be identified.

Packet switching is sometimes called "store and forward". In a multicomputer/multiprocessor system, latency is very important and packet switching as described incurs a significant latency since packets must be stored in buffers within each node, whether or not an outgoing link is available. This requirement is eliminated in *virtual cut-through*, a technique originally applied to computer networks. In virtual cut-through, if the outgoing link is available, the packet is immediately passed forward without being stored in the nodal buffer, i.e., it is "cut-through". Hence if the complete path is available, the packet would pass immediately through to the destination is the same manner as circuit switching. However each node must have buffer for the packets should a link be not available. The size of the packet is a compromise between the overhead of having to provide source and destination addresses and other information in the packet, and the size of the buffers/links.

Seitz introduced *wormhole* routing (Dally and Seitz, 1987) as an alternative to normal-store and forward routing to reduce the size of the buffers and decrease the latency. In store-and-forward routing, a packet is stored in a node and transmitted as a whole until an outgoing link becomes free. In wormhole routing, the packet is divided into smaller units called *flits* (flow control bits). Only the head of the packet is initially transmitted from the source node to the next node when the connecting link is available, and through the network to the destination. Subsequent parts of the packet are transmitted when links become available, and the parts can become distributed through the network. When the head flit moves forward, the next one can move forward and so on. A request/acknowledge system is necessary between nodes to "pull" the flits along as shown in Figure 9.3. When a flit is ready to move on from its buffer, it makes a request to the next node. When this node has a flit buffer empty, it calls for the flit from the sending node. It is necessary to reserve the complete path for the packet as the parts of the packet (the flits) are linked.

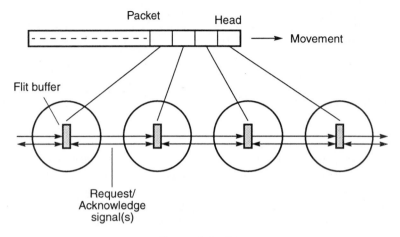

Figure 9.3 Flits

Other packets cannot be interleaved with the flits along the same links. Ni and McKinley (1993) describe a signaling system which only requires a single signal between the sending node and receiving node, called R/A (request/acknowledge). R/A is reset to a 0 only by the receiving node when is ready to receive the flit (its flit buffer is empty) and set to a 1 only by the sending node when it is about to send the flit. The sending node must wait for R/A = 0 before setting it to a 1 and sending the flit.

Wormhole routing requires less storage at each node and produces a latency which is independent of the path length. It is also easier to implement broadcast operations by simply copying the flit to two receiving nodes. (Broadcast in which the same information is sent to more than one destination is a common operation.) Ni and McKinley (1993) also presented the following analysis to show the independence of path length on latency in wormhole routing. Suppose the packet length is L, the bandwidth of the links B, and the number of links used is n, then circuit switching produces a latency of:

$$\text{Latency} = \left\lceil \frac{L_c}{B} \right\rceil n + \left\lceil \frac{L}{B} \right\rceil$$

where L_c is length of the control packet used to establish the circuit switched connection prior to launching the data packet. Store-and-forward packet switching produces a latency of:

$$\text{Latency} = \left\lceil \frac{L}{B} \right\rceil n$$

Virtual cut-through produces a latency of:

$$\text{Latency} = \left[\frac{L_h}{B}\right] n + \left(\frac{L}{B}\right)$$

where L_h is the length of the header field. Wormhole produces a latency of:

$$\text{Latency} = \left[\frac{L_f}{B}\right] n + \left(\frac{L}{B}\right)$$

where L_f is the length of each flit. In each case it is assumed that there is no contention in the network. If the length of a flit is much less than the total packet, then the latency of wormhole routing will be appropriately constant irrespective of the length of the route. The same is true of circuit switching. Store-and-forward packet switching produces a latency which is approximately proportional to the length of the route.

Routing

The path chosen for a packet could be established in various ways. First we can classify the routing as:

1. Source routing.
2. Distributed routing.

In *source routing*, the complete route is chosen prior to launching the packet, and routing information provided in the packet for nodes to use as the packet passes through the network. One variant of source routing is *street-map routing* in which the information carried are the links to turn into at a node (the streets). If a turn is not specified, the route continues straight through the node. However most systems use distributed routing. In *distributed routing*, each node could decide the next route from the source and destination addresses in the packet. Distributed routing can be completely *deterministic* in that the same route is always chosen between a source and a destination, or can be *adaptive* and different routes chosen dependent upon the traffic and other conditions found in the network.

A deterministic algorithm which always chooses the same route and the shortest route exists for all networks (a *minimal* path length routing algorithm). For example, packets can be routed in hypercube networks according to the following algorithm, which minimizes the path distance. Suppose the current nodal address is $P = p_{n-1}p_{n-2} \cdots p_1 p_0$ and the destination address is $D = d_{n-1}d_{n-2} \cdots d_1 d_0$. The exclusive-OR function $R = P \oplus D$ is performed operating on pairs of bits, to obtain $R = r_{n-1}r_{n-2} \cdots r_1 r_0$. Let r_i be the ith bit of R. The hypercube dimensions to use in the routing are given by those values of i for which $r_i = 1$. At each node in the path, the exclusive function $R = P \oplus D$ is performed. One of the bits in R which is 1, say r_k, identifies the kth dimension to select in passing the message forward until none of the bits is 1, and then the destination node has been found. The bits of R are usually scanned from most significant bit to least significant bit until a 1 is found. For example, suppose routing from node 5 (000101) to node 34 (100010) is sought in a six-dimensional hypercube. The route taken would be node 5 (000101) to node 21 (100101) to node 17 (100001) to node 19 (100011) to node 34 (100010). This hypercube routing algorithm is sometimes called the *e-cube routing algorithm*, or *left-to-right routing*. A two-dimensional mesh network also has a similar minimal routing algorithm, by first traversing up or down and then left or right to the destination.

There are many possible adaptive routing algorithms. The hypercube network, for example, has many possible routes from a source to a destination. There are even $k!$ minimal routes if there are k bits different between the source address and destination address. Similarly a mesh can have many routes. (It is left as an exercise to compute the number of minimal routes.) The total number of routes is very large, especially if backtracking is allowed. Unfortunately such adaptive routing algorithms are particularly prone to *livelock* which describes the situation in which a packet keeps going around the network without ever finding its destination.

Deadlock

Routing algorithms unless properly designed can also be prone to deadlock. *Deadlock* can occur in many networks if care is not taken and it is important to be able to identify possible deadlock in a routing algorithm. Deadlock occurs when packets cannot be forwarded to the next node because the packet buffers are filled with packets waiting to be forwarded and these packets are blocked by other packets waiting to be forwarded in such a way that none of the packets can move. Deadlock can occur in both store-and-forward and wormhole networks (and in circuit switched networks), and is characterized by cycles in the request patterns for buffers/links. Figure 9.4(a) shows deadlock in a group of four nodes connected as a unidirectional ring where each packet is requesting a nodal buffer already used by another packet. The current packet in node 0 is requesting node 3. The current packet in node 1 is requesting node 0. The current packet in node 2 is requesting node 1. The current packet in node 3 is requesting node 2.

The problem of deadlock appears in communication networks using store-and-forward routing and has been studied extensively in that context; for example, Gopal (1985). A general solution is to provide separate buffers at routing sites for classes of messages. Dally and Seitz (1987) developed the use of separate channels to avoid deadlock for wormhole networks. (Wormhole networks are particularly susceptible to deadlock.) The interconnections of processing nodes can be shown by a directed graph, called an *interconnection graph*, depicting the communication paths. Related to this is a *channel dependency graph* which is a directed graph showing the channels used for a particular routing function. In the channel dependency graph, the channels are depicted by the vertices of the graph and the connections of channels are depicted by the edges. Figure 9.4(b) shows the channel dependency graph for the 4-node ring. Here, one channel corresponds to one physical link. A network is deadlock-free if (and only if) there are no cycles in the channel dependency graph. Our ring has deadlock as shown by the cycle in the channel dependency graph.

For any network, if we number the channels in a way that the routing algorithm creates

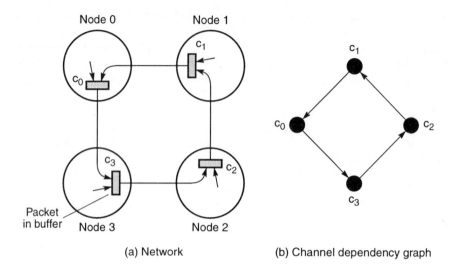

(a) Network   (b) Channel dependency graph

Figure 9.4 Deadlock cycle in a 4-node ring

a channel dependency graph without cycles, the routing algorithm is deadlock-free. Clearly a way of having no cycles is to have a channel dependency graph such as shown in Figure 9.5. Here the network has channels $c_{n-1} \ldots c_1, c_0$, with a linear channel dependency according to decreasing channel number. Therefore there are no cycles if messages are routed in decreasing channel numbers. (Increasing numbers will also work, if applied throughout.) The e-cube routing algorithm for the hypercube described previously has this characteristic and is deadlock-free. If we number the channels leaving node j as c_{ij} where i is the channel in the ith dimension, $0 \le i < n$ (for an n-dimensional hypercube) and scan bits of the channel number i from most significant bit to least significant bit, we naturally route in decreasing channel number. For example, the route from node 0001 (1) to node 1100 (12) is through node 1001 (9) and node 1101 (13). The channels would be $c_{1,2}, c_{2,9}$ and $c_{0,13}$. Notice that the hypercube has links in each direction between nodes.

The bidirectional mesh is also deadlock-free if we use Gray code to number the nodes and use the same routing algorithm as the hypercube. (In fact, the mesh is embedded in a

Figure 9.5 A channel dependency graph with no deadlock

hypercube by this numbering. Embedding means that all the links in the embedded network actually exist in the larger network.) Figure 9.6 shows a 8×8 mesh so numbered. To route from node 000010 (4) to node 001001 (9), for example, would use nodes 000001 (1), whereas to route from node 001001 (9) to node 000010 (4) would use node 000001 (1).

However, no matter how we number the nodes in our unidirectional ring, it has deadlock. Dally and Seitz introduced the concept of *virtual channels* to avoid deadlock in any network. A virtual channel shares the same physical link with other virtual channel(s) but has its own buffer. In effect, more channels are created by introducing numbered virtual channels. The problem is then to number the virtual channels so that the channel dependency graph for the network is totally ordered. To take the example in Dally and Seitz (1987), consider a unidirectional ring consisting of four nodes, 0, 1, 2 and 3. (It is not possible to avoid deadlock in unidirectional ring without additional mechanisms.) There are four physical channels, c_0, c_1, c_2 and c_3. To achieve a totally ordered channel dependency graph, each physical channel, c_i, is split into two "virtual" channels, a low channel, c_{0i}, and a high channel, c_{1i}. The low virtual channels are c_{00}, c_{01}, c_{02} and c_{03}, and the high channels are c_{10}, c_{11}, c_{12} and c_{13} as shown in Figure 9.7. Messages are routed on high channels from a node numbered less than the destination node, and to low

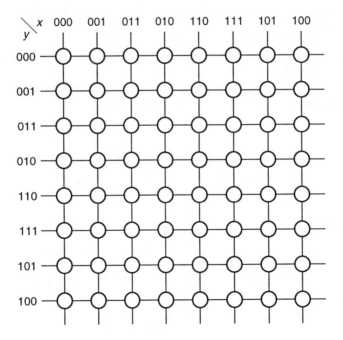

Figure 9.6 Mesh with Gray code numbering

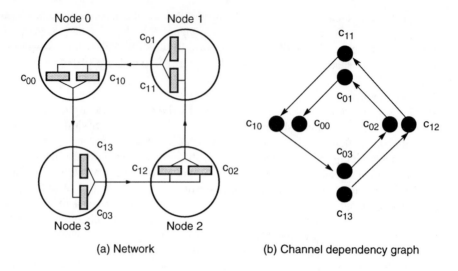

(a) Network   (b) Channel dependency graph

Figure 9.7 Virtual channels

channels from a node numbered greater than the destination node, and there are no cycles and hence no deadlock. Notice that the nodes are numbered so as to be connected in decreasing number. Channel c_{00} is not used. Figure 9.8 shows the routes taken for four messages, node 0 to 2, node 1 to 3, node 2 to 0, and node 3 to 1 (which would be completely deadlocked normally).

Sometimes deadlock can be eliminated simply by restricting the routing to break a cycle. Figure 9.9 shows a 4-node ring with separate links in each direction and deadlock-

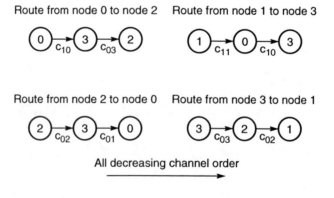

Figure 9.8 Deadlock free routing in a unidirectional ring

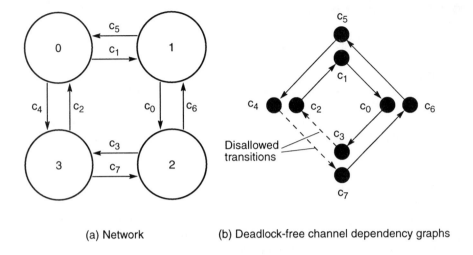

(a) Network   (b) Deadlock-free channel dependency graphs

Figure 9.9 4-node mesh with separate links in each direction

free channel dependency graph. Here we have broken each cycle by disallowing the transition from c_3 to c_0 and from c_7 to c_4. It is still possible to achieve minimal routing for all destinations, even though now no message can pass through node 0 (that is, from node 3 through node 0 to node 1, or vice versa). Of course we have also seen a way of making this ring deadlock-free by using Gray code numbering and the e-cube routing algorithm.

9.2 Programming

The key difference between programming a shared memory system as described in Chapter 6 and programming a message-passing system is the need to explicitly pass messages between concurrent processes being executed on different processors (or the same processor). Message passing can be achieved by:

1. Designing a special parallel programming language or more likely extensions to existing sequential languages in order to specify message passing (and process creation).
2. By using a normal high level language and provide a library of external procedures or system calls for message passing.

In this section we will review using a normal high level language with system calls. The reader is referred to Foster (1995) for examples of language extensions.

9.2.1 Message-passing routines

Send and receive message-passing procedure/system calls often have the form:

```
send(parameters)
recv(parameters)
```

where the parameters identify the source and destination processes, and the data. For example, in Fortran we might have:

```
send(destination_process_ID,type,buffer1,buffer_length)
recv(source_process_ID,type,buffer2,buffer_length)
```

which will send the data in buffer 1 in the source process to buffer 2 in the destination process. In this case, buffer 1 must have been preloaded with the data to be sent.

Message-passing send/receive routines can be divided into two types:

1. Synchronous or blocking.
2. Asynchronous or non-blocking.

Synchronous or *blocking* routines do not allow the process to proceed until the operation has been completed. *Asynchronous* or *non-blocking* routines allow the process to proceed even though the operation may not have been completed, i.e. statements after a routine are executed even though the routine may need further time to complete.

A blocking send routine will wait until the complete message has been transmitted and accepted by the receiving process. A blocking receive routine will wait until the message it is expecting is received. A pair of processes, one with a blocking send operation and one with a matching blocking receive operation, will be synchronized, with neither the source process nor the destination process being able to proceed until the message has been passed from the source process to the destination process. Hence, blocking routines intrinsically perform two actions; they transfer data and they synchronize processes. The term *rendezvous* is used to describe the meeting and synchronization of two processes through blocking send/receive operations.

A non-blocking message-passing send routine allows a process to continue immediately after the message has been constructed without waiting for it to be accepted or even received. A non-blocking receive routine will not wait for the message and will allow the process to proceed. This is not a common requirement as the process cannot usually do any more computation until the required message has been received. It could be used to test for blocking and to schedule another process while waiting for a message. The non-blocking routines generally decrease the process execution time. Both blocking and non-blocking variants may be available for programmer choice in systems that use routines to perform the message passing.

Non-blocking message passing implies that the routines have buffers to hold messages. In practice, buffers can only be of finite length and a point could be reached when a non-blocking routine is blocked because all the buffer space has been exhausted. Memory space needs to be allocated and deallocated and the messages and routines should be provided for this purpose; the send routine might automatically deallocate memory space. For low level message passing, it is necessary to provide an additional primitive routine to check whether a message buffer space is re-available.

9.2.2 Process structure

The basic programming technique for the system is to divide the problem into concurrent communicating processes. We can identify two possible methods of generating processes,

1. Static process structure.
2. Dynamic process structure.

In the *static process structure*, the processes are specified before the program is executed, and the system will execute a fixed number of processes. The programmer usually explicitly identifies the processes. It might be possible for a compiler to assist in the creation of concurrent message-passing processes, but this seems to be an open research problem. In the *dynamic process structure*, processes can be created during the execution of the program using process creation constructs; processes can also be destroyed. Process creation and destruction might be done conditionally. The number of processes may vary during execution. Processes can be created dynamically with FORK or spawn( ) types of system calls.

Process structure is independent of the message-passing types, and hence we have the following potential combinations in a language or system:

Synchronous communication with static process structure.
Synchronous communication with dynamic process structure.
Asynchronous communication with static process structure.
Asynchronous communication with dynamic process structure.

Language examples include Ada (having synchronous communication with static process structure), CSP (having asynchronous communication with static process structure) and MP (having synchronous communication with dynamic process structure) (Liskov, Herlihy and Gilbert, 1988). Asynchronous communication with dynamic process structure is used in message-passing systems using procedure call additions to standard sequential programming languages (e.g. Intel iPSC, see Section 9.3.1). The combination is not known together in specially designed languages, though it would give all possible features. Liskov, Herlihy and Gilbert suggest that either synchronous communication or static process structure should be abandoned but suggest that it is reasonable to retain one of them in a language. The particular advantage of asynchronous communication is that processes need not be delayed by messages, and static process structure may then be sufficient. Dynamic process structure can reduce the effects of delays incurred with synchronous communication by giving the facility to create a new process while a communication delay is in progress. The combination, synchronous communication with dynamic process structure, seems a good choice.

Program example

Suppose the integral of a function f(x) is required. The integration can be performed numerically by dividing the area under the curve f(x) into very small sections which are approximated to rectangles (or trapeziums). Then the area of each section is computed and added together to obtain the total area. One obvious parallel solution is to use one process for each area or group of areas, as shown in Figure 9.10. A single process is shown accepting the results generated by the other processes.

For simplicity suppose the basic blocking message-passing routines in the system using the C programming language are send(destination_process,message) and recv(source_process,message). With the integral processes numbered from 0 to $n-1$ and the accumulation process numbered n, we have two basic programs, one for the processes performing the integrals and one for the process performing the accumulation, i.e.:

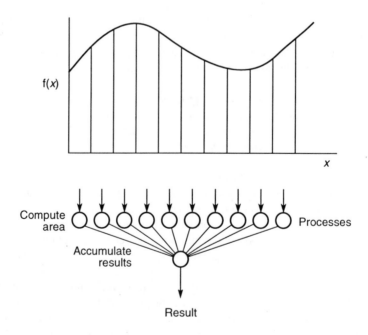

Figure 9.10 Integration using message-passing processes

Integral process *j*   Accumulation process

```
int area,n;                int area,i,n,acc;
    .                          .
    .                          .
    .                          .
compute jth area           for (i=0;i<n;i++) {
send (n,area);  ────────▶      receive (i,area);
    .                          acc = acc + area;
    .                      }
    .                          .
    .                          .
```

Variables are local and need to be declared in each process. The same names in different processes refer to different objects. Note that processes are referenced directly by number. The integral process requires information to compute the areas, namely the function, the interval size and number of intervals to be computed in each process. This information is passed to the integral processes perhaps via an initiation process prior to the integral processes starting their computation.

The accumulation process could also perform one integration while waiting for the results to be generated. A single program could be written for all processes using conditional statements to select the actions a particular process should take, and this program copied to all processes. This would be particularly advantageous if there is a global host-node broadcast mode in which all nodes can receive the same communication simultaneously. In this case, we have:

Composite process

```
int mynode,area,i,n,acc;
read input parameters
identify nodal address, mynode
if (mynode == n) {
    compute nth area
    for (i=0;i<n-1;i++) {
        recv(i,area);
        acc = acc + area;
    }
} else {
    compute jth area
    send(n,area);
}
```

Various enhancements can be made to improve the performance. For example, since the last accumulation is in fact a series of steps, it could be divided into groups of accumulations which are performed on separate processors. The number of areas computed by each process defines the process granularity and would be chosen to gain the greatest throughput taking into account the individual integration time and the communication time. In some cases, reducing the number of nodes involved has been found to decrease the computation time (see Pase and Larrabee, 1988). Host-node communication is usually much slower than node-node communication. If separate transactions need to be performed for each node loaded (i.e. there is no broadcast mode) the time to load the nodal program could be decreased by arranging the program to be sent to the first node, which then passes a copy on to the next node and so on. The most effective method to reduce the communication time is to arrange for each node to transmit its information according to a minimal spanning tree. Results could be collected in a pipeline or tree fashion with the results passed from one node to the next. Each node adds its contribution before passing the accumulation onwards. Pipeline structures are useful, especially if the computation is to be repeated several times, perhaps with different initial values.

9.3 Message-passing system examples

9.3.1 Cosmic Cube and derivatives

The Cosmic Cube is a research vehicle designed and constructed at Caltech (California Institute of Technology) under the direction of Seitz during the period 1981-5 (Seitz, 1985; Athas and Seitz, 1988) and is credited with being the first working hypercube multiprocessor system (Hayes, 1988) though the potential of hypercubes had been known for many years prior to its development. The Cosmic Cube significantly influenced subsequent commercial hypercube systems, notably the Intel iPSC hypercube system. Sixty-four-node and smaller Cosmic Cube systems have been constructed. The Intel 8086 processor is used as the nodal instruction processor with an Intel 8087 floating point coprocessor. Each node has 128 Kbytes of dynamic RAM, chosen as a balance between increasing the memory or increasing the number of nodes within given cost constraints. The memory has parity checking but not error correction. (A parity error was reported on the system once every several days!) Each node has 8 Kbytes of read-only memory to store the initialization and bootstrap loader programs. The kernel in each node occupies 9 Kbytes of code and 4 Kbytes of tables. The interconnection links operate in asynchronous full duplex mode at a relatively slow rate of 2 Mbits/sec. The basic packet size is sixty-four bits with queues at each node. Transmission is started with send and receive calls. These calls can be non-blocking, i.e. the calls return after the request is put in place. The request becomes "pending" until it can be completed. Hence a program can continue even though the message request may not have been completed.

The nodal kernel, called the Reactive Kernel, RK, has been divided into an inner kernel (written in assembly language) and an outer kernel. The inner kernel performs the send and receive message handling and queues messages. Local communication between processes in one node and between non-local processes is treated in a similar fashion, though of course local communication is through memory buffers and is much faster. The inner kernel also schedules processes in a node using a round robin selection. Each process executes for a fixed time period or until it is delayed by a system call. The outer kernel contains a set of processes for communication between user processes using messages. These outer kernel processes include processes to create, copy and stop processes.

The host run-time system, called the Cosmic Environment, CE, has routines to establish the set of processes for a computation and other routines for managing the whole system. The processes of a computation are called the process group. The system can be used by more than one user but is not time-shared; each user can specify the size of a hypercube required using a CE routine and will be allocated a part of the whole system not used by other users – this method has been called *space shared*. In a similar manner to a virtual memory system, users reference logical nodal addresses, which have corresponding physical nodal addresses. The logical nodal addresses for a requested n-cube could be numbered from 0 to $n - 1$.

Dynamic process structure with reactive process scheduling is employed. Programming is done in the C language, with support routines provided for both message passing and for process creation/destruction. The dynamic process creation function – spawn(parameters) – creates a process consisting of a compiled program in a node and process, all specified as function parameters. Specifying the node/process as function parameters rather than letting the operating system make this choice, enables predefined structures to be built up and allows changes to be made while the program is being executed. The send routine is xsend(parameters) where the parameters specify the node/process and a pointer to a message block. The xsend routine deallocates message space. Other functions available include blocking receive message, xrecvb, returning a pointer to the message block, allocating message memory space, xmalloc, and freeing message space, xfree. Later development of the system incorporated higher level message-passing mechanisms and fine grain programming. Statements such as:

```
IF i = 10 THEN SEND(i+1) TO self ELSE EXIT FI
```

can be found in programs in the programming environment Cantor (see Athas and Seitz, 1988, for further details).

The Intel Personal Supercomputer (iPSC) is a commercial hypercube system developed after the Cosmic Cube. The iPSC/1 system uses Intel 286 processors with 287 floating point coprocessors. The architecture of each node is shown in Figure 9.11. Each node consists of a single board computer, having two buses, a processor bus and an input/output bus. The nodes are controlled by a host computer system called a cube manager. As with the Cosmic Cube, each node has a small operating system (called NX). FORTRAN message-passing routines are provided. Eight communication channels are provided at each node, seven for links to other nodes in the hypercube and one used as a global Ethernet channel for communication with the cube manager. Typical systems have thirty-two nodes using five internode communication links. Internode communication

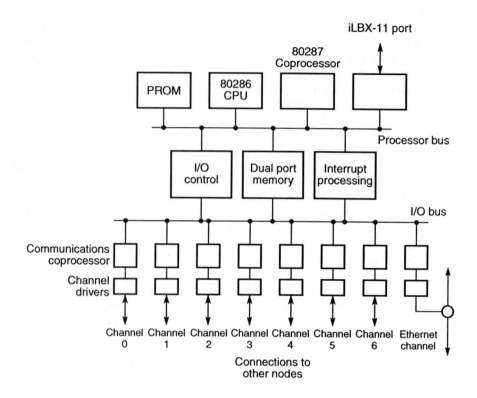

Figure 9.11 Intel iPSC node

takes between 1 and 2.2 ms for messages between 0 and 1024 bytes. Cube manager to node communication takes 18 ms for a 1 Kbyte message (Pase and Larrabee, 1988). The iPSC/2, an upgrade to the iPSC/1, uses Intel 386 processors and hardware wormhole routing. Additional vector features can be provided at each node or selected nodes on one separate board per node.

9.3.2 Workstation clusters

Powerful desktop computers are often connected together in a local network of workstations to share a file system and applications, and for information interchange (files, email etc.). Given the pervasiveness of such networks and that they are usually also connected together via national/international networks (Internet) forming a worldwide network, it is natural to see whether such clusters and networks can be used for message-passing parallel programming. One such attempt by Oak Ridge National Laboratories has lead to the pvm (parallel virtual machine) software which has become widely used partly because it has being made universally available at no charge.[1] Pvm enables an heterogeneous network of computers to be enrolled on a single problem. There are other examples of tools that can be provided for workstation cluster parallel programming, such as the Express software package from ParaSoft Corporation, and now a standard message-passing interface, MPI, has been created.

Let us briefly describe the pvm environment. As usual, the problem is decomposed into separate programs written in C (or Fortran) and compiled to run on individual computers. In a network of workstations, each workstation has access to the file system containing the compiled programs. It is only necessary to ensure that the programs are compiled for the specific workstations that will execute the programs. Pvm will automatically allocate computers if the user does not specify the specific computers that are to be used for executing the programs. The computers used on a problem first must be defined in a file (a hostfile) prior to running the programs, and form the "virtual parallel machine".

Programs communicate by message passing using pvm library procedure calls such as pvm_send() and pvm_rev(),[2] which are embedded into the programs prior to compilation. The routing of messages between computers is done by pvm daemon processes installed by pvm on the computers that form the virtual machine, as illustrated in Figure 9.12. Each pvm daemon requires sufficient information to be able to select the routing path, in fact it requires global information of all processes.

Processes are identified by a task ID, established when the process is enrolled into pvm (using the pvm system call pvm_mytid() which returns the task ID). The key operations of sending and receiving data are done through message buffers. First a message has to be formed in a message buffer. The message may be composed of various data items of different types and the data is packed into the message buffer. The receiving process must first unpack the message buffer according to the format in which it was packed. (This is rather tedious.) The following is an example of pvm code sequences for sending/receiving data (with the pvm system call parameters missing for clarity):

Send
.

```
pvm_initsend();              /* clear default send buffer */
                             /* & specify message encoding */
pvm_pkint();                 /* pack an integer into buffer */
pvm_pkint();                 /* pack an integer into buffer */
pvm_pkfloat();               /* pack a float into buffer */
msgtype = 5;                 /* include a message type tag */
proc1 = pvm_parent();        /* identify destination process*/
pvm_send(proc1,msgtype);     /* send message */
```

.

---

[1] It can be obtained by email from netlib@ornl.gov. Send message "send index from pvm" to get list of software/documentation.

[2] All pvm system calls in version 3 of pvm described here start with the letters pvm.

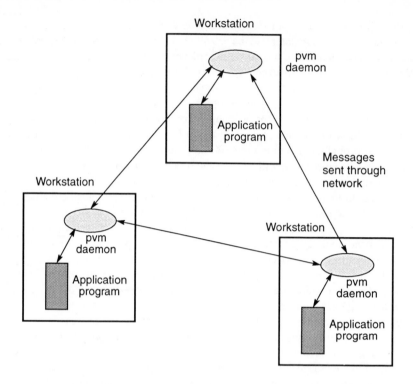

Figure 9.12 Message passing between workstations using pvm

Receive
.
```
msgtype = 0;
pvm_recv(-1, msgtype);      /* receive message */
pvm_upkint();               /* unpack message, integer */
pvm_upkint(tid, );          /* unpack next, integer */
pvm_upkfloat( );            /* unpack next, a float */
```
.

Further details of pvm can be found in Geist, Beguelin, Dongarra, Jiang, Manchek and Sunderam (1994a, 1994b). Similar features to pvm can be found in MPI. Details of MPI can be found in Gropp, Lusk and Skjellum (1994).

9.4 Transputer

In this section, we will present the details of the *transputer*, the first single chip computer designed for message-passing multiprocessor systems. A special high level programming language called *occam* has been developed as an integral part of the transputer development. Occam has a static process structure and synchronous communication, and is presented in Section 9.5.

9.4.1 Philosophy

The transputer is a VLSI processor produced by Inmos (Inmos, 1986) in 16- and 32-bit versions with high speed internal memory and serial interfaces. The device has a RISC type of instruction set though programming in machine instructions is not expected, as occam should be used.

Each transputer is provided with a processor, internal memory and originally four high speed DMA channels which enable it to connect to other transputers directly using synchronous send/receive types of commands. A link consists of two serial lines for bidirectional transfers. Data is transmitted as a single item or as a vector. When one serial line is used for a data package, the other is used for an acknowledgement package, which is generated as soon as a data package reaches the destination.

Various arrays of transputers can be constructed easily. Four links allow for a two-dimensional array with each transputer connecting to its four nearest neighbors. Other configurations are possible. For example, transputers can be formed into groups and linked to other groups. Two transputers could be interconnected and provide six free links, as shown in Figure 9.13(a). Similarly, a group of three transputers could be fully interconnected and have six links free for connecting to other groups, as shown in Figure

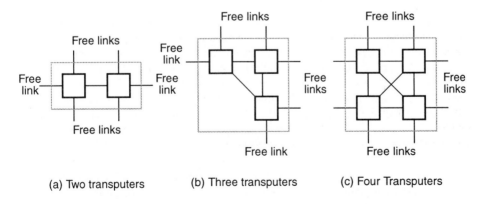

(a) Two transputers   (b) Three transputers   (c) Four Transputers

Figure 9.13 Groups of transputers fully interconnected

9.13(b). A group of four transputers could be fully interconnected and have four links to other groups, as shown in Figure 9.13(c). A group of five transputers, each having four links, could be fully interconnected but with no free links to other systems.

A key feature of the transputer is the programming language, *occam*, which was designed specifically for the transputer. The name occam comes from the fourteenth century philosopher, William of Occam, who presented the concept of Occam's Razor: "Entia non sunt multiplicanda praeter necessitatem", i.e. "Entities should not be multiplied beyond necessity" (May and Taylor, 1984). The language has been designed for simplicity and provides the necessary primitive operations for point-to-point data transfers and to specify explicit parallelism. The central concept in an occam program is the *process* consisting of one or more program statements, which can be executed in sequence or in parallel. Processes can be executed concurrently and one or more processes are allocated to each transputer in the system. There is hardware support for sharing one transputer among more than one process. The statements of one process are executed until a termination statement is reached or a point-to-point data transfer is held up by another process. Then, the process is descheduled and another process started automatically.

9.4.2 Processor architecture

The basic internal architecture of the processor is shown in Figure 9.14 and has the following subparts:

1. Processor.
2. Link interfaces.
3. Internal RAM.
4. Memory interface for external memory.
5. Event interface.
6. System services logic.

The first transputer product, the T212, announced in 1983, contained a 16-bit integer arithmetic processor. Subsequent products included a 32-bit integer arithmetic processor part (T414, announced in 1985) and floating point versions (the T800, announced in 1988, and later the T9000). The floating point versions are arranged such that both the integer processor and floating point processor can operate simultaneously. In addition to floating point capabilities and substantial upgrade in computational speeds (to 100 MIPS), the T9000 incorporates internal cache memory and a virtual channel processor. Though the processor itself is a RISC type, it is microprogrammed internally and instructions take one or more processor cycles. Simple operations such as add or subtract take one cycle but complex operations can take several cycles. Instructions are one or more bytes. Most versions of the transputer have four serial links, originally operating at 10 Mbits/sec serial link transfer rate. Subsequent products have increased transfer rates. The T9000 has a combined bandwidth of 70 Mbytes/sec across its four links. Internal memory capacity (originally 2 Kbytes) has also been increased. The T9000 has a 16-Kbyte

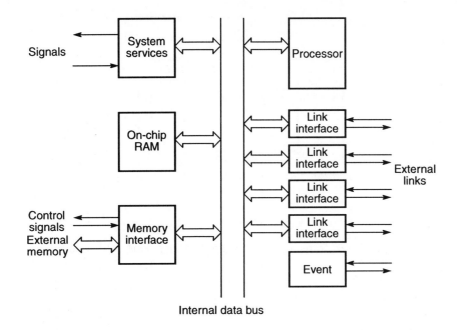

Signals

Figure 9.14 Basic internal architecture of transputer (On T9000, the link interfaces connect to an internal virtual channel processor and the internal bus is a crossbar.)

instruction and data cache. External memory can also be attached through a memory interface. The memory interface circuitry can be programmed to generate various signals to match external memory chips.

The transmission is synchronous and a common clock signal, or a separate clock at the same frequency, is applied to devices. Information is transmitted in the form of packets. Every time a data packet is sent, the destination responds by returning an acknowledge packet, as shown in Figure 9.15. Data packets consist of two 1s followed by an 8-bit data and terminated with a 0 (i.e. eleven bits in all). Acknowledge packets consist of a 1 followed by a 0 (i.e. two bits in all) and can be returned as soon as the data package can be identified by the internal link interface. The links provide the hardware for the input and output statements in occam (see later) and operate as DMA channels, i.e. data packets can be sent one after the other for vectors. Input/output statements use internal channels rather than external links for communication between processes within a transputer.

The event interface enables an external device to signal attention and to receive an acknowledgement. The event interface operates as an input channel and is programmed in a similar way.

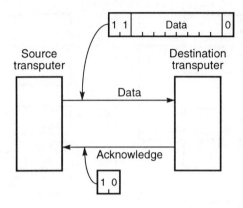

Figure 9.15 Transputer input/output handshaking technique

9.5 Occam

This section reviews the occam language, giving the main features, though not minor variations provided in the syntax. The reader is referred to May (1987) for a complete definition of the language.

9.5.1 Structure

Like all high level language programs, occam programs consist of statements, though only a limited number of different statements are provided. The first version of occam kept the facilities to a minimum on the principle that simple is best, but further facilities were added (and slight changes made in the syntax) in later versions called occam 2 and occam 3. We will restrict ourselves to the occam 2 syntax.

Occam is a block-structured language using indentation rather than brackets or BEGIN-END to show a compound structure. Each level of indentation consists of two spaces and each statement is normally placed on a separate line. Statements can be specified as being executed sequentially, in parallel or dependent upon some condition (including waiting for input or output). Explicit input and output statements are provided for passing data between processes. Communication between processes is dependent upon both the source and destination being ready, i.e. both the input and output statements on the respective processes must be encountered before the transfer of data commences. Occam uses prefix operators, i.e. operators are added to the head of a process to specify some condition or action or to declare variables. Comments can be included in the program by starting the comment with --. The comment can occupy a single line at the same level of indentation as the next statement or it can be added to the end of a statement. Termination symbols are not used at the end of statements on separate lines (i.e. redundant features are removed from the language).

9.5.2 Data types

The type of a variable is declared, as in other languages such as PASCAL or C, but using a colon to show that it is prefixing a process. The original reserved word was VAR which was subsequently changed to INT. The declaration:

```
INT x:
```

declares the variable x of a type appropriate for the transputer (32-bit 2's complement signed integer for 32-bit transputers). More explicit types are provided. INT16 x: declares x as a 16-bit integer; INT32 x: declares x as a 32-bit integer; INT64 x: declares x as a 64-bit integer; REAL32 x: declares x as a 32-bit floating point number using the 32-bit IEEE format; REAL64 x: declares x as a floating point number using the 64-bit IEEE format. Other types include BYTE (a number between 0 and +256) and BOOL (true or false).

Variables are always local variables; the concept of global variables has no meaning in a system without global memory. Variables are declared prior to processes or "subprocesses" and not only at the beginning of the complete program. They then have the scope given by the level of indentation.

Arrays in occam 2 can be declared by prefixing the declaration with the number of elements in the array (counting from zero). For example:

```
[10]INT x:
```

declares a one-dimensional array, x, having the elements x[0], x[1], x[9]. Multidimensional arrays can be declared by having more than one [ ] prefix.

Channels are also declared in the process before being used, originally using the reserved word CHAN and subsequently using the construct CHAN OF protocol where protocol can specify the data type of the data being sent across the channel. For example:

```
CHAN OF INT output:
```

declares a channel called output which will carry integer values. A set of channels can be formed into a vector of channels with the same name. We will omit the channel declaration in some simple programs, assuming that the declaration has been made in some higher level process.

9.5.3 Data transfer statements

Five *primitive processes* exist in occam for data transfer, three of which are actions concerned with data transfer, assignment, input and output.

The *assignment action* is conventional and allows the value of an expression to be assigned to a variable and has the general form:

```
variable := expression
```

where := means the usual "becomes equal to". (The type of the expression and the variable must be the same; type cohersion is not performed automatically in occam/occam 2, though occam 2 does have cohersion operations.) Multiple sequential assignments are possible in a single statement, by separating the variables and expressions with commas.

Transfer of data between processes through internal or external channels is achieved by having the *output action*:

```
channel ! expression
```

in the source process, where ! is the symbol for output (an output exclamation), and the *input action*:

```
channel ? variable
```

in the destination process, where ? is the symbol for input (a query for input). When both input and output have been encountered, the data transfer takes place. This *rendezvous* technique is illustrated in Figure 9.16. Processes can be synchronized using the rendezvous and, if the data value is unimportant, the variable and expression can be replaced with the occam word ANY, i.e. c?ANY and c!ANY have the effect of synchronizing processes. Multiple input/output can be specified by separating the variables and expressions with semicolons, or using a vector of variables, i.e. vect[ ] describes a one-dimensional array of variables with the name vect.

The two remaining primitive processes are STOP which "starts but never proceeds, and never terminates", and SKIP which "starts, performs no action, and terminates" (May, 1987). SKIP has a part to play in constructs which must have a terminating process.

9.5.4 Sequential, parallel and alternative processes

In most programming languages, it is assumed that statements are executed one after another in the sequence written unless control statements are used. In occam, the sequential nature of processes is not assumed; in fact processes can be specified as executed concurrently or sequentially. Concurrent processes on separate transputers can execute truly concurrently. Processes on one transputer simulate concurrent operation.

Sequential operation is specified with the sequence (SEQ) process:

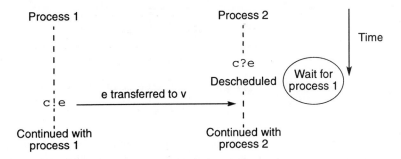

(a) Input encountered before output

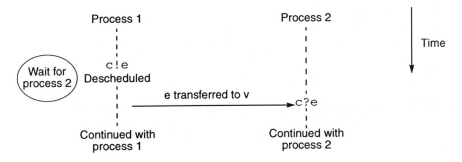

(b) Output encountered before input

Figure 9.16   Rendezvous technique

```
SEQ
   process1
   process2
```

Each component process is executed after the previous process has finished. For example, the following sequence process, as illustrated in Figure 9.17, takes data from an input channel c1 and sends it to an output channel c2:

```
INT x:
   SEQ
      c1?x
      c2!x
```

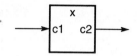

Figure 9.17 Single stage buffer

Notice that the declaration is at the same level of indentation as the SEQ process, but the component processes are at an extra level of indentation. Also, the input and output actions are performed in sequence.

Concurrent operation is specified with the parallel (PAR) process:

```
PAR
   process1
   process2
      .
      .
```

All component processes are executed simultaneously (conceptually if only one trans-puter is available). For example, the following parallel process, as illustrated in Figure 9.18, accepts two inputs and transfers the values from each input to a different output channel:

```
PAR
   INT x:
   SEQ
      c1?x
      c3!x
   INT y:
```

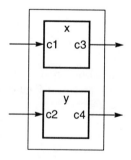

Figure 9.18 Parallel buffers

```
SEQ
   c2?y
   c4!y
```

In both SEQ and PAR processes, the syntax allows no processes to be specified and, in this unlikely case, they behave as SKIPs.

In the alternation process (ALT), a component process can be executed dependent upon an input proceeding. The first input to proceed enables the associated process to be executed; the others are discarded. The construction of the alternate process with input is:

```
ALT
   input
      process
   input
      process
```

Notice in particular the levels of indentation. The following alternate process, as illustrated in Figure 9.19, has three input channels and a single output channel. The first input to proceed passes the input value to the output:

```
INT x:
ALT
   c1?x
      cout!x
   c2?x
      cout!x
   c3?x
      cout!x
```

The general ALT syntax describes a "guard" (an input statement in the previous statement) where guard and process could be another alternate process. The guard is an input, or Boolean expression & (and) input, or Boolean expression &   SKIP (effectively a Boolean expression alone).

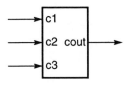

Figure 9.19 Alternate process

9.5.5 Repetitive processes

One construct, the WHILE construct, is provided for program loops and has the format:

```
WHILE Boolean expression
   process
```

While the Boolean expression yields a true value, the process is repeated.

Example
The following sequence will repeatedly accept data from channel c1 and transfer the value received to channel c2:

```
WHILE TRUE
   INT x:
   SEQ
      c1?x
      c2!x
```

Notice the two levels of indentation. To accept values between 0 and 9, we might try:

```
INT x:
SEQ
   x := 0
   WHILE (x >= 0) AND (x <= 9)
      SEQ
         c1?x
         c2!x
```

However, the first transfer from input to output would take place whether or not the input value is within the desired range. To remedy this fault, we could have:

```
INT x:
SEQ
   c1?x
   WHILE (x >= 0) AND (x <= 9)
      SEQ
         c2!x
         c1?x
```

Now we also leave the process with one more input than output action. Whether this is a problem depends upon the communicating processes.

9.5.6 Conditional processes

The conditional IF construct allows one of a series of component processes to be executed dependent upon a Boolean expression. The IF construct has the format:

```
IF
  Boolean expression
    process
  Boolean expression
    process
       .
       .
```

where the "Boolean expression - process" construct can be another IF construct. Notice that the Boolean expression is indented by two spaces and the component process is indented by a further two spaces. Each Boolean expression is evaluated in turn and the first found to be TRUE causes the associated process to be executed and the IF construct to terminate. If no Boolean expression is found to be true, the IF construct behaves as a STOP statement. Hence in these cases, one would need to include a NOT Boolean expression SKIP construct within the IF statement if the next statement is always to be executed or, more conveniently, simply TRUE SKIP at the end.

Example:
The following program sequence causes *x* to be output on channel c1 if an input is equal to 1, or on channel c2 if an input is equal to 2. Nothing is to happen if it is not equal to 1 or 2:

```
INT i,x:
SEQ
  input?i
  IF
    i = 1
      c1!x
      c2!x
    TRUE
      SKIP
```

Occam 2 has a CASE statement which allows a process to be selected according to an expression being evaluated to a particular value given in the statement.

The transputer has an internal real-time clock which enables variables to be declared as being of type TIMER and to be accessed by parallel processes. Timers are incremented at regular intervals dependent upon the external clock frequency applied. In the T212, for example, there are two timers – a high priority timer incrementing every 1 μs and a low priority timer incrementing every 64 ms if the applied frequency is 5 MHz. Both timers cycle after 23^2 increments and are of type INT. Timers are set to specific values by using input statements with literals. The timer will be incremented automatically after loading. Processes can be delayed until a specific value occurs.

9.5.7 Replicators

A replicator can be used in the SEQ construct, PAR construct, ALT construct or IF construct to specify that the component process is duplicated a number of times. The basic formats are:

```
SEQ   name = base FOR count
PAR   name = base FOR count
ALT   name = base FOR count
IF    name = base FOR count
```

where name is an integer variable and base and count are integer expressions. In each case, the component process is repeated count times and the variable name is incremented by one each time, starting at base.

Examples

Suppose that there are ten input channels and that each is examined in turn so that each value received is transferred to one output channel. We could have:

```
[10]CHAN OF INT c:    -- declares 10 channels c[0] to c[9]
CHAN OF INT cout:     -- declares channel cout
SEQ i = 0 FOR n
  INT x:
  SEQ
     c[i]?x
     cout!x
```

In Figure 9.20, there are four processes, each continually accepting an input from the previous process (except the first) and multiplying the value input by two. We could have:

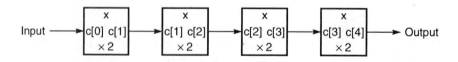

Figure 9.20 Four-stage buffer accepting continual input

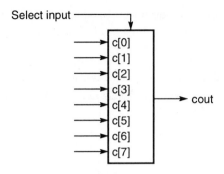

Figure 9.21 Eight-input multiplexer

```
[5]CHAN OF INT c:  -- declares five channels c[0] to c[4]
PAR i = 0 FOR 4
  WHILE TRUE
    INT x:
    SEQ
      c[i]?x
      x := 2*x    -- or use more efficient shift operator
      c[i+1]!x
```

To implement an eight-to-one line multiplexer, as shown in Figure 9.21, we could have:

```
[8]CHAN OF INT c:
CHAN OF INT cout, select:
INT x:
SEQ
  select?x
  IF i = 0 FOR 8
    x = 1
      SEQ
        c[i]?x
        cout!x
```

The program does not handle the situation $x < 0$ or $x > 7$. It is left as an exercise to incorporate this possibility.

9.5.8 Other features

Occam has the usual form of procedures using the construct PROC name(parameter list), and a number of other constructs including being able to create a message of different data types (see Burns, 1988, for a good description). A feature of occam and the transputer is that the program can be written irrespective of the number of transputers; the number of transputers and their actual interconnections via channels can be specified later. The program could be tested on a single transputer system before being put onto a multiprocessor system. Processes are allocated to processors using the PLACED PAR – PROCESSOR construct. For example:

```
PLACED PAR
  PROCESSOR 1
    Process1
  PROCESSOR 2
    Process2
```

allocates process 1 to processor 1 and process 2 to processor 2 and the processes are executed in parallel. Constructs are available to signify that particular processes are to be executed in preference to others, i.e. a priority is assigned to processes (PRI PAR construct).

The semantics of the language have been studied by Roscoe and Hoare (1986) leading to a set of algebraic laws. Also, it may be that complex programs can be transformed into other versions using formal mathematical transformations which can lead to improved programs. Occam transformations, though not necessarily difficult, are beyond the scope of this book (see May and Taylor, 1984).

We should mention that occam is a simple language; hence we are able to give the major details of the language in a section of a chapter. It lacks some features found in conventional high level languages, maybe purposely. The data structures are limited. Recursion is not allowed.

PROBLEMS

9.1 Design a multiprocessor architecture having both direct link message-passing characteristics and shared memory characteristics and make an evaluation of the design.

9.2 Deduce an equation for the network latency of a message-passing system, given that the bandwidth is B, the message length is L and the path set-up time per node is given by $t_{\text{set-up}}$. Plot the equation for fixed message length and for fixed path length. Under what conditions does the network latency approach a constant? Suggest an advantage of a constant network latency.

9.3 Produce a logic design for hardware routing in a hypercube according to the algorithm given in Section 9.1.2.

9.4 Draw the channel dependency graph for the *e*-cube routing algorithm in a 3-dimensional hypercube, and prove that the algorithm is deadlock-free. How many other similar deadlock-free routing algorithms are there?

9.5 Write a program to perform the numerical integration of an arbitrary function f(*x*), as given in Section 9.2.2, but using a tree structure to accumulate the results.

9.6 Deduce the actions of the following occam terminal screen handler program:

```
CHAN OF INT key.out,prog.out,screen:
INT ch,running,alarm.time,term.char:
SEQ
   running := TRUE
   term.char := 0
   WHILE running
     SEQ
       TIME ? alarm.time
       alarm.time := alarm.time + 5
       ALT
          key.out ? ch
            Screen ! ch
          prog . out ? ch
            IF
               ch = term.char
                  running := FALSE
               ch <> term.char
                  Screen ! ch
```

The period within a name is regarded as a normal symbol without any special meaning. It is used in the same way as the underscore in C programs, to clarify the name.

9.7 The declarations in the following occam program are incomplete. Add the required symbols and explain the operation of the program:

```
CHAN
PAR
  INT
  SEQ
     y := 1
     WHILE TRUE
        ALT
```

```
                  datainput ? x
                     output1 ! x * y
                  scaleinput ? y
                     SKIP
        INT
        WHILE TRUE
          SEQ
            output1 ? x
            IF
              x = 0
                output2 ! x
              x <> 0
                output2 ! -x
        INT
        SEQ
          y := 0
          WHILE TRUE
          ALT
            output2 ? x
              result ! x + y
            offsetinput ? y
              SKIP
```

9.8   Write a program in occam for each node in a three-dimensional hypercube to route a message from a source node to a destination node using the *e*-cube hypercube routing algorithm described in Section 9.1.2.

9.9   Design a message-passing routing algorithm for a mesh network which broadcasts a host message to all nodes in the mesh at the greatest speed. Further, design a message-passing routing algorithm which broadcasts a message from a node in the mesh to all other nodes in the mesh. Show how these algorithms can be implemented with message-passing routines.

9.10 Write a program in occam to broadcast a message from the host node to all other nodes in a hypercube.

9.11 Show how the statements:

```
IF Boolean_expression RECEIVE var_list FROM
   source_identifier
WHEN Boolean_expression RECEIVE var_list FROM
   source_identifier
```

could be implemented in occam.

9.12 Show how non-blocking send and receive routines could be constructed in occam.

9.13 Incorporate the possibility that $x < 0$ or $x > 7$ into the last program in Section 9.5.7.

10 | *Multiprocessor systems using the dataflow mechanism*

This chapter considers alternative computer designs to the (von Neumann) stored program systems described in previous chapters, concentrating upon the dataflow technique. The dataflow technique is a multiprocessor technique which enables parallelism to be found without being explicitly declared. The chapter concludes with a summary of the book.

10.1 General

The computer designs so far considered execute instructions, which are stored in a memory, in a particular sequence; the multiprocessor designs presented have more than one such sequence executed simultaneously to increase the execution speed, but do not change the basic mode of operation. A program counter is necessary within each processor to guide each sequence. The instruction execution within each processor is serial and hence inherently slow. To gain an advantage, the programmer, or a compiler, has to identify the independent instructions which can be passed to separate processors; the communication overhead also has to be sufficiently low.

The traditional "program counter controlled" stored program (von Neumann) computer system is sometimes called a *control flow* computer, especially when we wish to differentiate this computer system from alternative types in which the program execution sequence may not be controlled by a central control unit having a program counter. In alternative designs, the sequence is defined by some other mechanism. There are several alternative mechanisms that could be applied. If there is a program of instructions held in a memory, the following possibilities for execution can be identified:

1. An instruction is executed when the previous instruction in a defined sequence has been executed.
2. An instruction is executed when the operands required become available.
3. An instruction is executed when results of the instruction are required by other instructions.

414

4. An instruction is executed when particular data patterns appear.

The first method is the traditional control flow computer mechanism; the second method is known as *data driven* or *dataflow*; the third is *demand driven* and the fourth is *pattern driven.*

Computers do not necessarily need to perform operations specified by stored instructions at all. Neural networks, which attempt to model the human brain to some extent, do not have a stored program of instructions. Neural networks have a long history; the idea of copying the brain can be traced back many years to the 1940s, when Turing contemplated neural computers (Hodges, 1983). However, putting the concept into practice has eluded research workers until recently. Practical implementations of neural computers could arguably be classified as type four, though perhaps a separate category should be made for neural computers.

We will concentrate upon dataflow computers in this final chapter. The dataflow technique was originally developed in the 1960s by Karp and Miller (1966) as a graphical means of representing computations. In the early 1970s, Dennis (1974) and later others began to develop computer architectures based upon the dataflow computational model. Let us first examine the basic dataflow computational model, and then dataflow architectures.

10.2 Dataflow computational model

The dataflow computational model uses a directed graph, sometimes called a *data dependence graph* or *dataflow graph*, to describe a computation. This graph consists of nodes (vertices), which indicate operations, and arcs (edges) from one node to another node, which indicate the flow of data between them. Nodal operations are executed when all required information has been received from the arcs into the node. Typically, a nodal operation requires one or two operands and, for conditional operations, a Boolean input value, and produces one or two results. Hence one, two or three arcs enter a node and one or two arcs leave it. Once a node has been activated and the nodal operation performed (i.e. the node has *fired*) results are passed along the arcs to waiting nodes. This process is repeated until all of the nodes have fired and the final result has been created. More than one node can fire simultaneously, and generally any parallelism in the computational model will be found automatically.

Figure 10.1 shows a simple dataflow graph of the computation $f = A/B + B \times C$. The inputs to the computation are the variables A, B and C, shown entering at the top. The paths between the nodes indicate the route taken by the results of the nodal operations. The general flow of data is from top to bottom. There are three computational operations (add, multiply and divide). We notice that B is required by two nodes. An explicit COPY node is used to generate an additional copy of B.

Data operands/results move along the arcs contained in tokens. Figure 10.2 shows the movement of tokens between nodes. After the inputs are applied, the token containing the

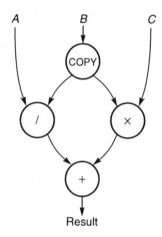

Figure 10.1 Dataflow graph of computation $A/B + B \times C$

A operand is applied to the division node, the token containing the B operand is applied to the COPY node and the token containing the C operand is applied to the multiply node. Only the COPY node can fire, as its single-input token is present at the node. The other nodes require a result token of the COPY node. Once the COPY tokens have become available, both the multiply and divide nodes have all their tokens and can fire. The final node waits for both the multiplication and division nodes to complete before it can commence. It may be that the multiplication operation is completed before the division operation but in any event both operations must produce a token before the final addition node can fire.

Clearly, one can build up in-line computations of this sort, but practical computations usually require additional features. For example, in control-flow computations, conditional instructions provide decision-making power. Similarly, conditional operations are provided in dataflow computations. Conditional operation nodes generally take one or two operands and one conditional input. They pass forward one or two results, which depend upon the value of the data input and the value of the condition. Condition nodes can be regarded as switches, passing a data input token to an output.

Two forms of switch or condition nodes are shown in Figure 10.3. In the MERGE node, there are two data inputs and one output. If the condition is true, the left-hand side input token is passed to the output; if the condition is false, the right-hand side input token is passed to the output. In the BRANCH instruction, the single-input token is passed to the left output path if the Boolean condition is true or to the right output path if the condition is false. It is not necessary to use both outputs in the BRANCH node. MERGE and BRANCH are not both strictly necessary, as MERGE can be achieved with two BRANCH nodes and BRANCH can be achieved with two MERGE nodes (Problem 10.2).

Once the first set of inputs has been used, a second set could be applied and processed behind the first in a pipeline fashion. However, it is important that partial results (tokens)

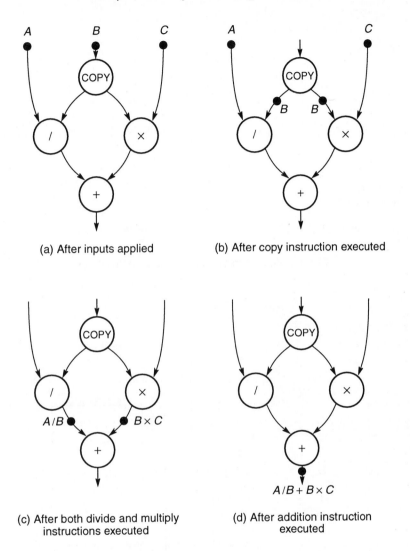

(a) After inputs applied

(b) After copy instruction executed

(c) After both divide and multiply
instructions executed

(d) After addition instruction
executed

Figure 10.2 Movement of data tokens in computation $A/B + B \times C$

of the first computation are not processed with partial results of the second or any other subsequent computation. The results are usually required in the sequence that the inputs are applied.

There are numerous instances in which a particular computation must be repeated with different data, notably with program loops. Program iteration loops of conventional pro-

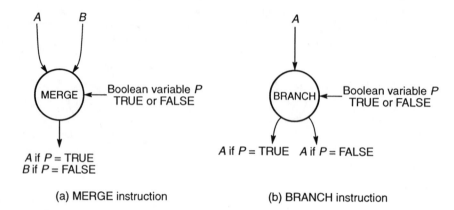

A if *P* = TRUE
B if *P* = FALSE

A if *P* = TRUE   *A* if *P* = FALSE

(a) MERGE instruction

(b) BRANCH instruction

Figure 10.3 Conditional dataflow instructions

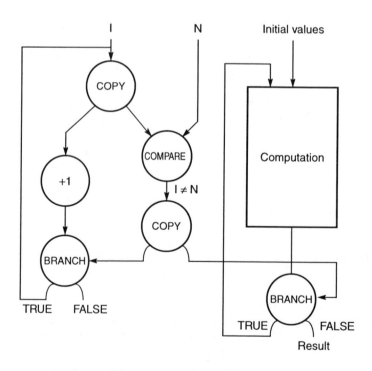

Figure 10.4 Dataflow loops

gramming languages can be reproduced by feeding results back to input nodes and tokens must be used only with those tokens of the same iteration. Loops are often formed in conventional languages using loop variables which are incremented each time the body of the computation is computed. The loop is terminated when the loop variable reaches a defined value. This method can be carried over to dataflow computations, as shown in Figure 10.4. It is important that a mechanism is in place to keep the two loops in step. Mechanisms should also be provided for function calls and handling data structures such as arrays.

A major problem with dataflow is dealing with data structures such as arrays. If we keep with the dataflow approach of consuming data tokens entirely and generating new result tokens, it follows that an array of elements would have to be consumed entirely and a completely new array created even if only one element of the array were to be changed. This would produce excessive coping of elements and reduced performance. The problem of course was recognized during the early years of dataflow, and a few approaches have been suggested to mitigate the effects. Separate memories have been proposed, accessed either directly or indirectly through pointers. Special instructions have to be provided to handle data structures, to read and write to elements of the data structure, and perhaps to fetch the complete data structure.

Another problem with dataflow is the constraint (in fine-grain dataflow) of nodes/operators only allowed two or three operands. This limits the complexity of the hardware and produces high speed of execution of individual instructions. However, it can be inefficient, especially in the use of the copy instruction, which is provided simply to create multiple instances of a token. Suppose n instances are need in a computation. Typically a tree of copy instruction is assembled so that $\log_2 n$ copy instructions would be needed. Such structures reduce the execution time of the program and increase the size of the program. One proposed solution is to provide iterative instructions which create multiple tokens, not just one or two. For example, the "tuplicate" instruction, TUP, on the Manchester machine (see later, Böhn and Gurd, 1990) generates n copies of the token. Each copy is sent to consecutive instructions in memory starting at the single output destination address. The TUP instruction accepts two tokens, one which is to be replicated, and a second a positive integer defining the number of copies of the token. Another solution is to have versions of arithmetic instructions which create a stream of identical tokens, each sent to successive destinations.

A number of dataflow system have been constructed. There are two general dataflow arrangements:

1. Static dataflow.
2. Dynamic dataflow.

which result in two types of dataflow system. In static dataflow, there can be only one instance of a particular node firing at a time, whereas in dynamic dataflow it is possible to have multiple instances of a node firing at run-time. This might occur in code sharing, multiple function calls and recursion. Hence, such operations are not possible in static dataflow. Let us first examine static dataflow.

10.3 Dataflow systems

10.3.1 Static dataflow

The static dataflow architecture has the *firing rules*:

1. Nodes fire when all input tokens appear and the previous output tokens have been consumed.
2. Input tokens are then removed and new output tokens are generated.

These rules allow for pipeline computations and loops but not recursion or code sharing. The machine generally requires a handshaking acknowledgement mechanism, as shown in Figure 10.5, to indicate to a node that the output token has been consumed. The acknowledgement mechanism can take the form of special control tokens sent from processors once they respond to a fired node.

The static mechanism was the first dataflow mechanism to receive attention for hardware realization at MIT (Dennis, 1974) though a system was not constructed then. Dennis conceived a packet-driven ring architecture, shown in Figure 10.6, consisting of a ring of processor and memory elements interconnected via routing networks. Processing elements would receive operation packets of the form:

Opcode	Operands	Destinations

where the opcode specifies the operation to be performed, the operands specify the numbers to be used in the operation, and the destinations specify where the result of the operation is to be sent.

Notice that the numbers to be used are literals and are always carried within the instruction. Numbers are never referred to by addresses in memory, as they are not stored in a globally accessible memory; this has advantages and disadvantages. It is an

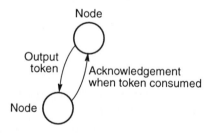

Figure 10.5 Static dataflow token-passing

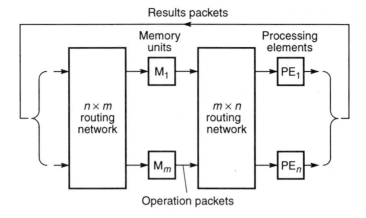

Figure 10.6 An early dataflow architecture

advantage that operands can only be affected by one selected node at a time. It is a disadvantage in that complex data structures, or even simple vectors or arrays, could not reasonably be carried in the instruction and hence cannot be handled in the mechanism (unless the mechanism is modified).

The result packet takes the form:

Value	Destination

where value is the value obtained after the operation has been executed. The result packets pass though a routing network to "instruction cells" in the memory unit, as identified by the destination address in the result packet. An instruction cell generates an operation packet when all of the input packets (tokens) have been received. Typically, two such packets are required in the instruction cell to generate an operation packet. The operation packet is then routed to a processing element. If all processing elements are identical (i.e. a homogeneous system) any free processing elements could be chosen. In a non-homogeneous system with specialized processing elements, each capable of performing particular functions, the opcode in the operation packet is used to select the processing element.

Dennis noted that the scheme, as he proposed it, was impractical if each instruction cell needed to be fabricated individually with a large number of instruction cells. Therefore, he proposed that instruction cells should be formed into groups (instruction blocks) each having a single input and a single output. The dataflow system can be further simplified by associating the instruction cells with processing elements, leading to the architecture shown in Figure 10.7. Here the processing elements (PEs) generate and receive packets and only one routing network is necessary to forward packets from PE outputs to PE

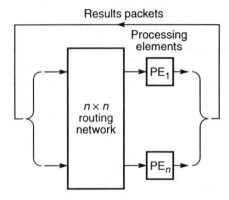

Figure 10.7 Simplified dataflow architecture

inputs. The destination PE is specified in the result packet.

Dataflow architectures generally use some form of routing network to transmit result packets on to a token matching mechanism. The packets usually consist of several bytes and could be sent one byte at a time, to reduce the interconnections. In the basic Dennis architecture, the matching mechanism is incorporated into the instruction cells or processing elements. The routing network must be capable of receiving byte-serial packets, with destinations encoded within the packets, and of forwarding the packets on to the required cells or processing elements. There are a number of possible candidates for the routing networks, as described in Chapter 8 (see especially dynamic multistage networks). The principal criterion is throughput of packets rather than the propagation time from the input of the routing network to the output, as the system is pipelined. Self-routing networks are particularly attractive for this application.

10.3.2 Dynamic dataflow

Dynamic dataflow describes a dataflow system in which the dataflow graph being executed is not fixed, but can be altered (dependent upon the executing code) through such actions as recursion and code sharing. Recursion and code sharing cannot be done in the static architecture as described but can be accomplished by simply copying the code every time a call is made. This is known as *dynamic code copying*. Alternatively, tags could be attached to the packets to identify tokens with particular computations (instances of shared code, recursive code, loops, functions, etc.); this is known as *dynamic token tagging*, and is the method normally associated with dynamic dataflow. Dynamic token tagging dataflow uses the firing rules:

1. A node fires when all input tokens with the same tag appear.
2. More than one token is allowed on each arc and previous output tokens need not be consumed before the node can fire again.

The dynamic token tagging dataflow system needs storage for unmatched tokens, hardware for matching the tokens and a hardware mechanism for generating the tags. Tokens may not be taken strictly in the order generated and a first-in first-out token queue for storing the tokens is not suitable. However, no acknowledgement mechanism is required. The term *coloring* has been used for the token labeling operation, and tokens with the same color belong together (Dennis, 1974). Token tagging can be extended to cover coloring elements of arrays so that the correct elements are processed. It implies that all tokens must now have a coloring tag and that machine operations must be provided to operate upon the coloring tags to generate new colors.

Token tags

To cover the three situations identified – functions and recursion, loops and array elements - each token tag could have three fields (Glauert, Gurd and Kirkham, 1985):

- - - -	Iteration level	Activation name	Index

Each field will hold a number, say, from zero onwards. Iteration level identifies the particular activation of a loop body, activation name identifies the particular function call and index identifies the particular element of an array. Iteration level and activation name might be combined into one field, activation name, referring to a loop body or function activation.

Individual fields of the tag need to be treated as data values and passed from one node to another. As a minimum requirement each field requires operations to extract the field value and to set the field to a value. For example, a "read token field" operation accepts a single token and produces a token with the value of the input token field. The "set token field" operation produces an output token corresponding to the input token except with its token field set to a value given as a literal in the operation. Increment and decrement operations can also be provided, particularly for iteration level. Often, after a particular routine has been completed using the coloring facility, the result is de-labeled by setting the token field(s) to 0. We note that it is possible for function call, a loop, and array index to occur in combination, for example, for a function call to occur with a different array index. It is also possible for nested function calls, loops, etc. to occur. Figure 10.8 shows one general arrangement for a loop with tagging of parameters before each activation of the loop, and re-tagging of the results.

Different instances of a function call can be colored with unique activation level numbers, but the mechanism needs to take into account that each call will be from a different place in the program and that it is necessary to return from these different places. In a normal von Neumann computer, a stack is used to hold the return address. In a dynamic token tagging dataflow system, a return operation can be provided to produce a token corresponding to one of the input tokens but having a specific destination address as given by a second input token, as shown in Figure 10.9. Further operations are

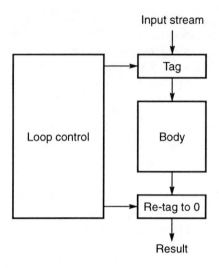

Figure 10.8 Token tagging in loops

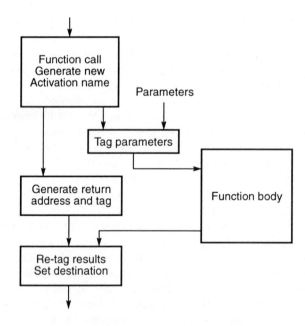

Figure 10.9 Function call using tags

necessary to allow complete generality of the function call in all situations (see Glauert, Gurd and Kirkham, 1985).

A simple approach to using the index field to access elements of an array would be to sequence through the elements until the specific element having the required index value has been found. Suppose the index field operations include "read index", RIX, and "set index", SIX. Read index, RIX, can be used on each element to find its index value, which can then be compared to the required value using a normal arithmetic compare operation. When the required value has been found, a set index operation, SIX, could be used to set the index to 0 and extract the token. However, this procedure is somewhat inefficient. Large data structures require alternative approaches, normally returning to globally stored data referenced by pointers in the tokens. Then, the pure form of dataflow with all data passed within the tokens is abandoned for large data structures (arrays, records, etc.). Performing arithmetic operations on elements from two arrays can be done efficiently using coloring by simply passing the pairs of elements through a normal arithmetic operation node. Only pairs of elements with the same index will be processed together.

System examples

The dynamic dataflow machine designed at MIT by Arvind in the late 1970s (Arvind and Nikhil, 1990) uses an array of processing elements interconnected the same way as the static dataflow architecture shown in Figure 10.7. The processing elements incorporate a program memory and instruction queue connected to an arithmetic and logic unit. A "waiting match" memory holds tokens as received at the input module of the processing element. When a full complement of tokens has been received, the appropriate instruction is fetched from the program memory and this instruction is executed with operands within the matched tokens. The result token is output to the Routing network and directed to the destination processing element. Each processing element in the MIT dynamic architecture incorporates a memory called an *I-structure memory*, to hold array data structures which cannot reasonably be transmitted within the tokens, thus alleviating the restriction on array data structures. Additional tags are stored with the data structures to control access to the data structures.

Figure 10.10 shows the architecture of the dynamic dataflow computer system constructed at Manchester University by Gurd and Watson (1980). This system also uses a pipelined ring architecture, but separates the computational functions from the token/tag matching functions. Each processor executes 166-bit packages consisting of two data operands, a tag, an opcode and one or two destinations (i.e. the address of the next instruction or instructions). A system/computation flag is associated with all packets to differentiate between a computational packet to be executed by a processor and a packet carrying a system message (such as to load an instruction into memory). Data operands can be 32-bit integers or floating point numbers.

Once an executable packet has been executed, a processor generates one or two result token packets. A result token packet contains one data operand, a tag and the destination address(es), 96 bits in all. Each result token packet enters a two-way switch which enables data to be input from an external source or output to an external destination

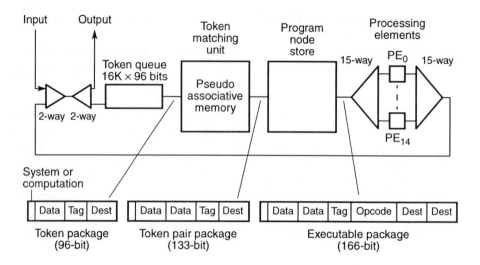

Figure 10.10 Manchester dataflow computer architecture

(peripheral device). Assuming the result token packet is to pass to another node, the packet is directed to a first-in first-out token queue and onto a matching unit. Here, a search is made to identify another token to complete the tokens necessary to fire a node (if the node requires two tokens). The search is done in hardware by comparing the destination and tag of the incoming token with all the stored tokens. If a match is found, a token-pair packet is formed, otherwise the incoming token is stored in the matching unit awaiting its matching token. Token pairs and single operand tokens are passed on to the program store which holds the nodal instructions, and the full executable packet is formed. Executable packets are sent to free processors in an array of fifteen processors when possible.

On average, packets into the program node store and executable packets are expected to be formed every 300 ns, and token packets produced by processors at an average rate of one every 200 ns, but this will depend on the program. These figures indicate that three tokens must enter the matching unit in the period that two token packets are generated, or that one in every three tokens is for a single input node. Similarly, as executable packets enter the processor array at a rate of one every 300 ns, every two executable tokens must generate three token packets if the generation rate is one every 200 ns. In fact, the processors are microprogrammable devices requiring 4.5 μs per machine operation and a throughput of one executable packet every 300 ns is achieved if all fifteen processors are active.

Hardware matching of a large number of tokens is problematical and is solved in the Manchester machine by employing a hardware hashing technique rather than by using a true associative memory because such memory would be uneconomic.

10.3.3 VLSI dataflow structures

The dataflow technique can be applied to VLSI (very large scale integration) arrays of interconnected cells. Each cell performs primitive dataflow operations on data received via direct links from neighboring cells, and consists of a processor, a small stored program and input/output communication. The array is connected to a host system which downloads the programs into the cells. A cell will fire when all the operands for one of its stored instructions are received, and internal logic is necessary to detect when such enabling conditions occur. Each cell will perform the operations of one or more nodes in a dataflow graph. A typical operation might require one or two input operands from neighboring cells and produce one output operand to a neighboring cell. Figure 10.11 illustrates how a dataflow graph might be mapped onto a hexagonal dataflow array. In this case, each cell in the array executes one primitive operation of the graph.

A VLSI dataflow array has been demonstrated by Koren *et al.* (1988). Their dataflow architecture uses a static hexagonal interconnection cell pattern. The array is connected to a host system, and communication buses, which are connected to the host, are provided within the array for loading the program memories and extracting the results. Each processing element has all the main features of a normal stored program computer, including familiar instructions within its instruction set, such as arithmetic and logic operations and input/output. In addition, instructions are provided for cell initialization. Instructions can operate upon six periphery registers, R1 through to R6, which are provided for communicating to adjacent cells. Up to six instructions can be stored in each cell at any instant in a small stored instruction memory. There is one instruction that can produce an output for each periphery register. The contents of these registers are automatically transferred to the neighboring cell when this can accept the data in the corresponding periphery register. Each cell operates on 8-bit numbers. Sixteen- and 32-bit numbers can be processed using carry propagation techniques. Carry values are passed through the periphery registers defined by initialization instructions.

Instructions have 16 bits and the format shown in Figure 10.12. A 9-bit opcode is provided. Each of the input register bits, B_6 through to B_1, can be set to 1 to indicate that the corresponding register holds one of the source operands. In fact, only up to three input registers can be specified in one instruction, two registers holding operands and one a carry-in value. Bit B_7, labeled Frst, is used when the order of the input operands is important, such as in subtraction and division, to specify which of two input registers holds the first operand. For example, subtraction could be $(A - B)$ or reverse subtraction $(B - A)$.

As in all the dataflow systems described so far, instructions are not necessarily executed in the program sequence but when the required operands become available. As soon as a new operand is received via one of its periphery registers, internal logic establishes whether any waiting instructions require the operand. This is achieved using a set of six *static flags* in the instruction memory, one for each instruction, and a two-dimensional array of *dynamic flags* with seven rows and six columns. The static flags indicate that the contents of the corresponding register have to be transferred to the corresponding register in the neighboring cell, i.e. that the instruction is present.

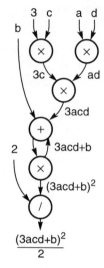

(a) Dataflow graph

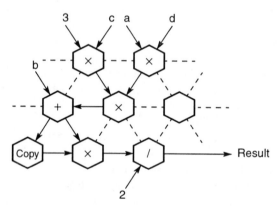

(b) Mapped onto hexagonal array

Figure 10.11 Dataflow graph mapped onto hexagonal array

Input registers								Frst	Operation code					
B_{15}	B_{14}	B_{13}	B_{12}	B_{11}	B_{10}	B_9	B_8	B_7	B_6	B_5	B_4	B_3	B_2	B_1

Figure 10.12 Hexagonal array processor instruction format

Each column in the dynamic flag array is assigned to one of the six registers. Each of the first six rows is assigned to one of the six instructions that might be present in the instruction memory. The seventh row in the dynamic array is used by the intercell register transfer logic. The flags in the jth column are set to 1 when a new operand arrives in the jth register and the corresponding instruction requires the operand. This is achieved by logically ANDing the operand arrival set signal with the static flags. Each time an instruction is executed, the flags in the corresponding row of the flag array are reset to 0. Hence, when all bits in a column have been reset to 0, the input operand has been used by all waiting instructions. The input register becomes "empty" and ready for new data to be loaded from adjacent cells. The conditions for an instruction to be executed ("fire") are as follows:

1. Input register dynamic flags values in instruction row = static flags values, indicating that all input operands are present.
2. Required output register is empty.

The dataflow graph from the application problem needs to be mapped onto the array; heuristics, as described by Koren *et al.* (1988), may be necessary to perform this mapping. In general, some cells are used simply to route operands towards their final destination. The PE (processing element) cell utilization percentage describes the percentage of cells that perform computations; Koren reports utilization percentages of between 7.4 and 75 per cent, depending on the method of mapping for a range of problems.

The array dataflow system is very similar to the message-passing systems described in Chapter 9, in that programs are loaded into independent nodes prior to execution and information passes from node to node. Indeed, a general purpose message-passing system could be programmed to operate on dataflow principles, though without operand matching facilities it would need to be at a reasonably coarse grain level.

10.3.4 Dataflow languages

Traditional procedural high level languages such as Pascal, C or FORTRAN could be pressed into service for dataflow computers, with some modifications or additions to the language. However, procedural languages grew from the development of sequential computations/computers and are not ideal as dataflow languages, particularly for the "fine grain" dataflow computing we have described so far.

Some key attributes of dataflow to be incorporated into dataflow languages are:

1. Parallelism constrained by data dependencies.
2. Locality of effect characteristic and freedom from side effects.
3. Lack of variables that can be altered.
4. Lack of stored values that can affect subsequent computations.

Locality of effect refers to operations only affecting values within a defined area. The phrase *freedom from side effects* has been coined to describe the general situation when an action in a program does not have unfortunate far-reaching consequences. These consequences might be unexpected and lead to errors. An example of side effects is a procedure which alters global variables in the calling program. The variables may be parameters passed to the procedure during the call, or worse, global variables directly referenced in the body of the procedure. Clearly, this effect could be avoided by not using global variables at all and by passing parameters by reference (name). Side effects cause difficulties in establishing program correctness and data dependencies for parallel computations. Problems can occur, particularly with data structures such as arrays and records, in which a change in one element of the structure at one part of a program might have significant effects in another part of the program.

Prime candidates for dataflow programming languages are those within the class of languages called *functional languages*. A program written in a functional language consists only of functions where a function is called by name, supplied with parameters and returns a value (or values), as in conventional high level languages. However, a functional language program is written entirely of functions. The program usually consists of a main function, which calls other functions, which may in turn call other functions, and so on, until a bottom level is reached in which the functions are composed of language primitives. There are no assignment statements, except that a program variable can be given a value once. The values of variables never change, i.e. variables are more like defined constants. There is research interest in functional languages because they might help write better structured programs, particularly parallel programs, and not necessarily for dataflow computers as the machine architecture. The reader is directed to Peyton Jones (1989) for details. We can make some general observations regarding functional languages.

Functional languages have several potential advantages, notably that a function cannot have any effect on the program except to return a value (or values, in the case of some function languages). They are free from side effects. Apart from eliminating a source of errors, freedom from side effects also helps parallel computations. As side effects are not present to alter expressions, the order of evaluation of expressions does not matter, and variables and their value can be interchanged at any time. This is known as *referential transparency*. Clearly, programmers could restrain themselves from using those features in a programming language which lead to possible side effects. A program could be written in a normal programming language as a series of functions. Hughes (1989) makes the point in his defence of functional languages that simply omitting features in a language cannot make the language more powerful; this is not sufficient. In addition to prohibiting programming styles which lead to side effects, functional languages also provide special program constructs to put together complex functions from simpler functions, and deal with lists (as in LISP, the first major functional language).

Functional languages have at the most one assignment for each program variable. Such languages are known as *single assignment languages*, and form the development of most, if not all, dataflow languages. There is a direct relationship between computations in dataflow graphs and single assignment. A program value is generated only at a dataflow node and cannot be altered elsewhere, except as a generated new data token. The single assignment convention carries over this concept that data operands can only be altered once, creating a new value. That is, variable names can only appear on the left hand side of an expression once. This implies that the program sequence in Pascal:[1]

```
A := 1;
A := A + 1;
A := A + B + C;
```

would be rewritten as:

```
A   := 1;
A'  := A + 1;
A"  := A' + B + C;
```

where A' and A" are new variables introduced to maintain the single assignment rule. Fortunately, by using language constructs, such transformations can be avoided in many instances when they occur in loops in single assignment languages.

Iterations in single assignment languages employ special notations so as not to break the single assignment rule. In normal languages, one makes use of a loop variable to count the number of iterations of a loop and perhaps also within expressions in the loop body. To take a very simple example, to generate factorial 10!, we might write:

```
fact := 1;
FOR i := 2 to 10 DO fact := fact*i;
```

However, this would be disallowed in a single assignment language because fact is re-assigned a new value on each iteration through the loop. One "solution" would be to unfold the iteration into separate computations, i.e. fact := 1; fact := fact*2; fact := fact*3; etc., and rename fact for each successive statement. We have seen that dynamic dataflow architectures can handle iterations by coloring tokens with an iteration tag, and hence there is a simple graphical transformation for the factorial loop. Some dataflow languages have reserved words such as NEW or OLD to identify successive values, for example:

```
i := OLD i + 1;
fact := OLD fact*i;
```

Several dataflow languages have been developed, often in connection with dataflow work on machine architectures. For example, the dataflow language VAL (Value-oriented Algorithmic Language) was developed in the late 1970s and early 1980s at MIT under the direction of Dennis, and also at Lawrence Livermore National Laboratory. A detailed description and analysis of VAL is given by McGraw (1982).

---

[1] Pascal is used here because the dataflow languages given here use a Pascal-type syntax.

Subsequently, SISAL (Streams and Iterations in a Single Assignment Language) was developed, though still as a research language. Details of the SISAL language are given by Allan and Oldehoeft (1985). SISAL was used in the development of the Manchester dataflow computer (Böhm and Sargeant, 1989). Streams and iterations are fundamental aspects of dataflow programming. A stream of tokens are used in dataflow to describe a sequence of data items like an array, except that the elements can be processed as they are generated rather than having to wait for the complete set of elements to be generated, as would be necessary with an array. The possibility of parallel computations on stream elements exists. We will briefly mention some of the unusual features of SISAL, which are characteristics of dataflow languages and are therefore representative. Of course, other dataflow languages may have different reserved words and syntax.

Functions can return more than one value, which are assigned to successive "variables". For example:

```
a,b,c := funct0(par1)
```

evaluates the function `funct0`, using the value of the parameter par1, returning three results which are assigned to a, b and c respectively. The function could return a stream.

Changing one element of an array implies that a completely new array is created in a functional language. In SISAL:

```
B := A[i:v]
```

creates a new array, B, which is the same as array A except that the ith element is changed to the value v. In a dataflow system which stores arrays, an alternative to copying the array is to modify the stored array, a decision that could be made by the compiler, dependent upon the use of the arrays.

Sequential expressions, which are similar to conventional programming languages except that each must return a value, exist in dataflow languages. For example, in SISAL, the IF THEN ELSE expression could be used in the statement:

```
a := IF b = c THEN funct1 ELSE funct2 END IF
```

If the Boolean expression $b = c$ is TRUE, `funct1` is evaluated and its result is returned to be assigned to a, otherwise `funct2` is evaluated and its result is returned and assigned to a. This construct is very similar to that allowed in ALGOL 68 and C.

Iterative sequential expressions, in which each evaluation within a loop has to be executed in strict sequence because of data dependencies, can use the FOR-INITIAL expression. The FOR-INITIAL expression consists of four parts, initialization with the reserved word INITIAL to specify the initial values, the body of the loop specifying the repetitive computation, loop termination conditions with WHILE or UNTIL placed before the loop body if tested before the loop begins, or after the loop body if tested at the end of each loop executed, and finally RETURNS followed by a return expression to specify the values returned. The return expression can be VALUE OF, ARRAY OF or STREAMS OF.

VALUE OF can also be extended to include VALUE OF SUM and other "reduction" operators. VALUE OF SUM var returns the value of the arithmetic summation of var. For example:

```
FOR INITIAL
   i := 1; j := 1
WHILE i < 10
REPEAT
   j := OLD j * i;
   i := OLD i + 1
RETURNS STREAM OF j
END FOR
```

returns a stream of factorial values 1, 2, 6, 24, ...

Iterations that can be performed in parallel (i.e. without any data dependencies) have a separate "for-all" FOR expression, for example:

```
FOR i IN 1,n
   sum1 := A[i]*i
   RETURNS VALUE OF SUM sum1
END FOR
```

returns the summation of the elements after each is multiplied by i. The construct IN 1, n specifies that there will be n activations of the loop, each with a successive value of i from 1 to n. Each activation can proceed in parallel. The construct VALUE OF SUM sum specifies that each value of sum computed is added together.

"For-all" iteration constructs are available to access multidimensional arrays, either with the inner (dot) product range of indices or the outer product range of indices, using DOT and CROSS respectively. For example i IN 1, 4 DOT j IN 8,11 generates the indices [1,8], [2,9], [3,10] and [4,11] and i IN 1, 5 CROSS j IN 11,15 generates the indices [1,1], [2,1], [3,1], [4,1], [1,2], [2,2], [3,2], [4,2], [1,3], [2,3], [3,3], [4,3], [1,4], [2,4], [3,4] and [4,4]. There is more than one method by which the system implements the VAL OF SUM summation (and other reduction operators). The method used may result in different values producing overflow conditions and the language definition fails to be sufficiently precise if the actual method is not specified, as in VAL (McGraw, 1982). For example, the summation could be done by adding successive values to an accumulating sum, the most likely method for a single processor system. Alternatively, a tree could be formed with pairs of values added at each node of the tree and partial results passed upwards towards the root of the tree. This method would allow each node to be done on a separate processor concurrently. It is possible that one method may produce an overflow not occurring in the other method. In SISAL, the associativity order can be specified using LEFT, RIGHT and TREE.

Internal error detection and recovery in a traditional computer often relies on errors being detected by processor hardware during the execution of an instruction. An interrupt

mechanism is activated to make the processor execute an error routine. This method may
be hard to do in a dataflow computer with substantial concurrency. In VAL and SISAL,
error handling is performed in a novel way by introducing error values within each data
type. When an error is produced at a node, the appropriate error value is generated in
place of a valid numeric or Boolean data value. For example, in VAL, positive and
negative overflow are indicated with the error values POS_OVER and NEG_OVER respectively. Underflow is indicated by POS_UNDER and NEG_UNDER. An error condition not
identified specifically has the error value UNDEF. Boolean values now become three-
valued, TRUE, FALSE and UNDEF. SISAL has the values UNDEF, to cover all arithmetic
errors, and BROKEN, to indicate some form of control flow error preventing the desired
result being generated. Error values are propagated through successive nodes. Both
languages have methods of testing for errors.

There are other languages for dataflow, for example the dataflow language Lucid
(Wadge and Ashcroft, 1985).

10.4 Macrodataflow

10.4.1 General

The dataflow mechanism as described operates at the instruction level, i.e. so-called *fine
grain dataflow*. However, there is a high communications overhead in passing operands.
A mechanism to reduce this communications overhead is to apply dataflow at the procedural level, so-called *coarse grain dataflow*. It is also possible to have variable grain
dataflow in which nodes might represent simple operations through to complete sequential procedures. A number of phrases have been invented in the literature to describe the
variations in dataflow. For example, coarse grain/variable grain dataflow can be described
as *combined dataflow/control flow*. We shall use the term *macrodataflow* (a term also used
by Gajski *et al.* (1983) and others) to cover dataflow in which each node can represent a
complex serial function. Macrodataflow graphs assume the same overall construction as
fine grain dataflow graphs, in that each node is interconnected to other nodes by arcs
carrying tokens. The tokens can carry single data items. Given that the nodes represent
procedures/functions, the input tokens carry procedure/function parameters, and the
output tokens carry procedure/function results.

Macrodataflow node firing rules can be:

1. Standard firing rule – node fires only when all of the operands are received.
2. Non-standard firing rule – node fires when certain specified operands are received.
   Each nodal operation is completed when all necessary operands are received. (The
   necessary operands may not be all of the operands.)

The second firing rule, a variation of the first, allows part of a procedure/function to be
executed while waiting for additional parameters to complete the procedure/function. The

firing rule would be inappropriate for a fine grain dataflow system because the fired operations of fine grain dataflow are of a simple type and would normally require all the inputs to perform any meaningful processing. The nonstandard firing rule includes the possibility that one or more of the input tokens need not ever be received for the node to fire. These tokens become "don't care" conditions. The tokens that must arrive to start the node firing, those which must arrive eventually and the "don't care" conditions can be specified in the nodal enabling conditions, for example, for each input arc, 1 = token must arrive to start, 0 = token can arrive later and X = "don't care" condition.

10.4.2 Macrodataflow architectures

The early fine grain dataflow systems, operating either as static or dynamic dataflow, employed ring structure architectures, the VLSI array dataflow systems being an exception. Macrodataflow (coarse grain) computing tends to suggest more conventional architectures containing a number of processing elements centrally controlled with access to a common memory. An example of a suitable system is the Cedar computer system (Gajski *et al.*, 1983) shown in Figure 10.13. A number of processor clusters connect to a global memory through a global routing network. Each processor cluster consists of a number of processing elements connecting to a number of local memory units through a local routing network and controlled by a cluster control unit within the processor cluster. The processor clusters are controlled by a global control unit. The program is a directed graph which is loaded into the global control unit which controls the execution of the program.

A macrodataflow architecture presented by Ayyad and Wilkinson (1987) employs a shared memory system but with the unusual characteristic that the memory provides access to specific locations, rather than the processor using bus arbitration to access the memory. Access to specific memory locations is offered and identified to the processors by broadcasting the memory addresses in a repeating sequence.

The sequence of locations offered can be found from knowledge of those nodes not yet satisfied. Figure 10.14(a) shows an implementation using a common bus interconnection system. A number of processors, each with local memory, are connected to a common memory through a single bus. Logic in each processor compares the incoming address from the common memory module with the address required by the processor. When a match is found, a data path is established between the common memory and the processor. Though a common bus is used here, no bus contention occurs and no arbitration logic is required. The cycling can operate at very high speed and is only limited by the address generation logic and the comparators; the address sequencing is only temporarily halted for memory accesses when necessary. Simultaneous writing to the same location in the common memory by more than one processor must be inhibited in the scheme. In macrodataflow, simultaneous writing of parameters into a common memory location should never occur.

An implementation for a crossbar switch architecture is shown in Figure 10.14(b) and requires each memory module to be provided with address generation logic but, significantly, no additional traditional arbitration logic is required. Typically, the upper address bits from the processing elements select the memory module. In the crossbar switch

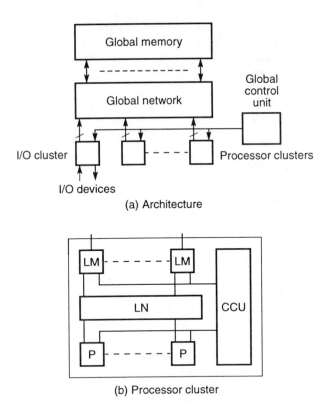

(a) Architecture

(b) Processor cluster

Figure 10.13 Cedar computer system (LM, local memory; LN, local network; P, processor; CCU, cluster control unit)

implementation it is possible for more than one processor to access the same memory module during the same address generation cycle. In a normal crossbar switch system this is prevented by the arbitration logic.

In dataflow, and in macrodataflow computations in particular, we would expect a processor to be waiting for more than one parameter on occasion. To accommodate multiple requests, the system can be provided with additional comparator circuits. As an alternative to using discrete comparators, particularly for multiple requests, content addressable memories (CAMs) could be employed, which compare all stored values with an applied value simultaneously. In this application, the addresses of locations required by the processor are loaded into a CAM as they are generated. Addresses generated by the cycling device are compared simultaneously with all stored addresses by the internal logic of the CAM. If any match is found, the processor is informed, perhaps by an interrupt signal. A signal is also passed to the cycling device to prevent it continuing with the next address and a data path is established.

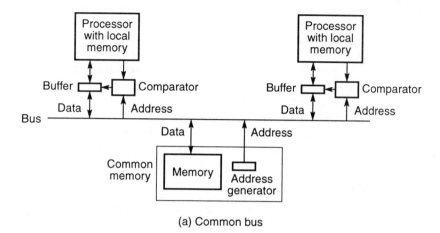

(a) Common bus

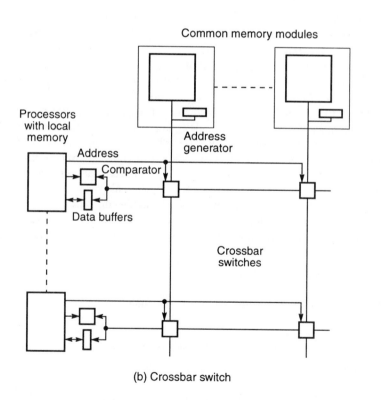

(b) Crossbar switch

Figure 10.14 Macrodataflow architecture

10.5 Summary and other directions

Dataflow has had a fairly long development time, with a few research groups studying the technique in earnest since the mid-1970s without it becoming widespread in commercial use. Admittedly, the pressure of market forces to maintain compatibility with existing systems greatly inhibit the introduction of a radically different computer system requiring a different style of programming and different programming languages. The dataflow idea of operations only being performed when the operands are available was applied to a traditional stored program computer in the IBM 360/91 in the form of internal forwarding (Chapter 5, Section 5.3.4) in the later 1960s and predates dataflow architectural developments. However, this early form of dataflow was abandoned after the introduction of cache memories, which achieved better performance with less complicated hardware. Subsequently, commercial computer manufacturers studied the technique for a while, for example Digital Equipment Corporation, with their initial involvement with the Manchester dataflow project. It would seem that dataflow will become a general computer technique just as pipelining is a general technique and will find some applications. Hence it is included in this text.

We have developed the designs of computers, starting from enhancements to the single processor stored program computer (Part I) through to the application of more than one processor sharing a memory (Part II) and finally to systems which do not share globally stored data (Part III). There are some other possible computer designs not dealt with, such as neural computers, computers based upon optical technology and architectures for implementing functional languages. There have been a few experimental systems for implementing functional languages, especially in England, including the ALICE machine at Imperial College, London and the GRIP (Graph Reduction in Parallel) machine at University College, London. For the most part, these experimental projects have used architectures that do not look significantly different to shared/local memory multiprocessor systems, except for the support given to the computational model. The specialized ring architectures such as the early dataflow computer architectures have not been used. The reader is referred to Peyton Jones (1989) and the references contained in this paper for further information on research directions on systems for functional programming.

PROBLEMS

10.1 Draw a dataflow graph to compute the function:

$$T = (x + y)(x - y)/(x^2 + y^2)$$

Show the movement of tokens through the graph.

10.2 Draw a dataflow graph to achieve a BRANCH operation using two MERGE operations and a dataflow graph to achieve a MERGE operation using two BRANCH operations.

10.3 Identify the situations in which both fields of a two-field tag, activation name and index, would need to change.

10.4 Determine the computation performed by the SISAL code segment:

```
FOR x IN data
RETURNS
    VALUE OF SUM x
END FOR
```

where data is a stream of integers.

10.5 The following is a code segment written in the VAL language:

```
FORALL i IN [1,n]
    x := IF i = 2 THEN x
    EVAL PLUS x*i
    PLUS x
ENDALL
```

which is similar to SISAL. Deduce the computation performed.

10.6 Draw a dataflow graph for the SISAL program:

```
FOR i IN 1,n
    x := IF (i/2)*2 = i THEN x
    RETURNS SUM OF x
END FOR
```

10.7 Write a program in SISAL to perform matrix multiplication of two $n \times n$ matrices.

10.8 Write a SISAL program to compute the numerical integration of a function $f(x)$ by dividing the integral into small areas and computing each area using trapezoidal approximation (see Section 9.2.2).

10.9 Draw dataflow graphs for the C programs:

(a)   if ((a == b) && (c < d)) c = c - a;
        else c = c + a;

(b)   for (i = 1; i < m; i++)
        d[i] = 0;
        for (j = 1; j < n; j++) d[i] = c[i] + a[i]b[i];

Rewrite (a) in SISAL.

10.10 Design a VLSI array dataflow system using a north-south-east-west mesh interconnection pattern. Give details of the instruction memory and matching logic.

10.11 Make a study of the viability of a variable grain dataflow system on a shared memory multiprocessor system. What types of hardware support would you envisage being required?

10.12 Discuss how a message-passing multiprocessor system could operate on dataflow principles.

References and further reading

Abraham, S. and K. Padmanabhan (1989), "Performance of the direct binary n-cube network for multiprocessors", *IEEE Trans. Comput.*, **38**, no. 7, 1000–11.

Adams, G., D. Agrawal and H. Siegel (1987), "A survey and comparison of fault-tolerant multistage interconnection networks", *IEEE Trans. Comput.*, **C-20**, no. 6, 1–29.

Advanced Micro Devices (1988), *32-bit Microprogrammable Products Am29C300/29300*, Data Book, Sunnyvale, California.

Adve, S and M. Hill (1990), "Weak ordering – a new definition", *Proc. 17th Annual Int. Symp. on Comp. Arch.*, 2–14.

Agarwal, A., M. Horowitz and J. Hennessy (1989), "An analytical cache model", *ACM Trans. Comp. Syst.*, **7**, no. 2, 184–215.

Agarwal, A., *et al.* (1988), "An evaluation of directory schemes for cache coherence", *Proc. 15th Int. Symp. Comput. Arch.*, 280–9.

Agrawal, P. D., V. K. Janakiram and G. C. Pathak (1986), "Evaluating the performance of multicomputer configurations", *IEEE Computer*, **19**, no. 5, 23–7.

Allan, S. J. and R. R. Oldehoeft (1985), "HEP SISAL: Parallel functional programming", in *MIMD Computation: The HEP supercomputer and its applications*, J. S. Kowalik (ed.), MIT Press: Cambridge, Massachusetts, 123–50.

Almasi, G. S. and A. Gottlieb (1994), *Highly Parallel Computing* (2nd ed.), Benjamin/Cummings Publishing Company, Inc.: Redwood City, California.

Amdahl, G. (1967), "Validity of the single-processor approach to achieving large-scale computing capabilities". *Proc. 1967 AFIPS Conf.*, **30**, p. 483.

Andrews, G. R. (1991), *Concurrent Programming*, Benjamin/Cummings Publishing Company Inc.: Redwood City, California.

Andrews, G. R. and F. B. Schneider (1983), "Concepts and notations for concurrent programming", *Computer Surveys*, **5**, no. 1, 3–43.

Arvind and R. S. Nikhil (1990), "Executing a program on the MIT tagged-token dataflow architecture", *IEEE Trans. Comput.*, **39**, no. 3, 300–18.

Athas, W. C. and C. L. Seitz (1988), "Multicomputers: Message-passing concurrent computers", *IEEE Computer*, **21**, no. 8, 9–24.

August, M. C., G. M. Brost, C. C. Hsiung and A. J. Schiffleger (1989), "Cray X-MP: The birth of a supercomputer", *IEEE Computer*, **22**, no. 1, 45–52.

Ayyad, A. and B. Wilkinson (1987), "Multiprocessor scheme with application to macrodataflow", *Microprocessors Microsyst.*, **11**, no. 5, 255–63.

Babb II, R. G. (1984), "Parallel processing with large-grain data flow techniques", *IEEE Computer*,

17, no. 7, 55—61.

Babb II, R. G. (1985), "Programming the HEP with large-grain data flow techniques", in *MIMD Computation: The HEP supercomputer and its applications*, J. S. Kowalik (ed.), MIT Press: Cambridge, Massachusetts, 203–27.

Babb II, R. G. (ed.) (1988), *Programming Parallel Processors*, Addison-Wesley: Reading, Massachusetts.

Bacon, J. (1992), *Concurrent Systems, An Integrated Approach to Operating Systems, Database, and Distributed Systems*, Addison-Wesley: Wokingham, England.

Baer, J.-L. (1980), *Computer Systems Architecture*, Computer Science Press: Rockville, Maryland.

Banning, J. (1979), "Z-bus and peripheral support packages tie distributed computer systems together", *Electronic Design*, **27**, no. 24.

Barron, I., P. Cavill and D. May (1983), "Transputer does 10 or more MIPS even when not used in parallel", *Electronics*, November, 109–15.

Baskett, F. and A. J. Smith (1976), "Interference in multiprocessor computer systems with interleaved memory", *Comm. ACM*, **19**, 327–34.

Batcher, K. E. (1980), "Design of a massively parallel processor", *IEEE Trans. Comput.*, **C-29**, 836–40.

Beetem, J., M. Denneau and D. Weingarten (1987), "The GF11 parallel computer", in *Experimental Parallel Computer Architectures*, J. J. Dongarra (ed.), North-Holland: Amsterdam, 255–98.

Beivide, R., E. Herrada, J. L. Balcázar and A. Arruabarrena (1991), "Optimal distance networks of low degree for parallel computers", *IEEE Trans. Comput.*, **40**, no. 10, 1109–24.

Belady, L. (1966), "A study of replacement algorithms for a virtual-store computer", *IBM Systems Journal*, **5**, no. 2, 78–101.

Bell, J., D. Casasent and C. G. Bell (1974), "An investigation of alternative cache organizations", *IEEE Trans. Comput.*, **C-23**, no. 4, 346–51.

Ben-Ari, M. (1990), *Principles of Concurrent and Distributed Programming*, Prentice Hall: New York.

Benes, V. E. (1965), *Mathematical Theory of Connecting Networks and Telephone Traffic*, Academic Press: New York.

Bernstein, A. J. (1966), "Analysis of programs for parallel processing", *IEEE Trans. Elec. Comput.*, **E-15**, 746–57.

Bertsekas, D. P. and J. N. Tsitsiklis, (1989), *Parallel and Distributed Computation Numerical Methods*, Prentice Hall: Englewood Cliffs, New Jersey.

Bhandarkar, D. P. (1975), "Analysis of memory interference in multiprocessors", *IEEE Trans. Comput.*, **C-24**, no. 9, 897–908.

Bhuyan, L. N. (1985), "An analysis of processor-memory interconnection networks", *IEEE Trans. Comput.*, **C-34**, no. 3, 279–83.

Bhuyan, L. N. (1987), "Interconnection networks for parallel and distributed processing", *IEEE Computer*, **20**, no. 5, 9–12.

Bhuyan, L. N. and D. P. Agrawal (1983), "Design and performance of generalized interconnection networks", *IEEE Trans. Comput.*, **C-32**, no. 12, 1081–9.

Bhuyan, L. N. and D. P. Agrawal (1984), "Generalized hypercube and hyperbus structures for a computer network", *IEEE Trans. Comput.*, **C-33**, no. 1, 323–33.

Blevins, D. W., E. W. Davis, R. A. Heaton and J. H. Reif (1988), "Blitzen: A highly integrated massively parallel machine", *Proc. 2nd Sym. Frontiers of Massively Parallel Computations*, October, Fairfax, Virginia.

Böhn, A. P. W. and J. R. Gurd (1990), "Iterative instructions in the Manchester dataflow computer", *IEEE Trans. Par. Distrib. Syst.*, **1**, no. 2, 129–39.

Böhm, A. P. W. and J. Sargeant (1989), "Code optimization for tagged-token dataflow machines", *IEEE Trans. Comput.*, **38**, no. 1, 4–14.

Bouknight, W. J., S. A. Denenberg, D. E. McIntyre, J. M. Randall, A. H. Sameh and D. L. Slotnick (1972), "The Illiac IV system", *Proc. IEEE*, April, 369–88. Reprinted (1982), in *Computer Structures Principles and Examples*, D. P. Siewiorek, C. G. Bell and A. Newell, McGraw-Hill: New York.

Brawer, S. (1989), *Introduction to Parallel Programming*, Academic Press Inc.: San Diego, California.

Broomell, G. and J. R. Heath (1983), "Classification categories and historical development of circuit switching topologies", *Computing Surveys*, **15**, no. 2, 95–133.

Buehrer, R. and K. Ekanadham (1987), "Incorporating data flow ideas into von Neumann processors for parallel execution", *IEEE Trans. Comput.*, **C-36**, no. 12, 1515–22.

Burns, A. (1988), *Programming in Occam 2*, Addison-Wesley: Wokingham, England.

Burns, A. and G. Davies (1993), *Concurrent Programming*, Addison-Wesley: Wokingham, England.

Buzbee, B. (1984), "Parallel processing makes tough demands", *Computer Design*, September, 137–40.

Carriero, N. and D. Gelernter (1990), *How to Write Parallel Programs*, MIT Press: Cambridge, Massachusetts.

Chaiken, D., C. Fields, K. Kurihara and A. Agarwal (1990), "Directory-based cache coherence in large-scale multiprocessors", *IEEE Computer*, **23**, no. 6, 49–58.

Chaitin, G. J., M. A. Auslander, A. K. Chandra, J. Cocke, M. E. Hopkins and P. W. Markstein (1981), "Register allocation via coloring", *Computer Languages*, **6**, 47–57.

Chandy, K. M. and S. Taylor (1992), *An Introduction to Parallel Programming*, Jones and Bartlett Publishers: Boston, MA.

Chang, D. Y., D. J. Kuck and D. H. Lawrie (1977), "On the effective bandwidth of parallel memories", *IEEE Trans. Comput.*, **C-26**, no. 5, 480–90.

Chen, T. C. (1980), "Overlap and pipeline processing", in *Introduction to Computer Architecture*, H. S. Stone *et al.*, 2nd ed., SRA: Chicago, 427–85.

Cheng, H. (1989), "Vector pipelining, chaining and speed on the IBM 3090 and Cray X-MP", *IEEE Computer*, **22**, no. 9, 31–46.

Cheong, H. and A. V. Veidenbaum (1990), "Compiler-directed cache management in multiprocessors", *IEEE Computer*, **23**, no. 6, 39–47.

Chu, W. W. and H. Opderbeck (1976), "Program behavior and the page-fault-frequency replacement algorithm", *IEEE Computer*, **9**, no. 11, 29–38.

Clark, D. W. and J. S. Emer (1985), "Performance of the VAX-11/780 translation buffer: Simulation and measurement", *ACM Trans. Comput. Syst.*, **3**, no. 2, 31–62.

Codenotti, B. and M. Leoncini (1992), *Introduction to Parallel Processing*, Addison- Wesley: Wokingham, England.

Conti, C. J., D. H. Gibson and S. H. Pikowsky (1968), "Structural aspects of the system 360/85: General organization", *IBM Systems Journal*, 2–14.

Conway, M. E. (1963), "A multiprocessor system design", *Proc. AFIPS Fall Joint Computer Conf.*, **4**, 139–46.

Cragon, H. G. (1992), *Branch Strategy Taxonomy and Performance Models*, IEEE Computer Society Press: Los Alamitos, California.

Dally, W. and C. L. Seitz (1987), "Deadlock-free message routing in multiprocessor interconnection networks", *IEEE Trans. Comput.*, **C-36**, no. 5, 547–53.

Das, C. R. and L. N. Bhuyan (1985), "Bandwidth availability of multiple-bus multiprocessors",

IEEE Trans. Comput., **C-34**, no. 10, 918–26.

Das, R., K. Mukhopadhyaya and B. P. Sinha (1994), "A new family of bridged and twisted hypercubes", *IEEE Trans. Comput.*, 43, no. 10, 1240–7.

Dasgupta, S. (1990), "A hierarchical taxonomic system for computer architectures", *IEEE Computer*, **23**, no. 3, 674.

Davidson, E. S. (1971), "The design and control of pipelined function generators", *Proc. 1971 Int. Conf. on Systems, Networks and Computers*, Oaxtepec, Mexico, 19–21.

Denning, P. J. (1968), "The working set model for program behavior", *Comm. ACM*, **11**, no. 11, 323–33.

Denning, P. J. (1970), "Virtual memory", *Computing Surveys*, **2**, no. 3, 153–89.

Denning, P. J. (1980), "Working sets past and present", *IEEE Trans. Soft. Eng.*, **SE-6**, no. 1, 684.

Denning, P. J. and D. R. Slutz (1978), "Generalized working sets for segmented reference strings", *Comm. ACM*, **21**, no. 9, 750–9.

Dennis, J. B. (1974), "First version of a data flow procedure language", *Lecture Notes in Computer Science*, **19**, 362.

Dettmer, R. (1985), "Chip architecture for parallel processing", *Electronics and Power*, March, 227–31.

Dijkstra, E. W. (1968), "Cooperating sequential processes", in *Programming Languages*, F. Genuys (ed.), Academic Press: New York, 43–112.

Dubois, M., C. Scheurich and F. A. Briggs (1988), "Synchronization, coherence and event ordering in multiprocessors", *IEEE Computer*, **21**, no. 2, 9–21.

Duncan, R. (1986), *Advanced MSDOS*, Microsoft Press: Redmond, Washington.

Easton, M. E. and P. A. Franaszek (1979), "Use bit scanning in replacement decisions", *IEEE Trans. Comput.*, **C-28**, no. 2, 133–41.

Efe, K. (1991), "A variation on the hypercube with lower diameter", *IEEE Trans. Comput.*, **40**, no. 11, 1312–16.

Efe, K. (1992), "The cross cube architecture for parallel computations", *IEEE Trans. Par. Distrib. Syst.*, **3**, no. 5, 513–24.

El-Amawy, A. and S. Latifi (1991), "Properties and performance of folded hypercubes", *IEEE Trans. Par. Distrib. Syst.*, **2**, no. 1, 31–42.

Estahanian, A.-H., L. M. Ni and B. E. Sagan (1991) "The twisted *n*-cube with application to multiprocessing", *IEEE Trans. Comput.*, **40**, no. 1, 88–93.

Farquhar, E. and P. Bunce (1994), *The MIPS Programmer's Handbook*, Morgan Kaufmann Publishers: San Francisco, California.

Feldman, J. M. and C. T. Retter (1994), *Computer Architecture, A Designer's Text Based on a Generic RISC*, McGraw-Hill: New York.

Feng, T.-Y. (1972), "Some characteristics of associative/parallel processing", *Proc. 1972 Sagamore Computing Conf.*, 5–16.

Feng, T.-Y. (1981), "A survey of interconnection networks", *IEEE Computer*, **14**, no. 12, 1 2–27.

Fernbach. S. (ed.) (1986), *Supercomputers Class VI Systems, Hardware and Software*, North Holland: Amsterdam.

Fisher, J. A. (1984), "The VLIW machine: A multiprocessor for compiling scientific code", *IEEE Computer*, **17**, no. 7, 45–54.

Flynn, M. J. (1966), "Very high speed computing systems", *Proc. IEEE*, **12**, 1901–9.

Flynn, M. J. (1995), *Computer Architecture Pipelined and Parallel Processor Design*, Jones and Bartlett Publishers: Boston, Massachusetts.

Foster, I. (1995), *Designing and Building Parallel Programs*, Addison-Wesley: Reading, Massachusetts.

Fox, G., M. Johnson, G. Lyzenga, S. Otto, J. Salmon and D. Walker (1988), *Solving Problems on Concurrent Processors, Vol. 1*, Prentice Hall: Englewood Cliffs, New Jersey.

Gabriel, J., T. Lindholm, E. L. Lusk and R. A. Overbeek (1985), "Logic programming on the HEP", in *MIMD Computation: The HEP supercomputer and its applications*, J. S. Kowalik (ed.), MIT Press: Cambridge, Massachusetts, 181–202.

Gajski, D., D. Kuck, D. Lawrie and A. Sameh (1983), "Cedar: A large scale multiprocessor", *Proc. 1983 Int. Conf. on Parallel Processing*, IEEE, 524–9.

Gajski, D. and J.-K. Peir (1985), "Essential issues in multiprocessor systems", *IEEE Computer*, **18**, no. 6, 9–27.

Gehani, N. and A. D. McGettrick (eds.) (1988), *Concurrent Programming*, Addison-Wesley: Wokingham, England.

Geist, A., A. Beguelin, J. Dongarra, W. Jiang, R. Manchek and V. Sunderam (1994a), *PVM3 User's Guide and Reference Manual*, Oak Ridge National Laboratory: Tennessee.

Geist, A., A. Beguelin, J. Dongarra, W. Jiang, R. Manchek and V. Sunderam (1994b), *PVM: Parallel Virtual Machine*, The MIT Press: Cambridge, Massachusetts.

Gimarc, C. E. and V. M. Milutinovic (1987), "A survey of RISC processors and computers of the mid 1980s", *IEEE Computer*, **20**, no. 9, 59–69.

Glauert, J. R. W., J. R. Gurd and C. C. Kirkham (1985), "Evolution of a dataflow architecture", in *Concurrent Languages in Distributed Systems*, G. L. Reijns and E. L. Daglass (eds.), Elsevier Science Publishers. B.V.: North-Holland, 1–15.

Goodman, J. R. and C. H. Séquin (1981), "Hypertree: A multiprocessor interconnection topology", *IEEE Trans. Comput.*, **C-30**, no. 12, 923–33.

Goodman, J. R. (1983), "Using cache memory to reduce processor-memory traffic," *Proc. 10th Symp. Comp. Arch.*, 124–31.

Gopal, I. S. (1985), "Prevention of store-and-forward deadlock in computer networks," *IEEE Trans. Comm.*, **COM-33**, no. 12, 1258–64.

Gottlieb, A., R. Grishman, C. P. Kruskal, K. P. McAuliffe, L. Rudolph and M. Snir (1983), "The NYU ultracomputer: designing an MIMD shared memory parallel computer", *IEEE Trans. Comput.*, **C-32**, no. 2, 175–89.

Goyal, A. and T. Agerwala (1984), "Performance analysis of future shared storage systems", *IBM J. Res. Develop.*, **28**, no. 1, 95–107.

Green, A. G. and P. E. Wright (1991), "Design and analysis of master/slave multiprocessors", *IEEE Trans. Comput.*, **40**, no. 8, 963–76.

Grimsdale, R. L. (1984), "Programming languages", in *Distributed Computing*, F. B. Chambers, D. A. Duce and G. P. Jones (eds.), Academic Press: London.

Gropp, W., E. Lusk, and A. Skjellum (1994), *Using MPI Portable Parallel Programming with the Message-Passing Interface*, MIT Press: Cambridge, Massachusetts.

Grossman, C. P. (1985), "Cache-DASD storage design for improving system performance", *IBM Systems Journal*, **24**, no. 314, 316–34.

Gupta, A. (ed.) (1987), *Multi-Microprocessors*, IEEE Press: New York.

Gupta, A. and H.-M. D. Toong (1985), "Increasing throughput of multiprocessor systems", *IEEE Trans. Ind. Electronics*, **IE-32**, no. 3, 267.

Gurd, J. R., C. C. Kirkharn and I. Watson (1985), "The Manchester prototype dataflow computer", *Comm. ACM*, **28**, no. 1, 34–52.

Gurd, J. R. and I. Watson (1980), "Data driven system for high speed parallel computing: Part 2 – Hardware design", *Computer Design*, July, 97–106.

Hagwersen, E., A. Landin and S. Haridi (1992), "DDM – A cache-only memory architecture", *IEEE Computer*, **25**, no. 9, 44–54.

Halfhill, T. R. (1995), "Intel's P6", *Byte*, **20**, no. 4, 42–58.

Hallin, T. G. and M. J. Flynn (1972), "Pipelining of arithmetic functions", *IEEE Trans. Comput.*, August, 880–6.

Händler, W. (1977), "The impact of classification schemes on computer architecture", *Proc. Int. Conf. Parallel Processing*, August, 7–15.

Hayes, J. P. (1988), *Computer Architecture and Organization*, 2nd ed., McGraw-Hill: New York.

Hellerman, H. (1966), "On the average speed of a multiple-module storage system", *IEEE Trans. Electronic Comput.*, August, 670.

Hennessy, J. L. (1984), "VLSI processor architecture", *IEEE Trans. Comput.*, **C-33**, no. 12, 1221–46.

Hennessy, J. L. and D. A. Patterson (1990), *Computer Architecture: A Quantitative Approach*, Morgan Kaufmann: San Mateo, California.

Hennessy, J. L. and D. A. Patterson (1994), *Computer Organization & Design, the Hardware/Software Interface*, Morgan Kaufmann: San Mateo, California.

Hilberts, P. A. J., M. R. J. Koopman and J. L. A. van de Snepscheut (1987), "The twisted cube" in *Parallel Architectures and Languages Europe, Lecture Notes in Computer Science*, Berlin: Springer-Verlag, 152–9.

Hill, M. D. (1988), "A case for direct-mapped caches", *IEEE Computer*, **21**, no. 12, 25–40.

Hillis, W. D. (1985), *The Connection Machine*, MIT Press: Cambridge, Massachusetts.

Hoare, C. A. R. (1974), "Monitors: An operating system structuring concept", *Comm. ACM*, **17**, no. 10, 549–57.

Hoare, C. A. R. (1978), "Communicating sequential processes", *Comm. ACM*, 21, no. 8, 666–77.

Hodges, A. (1983), *Allan Turing the Enigma*, Simon and Schuster: New York.

Holliday, M. A. and M. K. Vernon (1987), "Exact performance estimates for multiprocessor memory and bus interference", *IEEE Trans. Comput.*, **C-36**, no. 1, 76–84.

Hoogendoorn, C. H. (1977), "A general model for memory interference in multiprocessors", *IEEE Trans. Comput.*, **C-26**, no. 10, 998–1005.

Howe, C. D. and B. Moxon (1987), "How to program parallel processors", *IEEE Spectrum*, **24**, no. 9, 36–41.

Hughes, J. (1989), "Why functional programming matters", *The Computer Journal*, **32**, no. 2, 98–107.

Hwang, K. (1979), "Global and modular two's complement cellular array multipliers", *IEEE Trans. Comput.*, **C-28**, no. 4, 300–6.

Hwang, K. (1985), "Multiprocessor supercomputers for scientific/engineering applications", *IEEE Computer*, **18**, no. 6, 57–73.

Hwang, K. (1993), *Advanced Computer Architecture, Parallelism, Scalability, Programmability*, McGraw-Hill: New York.

Hwang, K. and F. A. Briggs (1984), *Computer Architecture and Parallel Processing*, McGraw-Hill: New York.

Hwang, K., J. Ghosh and R. Chowkwanyun (1987), "Computer architectures for artificial intelligence processing", *IEEE Computer*, **20**, no. 1, 19–27.

Hwang, K., P.-S. Tseng and D. Kim (1989), "An orthogonal multiprocessor for parallel scientific computations", *IEEE Trans. Comput.*, **38**, no. 1, 47–61.

Hwu, W. W. and Y. N. Patt (1987), "Checkpoint repair for high performance out-of-order execution machines", *IEEE Trans. Comput.*, **C-36**, no. 12, 1496–1514.

Hwu, W.-M. and P. P. Chang (1992), "Efficient instruction sequencing with inline target insertion", *IEEE Trans. Comput.*, **41**, no. 12, 1537–51.

Inmos Ltd. (1984a), "IMS T424 transputer preliminary data", Bristol, England.

Inmos Ltd. (1984b), *Occam Programming Manual*, Prentice Hall: Englewood Cliffs, New Jersey.

Inmos Ltd. (1986), *Transputer Reference Manual*, Bristol, England.

Inmos Ltd. (1987), *IMS T800 Architecture*, Technical Note 6, Bristol, England.

Intel Corp. (1987a), *80286 High Performance Microprocessor with Memory Management and Protection*, Santa Clara, California.

Intel Corp. (1987b), *82385 High-Performance 32-bit Cache Controller Architectural Overview*, Santa Clara, California.

Intel Corp. (1992a), *Intel486™ Microprocessor Family Programmer's Reference Manual 1992*, Mt. Prospect, IL.

Intel Corp. (1992b), *i860™ Microprocessor Family Programmer's Reference Manual 1992*, Mt. Prospect, IL.

Intel Corp. (1994a), *Microprocessors: Volume I Intel386™ 80286 & 8086 Microprocessor 1994*, Mt. Prospect, IL.

Intel Corp. (1994b), *Microprocessors: Volume II Intel486™ Microprocessor 1994*, Mt. Prospect, IL.

Intel Corp. (1994c), *Microprocessors: Volume III Pentium™ Processors 1994*, Mt. Prospect, IL.

Irani, K. B. and I. H. Önyüksel (1984), "A closed-form solution for the performance analysis of multiple-bus multiprocessor systems", *IEEE Trans. Comput.*, **C-33**, no. 11, 1004–12.

JáJá, J. (1992), *An Introduction to Parallel Algorithms*, Addison Wesley: Reading Massachusetts.

Johnson, M. (1991), *Superscalar Microprocessor Design*, Prentice Hall: Englewood Cliffs, New Jersey.

Jordan, H. F. (1985), "HEP architecture programming and performance", in *MIMD Computation: The HEP supercomputer and its applications*, J. S. Kowalik (ed.), MIT Press: Cambridge, Massachusetts, 1–40.

Jouppi, N. P. and D. W. Wall (1989), "Available instruction-level parallelism for superscalar and superpipelined machines", *Int. Conf. on Architectural Support for Programming Languages and Operating Systems*, 272–82.

Jump, J. R. and S. R. Ahuja (1978), "Effective pipelining of digital systems", *IEEE Trans. Comput.*, **C-27**, no. 9, 855–65.

Karp, A. H. (1987), "Programming for parallelism", *IEEE Computer*, **20**, no. 5, 43–51.

Karp, R. M. and R. E. Miller (1966), "Properties of a model for parallel computations: Determinacy, termination, queueing", *SIAM Journal of Applied Mathematics*, **14**, no. 6, 1390.

Katevenis, M. G. H. (1985), *Reduced Instruction Set Computer Architectures for VLSI*, MIT Press: Cambridge, Massachusetts.

Katseff, H. P. (1988), "Incomplete hypercubes", *IEEE Trans. Comput.*, **37**, no. 5, 604–8.

Katz, R. H., G. A. Gibson and D. A. Patterson (1989) "Disk system architectures for high performance computing," *Proc IEEE*, **77**, 1842–58.

Kernighan, B. W. and D. M. Ritchie (1988), *The C Programming Language* (2nd ed.), Prentice Hall: Englewood Cliffs, New Jersey.

Kilburn, T., D. B. G. Edwards, M. J. Lanigan and F. H. Sumner (1962), "One-level storage system", *IRE Trans.*, **EC-11**, 223–35. Reprinted (1982), in *Computer Structures Principles and Examples*, D. P. Siewiorek, C. G. Bell and A. Newell, McGraw-Hill: New York.

Kogge, P. M. (1981), *The Architecture of Pipelined Computers*, McGraw-Hill: New York.

Koren, I., B. Mendelson, I. Peled and G. M. Silberman (1988), "A data-driven VLSI array for arbitrary algorithms", *IEEE Computer*, **21**, no. 10, 30–43.

Krishnamoorthy, M. S. and B. Krishnamurthy (1987), "Fault diameter of interconnection networks", *Comput. Math. Appl.*, **13**, no 5/6, 577–82.

Krothapalli, V. P. and P. Sadayappan (1991), "Removal of redundant dependencies in DOACROSS loops with constant dependencies", *IEEE Trans. Par. Distrib. Syst.*, **2**, no. 3, 281–9.

Kumar, V., A. Grama, A. Gupta, and G. Karypis (1994), *Introduction to Parallel Computing*, Benjamin/Cummings Publishing Company Inc.: Redwood City, California.

Kung, H. T. (1982), "Why systolic architectures", *IEEE Computer*, **15**, no. 1, 37–46.

Kung, S.-Y., K. S. Arun, R. J. Gal-Ezer and D. V. B. Rao (1982), "Wavefront array processor: Language, architecture and applications", *IEEE Trans. Comput.*, **C-31**, no. 11,1054–65.

Lamport, L. (1974). "The parallel execution of DO loops", *Comm. ACM*, **17**, no. 2, 83–93.

Lamport, L. (1979), "How to make a multiprocessor computer that correctly executes multiprocess programs", *IEEE Trans. Comput.*, **C-28**, no. 9, 690–1.

Lang, G. R., M. Dharssi, F. M. Longstaff, P. S. Longstaff, P. A. S. Metford and M. T. Rimmer (1988), "An optimum parallel architecture for high-speed real-time digital signal processing", *IEEE Computer*, **21**, no. 2, 47–57.

Lang, T., M. Valero and I. Alegre (1982), "Bandwidth of crossbar and multiple-bus connections for multiprocessors", *IEEE Trans. Comput.*, **C-31**, no. 12, 1227–34.

Lang, T., M. Valero and M. A. Fiol (1983), "Reduction of connections for multibus organizations", *IEEE Trans. Comput.*, **C-32**, no. 8, 707–16.

Lea, R. M. (1986), "VLSI and WSI associative string processors for cost-effective parallel processing", *The Computer Journal*, **29**, no. 6, 486–94.

Leighton, F. T. (1992), *Introduction to Parallel Algorithms and Architectures*, Morgan Kaufmann Publishers, Inc.: San Mateo, California.

Leiserson, C. L. (1985), "Fat-trees: Universal networks for hardware-efficient supercomputing", *IEEE Trans. Comput.*, **C-34**, no. 10, 892–901.

Lester, B. (1993), *The Art of Parallel Programming*, Prentice Hall: Englewood Cliffs, New Jersey.

Lewis, T. G. and H. El-Rewini (1992), *Introduction to Parallel Computing*, Prentice Hall: Englewood Cliffs, New Jersey.

Lilja, D. J. (1988), "Reducing the branch penalty in pipelined processors", *IEEE Computer*, **21**, no. 7, 47–55.

Lilja, D. J. (1991), *Architectural Alternatives for Exploiting Parallelism*, IEEE Computer Society Press: Los Alamitos, California.

Lipovski, G. J. and M. Malek (1987), *Parallel Computing Theory and Comparisons*, Wiley: New York.

Liskov, B., M. Herlihy and L. Gilbert (1988), "Limitations of synchronous communication with static process structure in languages for distributed computing", in *Concurrent Programming*, N. Gehani and A. D. McGettrick (eds.), Addison-Wesley: Wokingham, England, 545–64.

Liu, Y.-C. and C.-J. Jou (1987), "Effective memory bandwidth and processor blocking probability in multiple-bus systems", *IEEE Trans. Comput.*, **C-36**, no. 6, 761–4.

Mano, N. M. (1982), *Computer System Architecture*, Prentice Hall: Englewood Cliffs, New Jersey.

Maruyama, K. (1975), "mLRU page replacement algorithm in terms of the reference matrix", *IBM Tech. Disclosure Bulletin*, **17**, no. 10, 3101–3.

Matsen, F. A. and T. Tajima (eds.) (1986), *Supercomputers, and Scientific Computations*, University of Texas Press: Austin, Texas.

Mattos, P. (1987a), "Applying the transputer", *Electronics and Power*, June, 397–401.

Mattos, P. (1987b), "Program design for concurrent systems", Inmos Ltd., Technical Note 5, Bristol, England.

May, D. (1987), *Occam 2 Language Definition*, Inmos Ltd.: Bristol, England.

May, D. and R. Taylor (1984), "OCCAM: an overview", *Microprocessors Microsyst.*, **8**, no. 2, 73–80.

Maytal, B., S. Iacobovici, D. B. Alpert, D. Biran, J. Levy and S. Y. Tov (1989), "Design considerations for a general-purpose microprocessor", *IEEE Computer*, **22**, no. 1, 66–76.

McGraw, J. R. (1982), "The VAL language: description and analysis", *ACM Trans. Program. Lang. Syst.*, **4**, no. 1, 44–82.

Microsoft Inc. (1987), *Microsoft Macro Assembler 5.1 Microsoft CodeView and Utilities*, Microsoft Press: Redmond, Washington.

Milulinovic, V. M. (1989), *High Level Language Computer Archiectures*, Computer Science Press, Freeman and Co.: New York.

Moldovan, D. I. (1993), *Parallel Processing from Applications to Systems*, Morgan Kaufmann: San Mateo, California.

Motorola Inc. (1984), *MC68000 16-32-bit Microprocessor Programmer's Reference Manual*, 4th ed.

Motorola Inc. (1988a), *MC88100 RISC Microprocessor User's Manual*, Phoenix, Arizona.

Motorola Inc. (1988b), *MC88200 Cache/Memory Management Unit User's Manual*, Phoenix, Arizona.

Motorola Inc. (1989), *MC68040 32-bit Microprocessor User's Manual*, Phoenix, Arizona.

Mudge, T. N., J. P. Hayes, G. D. Buzzard and D. C. Winsor (1984), "Analysis of multiple bus interconnection networks", *Proc. 1984 Int. Conf. on Parallel Processing*, IEEE, 228–32.

National Semiconductor Inc. (1981), *COP2440/COP2441/COP2442 and COP2340/COP2341/ COP2342 Single-Chip Dual CPU Microcontrollers*.

Nelson, J. C. C. and M. K. Refai (1984), "Design of a hardware arbiter for multimicroprocessor systems", *Microprocessors Microsyst.*, **8**, no. 1, 21–4.

Ni, L. M. and P. K. McKinley (1993), "A survey of wormhole routing techniques in direct networks", *IEEE Computer*, **26**, no. 2, 62–76.

Ottenstein, K. J. (1985), "A brief survey of implicit parallelism detection", in *MIMD Computation: The HEP supercomputer and its applications*, J. S. Kowalik (ed.), MIT Press: Cambridge, Massachusetts, 93–122.

Oxley, D. (1981), "Motivation for a combined data flow-control flow processor", *25th Annual Symposium of the Society of Photo-Optical Instrumentation Engineers – Sessions on Real-Time Signal Processing IV*, San Diego, California, 305–11.

Padua, D. A., D. J. Kuck and D. H. Lawrie (1980), "High-speed multiprocessors and compilation techniques", *IEEE Trans. Comput.*, **C-29**, no. 9, 763–76.

Padua, D. A. and M. J. Wolfe (1986), "Advanced compiler optimizations for supercomputers", *Comm. ACM*, **29**, no. 12, 1184–1201.

Padmanabhan, K. (1991), "Design and analysis of even-sized binary shuffle-exchange networks for multiprocessors", *IEEE Trans. Par. Distrib. Syst.*, **2**, no. 4, 385–97.

Pase, D. M. and A. R. Larrabee (1988), "Intel iPSC Concurrent Computer", in *Programming Parallel Processors*, R. G. Babb II (ed.), Addison-Wesley: Reading, Massachusetts, 105–23.

Patel, J. H. (1981), "Performance of processor-memory interconnections for multiprocessors", *IEEE Trans. Comput.*, **C-30**, 771–80.

Patterson, D. A. (1985), "Reduced instruction set computers", *Comm. ACM*, **28**, no. 1, 8–21.

Patterson, D. A. and J. L. Hennessy (1985), "Response to 'computers, complexity and controversy'", *IEEE Computer*, **18**, no. 11, 142–3.

Patton, P. C. (1985), "Multiprocessors: architecture and applications", *IEEE Computer*, **18**, no. 5, 29–40.

Paul, G. and G. S. Almasi (eds.) (1988), *Parallel Systems and Computations*, North-Holland: Amsterdam.

Pease III, M. C. (1977), "The indirect binary *n*-cube microprocessor array", *IEEE Trans. Comput.*, **C-26**, no. 5, 458–73.

Perleberg, C. H. and A. J. Smith (1993), "Branch target buffer design and optimization", *IEEE Trans. Comput.*, **42**, no. 4, 396–412.

Perrott, R. H. and A. Zarea-Aliabadi (1986), "Supercomputer languages", *Computing Surveys*, **18**, no. 1, 5–22.

Peyton Jones, S. L. (1989), "Parallel implementation of functional programming languages", *The Computer Journal*, **32**, no. 2, 175–86.

Pfister, G. F. and V. A. Norton (1985), "Hot spot contention and combining in multistage interconnection networks", *IEEE Trans. Comput.*, **C-34**, no. 10, 943–8.

Pohm, A. V. and O. P. Agrawal (1983), *High-speed Memory Systems*, Reston: Virginia.

Polychronopoulos, C. D. (1988), *Parallel Programming and Compilers*, Kluwer Academic: Norwell, MA.

Prieve, B. G. and R. S. Fabry (1976), "VMIN: an optimal variable-space page replacement algorithm", *Comm. ACM*, **19**, no. 5, 295–7.

Quinn, M. J. (1994), *Parallel Computing Theory and Practice*, McGraw-Hill: New York.

Radin, G. (1983), "The 801 minicomputer", *IBM J. Res. Develop.*, **27**, no. 3, 237–46.

Raghavendra, C. S. and A. Varma (1986), "Fault-tolerant multiprocessors with redundant path interconnection networks", *IEEE Trans. Comput.*, **C-35**, no. 4, 307–16.

Ravi, C. V. (1972), "On the bandwidth and interference in interleaved memory systems", *IEEE Trans. Comput.*, **C21**, no. 4, 899–901.

Reed, D. A. and R. M. Fujimoto (1989), *Multicomputer Networks: Message-Based Parallel Processing*, MIT Press: Cambridge, Massachusetts.

Reddy, A. L. N. and P. Banerjee (1991), "Design, analysis, and simulation of I/O architectures for hypercube multiprocessors", *IEEE Trans. Par. Distrib. Syst.*, **1**, no. 2, 140–51.

Reddi, S. S. and E. A. Feurstel (1976), "A conceptual framework for computer architecture", *Computing Surveys*, **8**, no. 2, 277–300.

Rettberg, R. and R. Thomas (1986), "Contention is no obstacle to shared-memory multiprocessing", *Comm. ACM*, **29**, no. 12, 1202–12.

Roscoe, A. W. and C. A. R. Hoare (1986), *The Laws of Occam Programming*, Oxford University Computing Laboratory, Technical Monograph PRG-53.

Seitz, C. L. (1984), "Concurrent VLSI architectures", *IEEE Trans. Comput.*, **C-33**, no. 12, 1247–65.

Seitz, C. L. (1985), "The cosmic cube", *Comm. ACM*, **28**, no. 1, 22–33.

Skillicorn, D. B. (1988), "A taxonomy for computer architectures", *IEEE Computer*, **21**, no. 1 1, 46–57.

Smith, A. J. (1982), "Cache memories", *Computing Surveys*, **14**, no. 3, 473–530.

Smith, A. J. (1985), "Disk cache: miss ratio analysis and design considerations", *ACM Trans. Comput. Systems*, **3**, no. 3, 161–203.

Smith, A. J. (1987a), "Line (block) size selection in CPU cache memories", *IEEE Trans. Comput.*, **C-36**, no. 9, 1063–75.

Smith, A. J. (1987b), "Cache memory design: An evolving art", *IEEE Spectrum*, **24**, no. 12, 40–4.

Smith, J. E. and A. R. Pleszkum (1988), "Implementing precise interrupts in pipelined processors," *IEEE Trans. Comput.*, **C-37**, no. 5, 562–73.

Snyder, L. (1982), "Introduction to the configurable highly parallel computer", *IEEE Computer*, **15**, no. 1, 47–56.

Srini, V. P. (1986), "An architectural comparison of dataflow systems", *IEEE Computer*, **19**, no. 3, 68–87.

Stallings, W. (1987), *Computer Organization and Architecture*, Macmillan: New York.

Stone, H. S. *et al.* (1980), *Introduction to Computer Architecture* (2nd ed.), SRA: Chicago.

Stone, H. S. (1987), *High Performance Computer Architecture* (1st ed.), Addison-Wesley: Reading, Massachusetts.

Stone, H. S. (1993), *High Performance Computer Architecture* (3rd ed.), Addison-Wesley: Reading, Massachusetts.

Strecker, W. D. (1978), "VAX-11/780: A virtual address extension to the DEC PDP-11 family", *AFIPS Proc. NCC*, 967–80. Reprinted (1982), in *Computer Structures Principles and Examples*, by D. P. Siewiorek, C. G. Bell and A. Newell, McGraw-Hill: New York.

Strecker, W. D. (1983), "Transient behavior of cache memories", *ACM Trans. Comput. Systems*, **1**, no. 4, 281–93.

Sunderam, V. (1990), "PVM: A framework for parallel distributed computing", *Concurrency: Practice and Experience*, **2**, no. 4, 315–39.

Tabak, D. (1987), *Reduced Instruction Set Computer RISC Architecture*, Research Studies Press Ltd.: Letchworth, England.

Teller, P. J. (1990), "Translation-lookaside buffer consistency", *IEEE Computer*, **23**, no. 6, 26–36.

Tanenbaum, A. S. (1984), *Structured Computer Organization* (2nd ed.), Prentice Hall: Englewood Cliffs, New Jersey.

Tanenbaum, A. S. (1990), *Structured Computer Organization* (3rd ed.), Prentice Hall: Englewood Cliffs, New Jersey.

Terrano, A. E., S. M. Dunn and J. E. Peters (1989), "Using an architectural knowledge base to generate code for parallel computers", *Comm. ACM*, **32**, no. 9, 1065–72.

Texas Instruments (1984), *The TTL Data Book for Design Engineers*, Dallas, Texas.

Thacker, C. P., L. C. Stewart and E. H. Satterthwaite (1988), "Firefly: A multiprocessor workstation", *IEEE Trans. Comput.*, **C-37**, no. 8, 909–20.

Thiebaut, D. and H. S. Stone (1987), "Footprints in the cache", *ACM Trans. Comput. Systems*, **5**, no. 4, 305–29.

Thornton, J. E. (1970), *Design of a Computer: The Control Data 6600*, Scott, Foresman and Company: Glenview, Illinois.

Tomasevic M. and V. Milutinovic (1993), *The Cache Coherence Problem in Shared-Memory Multiprocessors: Hardware Solutions*, IEEE Computer Society Press: Los Alamitos, California.

Tomasulo, R. M. (1967), "An efficient algorithm for exploiting multiple arithmetic units", *IBM Journal*, **11**, 25–33. Reprinted (1982), in *Computer Structures Principles and Examples*, by D. P. Siewiorek, C. G. Bell and A. Newell, McGraw-Hill: New York.

Torng, H. C. and M. Day (1993), "Interrupt handling for out-of-order execution processors," *IEEE Trans. Comput.*, **42**, no. 1, 122–7.

Treleaven, P. C., D. R. Brownbridge and R. P. Hopkins (1982), "Data driven and demand driven computer architectures", *Computing Surveys*, **14**, no. 1, 93–143.

Tucker, S. G. (1986), "The IBM 3090 System: an overview", *IBM Systems Journal*, **25**, no. 1, 4–18.

Tzeng, N.-F. and H.-L. Chen (1994), "Structural and tree embedding aspects of incomplete hypercubes", *IEEE Trans. Comput.*, **43**, no. 12, 1434–44.

Varma, A., and C. S. Raghavendra (1994), *Interconnection Networks for Multiprocessors and Multicomputers: Theory and Practice*, IEEE Computer Society Press: Los Alamitos, California.

Vegdahl, S. (1984), "A survey of proposed architectures for the execution of functional languages", *IEEE Trans. Comput.*, **C-33**, no. 12, 1050–71.

Wadge, W. W. and E. A. Ashcroft (1985), *Lucid, the Dataflow Programming Language*, Academic Press: London.

Walker, W. and H. G. Cragon (1995), "Interrupt processing in concurrent processors", *IEEE Computer*, **28**, no. 6, 36–46.

Watson, I. and J. R. Gurd (1979), "A prototype data flow computer with token labelling", *AFIPS*

National Computer Conference, June 4-7, New York, 623–8.

Weiss, S. and J. E. Smith (1984), "Instruction issue logic in pipelined supercomputers", *IEEE Trans. Comput.*, **C-33**, no. 11, 1013–22.

Wilkes, M. V. (1951), "The best way to design an automatic calculating machine", *Rept. Manchester University Computer Inaugural Conf*, 16–18. Reprinted (1976), in *Computer Design Development: Principal Papers*, E. E. Schwartzenlander (ed.), Hayden: Rochelle Park, New Jersey, 266–70.

Wilkes, M. V. (1965), "Slave memories and dynamic storage allocation", *IEEE Trans. Elect. Comput.*, **41**, no. 3, 270–71.

Wilkinson, B. (1989), "Simulation of rhombic cross-bar switch networks for multiprocessors", *Proc. 20th Annual Pittsburgh Conf. on Modeling and Simulation*, 1213–18.

Wilkinson, B. (1990a), "Cascaded rhombic crossbar interconnection networks", *J. Par. Dist. Comput.*, **10**, no. 1, 96–101.

Wilkinson, B. (1990b), "Increasing the number of links in mesh and hypercube networks", unpublished paper, University of North Carolina at Charlotte.

Wilkinson, B. (1991a), "Comparative performance of overlapping connectivity multiprocessor interconnection networks", *The Computer Journal*, **34**, no. 3, 207–14.

Wilkinson, B. (1991b), "Multiple bus network with overlapping connectivity", *IEE Proceedings Pt. E: Computers and Digital Techniques*, **138**, no. 4, 281–4.

Wilkinson, B. (1992a), "Comments on 'Design and analysis of arbitration protocols' ", *IEEE Trans. Comput.* , **41**, no. 3, 348–51.

Wilkinson, B. (1992b), "Overlapping connectivity interconnection networks for shared memory multiprocessor systems", *J. Par. Dist. Comput.*, **15**, no. 1, 49–61.

Wilkinson, B. (1992c), *Digital System Design* (2nd ed.), Prentice Hall: London.

Wilkinson, B. (1993), "On crossbar switch and multiple bus interconnection networks with overlapping connectivity", *IEEE Trans. Comput*, **41**, no. 6, 738–46.

Wilkinson, B. and H. Abachi (1983), "Cross-bar switch multiprocessor system", *Microprocessors Microsyst.*, **7**, no. 2, 75–9.

Wilkinson, B. and J. M. Farmer (1994), "Reflective interconnection networks", *Comput. Elect. Eng.*, **20**, no. 4, 289–308.

Wittie, L. D. (1981), "Communication structures for large networks of microcomputers", *IEEE Trans. Comput.*, **C-30**, no. 4, 264–73.

Wong, F. S. and M. R. Ito (1984), "Design and evaluation of the event-driven computer", *Proc. IEE*, **131**, no. 6, 209–22.

Wulf, W. A. and S. P. Harbison (1978), "Reflections in a pool of processors: an experience report on C.mmp/Hydra", *Carnegie-Mellon University Dept. of Computer Science Report CMU-CS-78-103*.

Yalamanchili, S. and J. K. Aggarwal (1985), "Reconfiguration strategies for parallel architectures", *IEEE Computer*, **18**, no. 12, 44–61.

Yang, Q., L. N. Bhuyan and B.-C. Liu (1989), "Analysis and comparison of cache coherence protocols for a packet-switched multiprocessor", *IEEE Trans. Comput.*, **38**, no. 8, 1143–53.

Yen, D. W. L., J. H. Patel and E. S. Davidson (1982), "Memory interference in synchronous multiprocessor systems", *IEEE Trans. Comput.*, **C-31**, no. 11, 1116–21.

Yew, P.-C., N.-F. Teng and D. H. Lawrie (1987), "Distributing hot-spot addressing in largescale multiprocessors", *IEEE Trans. Comput.*, **C-36**, no. 4, 388–95.

Index

Absolute addressing, 9
Accessed bit, 131
Access time, 26, 80, 139, 145
   average, 82–6, 96–99
   cache, 80–6, 96–99
   memory, 80
   single bus network, 297
Accumulator, 7
Acknowledge signal, 277
Active low signal, 276
Adder:
   carry-look-ahead, 208
   full adder, 208
   parallel, 208
   ripple, 208
Address, 5
   effective, 9, 50
   lines, 18
   logical, 147
   physical, 147
   real, 117
   register, 9, 55
   return, 57
   virtual, 117
Addressing:
   absolute, 9, 32
   CISC, 30–1
   immediate, 9, 32, 46–7
   modes, 9
   PC-relative, 50
   register (direct), 9, 32, 44–7
   register indirect, 9, 32, 47–9, 55-6
Address translation:
   cache, 122, 126
   paging, 117–30
Ageing registers, 101
ALGOL-68, 257
ALICE computer system, 438
Allocate on write, cache, 97
Alpha 21164, 39
ALU (arithmetic and logic unit), 10, 42, 50, 62, 63
Amdahl's law, 247
Antidependency, 183, 258
Applied parallelism, 249
Arbitration:
   bus *see* Bus arbitration
   crossbar switch network, 301–2
   multiple bus network, 306–7
Arithmetic pipeline, 204–9
Array computer, 230, 233–6
   bit-organized, 236–8
   word-organized, 236
ASCII, 5, 43
Assembly language, 5, 45
Associative mapping, 86–8
Associative memory, 124
Associativity, 91, 125
Asymmetric multiprocessor, 240
Asynchronous message passing, 388
Asynchronous pipeline, 159
Atlas computer, 118
Average distance, in networks, 367
Average latency, 212

Babbage, 3
Backing store, 6
Backside bus, 110

Bandwidth, 22, 335, 379
  crossbar switch, 303
  multiple bus, 308
  multistage networks, 346
  overlapping networks, 311
  single bus network, 295
  static networks, 368
Base, floating point, 16, 206
Baseline network, 340
Benchmark, 14, 33
Benes' network, 339
Bernstein's conditions, 185, 258
Best fit replacement algorithm, 150
Big endian, 5
Binary tree network, 360
Bisection width, 368
Bit selection, 92
BLITZEN computer, 237
Block, cache, 83
Block address translation cache, 125
Blocking, message passing routine, 388
Blocking networks, 336
Branch bypassing, 177
Branch folding, 177
Branch history table, 178
Branch instructions, 68, 173
  array computer, 233
  effect on pipelines, 173–4
  frequency, 173, 174
  format, 49
Branch prediction logic, 177
Branch target buffer, 178
Broadcast, hypercube, 391
Broadcast instruction, array computer, 233
Broadcast writes, cache, 322–3
Burroughs' computers:
  B5000, 147
  D-825, 302
  BSP, 235
Bus, 17
  arbitration, 277–293
  asynchronous, 277
  busy signal, 277
  contention, 274
  local, 299–300
  synchronous, 277
  system, 299–300
Busy waiting, 264

Butterfly multiprocessor, 250
Byte, 5

Cache, 26, 80
  access time, 26, 80–6, 96–9
  address translation, 122, 125
  associativity, 91
  block see line
  broadcast writes, 322
  code, 26, 94
  coherence, 318, 322
  cold start, 105
  consistency, 318
  context switch misses, 105
  controller, 323, 324,
  data, 26, 94, 322
  direct mapped, 89–91
  disk, 110–12
  fetch policy, 94
  instruction see code
  invalidate, 319, 323
  line, 83
  multiprocessor system, 316
  performance 105–9
  real addresses, 141
  replacement policy, 99–104
  second level (secondary), 109–10
  sector mapped, 93
  set-associative, 91–3
  shared, 322
  unified, 26, 94
  update, 319, 323
  virtual addresses, 143
  write policy, 96–9
Cache-only memory architecture (COMA), 244
Carry (C) flag, 50
Cedar computer system, 435–6
Cell-based network, 339–42
Central processing unit (CPU), 4
Chaining, pipeline, 219
Changed bit, page, 131
Channel dependency graph, 383–7
Channel, occam, 377
Checkerboard effect, in segmentation, 150
Chordal ring network, 357
Circuit switched network, 336, 379
CISC (complex instruction set computer), 9, 30–6, 42, 173

CLIP computer, 237
Clock doubling, 16
Clock period, 13
Clock replacement algorithm, 134
Clock tripling, 16
Clos networks, 337–9
CM5, 361
C.mmp, 302
CMOS, 13
Collision vector, 212
Collision, in a pipeline, 211
Coloring, in dataflow, 423
Combining circuits, hardware, 349–51
Compare instruction, 50
Compiler, 5
  optimizing for RISCs, 35, 36
  parallelizing, 253, 260
Completely connected network, 357
Complex Instruction Set Computer *see* CISC
Computer:
  control flow, 414
  dataflow, 415
  neural, 415
  parallel, 228
  pattern driven, 415
  program, 5
  stored program, 3
  von Neumann, 4
Concurrency, 227
Concurrent programming, 228
Condition code register, 50, 73
Conditional critical section, 270
Conditional process, 407
Conditional synchronization, 270
Content addressable (CAM) memory, 124
Context switch, 42, 52, 105
Conti, C. J., 81
Control Data computer:
  CDC 6600, 188
Control flow computer, 414
Control lines, 18, 20
Control memory 12, 73–4
Control unit, 62, 64
  design, 70–7
Conway, M. E., 28
Coprocessor, 300
Copyback, in cache, 96
Cosmic Cube, 392

Cost:
  memory system, 138–9
  pipeline, 160–3
  multiprocessor, 228
  trade-offs, 29
Cray computers:
  Cray 1, 13, 177, 219
  Cray 2, 13, 14, 219, 228
  Cray 3, 14
  Cray X-MP, 13, 14, 219
  Cray Y-MP, 219
Critical section, 263
Crossbar switch:
  multiprocessor systems, 301–3
  network, 235, 240–1, 300, 337
  system, 240
CSP (programming language), 389
Cube connected cycles network, 362
Cube network, 362
Cyber 205, 219
Cycle time:
  memory, 80
  processor, 13

Daisy chain, 277, 285
DAP (Distributed Array Processor), 237
Data bus, 18
Data cache, 94
Data dependence graph, 415
Data dependency, 182–4
Data driven computer, 415
Data lines, 18
Dataflow, 414–38
  dynamic, 422
  graph, 415
  languages, 429–34
  macro, 434–7
  static, 420
  systems 420–9
  VLSI structures, 427–9
Davidson's pipeline control algorithm, 213
Deadlock, 269, 383
DEC (Digital Equipment Corp.) computers:
  21064 (Alpha), 39
  PDP 11, 18, 130, 302
  PDP 8E, 18
  VAX-11/780, 31, 33, 130, 132
  VAX-32, 32

DEC computers (*continued*)
  VAX-8600, 126
Decode history table, 179
Delay, adding in a pipeline, 216–17
Delayed branch instruction, 179
Delta network, 343–6, 353
Demand driven computer, 415
Demand fetch, 94
Demand paging, 131
Denning, P. J., 136
Dennis, J. B., 415, 420
Dependency:
  anti-, 183–4
  data, 182–4
  detection, 184–6
  loop-carried, 261
  loop-independent, 261
  output, 184
  procedural, 260
  read-after write, 182–3
  true, 182–3
  write-after-read, 183–4
  write-after-write, 184
Destination tag algorithm, 340
Dhrystone, 33
Dijkstra, E. W., 267
Direct binary *n*-cube, 343
Direct mapping, 89, 123
Directed acyclic graph, 262
Directory look-aside table, 122
Directory method, for cache coherence, 328–31
Dirty bit, 131, 328–31
Disk cache, 110–12
Disk controller, microprocessor, 17
Disk memory, 16, 26–7, 110–12, 115–17
Displacement, in segmentation, 147
Distributed shared memory architecture, 240, 242
DLT (directory look-aside buffer) *see* TLB
DMA (direct memory access), 116, 130, 145, 149, 322, 397, 399
DOALL construct, 257
DOPAR construct, 256
Double reflective networks, 353
Dual port memory, used as pipeline delay, 216
Dynamic code copying, dataflow, 422
Dynamic dataflow, 422
Dynamic interconnection network, 335

Dynamic process structure, 389
Dynamic token tagging, dataflow, 422–3

ECL, 13, 36, 228, 303
E-cube routing algorithm, 383
Edge disjoint, 368
EDVAC, 6
Effective address, 9, 50
Efficiency:
  multiprocessor, 246
  pipeline, 162
Emulation, 12
Ethernet, 393–4
Exception, 203
Execute cycle, 10, 66
Exhaustive network, 357
Exponent, 16, 206
  biased, 206
External fragmentation, 150
Extra stage networks, 344–5

False sharing, 321
Fat tree network, 361
Fault tolerance:
  multistage networks, 344, 345, 354
  static networks, 368
  systems, 244
Fetch-and-add operation, 349
Fetch cycle, 10, 65
Fetch/execute overlap, 21, 163–5
Fetch on write, 97, 324
File striping, 27
Finite state diagram, 70
First fit replacement algorithm, 150
First-in first-out replacement algorithm, 100, 133
First-in-not-used-first-out replacement algorithm, 134
Fixed partition replacement algorithm, 132
Fixed point numbers, 208
Fixed priority, 280
Flit, 380
Floating point number, 16, 45, 205
Flow dependency, 182
Flynn's classification, 229
Footprint, in cache, 109
Forbidden latency, 212
FORK, 253

Forwarding, 188, 189
Freedom from side effects, 430
Frontside bus, 110
Fully associative mapping, 86, 124
Function, 57
Functional languages, 430

GaAs processor, 34
Generalized shuffle network, 343
GF-11, 236
GFLOPS, 13
Global replacement algorithms, 132
Granularity, process, 377
Greedy strategy, in a pipeline, 213
GRIP (Graph Reduction in Parallel) machine, 438

Handshaking, 159, 276–7
Harvard architecture, 6
Hashing, 126–7
Hazard detection, in a pipeline, 184
Heavyweight process, 258
Hexagonal array, 358–9
High order interleaving, 23
Hit ratio, 84, 85, 139
Hot spots, 347
Hypercube:
   cosmic cube, 392–3
   crossed, 366
   incomplete, 366
   iPSC, 393–4
   network, 362, 378
   routing, 382–3
   spanning bus, 363
Hypertree networks, 361

IBM computers:
   801, 36
   360/85, 81, 93, 191
   360/91, 177, 191, 438
   360/195, 177, 191
   370/168-3, 103
   3033, 100, 127
   308X, 14
   3090, 14
   RS6000, 39, 177
IEEE 896 Future+ bus, 299
Illiac IV, 234–5

Immediate addressing, 9, 46
Implicit parallelism, 253
Imprecise interrupts, 204
Index, cache, 90
Indirect addressing, 9, 31, 32, 55, 69
Indirect binary n-cube network, 343
Initial collision vector, 212
Initiation, in a pipeline, 211
Inmos, 397
In-order issue, 195
Input/output interface, 17
Instruction cache, see cache, code
Instruction fetch/execute overlap, 21, 163
Instruction level parallelism, 228
Instruction pointer, 10
Instruction register, 10, 63
Instruction set, 5
Instruction window, 197
Instructions:
   arithmetic and logic, 44, 66
   branch, 49–55, 68–9, 173–82, see also jump
   buffers, 176
   formats, 6–10, 33, 42–3, 44–62
   indivisible, 265, 266
   jump, 50, 55, 69, 173
   jump and link, JAL, 61, 69
   usage, 32
Instruction-time diagram, 167
Intel processors:
   186, 16
   286, 16, 152, 393
   287, 393
   386, 16, 19, 31, 152
   432, 31
   486, 5, 6, 16, 19, 26, 31, 93, 95, 98, 104, 110, 152
   486 DX2, 16
   486 DX4, 16
   4004, 15
   8051, 16
   8080, 15
   8086, 5, 10, 16, 30, 33, 44, 52, 105, 151, 265, 322, 392
   8087, 392
   80960, 182
   i860, 43, 93, 126, 132, 324
   iPSC, 392–3
   P6, 110, 194

Intel processors (*continued*)
  Pentium, 18, 19, 20, 93, 128, 324
Interconnection network:
  message-passing, 375–6
  shared memory, 232–3, 238–9, 244, 318–20
Interleaved memory, 23–5, 304
Internal forwarding, 190–2
Internal fragmentation, 128
Interrupts, 203–4
Inverse translation buffer (ITB), 145
IP-1, 302
I-structure, in dataflow, 425
Iteration space dependence graph, 262

JOIN, 253

Katevenis, M. G. H., 34, 38
Kendal Square Research KRS1, 243–4
Kilburn, T., 117, 120
Koren, I., 427, 429

Lamport's conditions, 266–7
Lang, T., 307, 308
Latency, 22, 162, 379
Latency, pipeline, 212
Least recently used:
  arbitration, 284
  implementation, 101–3, 135
  replacement algorithm, 93, 101, 134, 179,
    284
Left-to-right routing, 383
Lifetime, of a variable, 37
Lightweight process, 258
Line, cache, 83
Line, in paging, 118
Linear array, 357
Linear pipeline, 205
Literal, 46
Little endian, 5
Livelock, 383
Load instructions, 42, 47, 67
Local algorithm, 132
Local bus, 299–300
Local replacement algorithm, 132
Locality of effect, 429
Lock, 264–7
Logical address, 147
Logical operations, 45

Loop buffer, 177
Low order interleaving 23
LRU, *see* least recent used
LSI, 15

Machine instruction, 4
Macrodataflow, 434
  architectures, 435–7
MAL (minimum average latency), 213
Mantissa, 16, 205–8
M-ary tree, 361
Master-slave operation, crossbar switch system,
    301–2
Memory:
  access time, 80
  address, 44
  address register, 63
  cache *see* cache memory
  contention, 173
  cycle time, 80
  data register, 63
  hierarchy, 115
  interleaving *see* interleaved memory
  main, 5
  management, 115–16
  management unit, 117
  multiport, 302
  pollution, 106
  protection, 117, 148, 149
  random access, 5
  read-only, 5
  read-write, 5
Mesh network, 357, 378
MESI protocol, 324
Message-passing:
  blocking routines, 388
  format, 379–80
  multicomputers, 376
  multiprocessor, 238, 375
  networks, 356–66
  non-blocking routines, 388
  programming, 387–92
  systems, 28–9, 392–6.
  transputer, 397–410
MFLOPS, 13
Microcode, 12, 34
Microinstruction, 12, 72

Microinstruction (*continued*)
  program counter, 73
Micro-order, 74
Microprocessor systems, 14–20
Microprogram, 12, 72
Microprogramming, 34
Midimew network, 358
MIMD (multiple instruction stream-multiple data stream) computer, 229, 238
MIN (minimum page fault) replacement algorithm, 137–8
MIN *see* multistage interconnection network
Minsky's conjecture, 249
MIPS (millions of instructions per second), 13
MIPS (microprocessor without interlocking pipeline stages), 38, 54
MIPS 10 000, 39
MISD (multiple instruction stream-single data stream) computer, 230
Miss penalty, 86
Miss rate (ratio), 85
MMU (memory management unit), 117
Modified bit, 131, *see also* dirty bit
Monitor (suite of procedures), 270
MOPS (millions of operations per second), 13
Motorola:
  MC6800, 15, 275
  MC68000, 5, 9, 16, 19, 30, 31, 33, 52, 172, 265, 322
  MC68010, 16
  MC68020, 16,19, 31, 44, 266
  MC68030, 16, 19, 266
  MC68040, 16, 19, 26, 93, 95, 129, 266, 322
  MC88100, 38, 125, 187
  MC88200, 125, 128, 324
MP programming language, 389
MPI (message-passing interface), 395
MPP (massively parallel processor), 237
MSI, 15, 36
MSISD (multiple single instruction stream-single data stream) computer, 231
Multicomputer, 238
Multiple bus:
  bandwidth, 308–9
  network, 240–1, 306
  overlapping connectivity, 314–15
  partial, 307
Multiport memory, 240
multiprocessor

Multiprocessor system, 227
  asymmetric, 240
  classifications, 229–31
  efficiency, 246
  message-passing, 238–9,
  programming, 252–70
  shared memory, 238, 240–5
  speed-up factor, 245–6
Multiprogramming, 27
Multistage interconnection network (MIN), 242, 337
  arbitrary sized, 345
  bandwidth, 346-7
  Baseline, 340
  Benes, 339
  blocking, 336
  cell based, 337, 339
  Clos, 337–9
  Delta, 343–6, 353
  fault tolerant, 344, 345, 354
  generalized shuffle, 343
  hot spots, 347–51
  indirect binary n-cube, 343
  non-blocking, 343
  Omega, 341–3
  rearrangeable, 336
  recirculating, 341
  shuffle, 341–3
Multistreaming, 192
Multithreaded processor, 192
Mutual exclusion, 264

Natural parallelism, 249
Network:
  average distance, 367
  crossbar switch, 235, 240–1, 300, 337
  blocking, 336
  chordal ring, 357
  completely connected, 357
  cube, 362
  cube connected cycles, 362
  exhaustive, 357
  folded, 358
  hexagonal array, 358–9
  hypercube, 362, 382

Network (*continued*)
   hypertree, 361
   linear array, 357
   mesh, 357–8
   midimew, 358
   multiple bus, 306–7
   multistage, 240, 337–55
   near(est) neighbor, 357
   non-blocking, 336
   overlapping connectivity, 309–17, 351–5
   shuffle exchange, 341–5
   single bus, 240, 274
   single stage, 337
   spanning bus hypercube, 363
   star network, 360
   static, 356
   tree, 360–1
Neural computer, 415
Nibble, 15
Node disjoint, fault tolerance, 368
No fetch on write, cache policy, 97
Non-allocate on write, cache policy, 97
Non-blocking message passing, 388
Non-blocking network, 336
Non-cacheable items, 322
Non-usage-based replacement algorithms, 131
No-op instruction, 69
Nova minicomputer, 30
Nullification method, for branch instructions, 181

Occam, 397, 398, 400–10
   razor, 398
Offset:
   branch instruction, 50, 55
   jump instruction, 55–6
   load/store instruction, 47–49
   segmentation, 147
Omega network, 341, 346, 353
Omnibus, 18
One-address instruction format, 7
One-and-a-half-address instruction format, 7
One-level store, 117, 124
Opcode, 6
Orthogonal multiprocessor, 303
Out-of-order completion, instruction, 195

Out-of-order issue, instruction, 195
Output dependency, 184, 258
Overflow (O) flag, 50
Overlap, 157
Overlapping connectivity network, 309
   crossbar switch, 310–14
   generalized arrays, 315–17
   multiple bus, 314–15
   multistage (reflective), 351–5
   two-dimensional, 313–14
Overlaying, 116

P (operation), 267–70
Packet switching, 336, 379
Page, 118
   address translation cache, 125
   fault, 118, 130
   fault frequency algorithm, 137
   replacement algorithm, 120, 130–41
   size, 127–8
   table, 118
Paged segmentation, 150–3
Paging, 117
Parallel adder, 208
Parallel arbiter, 279–82
Parallel computer, 228
Parallel programming, 227
Parallelism, 227
   explicit, 253
   implicit, 253
   in loops, 260–3
Pattern driven computer, 415
PC-relative addressing, 50, 55
PDP computers *see* DEC computers
Pease, M. C., 341
Pentium, 26, 110, 194
Perfect shuffle, 341
Physical address, 147
Pipeline, 20, 157
   arithmetic pipelines, 204–9
   asynchronous, 159–60
   collision, 211
   control, 212–17
   dynamic, 205, 211
   efficiency, 162
   feedback, 205
   five-stage, 167
   floating point, 205

Pipeline (*continued*)
　four-stage, 165, 182
　hazards, 171
　initiation, 211
　interlock, 186
　latch, 160, 169
　linear, 205
　maximum-rate, 160
　multifunction, 205
　RISC processor, 168–71
　scheduling, 212–17
　speed-up factor, 161–2
　synchronous, 159–60
Pipelining, 157
Placement algorithm, in paging, 120
Polling, for bus arbitration, 291–3
PowerPC, 39
Precise interrupts, 204
Prefetch, cache, 94
Prefetch buffer, 26
Primary memory *see* Memory, main
Principle of inclusion, in cache memory, 110
Principle of locality, 82, 121
Principle of optimality, in paging, 137
Private bit, 328
Procedural dependency, 260
Procedure call, 56
Process, 252, 376, 398
Processor, 4, 41
Program counter, 63
program counter, 10, 62, 68
Programmer, 5
Programming:
　shared memory systems, 252–70
　message-passing systems, 387–92
Pvm (parallel virtual machine), 394

Queue:
　in dataflow, 423
　in replacement algorithm, 133, 134, 136

Radin, G., 36
RAID, 27
Random access memory (RAM), 5
Random logic, 11
Random replacement algorithm, 100, 132
Read-after-write hazard, 182, 185, 258
Read-only memory, 5

Read-through, in cache, 90
Real address, 117
Real-time clock, in transputer, 407
Rearrangeable network, 336
Recirculating network, 341
Recursive procedure, 56
Reduced instruction set computer (RISC), 9, 17,
　30–9, 41
Reference matrix, 102–3
Referential transparency, 430
Reflective interconnection network, 352
Register, 7
Register direct addressing, 9
Register file, 42, 62, 63
Register indirect addressing 9, 47, 55
Register renaming, 200, 201
Register stack, 101
Register transfer notation, 64
Register window, 59
Relative addressing, 9
Relocatable, code, 50
Rendezvous, 388, 402
Reorder buffer, 201
Replacement algorithms, 88, 90, 92, 100–4,
　130–8, 150
Reservation station, 199, 210
Resource conflicts, 171
Return address, 57
Reverse translation buffer (RTB), 145
RISC I/II, 38, 60
Routing
　adaptive, 382
　deterministic, 382
　distributed, 382
　e-cube, 383
　source, 382
　store-and-forward, 380
　street-map, 382
　virtual cut-through, 380
　wormhole, 380

S1 multiprocessor system, 303
Scalability, 251
Scalarity, 39
Scalar processor, 16
Scale up function, 251
Scoreboard, 188
Secondary cache, 109

Secondary memory, 6
Second-level cache, 109
Sector, 93
Sector mapping, cache, 93
Segment, 147
Segmentation, 147–53
Seitz, C. L., 377, 380, 392
Selective fetch, in cache, 94
Self-modifying code, 95
Self-routing network, 340–5
Semaphore, 267
Sequential consistency, 321
Sequential locality, 82
Serialization principle, 350
Set-associative, 91, 125
Shared caches, 322
Shared memory architecture, 238, 240
    cache-only (COMA), 244
    non-uniform memory access (NUMA), 242
    uniform memory access (UMA), 240
Shuffle interconnection, 341, 343
Sign (S) flag, 50
SIMD (Single instruction stream-multiple data
stream) computer, 229
Simple cycle, pipeline, 213
Single assignment language, 430
Single bus system, 240, 274
    performance, 293
Single stage network, 337
SISAL (Streams and Iterations in a Single
        Assignment Language), 432
Smith, A. J., 106, 108, 112
Snoop bus, 323
Software combining trees, 349
Source routing, 382
Space-shared, message-passing system, 393
Space-time diagram, 157
Space-time product, 138
Spanning bus hypercube network, 363
Spatial locality, 82, 121
SPECfp92/int92, 14, 33
Speed-up factor, 245
    pipeline, 161
    single bus network, 296
Spin lock, 264
SSI, 15, 36
Stack, 57
    algorithm, 138

    pointer, 57
Staging latch, in pipelines, 160, 169
Stall, in a pipeline, 171
Star network, 360
State diagram, 70, 213
Static interconnection network, 356–66
    evaluation, 367–70
Static prediction, branch instruction, 181
Static priority, 280
Static process structure, 389
Status vector, 213
Stone, H. S., 106, 108, 109, 137
Store-and-forward routing, 380
Stored program computer, 3, 229
Store instructions, 47, 67
Streams, dataflow, 432
Street-map routing, 382
Strict consistency, 321
Strong ordering, 321
Sub-block, 89
Sub-opcode, 44
SUN Sparc processor, 38, 59
Supercomputer, 13, 218
Superpipelining, 193
Superscalar processor, 16, 192–203
Symmetric multiprocessor, 240
Synchronous pipeline, 159
Synonyms, 144
System bus, 299
System mode, 149

Table fragmentation, 128
Tag:
    in cache, 90
    dataflow token, 422–4
Tagged architecture, 15
Temporal locality, 82, 121
Test and set (TAS) instruction, 265–6
Thrashing, 132
Thread, 258
Three-address instruction format, 7
Three-cube network, 362
Three-level overlap, 165
Throughput, 162
Tomasulo, R. M., 191
Translation look-aside buffer (TLB), 121, 122
Transputer, 397
True data dependency, 182, 258

Tree network:
  binary, 360–1
  fat, 361
  hyper-, 361
  m-ary, 361
  saturation, 348
TTL, 13
Twisted hypercube, 366
Two-address instruction format, 7
Two's complement numbers, 48, 51, 208

Ultracomputer, NYU, 351
UltraSparc, 39
Unibus, 18
Universal fat tree, 361
Use bit, 131, 134–5

V (operation), 267–70
VAL (Value-oriented Algorithmic Language), 431
valid bit:
  cache, 88–9, 328
  pipeline, 186–8
Variable partition, in paging, 132
VAX *see* DEC computers
Vector computer, 205, 217
Vector instruction, 217–18, 233
Vector processor, 218
Virtual addresses, 117
Virtual channel, 385
Virtual cut-through, 380
Virtual memory, 28, 117

  with cache memory, 141
VLSI, 13, 15, 42
VMIN replacement algorithm, 137
Von Neumann computer, 4
Voter, in triplicated system, 245

Warm start, in cache, 105
Weak ordering, 321
Whetstone benchmark, 33
Wilkes, M. V., 12
Wire bisection width, 368
Working set, 135
  algorithm, 136
Workstation cluster, 394
Wormhole routing, 380
Worst fit replacement algorithm, 150
Write-after-read hazard, 184, 185, 258
Write-after-write hazard, 184, 185, 258
Write-back, in cache, 98
Write-through, in cache, 90, 96, 319
Written bit, 131

X-grid interconnection network, 237
X-MP *see* Cray computers

Y-MP *see* Cray computers

Zero (Z) flag, 50
Zero-address instruction format, 7
Zilog Z-80, 15, 287
Zuse, 4